Segmental Phonology in Optimality Theory

Optimality Theory has rapidly become the dominant framework in formal phonological theory. OT fundamentally revises the basic notions of generative grammar, replacing rules and derivations with a system of interacting constraints. Early work in OT tended to concentrate mainly on prosodic phonology and the phonology-morphology interface, and it was not initially clear how the theory could attack the rich range of phenomena found in segmental alternations. However, there is now a body of work that concentrates on working out the details of featural phonology with OT, and this work shows that the theory allows superior explanations of the typological possibilities and the underlying motivations for these phenomena. This volume brings together current work by some of the leading researchers in this area, ranging from the authors of recent influential dissertations to prominent senior faculty.

Linda Lombardi is an Associate Professor of Linguistics at the University of Maryland, College Park, and the author of *Laryngeal Features and Laryngeal Neutralization* (1994).

Segmental Phonology in Optimality Theory

Constraints and Representations

Edited by

LINDA LOMBARDI

University of Maryland

CAMBRIDGE
UNIVERSITY PRESS

PUBLISHED BY THE PRESS SYNDICATE OF THE UNIVERSITY OF CAMBRIDGE
The Pitt Building, Trumpington Street, Cambridge, United Kingdom

CAMBRIDGE UNIVERSITY PRESS
The Edinburgh Building, Cambridge CB2 2RU, UK
40 West 20th Street, New York, NY 10011-4211, USA
10 Stamford Road, Oakleigh, VIC 3166, Australia
Ruiz de Alarcón 13, 28014 Madrid, Spain
Dock House, The Waterfront, Cape Town 8001, South Africa

http://www.cambridge.org

© Cambridge University Press 2001

First published 2001

Printed in the United States of America

Typeface Times Roman 10/12.5 pt.   *System* QuarkXPress [BTS]

A catalog record for this book is available from the British Library.

Library of Congress Cataloging in Publication Data
Segmental phonology in Optimality Theory : constraints and representations / edited by
Linda Lombardi.
    p.   cm.
    Includes bibliographical references and index.
    ISBN 0-521-79057-3
    1. Grammar, Comparative and general – Phonology.   2. Optimality theory
(Linguistics)   I. Lombardi, Linda, 1961–

    P217.3   S43   2001
    414′.6 – dc21

                                                                00–052895

ISBN   0 521 79057 3   hardback

Contents

III The Structure of the Grammar: Approaches to Opacity

Contributors

Haruka Fukazawa, Kyushu Institute of Technology
Chip Gerfen, University of North Carolina, Chapel Hill
Junko Ito, University of California, Santa Cruz
Robert Kirchner, University of Alberta
Linda Lombardi, University of Maryland, College Park
Armin Mester, University of California, Santa Cruz
Máire NíChiosáin, University College, Dublin
Jaye Padgett, University of California, Santa Cruz
Joe Pater, University of Alberta and University of Massachusetts, Amherst
Moira Yip, University of California, Irvine, and University College London
Cheryl Zoll, Massachusetts Institute of Technology

Introduction

LINDA LOMBARDI

Optimality Theory (OT) (Prince and Smolensky 1993; McCarthy and Prince 1993) has rapidly become the dominant framework in formal phonological theory. In OT fundamental notions of generative grammar are revised by replacing rules and derivations with interacting well-formedness constraints. The phonological literature immediately prior to OT had shown that such constraints were crucial to the construction of explanatory analyses. (Prince and Smolensky 1993 give nearly half a page of such references; limiting ourselves just to works on segmental phonology by authors represented in this volume, we can point to such works as Ito 1986, 1989; Lombardi 1991, 1995; Mester 1986; Yip 1988.) But incorporating such constraints into derivational theory posed a number of problems.

One problem was that it was difficult to make a formal connection between constraints and the rules that accounted for the related alternations. (See Prince and Smolensky 1993, ch. 10, for discussion of some attempts.) It has long been observed that many languages exhibit phonological conspiracies (Kisseberth 1970): that is, there are different rules that have the effect of making forms obey the same surface well-formedness constraints. And many languages have been observed to have a kind of duplication problem: the constraints needed to restrict underlying forms and the rules that give the correct surface forms have the same effects. But in derivational theory the rules and the constraints were stated separately from each other, and also stated separately on the different levels, and were not formally linked.

Another difficulty was the issue of universality. The assumption that the constraints were constructed anew in each grammar, like rules, was unsatisfactory since the same constraints tended to recur in many different languages. But most constraints were not obeyed in all languages, seemingly contradicting the idea that they could be part of Universal Grammar (UG). (For discussion of this in the literature see, for example, the debate on the Obligatory Contour Principle (OCP) (Odden 1986, 1988; McCarthy 1986).)

Given that rules alone were not sufficient to provide explanatory analyses, but that rules and constraints were difficult to combine formally, in hindsight it may seem to have been an obvious alternative to try using constraints alone. But how could this work? Constraints could describe static patterns, but what about phonological alternations?

Prince and Smolensky's proposals made it possible to construct the grammar entirely from constraints in a way that both allowed constraints to account for alternations and to be universal. Prince and Smolensky achieve this by claiming that constraints are violable and ranked: although all languages have a given constraint in their grammar, that constraint may be violated if necessary to obey a higher-ranked constraint. Constraint ranking and constraint violability thus allow language variation while using universal constraints: when two constraints make conflicting demands, languages differ in how the conflict is resolved. And one of the basic types of constraint conflict is that between markedness and faithfulness: when violation of faithfulness is forced, forms change, giving us phonological alternations.

The original work in OT (cited earlier) concentrated mainly on prosodic phonology and on the phonology-morphology interface. The clearest and perhaps most convincing success was Prince and Smolensky's analysis of crosslinguistic syllable structure requirements. Prince and Smolensky showed that these patterns were due to the interaction of a limited set of markedness constraints, which defined the well-formed structures, and faithfulness constraints, which regulated the extent of possible differences between underlying and surface forms. This analysis is a model for all work in the framework.

The immediate impact of Prince and Smolensky's syllable structure analysis was partly due to the fact that it was clear to all phonologists that there is indeed a restricted, well-attested pattern of syllable structure requirements across languages; their basic observations go back to Jakobson. And at the point when OT was introduced, prosodic phenomena were already being spoken of largely in constraint-based terms even in derivational phonology, using templates as constraints on prosodic shape (for example, Ito 1986 for syllables and McCarthy 1981 for prosodic morphology). Thus, these cases were ripe for translation into a framework where constraints are primary, and where a crucial limiting factor is that reranking of the proposed constraints should result in the appropriate crosslinguistic typology.

In contrast, segmental phonology was in a rather different position. Many analyses (like those cited earlier) did invoke constraints. But many phenomena were still generally analyzed exclusively in terms of rewrite rules. It was also much less clear what the restrictions were on the crosslinguistic typology of segmental processes. Segmental feature-changing alternations appear to show a good deal more variation than prosodic patterns do. There are simply more different features than there are prosodic constituents, and they do not all obviously have the same behavior. Vowel features and nasality assimilate long-distance; in contrast, Voice and Place assimilate only locally, but may dissimilate long-distance. Consonant features usually spread regressively, except that many languages have (progressive) postnasal voicing of obstruents. Neutralization of featural distinctions is common, but the context where it occurs differs depending on the particular feature involved. In sum, there are more kinds of interactions and patterns possible for features than there are for syllable structure constituents, and it was not as clear what the typological restrictions on their variation are, or how they can be accounted for.[1]

But although initially progress in OT phonology was concentrated in prosodic phenomena, there is now a body of work and a core research community that focuses on working out the details of featural phonology in the OT framework. This work shows that, with appropriate depth of analysis, there is in fact a restricted, universal set of possibilities for segmental phonology. The papers in this volume show us both what OT can tell us about segmental phonology, and what analysis of segmental phenomena has to contribute theoretically to OT.

The first part of this volume is "The Content of Representations." The tenets of OT, regarding constraint violability and ranking, make no particular claims about phonological representations. We could, for example, do OT with any kind of feature theory: SPE feature bundles or feature geometric representations, privative or binary features, and so on. Much early work in OT paid little attention to representational questions, simply taking over assumptions from previous work in derivational autosegmental phonology. But representational arguments are theory-internal and need to be reexamined in light of fundamental theoretical changes; the choice of correct representations to use in OT analyses must be based on arguments couched in OT terms. The chapters in the first part of the book make such arguments, and they show the additional insight into phonological patterns that can be gained by applying OT to these facts.

The first chapter, my "Why Place and Voice Are Different," gives an OT-internal argument that in order to explain certain asymmetries in phonological patterns, Voice must be a privative feature, and the laryngeal consonants [h, ʔ] cannot be literally Placeless, but rather have a relatively unmarked Place feature. The former argument confirms earlier derivationally based work, but the latter contradicts it and shows that making this representational assumption within an OT grammar solves problems that were intractable in earlier frameworks.

Representational arguments are also central to Zoll's contribution, "Constraints and Representation in Subsegmental Phonology." This chapter is based on work in her dissertation, a crosslinguistic study of ghost segments and floating features that was one of the first in-depth OT studies of an area of featural phonology. Zoll shows that within OT, we can account for all of these phenomena with more restricted representational differences than those proposed in pre-OT analyses. Zoll's chapter shows that these subsegmental constituents submit to a more insightful and appropriately restrictive analysis in an OT framework.

Kirchner's chapter, "Phonological Contrast and Articulatory Effort," takes a novel approach to representations. He argues that phonological representations in an OT grammar can contain much richer phonetic detail than is normally assumed, without predicting unattested systems of contrasts. Constraints can then refer to more specifically phonetic properties than is otherwise possible. Using constraints regulating faithfulness to auditory features, and triggering constraints referring to articulatory effort and to a perceptually based fortition requirement, Kirchner gives a unified account of lenition, a segmental phenomenon that has been problematic for almost all previous phonological frameworks. This chapter thus represents an important alternative approach to segmental representations that has been made possible by the assumptions of OT.

In rule-based autosegmental theory, transparency and opacity phenomena were a crucial type of evidence for representational claims. Transparency effects were used to argue for lack of feature specifications (privative features or underspecification); opacity, in contrast, was often explained as due to the presence of a feature value blocking spread. These representational assumptions must be reexamined in light of our new theoretical assumptions. NíChiosáin and Padgett's chapter, "Markedness, Segment Realization, and Locality in Spreading," addresses the fundamental question of the locality of spreading, and what it means for a segment to be "transparent." Their paper is couched in terms of Dispersion Theory (Flemming 1995), an important line of research within OT segmental phonology. Similar to Kirchner's approach, the representations are assumed to contain rich phonetic detail. In addition, an important difference between this framework and standard OT is that phonological contrasts arise directly from output constraints requiring the maintenance of contrasts; the distinctiveness of contrasts is also controlled by output constraints. Using these assumptions NíChiosáin and Padgett propose that at least some apparently long-distance spreading is actually local, and that the apparent fact of transparency can be an artifact of the phonological framework underlying the analysis.

Of course, all analyses must call on assumptions about both the form of phonological constraints and the form of representations, so along the way to their main points, these chapters also make theoretical contributions to topics in other parts of the book, particularly the second part on the form of phonological constraints. For example, along with arguments for the representations of voiceless sounds and laryngeal consonants, my chapter also argues for the existence of MaxFeature constraints and for the existence of CodaCond for Place but not for Voice. NíChiosáin and Padgett's chapter and Kirchner's as well, because of their different view of representations, must make novel claims about both faithfulness constraints and the markedness constraints triggering alternations.

The second part of the volume, "The Content of Constraints," addresses what can be seen as the central issue of what the content of UG is in OT. The basic tenets of OT are very general claims about constraint violability and interaction. They may imply the existence of the two basic conflicting categories of constraints, Markedness and Faithfulness, which give the conflict between well-formedness requirements and the constraints that penalize changes to input (although even this may not be required, as in Dispersion Theory, used in NíChiosáin and Padgett's chapter). But the specific formulation of the constraints can be worked out in many different ways. Many of the chapters in this volume assume the faithfulness theory of Correspondence (McCarthy and Prince 1995), for example, but within this theory there are still open questions about what kinds of correspondences are regulated by faithfulness relations. Similar questions arise perhaps even more strongly for the content of markedness constraints, which are the triggers of phonological alternations, since there is no general theory like Correspondence that constrains their form.

Pater's chapter, "Austronesian Nasal Substitution Revisited," is a continuation of research begun in his earlier paper, "Austronesian Nasal Substitution and other NC̥ Effects" (Pater 1999). This paper was one of the earliest detailed treatments of the question of what constraints trigger a particular featural alternation, and what might be the explanation for the existence of such constraints. In it, Pater proposes a constraint *NC̥ that penalizes a cluster of a nasal and a voiceless stop. He shows that such a constraint is phonetically motivated: it is grounded in the articulatory difficulty of such sequences compared to nasal–voiced stop clusters. The need for a constraint like *NC̥ to trigger simple postnasal voicing seems clear. But in the present volume, Pater re-examines the Austronesian nasal substitution data and suggests that the triggering factors for these more complex alternations must be seen in a different way.

Gerfen's chapter, "A Critical View of Licensing by Cue," addresses the question of the form of the constraints licensing contrast, which are crucial to achieving positional neutralization of phonological distinctions in OT analyses. As shown by the chapters by Kirchner and by NíChiosáin and Padgett in the first part, OT allows some novel approaches to the interaction of phonetics and phonology and to the issue of where the boundary between the two lies. This leads to the idea that instead of referring to traditional phonological elements, constraints refer directly to phonetic cues. As Gerfen points out, a problem with assessing these alternatives is that they often have the same empirical coverage. He examines in detail a particular case in Eastern Andalusian Spanish that he argues allows us to distinguish the two possibilities, and he shows that it can be best explained by licensing constraints that refer to syllable position rather than to phonetic cues. Gerfen's chapter is of particular interest in that its arguments are supported by both phonological patterning and phonetic data: measurements of duration support the proposed syllabification analysis, and thus, the argument that the context of neutralization is best described in terms of syllabic position.

Yip's chapter, "Segmental Markedness versus Input Preservation in Reduplication," looks at the segmental alternations involved in several types of reduplication in Chinese languages. Her chapter shows that these alternations can be seen as a direct result of contextual featural markedness; the segments that appear are the least marked for the various syllable positions involved. On the basis of this, she argues that the only faithfulness relationship that should be recognized is that between input and output (IO); there is no Base-Reduplicant faithfulness relation specific to reduplication. Thus, IO faithfulness is fully satisfied by a faithful realization in just one copy of the pair, leaving the other copy free to alternate under pressure of markedness.

The third and final part of this volume looks at broader questions of "The Structure of the Grammar," concentrating on how we should account for opaque phonological interactions.

Fukazawa's "Local Conjunction and Extending Sympathy Theory" shows that McCarthy's (1998) proposal of Sympathy, a type of candidate-to-candidate correspondence, can be shown to account for phenomena beyond the residual derivational opacity problems that it was designed to solve. This is an important point, showing that Sympathy has broader OT-internal application and is not just an appendage to explain away troublesome cases. The argument is based on a complicated OCP-triggered alternation in Yucatec Maya that is restricted to homorganic consonants. The analysis also contributes to the question of the constraints that trigger alternations, the topic of the second part, as it is shown that the combined requirements for violating this OCP constraint are accounted for by Smolensky's (1993) Local Conjunction of constraints.

Ito and Mester's chapter, "Structure Preservation and Stratal Opacity in German," addresses the details of an opaque interaction between two allophonic rules in German and shows that this type of interaction, where both rules are allophonic and affect each other's environment, cannot be accounted for using Sympathy Theory. From this interaction they draw the important and likely controversial conclusion that we must recognize some serialism within the phonology in OT. The two alternations, although both nondistinctive, otherwise differ in precisely the properties that are used to distinguish lexical and postlexical rules in Lexical Phonology. Ito and Mester show that if the two are the result of two different constraint rankings, one feeding into the other, the facts can be accounted for straightforwardly. Their model formalizes many of the key insights of Lexical Phonology, but within an OT grammar.

The chapters in this volume show both that OT allows new insights into segmental phonology, and that the details of segmental phonology provide insight into the broadest possible issues in the structure of UG. From basic questions of the representation of a segment to whether the fundamental architecture of the grammar is serial or fully parallel, these are important contributions to our formal understanding of the language faculty.

Notes

For their hard work on this volume, the editor would like to thank all of the contributors as well as our erstwhile representative at Cambridge University Press, Christine Bartels. Thanks also to Jill Beckman and Donca Steriade for their consideration early on in the project, although they were ultimately unable to contribute for reasons of scheduling. I would especially like to thank

John McCarthy for encouraging me to persist at some discouraging junctures. The usual caveats apply about none of the aforementioned being responsible for my or each other's errors and misconceptions. Finally, thanks to the technical support department at Three Cats Software for crucial assistance in coping with the many ways in which computers have made our lives so much easier.

1. Some earlier attempts at crosslinguistic typologies include Lombardi (1991, 1995) and Cho (1991). Of course, the intent of work in feature geometry and underspecification was also originally to achieve crosslinguistic restrictions on featural phonology by arriving at the correct structure for the segment. However, given the proliferation of different proposals for the representation of the same distinctions in this literature, it was unclear that this framework was approaching an agreed-upon and appropriately restrictive account.

References

Cho, Young-Mee Yu. 1991. Parameters of Consonantal Assimilation. PhD dissertation, Stanford University.

Ito, Junko. 1986. Syllable Theory in Prosodic Phonology. PhD dissertation, University of Massachusetts at Amherst.

Ito, Junko. 1989. A Prosodic Theory of Epenthesis. *Natural Language and Linguistic Theory* 7:217–259.

Flemming, Edward. 1995. Auditory Representations in Phonology. PhD dissertation, UCLA.

Kisseberth, Charles. 1970. On the Functional Unity of Phonological Rules. *Linguistic Inquiry* 1:291–306.

Lombardi, Linda. 1991. Laryngeal Features and Laryngeal Neutralization. PhD dissertation, University of Massachusetts, Amherst. Published by Garland, 1994.

Lombardi, Linda. 1995. Laryngeal Neutralization and Syllable Wellformedness. *Natural Language and Linguistic Theory* 13:39–74.

McCarthy, John J. 1981. A Prosodic Theory of Nonconcatenative Morphology. *Linguistic Inquiry* 10:433–466.

McCarthy, John J. 1986. OCP Effects: Gemination and Antigemination. *Linguistic Inquiry* 17:207–263.

McCarthy, John J. 1999. Sympathy and Phonological Opacity. *Phonology* 16:331–399.

McCarthy, John J., and Alan Prince. 1993. Prosodic Morphology I: Constraint Interaction and Satisfaction. Technical Report No. 3, Rutgers University Center for Cognitive Science.

McCarthy, John, J., and Alan Prince. 1995. Faithfulness and Reduplicative Identity. University of Massachusetts Occasional Papers 18, pp. 249–384. Amherst, MA: GLSA. ROA 60-0000, http://ruccs.rutgers.edu/roa.html.

Mester, R. Armin. 1986. Studies in Tier Structure. PhD dissertation, University of Massachusetts, Amherst.

Odden, David. 1986. On the Obligatory Contour Principle. *Language* 62:353–383.

Odden, David. 1988. AntiAntigemination and the OCP. *Linguistic Inquiry* 19:451–475.

Pater, Joe. 1999. Austronesian Nasal Substitution and other *NC̥ Effects. In *The Prosody-Morphology Interface*, ed. R. Kager, H. van der Hulst, and W. Zonneveld, pp. 310–343. Cambridge: Cambridge University Press.

Prince, Alan, and Paul Smolensky. 1993. Optimality Theory: Constraint Interaction in Generative Grammar. To appear, MIT Press.

Smolensky, Paul. 1993. Harmony, Markedness, and Phonological Activity. Paper presented at Rutgers Optimality Workshop 1 and revised handout.

Yip, Moira. 1988. The Obligatory Contour Principle and Phonological Rules: A Loss of Identity. *Linguistic Inquiry* 19:65–100.

PART I

THE CONTENT OF REPRESENTATIONS

1

Why Place and Voice Are Different: Constraint-Specific Alternations in Optimality Theory

LINDA LOMBARDI

1. Introduction

Both Place and Laryngeal features are often restricted in coda position. The laryngeal distinctions of voicing, aspiration, and glottalization are often neutralized to plain voiceless in coda position. The phonology of Place often shows the Coda Condition pattern of Ito (1986), according to which syllables cannot end in a consonant other than the nasal of a homorganic NC cluster or the first half of a geminate. This is analyzed by Ito as due to a constraint against singly linked Place in a coda.

Both laryngeal neutralization and the alternations involving place have been seen as the result of similar restrictions: constraints that restrict features from appearing in coda position, whether these constraints are negative (as in Ito 1986) or positive (as in Lombardi 1991, 1995a, and the Alignment analysis of the Coda Condition in Ito and Mester 1994). However, the types of alternations that languages exhibit in association with these coda restrictions differ. Although both Laryngeal Constraint and Coda Condition languages may show codas in assimilated clusters escaping the constraint, beyond that there seem to be more differences than similarities in the behavior of Place and Voice. Both types of features may be subject to neutralization. But coda restrictions on Place may result in either epenthesis or deletion, while forbidden coda Voice never triggers these alternations.[1]

In a theory where phonological rules specify both context and change, as in SPE and much work following it, it is not possible to account for this asymmetry of patterns except by stipulation. For example, an autosegmental rule deleting a voiced consonant from coda position is as well formed as a rule deleting a consonant with Place from the coda, even though the former is unattested. But since it is possible to write all the rules that do exist with the machinery of the theory, we can easily construct analyses of any given language, and the gaps in the crosslinguistic typology are not made obvious.

A theory that tries to combine constraints and rules runs into similar difficulty. For example, Lombardi (1991, 1995a), following Mester and Ito (1989), suggests that Laryngeal neutralization is an automatic consequence of the violation of a constraint that rules out Laryngeal features except in a certain position, and that delinking the feature repairs the violation without requiring any additional information. However, delinking is not an automatic consequence of having Place in coda; either epenthesis or deletion are also possible. Delinking may be the universal reaction to Laryngeal violations, but it is not the universal reaction to Place violations. Conversely, the other possible responses to Place violations do not occur in response to voicing. Thus we must stipulate that certain repairs can be connected only to certain constraints.

Optimality Theory (Prince and Smolensky 1993) focuses our attention on this kind of asymmetry for two reasons. First, it is not possible even to stipulate a connection between particular constraints and associated alternations. Since we cannot avoid the problem by stipulation, we are forced to look for a more satisfactory approach. Second, it is not possible to ignore the problem of the asymmetry in OT because crosslinguistic typology is absolutely central to the theory. One fundamental premise of OT is that UG consists of a set of constraints, and that languages differ only in how they rank these constraints; all language-particular variation comes from the different effects of constraint interactions in different rankings. Thus, in order to argue that a certain set of constraints exists, we must show that rerankings of these constraints give all and only attested grammars. If rerankings do not give the appropriate crosslinguistic typology, the proposed constraints must not be the correct analysis of the phenomena in question.

For instance, suppose that there is a Coda Condition on Place, and that we can rank it above the anti-insertion constraint so that epenthesis is optimal. If there is a similar coda constraint on Voice, the same ranking should be possible, incorrectly predicting the possibility of epenthesis. We cannot stipulate that the connection between the voicing constraint and the epenthetic repair is impossible. Thus, this first, most obvious attempt at a constraint-based analysis – that both features are subject to a Coda Condition – must be incorrect, and we are forced to find an alternate account that makes the correct typological predictions.

I will argue in this chapter that if we propose that UG contains the appropriate constraints and representational properties, OT can provide an appropriately restrictive account of the alternations involving Place and Voice. The analysis will be based on the following substantive claims:

1. Although both types of features are subject to position-independent markedness constraints like *Voice and *Dor, only Place is subject to a positional markedness constraint, CodaCond.
2. There are consonants that are not marked with any Laryngeal specification, but none that are truly Placeless: /h,ʔ/ are marked with Pharyngeal place and are subject to a low-ranked Place markedness constraint. This not only solves part of the problem regarding the differences in alternations, but is important with respect to long-standing problems with the representation of /h/ and /ʔ/.
3. It is necessary to recognize the existence of MaxFeature constraints that ensure realization of underlying feature specification, as suggested in McCarthy and Prince (1995).

The particulars of the analysis are important for featural phonology in general since they speak to issues of neutralization, markedness, and faithfulness that are relevant for the treatment of features other than Place and Laryngeal. In addition, the results also have broad implications for other cases where we see similar asymmetries and limits on the attested types of alternations associated with a constraint.

2. Differences between Place and Voice: The Data

In this section I review the data that show the different patterns of alternations in response to Place and Voice in coda position.

2.1. Laryngeal Neutralization

In many languages, syllable-final consonants cannot bear the laryngeal distinctions of voicing, aspiration, or glottalization. For the present purpose the most interesting cases are those that show active alternations, such as the well-known case of syllable-final devoicing in German (see (1)). In German, syllables may not end in a voiced consonant. If the final consonant of a morpheme like /veg/ becomes syllable-final at the surface, it is devoiced. See Lombardi (1991, 1995a) for additional data.

(1) German: syllable-final laryngeal neutralization

a. /rund/   b.   /veg/

run[d]e   'round pl.'   We[g]e   'way pl.'

run[t]   'round sg.'   We[k]   'way sg.'

Run[tv]urm   'roundworm'   We[kš]necke   'slug (path+snail)'

2.2. Coda Condition on Place

It is also possible for a language to forbid Place features in a coda. In
the analysis of Ito (1986, 1989), geminates and place-assimilated clusters
escape the Coda Condition on Place because there is not a single link
from the coda position to a Place feature; Ito and Mester (1994) discuss
how to analyze this effect in OT by refining the definition of Alignment.
What I am most concerned with here is what happens when such double
linking does not exist. That is, what happens when the consonant cannot
have its own Place, but also does not come to share Place with the following consonant?

The alternations triggered by the coda constraint on Place are more
varied than those triggered by the impossibility of coda Voice. Ito gives
examples of two: epenthesis of a vowel (making the consonant syllable-
initial) and deletion of the offending consonant. I will give examples of
these and then turn to the possibility of coda Place neutralization.

2.2.1. Epenthesis. In Ponapean (Rehg 1984, Rehg and Sohl 1981) word-
internal syllables are either open, closed by the first segment of a geminate, or closed by a nasal in a homorganic cluster (see (2)).

(2) Ponapean syllable types

        pereki   'to order'   urenna   'lobster'

        lusida   'to jump upwards'   rerrer   'to be trembling'

        nampar   'trade wind season'

When two consonants come together by morpheme concatenation,
various alternations ensure that these syllable constraints are met. Nasals
assimilate in Place, and in some cases there is nasal substitution, creating homorganic nasal-stop clusters. In the absence of the environment
for these processes, a vowel is epenthesized, making the consonant syllable-initial (the quality of the vowel differs in different circumstances,

but is predictable). Word-final consonants escape the Coda Condition by final extraprosodicity.[2] These processes are illustrated in (3).

(3) Ponapean epenthesis   reduplicated:

/kitik men/	kitikimen	'rat'		net	netenet	'smell'
/ak dei/	akedei			tep	tepitep	'start'
/ak tantat/	akatantat	(Rehg and Sohl, p. 92; no glosses)		kos	kosokos	'throw'

Ito's (1989) analysis of this set of facts brings them all together as the result of a prohibition on Place syllable-finally, stated in (4).

(4) Coda Condition (CodaCond): $*\text{C}]_\sigma$
$$\mid$$
Place

Doubly linked structures such as Place-assimilated clusters and geminates escape this constraint; for other consonants, epenthesis renders them syllable-initial, so the constraint is not violated.

    Ito (1986) also discusses alternations in Sino-Japanese compounds, where the facts are essentially the same except for the absence of final extraprosodicity. Another case is Axininca Campa, except for person prefixes (Payne 1981).

2.2.2. Deletion. Diola deletion (Sapir 1965) is analyzed by Ito as triggered by the coda condition on Place, with deletion of unlicensed consonants following from Stray Erasure, as first suggested by Steriade (1982) in her analysis of this language. Like Ponapean, Diola allows homorganic nasal-stop clusters and geminates, but no other coda consonants. Nasals may be preserved by assimilating to the following consonant, but where assimilation is inapplicable, the coda consonant deletes (see (5)).[3] Additional cases of this type are Akan (Schachter and Fromkin 1968) and Axininca person prefixes (Payne 1981).

(5)   Diola consonant deletion

/let+ku+jaw/	lekujaw	'they won't go'
/ujuk+ja/	ujuja	'if you see'
/-kob kob en/	kokoben	'yearn'

2.2.3. Place neutralization. A final pattern that disallows Place distinctions in coda position is neutralization to an unmarked Place. For example, in Slave (Athabaskan) all nonsonorant consonants surface as /h/ when syllable-final (Rice 1989), as shown in (6). Sonorants are treated differently, but also do not allow Place distinctions in coda: nasals delete and nasalize the preceding vowel, and the only possible syllable-final non-nasal sonorant is /y/.

(6) Slave syllable-final Place neutralization

/ts'ad/	ts'ah	'hat'	/xaz/	xah	'scar'
	-ts'ade			-ɣaze	
/seeɣ/	seeh	'saliva'	/tl'uɬ/	tl'uh	'rope'
	-zeeɣe			-tl'uɬe	

Another example is the Kelantan dialect of Malay (Teoh 1988), where /k,t,p/ become /ʔ/ in coda position, and /s/ (and borrowed /f/) become /h/, as in (7). (As in Slave, sonorants are also treated differently, but the result is that there are also no Place distinctions in coda.)

(7) Kelantan Malay

/ikat/	ikaʔ	'tie'	/səsak/	səsaʔ	'crowded'
/dakap/	dakaʔ	'embrace'	/tapis/	tapɪh	'to filter'

As we see, in both of these languages, codas neutralize to some segment that has an unmarked Place. Other distinctions may be possible in coda – the sonorant/obstruent distinction in Slave, the stop/fricative distinction in Malay – but Place distinctions are not: corresponding to the obstruents, we see only /h,ʔ/. Neutralization of all distinctions to /ʔ/ is also possible, as in Burmese, for example (Okell 1969), where /ʔ/ is the only possible coda. I will concentrate here on neutralization to /ʔ/ as the representative case, to simplify comparison of the overall patterns to those for Voice. Additional cases are numerous; some examples are Austronesian languages such as Selayarese (Mithrun and Basri 1986), Buginese, Makasserese (Mills 1975), and Sangir (Maryott 1961), the Carib language Macushi (Macuxi), (Abbott 1986, Carson 1982), the New Guinea languages Kanite, Kamano, and Fore (Nicholson 1962, Young 1962), Usarufa (Bee and Glasgow 1973), Tucana (West and Welch 1967), and Guanano (Waltz 1967).

2.3. Summary

We can sum up the data in the following way. I use hypothetical examples to facilitate comparison. Of the three logical possibilities for avoiding a feature in coda position, in response to coda Voice only the first is attested (see (8)). In contrast, in response to coda Place all three possibilities occur (see (9)).

(8) /pig/ - > pik, /pik/ -> pik Neutralization: German

/pig/ -> pigi, /pik/ -> pik Epenthesis: unattested

/pig/ -> pi, /pik/ -> pik Deletion: unattested

(9) /pip, pit, pik/ -> pi? Neutralization: Slave

/pip, pit, pik/ -> pipi, piti, piki Epenthesis: Ponapean

/pip, pit, pik/ -> pi Deletion: Diola

2.4. Place Assimilation

A final detail should be noted about the facts regarding Place. Assimilation is another way of avoiding violations of the Coda Condition, as shown by Ito (1986). Indeed, unless a language has such assimilation, we have no evidence that CodaCond is active. Deletion and epenthesis can also be an effect of NoCoda, which rules out all syllable-final consonants. We have evidence for active CodaCond only when a language has the pattern described by Ito (1986) where syllables closed by the first half of geminates and/or assimilated NC clusters are permitted.

This means that the languages relevant to the consideration of Place phonology all have certain types of assimilation, in addition to the alternations that I will concentrate on. There are some environments where Place or total assimilation takes place; outside of these environments, then, is where we see the other types of alternations forced by the need to satisfy CodaCond.

A detailed analysis of Place assimilation is beyond the scope of this (see Padgett 1995a for an approach). This means that except for Place neutralization languages like Slave, where assimilation is not an issue, I will give only a partial analysis of coda Place phonology for a given language. Consider the contrast between nasal-stop clusters and all other clusters in Diola, for example. Nasals are obviously the consonants most susceptible to assimilation, and any analysis of Place assimilation will need to account for this. Perhaps there are separately ranked constraints triggering assimilation for stops and nasals; perhaps there are differently ranked Faithfulness constraints for stop and nasal Place. Either way, we simply need to concentrate on those cases where the consonants are non-nasal, and we will be able to see the interactions of the other constraints, which are the focus of interest here.

2.5. Outline

In Section 3 I review the analysis of laryngeal neutralization proposed by Lombardi (1999). I then explain how this analysis can be used to explain why we do not see epenthesis or deletion in response to coda Voice restrictions. Section 4 argues that the existence of epenthesis in response to coda Place shows that there must be an explicit Coda Condition constraint as in Ito (1986). Section 5 then turns to the question of deletion. I first show how neutralization of Place can be analyzed with fully Place-specified consonants, therefore arguing that there are no Placeless consonants. Then I show how this difference in representation – there are Laryngeally unmarked consonants, since voice is privative – accounts for the existence of deletion in response to Place but not Voice. Section 6 sums up the analysis of the differences in the phonological patterns.

3. Laryngeal Patterns

3.1. Analysis of Lombardi (1999)

The analysis of Lombardi (1999) first of all assumes privative [voice]: a voiced obstruent is marked Voice, whereas a voiceless obstruent has no Laryngeal specification. This was also argued for by Lombardi (1991, 1995a,b), Mester and Ito (1989), and Cho (1990). We will see that this assumption is crucial to the argument in Section 5.

Central to the present analysis is the Correspondence Theory framework of faithfulness constraints (McCarthy and Prince 1995). I will assume the constraint MaxIOSeg, penalizing deletion, and DepIOSeg, penalizing epenthesis, abbreviated Max and Dep. I will also argue that we must recognize a type of MaxIO constraint that regulates direct correspondence between features, unlike McCarthy and Prince's IdentF family, which only penalizes feature changing, regulated through the segment.

For the analysis of laryngeal neutralization, I will define only the constraints and basic interactions that are crucial to the present arguments (see (10)–(12)). For more detailed discussion of these constraints and others affecting voice assimilation, including the complete factorial typology, see Lombardi (1999).

(10) IdentOnset(Laryngeal)   (Abbreviated: IDOnsLar)

A is a segment in the Input and B in the Output:

If B is in onset position, it must be faithful to the Laryngeal specification of A.

This member of the Ident family is specified for position. Such positional faithfulness constraints are also proposed by Beckman (1995, 1998) and Padgett (1995a) to account for a range of different cases crosslinguistically where certain features have a preference for certain positions, often resulting in neutralization of some kind in other positions. ("Onset" is a shorthand for the released prenuclear position described by the Laryngeal Constraint of Lombardi (1991, 1995a); see Lombardi (1999) for additional discussion. Examples in this chapter are chosen so that the simplified version in (10) is sufficient.)

Given privative [voice], I assume that even though voiceless consonants have no feature marking, the Ident constraint can tell the difference between voiced and voiceless: a segment with either an added Laryngeal feature or a missing one will cause a violation of Ident.

(11) MaxLaryngeal   (MaxLar)

Every Laryngeal autosegment in the input has a correspondent in the output.

As we will see, the additional type of featural faithfulness in (11) will be crucial to the results here. Although their analyses employ Ident constraints for featural faithfulness, McCarthy and Prince do suggest that MaxFeature constraints may exist, and that Ident may actually be decomposed into MaxF and DepF components (1995:71). Other authors have used these constraints (LaMontagne and Rice 1995, Causley 1997, Walker 1997) or ones with a similar effect (Pater 1995).

(12) *Lar : Don't have Laryngeal features

(12) is one of the family of featural markedness constraints proposed by Prince and Smolensky (1993). A consonant bearing a Laryngeal feature violates this constraint, but since voice is assumed to be privative, a voiceless consonant does not.

The interaction of *Lar with the positional faithfulness constraint may result in the possibility of voicing in the onset and not the coda. This is the result of the ranking IDOnsLar » *Lar » MaxLar. Consider first a simple monosyllable. The ranking in (13) gives syllable-final devoicing.

(13a) Syllable-final Laryngeal neutralization   (German)

/veg/	IDOnsLar	*Lar	MaxLar
veg		*!	
☞vek			*

(13b)

/der/	IDOnsLar	*Lar	MaxLar
☞der		*	
ter	*!		*

The *Lar violation for the syllable-final consonant in [veg] is more serious than the MaxLar violation incurred when the consonant is devoiced; the devoiced consonant has no Laryngeal features, and so does not violate *Lar. Syllable-initially, however, voicing is maintained, because IDOnsLar outranks *Lar. In the onset it is more important for the correspondent input and output segments to agree in laryngeal specification, as required by IDOnsLar, than it is for them to lack laryngeal marking, as required by *Lar.

If *Lar is ranked above both faithfulness constraints, voicing will be entirely prohibited in obstruents. As the tableau in (14) shows, *Lar gives a mark for each voiced consonant. Thus the candidate with all voiceless consonants will be optimal regardless of faithfulness violations. This gives the common type of language that has only plain voiceless obstruents.

(14)   Voiceless obstruents only (Hypothetical input)

/big/	*Lar	IDOnsLar	MaxLar
☞pik		*	**
big	*!*		
bik	*!		*
pig	*!	*	*

Thus the proposed constraints can produce languages that allow voicing in onset but not coda, as well as languages without voiced consonants. In addition, where *Lar is lowest ranked, the result is a language without voicing restrictions on obstruents. The remaining logically possible pattern – voicing in the coda but not in the onset – is impossible, which is correct, since there are no such languages. As we see, even if we reverse the ranking of the faithfulness constraints there is no ranking that gives this pattern; either voicing is possible everywhere, as in (15), or voicing is prohibited entirely, as in (16).

(15)   Voice unrestricted

/big/	MaxLar	*Lar	IDOnsLar
pik	*!*		*
☞big		**	
bik	*!	*	
pig	*!	*	*

(16) Voice prohibited

/big/	*Lar	MaxLar	IDOnsLar
☞pik		**	*
big	*!*		
bik	*!	*	
pig	*!	*	*

These constraints generate the correct typology without a specific constraint against laryngeal features that mentions the syllable-final position. Neither is there a licensing constraint as in Lombardi (1991, 1995a) that describes the licensed position. There is a constraint that mentions position, but it is the faithfulness constraint: onset is the position where it is important to be faithful. The constraint that may trigger devoicing is simply the markedness constraint *Lar, which is independently necessary to account for the relative markedness of voiced and voiceless consonants. For more discussion, see Lombardi (1995b), where it is shown that this approach gives the correct typology of voicing assimilation and neutralization.[4]

Thus, under this analysis, devoicing is a result of markedness of [voice] interacting with positional faithfulness constraints. There is no specific licensing or Coda Condition type of constraint. As we will see, Place will differ. Although most of the constraints affecting Place are parallel to the ones affecting laryngeal features, the wider variety of Place alternations will be evidence for additional constraints.

3.2. MaxLar and Faithfulness "Overkill"

I now will turn to the question of why there is only one possible response to the prohibition on syllable-final voiced consonants. We know that impermissible Place seems to be able to trigger epenthesis (Ponapean) or deletion (Diola). Why does this never happen with impermissible voiced consonants?

Assuming a language with the ranking of laryngeal constraints that rules out voiced coda consonants, what repair options are possible when an underlying voiced consonant is in danger of being in coda position? Example (17) shows the violations incurred by the relevant candidates.

(17) No epenthesis or deletion due to *Lar: hypothetical input /pig/

/pig/	*Lar	MaxLar	Dep	Max
pig	*			
pik		*		
pigi	*		*	
pi		*		*

As we see by examining these marks, no ranking of Dep and Max with respect to these constraints can cause deletion or epenthesis to be optimal. First of all, in the languages of interest, where *Lar is high ranked, both the faithful [pig] and the epenthesized [pigi] have a fatal *Lar violation. Since *Lar applies regardless of the position of the consonant, moving the voiced consonant to an onset does not eliminate the violation. The choice then must be made between [pik] and [pi]. [pi] will never be optimal, no matter how the constraints are ranked, because it has more Faithfulness violations than are necessary to satisfy the markedness constraints. Both [pik] and [pi] violate MaxLar since their laryngeal feature is not parsed, but [pi] has an additional Max violation that [pik] does not have. So Max will make the decision in favor of the devoiced [pik] regardless of where it is ranked.

What we see, then, is that given the proposed constraints and representations, segment deletion will always be "overkill" as a way of satisfying the markedness constraint and will never be optimal. This situation corresponds to that described in Legendre, Raymond, and Smolensky's (1993) discussion of the typology of case systems: if the marks of candidate A are a subset of the marks of candidate B, B will never be optimal in any grammar.

Using the MaxF constraint for featural faithfulness is crucial to this result. With Ident, it would be impossible to rule out deletion or epenthesis in response to coda voicing. As seen in the tableau in (18), if faithfulness to [voice] in non-onset position were governed by an Ident constraint, there would be no featural faithfulness violation in the last candidate, in which the final consonant is deleted. This is due to the definition of McCarthy and Prince's Ident constraints, which refer to correspondent segments. Since /g/ has no output correspondent in the last candidate, it does not violate any Ident constraint for the features of the input.

(18)

/pig/	*Lar	IDLar	Dep	Max
pig	*!			
pik		*!		
pigi	*!		*	
☞pi				*

Without MaxLar, then, we cannot account for the absence of languages where the Laryngeal Constraint is satisfied by deletion: that is, of languages with a voicing distinction in obstruents where coda voiced consonants delete, but coda voiceless consonants do not. It would be possible to construct a grammar for such a language. It would have the ranking in the tableau in (18), along with high-ranked Onset to prevent deletion of voiced onset consonants. As we see in the tableau in (19), this ranking, which deletes voiced coda consonants, would not delete voiceless coda consonants. But such a language is unknown; thus, the MaxF constraint is essential.[5]

(19)

/pik/	*Lar	IDLar	Dep	Max
☞pik				
pi				*!

4. Place and Epenthesis: The Need for CodaCond

We have seen why deletion and epenthesis are impossible if we assume the analysis of voicing neutralization proposed in Lombardi (1999). However, these additional patterns are possible for Place. We now turn to the question of what differs about Place that allows this. I will propose that there are two differences. One involves what constraints exist that refer to each type of feature. The other is a representational difference.

First, in this section, I discuss epenthesis. I will show that the relevant crucial difference is that there are different constraints affecting the two types of features. I further show that we can account for some of the differences in phonological behavior by recognizing that while both Place and Voice are subject to position-neutral markedness constraints like *Voice and *Dor, only Place is subject to a positional markedness constraint, CodaCond (Ito 1986).

In Section 5, we turn to deletion. I will show that the difference here turns on a representational difference, based partly on the assumption of privative [voice] made earlier: namely, that plain voiceless consonants have no Laryngeal features at all, but that there are no truly Placeless consonants. The latter is a claim that I will show is possible in OT, despite the arguments of previous theories that [h,ʔ] must be Placeless.

The analysis of voice neutralization given earlier uses no constraint that specifically forbids Voice in coda. Rather, the alternation is shown to be a result of the interaction of context-free markedness – *Lar – with positional and general faithfulness – IdentOnsLar and MaxLar. So we have seen that some coda effects, abstracting away from the particular feature, can be the result of the type of constraint interaction shown in (20).

(20)   Onset Feature Faithfulness >> *Feature >> General feature faithfulness

For Place features, parallel constraints must exist to account for markedness facts. For instance, the family of *F constraints on Place features (e.g., *Dor, *Cor) was proposed in the original work on OT (Prince and Smolensky 1993). Furthermore, in Section 5, we will see that the existence of such constraints and of positional faithfulness (IdentOnsetPlace) is crucial to part of the present argument.

So why do we need CodaCond, if we could analyze coda effects for Voice without a constraint referring to codas?

While it is possible to derive certain of the Place alternations from a markedness/faithfulness interaction parallel to that proposed for laryngeal alternations, the facts about the difference between Place and Voice show that such constraints are not sufficient to account for the phonology of Place. As we saw in Section 3, the interaction of faithfulness and context-free markedness will never result in epenthesis in response to a prohibition on a feature in coda. But Place shows exactly this kind of alternation.

The solution to this is simple: we must simply assume in OT the existence of the constraint proposed in Ito (1989), stated earlier in (4) and repeated here as (21).[6]

(21) Coda Condition (CodaCond): $*C]_\sigma$
$$|$$
$$\text{Place}$$

Interactions of Dep, Max and CodaCond can give languages where vowel epenthesis is optimal (I use the same hypothetical input throughout to facilitate comparison). If Dep is ranked below CodaCond, then a language can avoid violating the coda condition by inserting a vowel (see (22)).

(22)

/pik/	CodaCond	Dep
pik	*!	
☞piki		*

The opposite ranking disallows this type of alternation (see (23)).

(23)

/pik/	Dep	CodaCond
☞pik		*
piki	*!	

Max must also be high ranked for epenthesis to be optimal, in order to rule out the candidate that deletes the offending consonant. The full ranking, then, is as in (24).[7]

(24) Languages with epenthesis in response to CodaCond

/pik/	Max	CodaCond	Dep
pik		*!	
pi	*!		
☞piki			*

Thus, with the addition of CodaCond, we can produce a grammar with the epenthesis alternation. Why does this differ from the result using positional faithfulness alone?

The markedness constraints give a mark to a consonant whether it is syllable-final or syllable-initial: thus, high-ranking markedness will never result in epenthesis. As we saw earlier with *Voice, both [pig] and [pigi] have a mark for the *F constraint *Dor. Epenthesis does nothing to solve the *Dor problem, so it will never be prompted by place-neutral markedness. This is in clear contrast to the interaction of CodaCond and epenthesis: if Dep is low ranked, epenthesis allows satisfaction of Coda-Cond (see (25)).

(25) CodaCond and Markedness effects difference

/pik/	CodaCond	Dep
pik	*	
piki		*

/pik/	*Dor	Dep
pik	*	
piki	*	*

Thus, epenthesis can be optimal when CodaCond is high ranking, since those two candidates differ in their violations of CodaCond. They do not differ in their violations of *Dor, so no ranking of *Dor can motivate epenthesis.

We see, then, that all of Place constraints are necessary. Although the markedness and faithfulness constraints are independently required, they cannot account for the existence of the epenthesis alternation, and therefore CodaCond is necessary as well.[8]

5. Neutralization and Deletion with Place Coda Restriction

We now turn to the question of why we see deletion in response to coda Place, but not in response to coda Voice. Understanding the nature of the Place-unmarked consonant is crucial to the explanation.

5.1. Place of /h,ʔ/

It has often been argued that /h,ʔ/ are Placeless, based on phenomena such as transparency to spreading (Steriade 1987) and apparent Place delinking, as in the cases discussed in Section 2.2.3. Unfortunately, this proposal is inconsistent with the evidence from languages that show the natural class of gutturals – uvulars, glottals, and pharyngeals – which has been amply documented by McCarthy (1989, 1994a). It has been impos-

sible to reconcile these two approaches in previous theoretical frameworks, forcing the conclusion that different languages differ in their representations of [h,ʔ]: in some they are Placeless, and in some they have
Pharyngeal place.

I will suggest that OT allows a resolution of this problem that does
not require language-specific representations for these consonants, and
that will be crucial to the analysis of the phonological asymmetries
described in this paper.

Following Prince and Smolensky (1993) and Smolensky (1993), I
assume that Place markedness is not due to underspecification, but rather
to a universally ranked family of markedness constraints. So the fact that
Coronals are more unmarked than Dorsals and Labials is due to the universally ranked constraints in (26). It is proposed that this family of constraints is not freely rerankable by individual languages, but is fixed by
UG, since all languages show the same Place markedness relations.

(26) *Dor , *Lab >> *Cor

Next, following McCarthy (1989, 1994a), I will assume that the place
feature that defines /h,ʔ/ is Pharyngeal. This accounts for the fact that
these consonants pattern as part of the natural class of gutturals. In order
to distinguish the different Pharyngeal consonants I call on a dependent
Place feature, following McCarthy (1989) for concreteness, as in (27).[9]

(27)   [ʔ, h]:   Phar   [ʕ ,ʜ]:   Phar
            | |
         [+glottal]   [-glottal]

Then, to the hierarchy of markedness constraints I will add Pharyngeal
place as the least marked (see (28)).

(28) Place Hierarchy (PLHier):   *Dor, *Lab >> *Cor >> *Phar

Although it may seem odd for Phar to be the least marked place given the
crosslinguistic rarity of the true Pharyngeals, I suggest that the markedness of the gutturals must be due not to their primary Place, but to other
features or combination of features that they bear – in the simplest case
that perhaps [-glottal] is highly marked. We can usefully compare this to
a consonant like English /ð/, which is highly marked crosslinguistically,
despite its relatively low-marked Coronal primary Place.

This constraint-ranking approach to markedness allows us to analyze
the special behavior of glottals and coronals in epenthesis (Lombardi
1997) and transparency (Gafos and Lombardi 1999). It thus allows a

uniform representation for /h,ʔ/ in all languages: they are Phar in languages where they form a natural class with gutturals, and they are also Phar in languages with neutralization, /ʔ/ epenthesis, and transparency effects.[10]

For the purposes of this chapter, this approach will help explain the remaining differences between Place and Voice phonology. I assume that a well-formed consonant must always have Place – in OT terms, that a constraint HavePlace is never violated. But given privative Voice there are truly laryngeally unmarked consonants; there is no constraint HaveLar. Therefore a glottal stop will get a mark for violating some constraint against Place, even if it is the most unmarked Place, but a voiceless unaspirated stop will violate no constraint on laryngeal features. Obviously this will have crucial repercussions.

5.2. Neutralization

These assumptions will allow us to analyze Place neutralization without Placelessness, but rather as a change to the least marked Place. I assume faithfullness constraints parallel to those for laryngeal features. IDent-OnsPlace requires that an onset consonant have the Place of its input correspondent. MaxPlace requires that an underlying Place feature have an output correspondent. The universal ranking of these constraints, as for laryngeal features, is as in (29).

(29) IDOnsPlace >> MaxPlace

The interactions of markedness and faithfulness do not have the same freedom for Place as they do for Laryngeal features. Since all languages have Place in consonants at least syllable-initially, the ranking IDOnsPlace » PLHier must be fixed. This is in contrast to Laryngeal features, where *Lar » IDOnsLar is possible, yielding a language with only plain voiceless consonants.

Since the Place ranking is fixed, the constraint IDOnsPlace will generally be omitted in the following tableaus. All languages have Place distinctions syllable-initially, and syllable-initial consonants will not be involved in the alternations to be examined.

We can now analyze the loss of Place distinctions in coda, as exemplified by Slave in Section 2.2.3. With the constraints proposed so far, Place neutralization can be optimal when MaxPlace is too low ranked to force the original Place feature to be parsed, and Max and Dep are too high for deletion or epenthesis to be an option. McCarthy and Prince's definition of the Max constraint is crucial to the analysis: Max requires that there be some consonant is correspondence with the input consonant, but not that the correspondents agree in all features. Thus, [ʔ] satisfies Max as a correspondent for the underlying /g/. (*F marks for syllable-initial consonants, which are irrelevant to the outcome, are omitted in the tableaus in (30) and (31).)

(30) Syllable-final Place neutralization (Malay)

/ikat/	Max	Dep	CodaCond	*Cor	*Phar	MaxPlace
ikat			*	*!		
ikati		*!		*		
ika	*!					*
☞ikaʔ			*		*	*

As we see in the tableau in (30), both epenthesis and deletion are ruled out by Max and Dep. Both faithful [ikat] and debuccalized [ikaʔ] satisfy Max, however, since both have some consonant corresponding to the underlying /t/. Both of these candidates fail CodaCond, so the decision falls to the markedness constraints, which pick [ikaʔ]. MaxPlace is ranked too low to force faithful parsing of the underlying place feature, so the markedness constraints cause the consonant to have the least marked possible Place, resulting in /ikat/ → [ikaʔ]. The relative rankings of Coda-Cond and PLHier » MaxPlace do not matter; we can see this most clearly by comparing (28) to the tableau in (31), which yields the same result even though CodaCond is low ranked.

(31)

/ikat/	Max	Dep	*Cor	*Phar	MaxPlace	CodaCond
ikat			*!			*
ikati		*!	*			
ika	*!				*	
☞ikaʔ				*	*	*

A language with coda Place neutralization will still be able to maintain a place distinction in onsets. Recall that IDOnsPlace always outranks PLHier, and that, in addition, in this grammar Max is high ranked. Max thus forces syllable-initial consonants to remain, and IDOnsPlace forces them too keep their underlying Place (see (32)). The high ranking of IDOnsPlace also means that there will be no languages that avoid coda place while satisfying MaxPlace by moving the coda Place feature to an onset consonant, since this would result in unfaithfulness to the underlying Place of the onset.[11]

(32) Onsets in syllable-final Place neutralization language

/dakap/	IDOnsPl	Max	Dep	CodaCond	*Cor	*Phar	MaxPlace
☞dakap					*		
akap		*!					*
ʔakap	*!					*	*

5.3. Deletion: Place and Voice

Having seen the analysis of Place neutralization, we can now account for the difference in Place and Voice with respect to deletion. If Max is ranked below CodaCond, the latter can be satisfied by deletion of the offending consonant (see (33)).

(33)

/pik/	CodaCond	Max
pik	*!	
☞pi		*

The same effect can be caused by the interaction of MaxPlace and Coda-Cond. In order to satisfy MaxPlace, the consonant must remain, since the Place feature must be associated to a consonant. Thus, if MaxPlace outranks CodaCond, the consonant must be retained despite the CodaCond violation (see (34)).

(34)

/pik/	MaxPlace	CodaCond
☞pik		*
pi	*!	

Thus, both Max and MaxPlace must be low ranked for deletion to be optimal: the ranking must be Dep, CodaCond » MaxPlace, Max. In this grammar, the constraints MaxPlace and Max that force the consonant to remain are lowest ranked. CodaCond prevents the consonant from remaining with syllable-final Place, and Dep forbids epenthesis as a way to change the consonant's syllable position. So deletion is optimal (see (35)).

(35) Syllable-final deletion language

/pik/	Dep	CodaCond	Max	MaxPlace
pik		*!		
☞pi			*	*
piki	*!			

Why is this result possible, when it is not possible for Voice?

The representational difference between the unmarked consonants is the crucial point here. As we saw earlier, neutralization of Place results in a consonant that does have a Place feature. It still violates some Place markedness constraint, albeit a low-ranked one. In contrast, we saw in Section 3 that the Laryngeally neutralized consonant was truly unmarked: given the assumption of privative Voice, the plain voiced obstruent has no Laryngeal specification at all and violates no Laryngeal markedness constraint.

This difference means that if Max is low ranked, deletion may be the only way to obey the high-ranked constraints: even /ʔ/ will violate CodaCond (as well as the markedness constraint) since it does have a Place feature in the coda (see (36)).

(36) CodaCond interaction with Dep, Max

/pik/	CodaCond	Dep	Max	MaxPlace
pik	*!			
piʔ	*!			*
☞pi			*	*
piki		*!		

This differs from the situation for Voice, where even if Max is low, deletion of the entire consonant will never be optimal. Devoiced [pik] in the tableau in (37) satisfies both *Lar and Max, so no reranking of them will make [pi], with deletion, the winner.

(37)   Effect of Place and Lar representational difference

/pig/	*Lar	Max
pig	*	
pik		
pi		*

5.4. Comparison between CodaCond and Place Markedness

Now that we have seen the interactions of the Place markedness constraints, one final comparison must be made for completeness. We have seen CodaCond triggering epenthesis, deletion, and neutralization. But we have also seen that there are *F and positional faithfulness constraints for Place, and we saw in Section 3 that the latter type of constraint was sufficient to trigger Voice alternations.

It is true that deletion and Place neutralization both can have an alternation analysis without CodaCond. We saw in Section 5.2 that we could produce Place neutralization by the effects of the ranking PLHier » MaxPlace even when CodaCond was low ranked (see (38)).

(38)   Place neutralization language: a second possibility

/ikat/	Max	*Cor	*Phar	MaxPlace	Dep	CodaCond
ikat		*!				*
☞ika?			*	*		*
ika	*!			*		
ikati		*!			*	

Similarly the ranking IDOnsPlace » PLHier » Max, MaxPlace, Dep will give a language with deletion, without the need for CodaCond (see (39)). Deletion is optimal here because all consonants, even /?/, violate a PLHier constraint, and since these outrank Max, deleting the consonant entirely incurs the lowest-ranked violation.

However, recall that Place and Voice alternations differ. These two alternations are possible without CodaCond, but remember the results of Section 3: there is never epenthesis to save syllable-final voiced consonants, but there are languages with epenthesis in response to the coda constraint on Place. As shown there, such a grammar cannot be the result of positional faithfulness, but is only possible given the existence of the CodaCond constraint.

(39) Deletion languages: a second possibility

/pik/	IDOnsPl	*Dor	*Phar	Max	MaxPlace	Dep
pik		*!				
pi?			*!		*	
☞pi				*	*	
piki		*!				*

6. Summary: Why Different Patterns?

Now that we have seen the analyses of the relevant Place alternations, we can sum up why Place and Voice show different phonological patterns.

For Voice, we made two assumptions. One is that Voice is privative. The other is that the Voice alternations were the result of context-free markedness (*Lar) interacting with positional faithfulness. The table in (40), repeated from Section 3.2, shows the marks incurred by the faithful, devoiced, deleted, and epenthesized candidates.

(40) Laryngeal constraints interaction with Dep, Max

/pig/	*Lar	MaxLar	Dep	Max
pig	*			
pik		*		
pigi	*		*	
pi		*		*

Examining these marks, we see that the only possible grammars are those where [pig] and [pik] are optimal. [pigi] will never win because its marks are a superset of those incurred by [pig]: both violate *Lar, so that the additional Dep mark incurred by [pigi] will be decisive wherever it is ranked. Thus, we will be able to construct a ranking where [pig] is optimal, but never one where [pigi] is. Comparing the remaining two candidates, then, we see that a similar relationship holds between [pi] and [pik]. Both violate MaxLar; thus the additional Max violation incurred by [pi] will always be decisive. So we will be able to construct a ranking where [pik] is optimal, but never one where [pi] is.

Thus, there are only two possible grammars for Laryngeal coda effects: the one where faithful [pig] wins, giving the languages with no voicing alternations in coda, and the one where [pik] wins, giving the languages with final devoicing.

The alternations shown by Place restrictions differ for two reasons. One is that there are no truly Placeless consonants. Thus, if Max is low, deletion may be the only way to obey the high-ranked constraints: even /ʔ/ will violate CodaCond (as well as the markedness constraint), since it does have a Place feature in the coda (see (41)).

(41) CodaCond interaction with Dep, Max

/pik/	CodaCond	Dep	Max	MaxPlace
pik	*!			
piʔ	*!			*
☞pi			*	*
piki		*!		

This differs from the situation for Voice, where even if Max is low, deletion of the entire consonant will never be optimal. Devoiced [pik] in the tableau in (42) satisfies both *Lar and Max, so no reranking of them will make [pi], with deletion, the winner.

(42)   Effect of Place and Lar representational difference

/pig/	*Lar	Max
pig	*	
pik		
pi		*

The other difference between Place and Voice is due to the fact that there is a CodaCond constraint for Place but not for Laryngeal, with the result that epenthesis is only possible in response to Place. A context-free constraint like *Lar cannot result in epenthesis, as it does not treat the epenthesized and non-epenthesized candidates differently. The table in (43) summarizes the marks for the relevant constraints.

(43) Different effects of CodaCond and markedness

a.

/pik/	CodaCond	Dep
pik	*	
piki		*

/pik/	*Dor	Dep
pik	*	
piki	*	*

b.

No CodaCond

/pig/	*Lar	Dep
pig	*	
pigi	*	*

As we see in (43a), then, epenthesis may sometimes arise for place features due to the effect of CodaCond, although it cannot be an effect of markedness. But as shown in (43b), since there is no such additional CodaCond constraint for laryngeal features, and since markedness constraints alone cannot trigger insertion, there will never be epenthesis to save laryngeal features. Thus, the correct patterns are generated for the different features.

If we now sum up the proposed constraints affecting Place in a single tableau and compare the marks given for the candidates, we see that their relationship is quite different from the one that holds among the Voice candidates (see (44)). As is clear, there is no subset relation between the marks of any pair of the candidates in (44). For example, although both [pik] and [piʔ] violate CodaCond, they differ in marks incurred for other constraints; thus, depending on the rankings, either may be optimal. So, as we have already seen in Section 5, we can construct grammars that will make any one of these candidates optimal. This is the correct result, since each type of language is attested: the types that allow coda Place, that neutralize coda Place, that epenthesize in response to coda Place, and that delete in response to it.

(44)

/pik/	Max	Dep	CodaCond	*Dor	*Phar	MaxPlace
pik			*	*		
piki		*		*		
pi	*					*
piʔ			*		*	*

Thus, the resulting typology confirms the correctness of the proposed constraints for both Place and Voice; in both cases we generate all and only the attested languages.

7. Conclusion

These results are important for a number of reasons. The specifics of the analysis attest to the importance of the MaxF family of constraints and positional faithfulness constraints, and they imply that these constraint families will be found for other features. Markedness constraints (the *F family) are used to account for phenomena that formerly were analyzed using underspecification; it is shown that this can be a fruitful way of resolving underspecification paradoxes like the problems with the hypothesis that /h,ʔ/ have no Place features.

But a broader point is perhaps even more important. This is not the only case in featural phonology where there are asymmetries in the types of alternations associated with a constraint. This paper has made at least three points regarding the analysis of such asymmetries.

One is the fact that constraints are not purely formal in nature, but can have substantive differences: just because UG contains a Coda Condition on a certain feature does not inevitably mean that it contains a Coda Condition on some other feature. Rather, we must demonstrate the existence of proposed constraints in UG by phonological argumentation. As we have seen, the facts point toward the existence of a Coda Condition for Place, but not for Voice.[12]

The second line of argument is based on a representational difference: there are no Placeless consonants, but there are consonants without Laryngeal features. Thus, although I have argued against underspecification of Place, I have also shown that we cannot necessarily retreat to the assumption that representations are always composed of fully specified binary features. Proposals like the privative nature of the feature Voice and the resulting lack of specification of voiceless obstruents still have a role to play in the OT framework.

The general form of the interaction that results from the representational possibilities for Laryngeal features is a significant one. Because *Lar can be satisfied by simply deleting the offending Laryngeal feature, deletion of the whole segment is overkill: it incurs additional unnecessary Max violations. Thus, no ranking can make segment deletion an optimal way of satisfying *Lar. As a result, we see a type of alternation universally ruled out without any additional stipulation: it falls out from the basic constraints that are needed and from the proposed representations, because of the resulting subset relationship between the marks of the two candidates. It is clear that this type of interaction should be considered as a possible line of attack on other such phonological asymmetries.

Finally, further research is needed to determine the status of IdentF constraints, given the demonstration here that MaxF constraints are necessary. It may be preferable to have only one family of featural faithfulness constraints if possible, but replacing Ident with MaxF in all situations is not trivial.

Notes

Thanks to Jill Beckman, Jaye Padgett, Joe Pater, Alan Prince, Keren Rice, Paul Smolensky, and especially John McCarthy, and to audiences at Rutgers, the University of Massachusetts at Amherst, the University of Pennsylvania, Johns Hopkins, and my graduate classes at the University of Maryland. Thanks also to several reviewers whose comments were useful and apologies to anyone whose assistance during the long life of the manuscript I may have omitted.

1. Interlanguage sometimes shows a pattern of syllable simplification where final voiced consonants trigger epenthesis and final voiceless ones do not, when the native language does not allow final voiced consonants (Edge 1991; Eckman 1981). Eckman (1981) notes that no such pattern occurs in natural languages and uses this as support to argue that interlanguages are not necessarily natural languages. As several researchers have noticed, there is a strong effect of experimental task (Eckman 1981; Weinberger 1987, 1994; Edge 1991): epenthesis is found with elicitation by reading of word lists, whereas in spontaneous speech there tends to be deletion of all syllable-final consonants and/or final devoicing of voiced obstruents.

2. I assume that in an OT framework this will be due to an overriding right-alignment constraint as in McCarthy (1993) or RightAnchor as in McCarthy and Prince (1995) (although see Lombardi 1999 for a different approach to a similar type of pattern for laryngeal features). The restrictions on nasal substitution include that it only applies to clusters with identical Place, clearly reflecting the importance of faithfulness to Place. It does not apply to coronal clusters for various reasons. For further details see Rehg (1984), Rehg and Sohl (1981), Ito (1986), Lombardi (1994), and Blevins and Garrett (1993).

3. Again, word-final consonants are unaffected (see note 2). Note that for Diola the coda constraint is on [+cons] in Ito (1986), but this language is listed as a case of the coda filter in Ito (1989), which does not appear to recognize any but Place coda filter. Diola also has epenthesis when total reduplication takes place and possibly in other morphological situations; Sapir (1965) is unclear on further details, saying only that they occur in different grammatical situations.

4. Lombardi (1999) uses IdentVoice for the general (nonpositional) faithfulness constraint. This results in a very minor difference in predictions for the crosslinguistic typology of voicing assimilation and neutralization, which is of no concern for the issues in this paper.

5. There is an apparent exception to this generalization in Slave unless we are attentive to the details of Rice's (1995) analysis. As seen in Section 2.2.3, Slave has syllable-final debuccalization. We can see this in imperfective stems ([l] is a voiced lateral fricative).

With V-initial suffix   Syllable-final form
-ji[l]e   -ji[h]   'breathe'

Perfective forms of the same stems show a different alternation: the voiced fricative deletes in the syllable-final form: -ji 'breathe, perf.' Superficially this looks like deletion of impermissible syllable-final voiced consonants, but it is clearly not as simple as that. We see different effects in different morphological forms of the same verb even though the phonological environment – syllable-final – is the same. Thus, this cannot be simply a phonological rule deleting all syllable-final voiced consonants, but must have some additional phonological or morphological conditioning that only occurs in the perfective. Rice's account is that there is an underspecified perfective suffix in Athabaskan, and that this is a phonological effect resulting from the illformedness of the resulting consonant when a voiced fricative is fused with the suffix; the resulting ill-formed consonant is what is subject to deletion, or more precisely, it is impossible to phonetically realize it (Rice 1995:24). Thus, this is not a general process deleting syllabically impermissible voiced consonants, but rather deletion of a particular voiced segment that is ruled out generally in the language. (Thanks to Keren Rice for pointing out this example.)

6. Ito and Mester (1994) propose in an OT framework that CodaCond should be stated as a positive constraint requiring left alignment of CPlace and the syllable edge; they also discuss how to formulate the double linking effects. As far as I can tell, either a negative formulation as in Ito (1986, 1989) or the formulation in Ito and Mester (1994) will interact in the same way with the constraints I will discuss. I call the constraint CodaCond, rather than using an alignment formulation, for the sake of familiarity.

7. If we assume a MaxPlace constraint (rather than IdentPlace) parallel to MaxVoice, either high ranking of Max or of MaxPlace will give the result that epenthesis is optimal. This may seem redundant in that there are different grammars that appear to give the same languages. It is not clear that this is truly a problem, however. The different rankings may in fact give different results elsewhere – in assimilation, where Place changes, but there is no segment deletion; ghost consonants might show differences between Max violations and MaxPlace violations, if Max does not apply to a ghost since it is not a full segment (Zoll, this volume). One might also consider, in this context, whether it is necessarily the case that all speakers of a given language in fact have identical grammars; for some discussion, see Mohanan (1992).

8. Although the facts lead inexorably to this conclusion, we might ask why such a constraint exists for Place and not Voice. I am unable at this point to give a simple explanation, but perhaps this is not unexpected given fundamental differences between Place and Voice. It is truly marked to have laryngeal features: many languages have only voiceless unaspirated consonants. On the contrary, it is not marked in the same way for a consonant to have a Place feature: rather, it is the normal situation for a consonant to have Place. Place is a fundamental requirement for being a consonant and realizing other consonantal features such as stricture. And all languages have Place distinctions: unlike the case with Laryngeal distinctions, there is no language where all consonants have the unmarked Place. Certainly particular Places differ in their respective markedness, but it is not the case that simply to have Place is a marked situation, for a consonant. However, it is marked to have Place in a coda, and CodaCond expresses this.

9. While I am adopting McCarthy's features, I am not necessarily assuming his oral/pharyngeal node feature geometry as well, given Padgett's (1995b) convincing arguments for using feature classes rather than class nodes in OT. In addition to languages that show the guttural natural class (Phar), there are Salish languages where we see a natural class of uvulars and pharyngeals excluding the laryngeals (Bessell 1992). The proposed features also allow this, as this is the class [–glottal].

10. See Smolensky (1993), Cole and Kisseberth (1994), McCarthy (1994b), and NíChiosáin and Padgett (this volume) for different accounts of transparency effects that also do not require underspecification.

11. A remaining possible typological problem is that if both Max and MaxPlace are ranked below the *F constraints on Place, we can generate an unattested language that deletes all syllable-initial consonants. This may be an accidental gap, since the resulting languages has obvious functional problems. However, it seems possible that this problem only exists because we have incorrectly defined the onset faithfulness constraints. If IdentOnsPlace were replaced by MaxOnsPlace and DepOnsPlace, deleted onsets would violate universally high-ranking MaxOnsPlace, and such a language would no longer be predicated. For reasons of space I do not pursue this option here.

12. Smolensky has suggested in presentations that the Coda Condition should be analyzed as a conjunction of the more basic constraints *Place and NoCoda. This predicts that we could also construct the constraint *Voice & NoCoda and use it to account for coda Voice effects, which has in fact been done by Ito and Mester (1997); see also Ito and Mester (this volume). The latter is equivalent to a coda condition on Voice, which, as I have shown in this paper, makes incorrect predictions. This suggests that we should rule out conjunctions of this type. Fukazawa and Miglio (1998) (see also Fukazawa, this volume) propose that we restrict conjunction to constraints within the same constraint family, which would rule out such a conjunction. The question remains how we would then account for the results of Ito and Mester (this volume).

References

Abbott, Miriam. 1986. Macushi. In *Handbook of Amazonian Languages*, vol. 3, ed. G. Pullum and D. Derbeyshire, pp. 23–160. The Hague: Mouton de Gruyter.

Beckman, Jill. 1998. Positional Faithfulness. PhD dissertation, University of Massachusetts, Amherst.

Beckman, Jill. 1995. Shona Height Harmony: Markedness and Positional Identity. *University of Massachusetts Occasional Papers* 18:53–75.

Bee, Darlene, and Kathleen Barker Glasgow. 1973. Usarufa Tone and Segmental Phonemes. *The Languages of the Eastern Family of the East New Guinea Highland Stock*, ed. Howard McKaughan, pp. 190–224. Seattle, WA: University of Washington Press.

Bessell, Nicola. 1992. Towards a Phonetic and Phonological Typology of Post-Velar Articulation. PhD dissertation, University of British Columbia.

Blevins, Juliette, and Andrew Garrett. 1993. The Evolution of Ponapeaic Nasal Substitution. *Oceanic Linguistics* 32:199–236.

Carson, Neusa M. 1982. Phonology and Morphosyntax of Macuxi (Carib). PhD dissertation, University of Kansas.

Causley, Trisha. 1997. Identity and Featural Correspondence: The Athapaskan Case. In *Proceedings of NELS 27*, pp. 93–101. Amherst, MA: GLSA.

Cho, Young-Mee Y. 1990. Parameters of Consonantal Assimilation. PhD dissertation, Stanford University.

Cole, Jennifer, and Charles Kisseberth. 1994. An Optimal Domains Theory of Harmony. *Studies in the Linguistic Sciences* 24:101–114.

Eckman, Fred R. 1981. On the Naturalness of Interlanguage Phonological Rules. *Language Learning* 31:195–216.

Edge, Beverley A. 1991. The Production of Word-Final Voiced Obstruents by L1 Speakers of Japanese and Cantonese. *Studies in Second Language Acquisition* 13:377–393.

Fukazawa, Haruka, and Viola Miglio. 1998. Restricting Conjunction to Constraint Families. In *Proceedings of Western Conference on Linguistics 96*, vol. 9, pp. 102–117.

Gafos, Adamantios, and Linda Lombardi. 1997. Consonant Transparency and Vowel Echo. In *Proceedings of NELS 29*, vol. 2, pp. 81–95. Amherst MA: GLSA.

Ito, Junko. 1986. Syllable Theory in Prosodic Phonology. PhD dissertation, University of Massachusetts at Amherst.

Ito, Junko. 1989. A Prosodic Theory of Epenthesis. *Natural Language and Linguistic Theory* 7:217–259.

Ito, Junko, and Armin Mester. 1994. Reflections on CodaCond and Alignment. *Phonology at Santa Cruz 3*, ed. Jason Merchant, Jaye Padgett, and Rachel Walker, pp. 27–46. Santa Cruz, CA: Linguistics Research Center.

Ito, Junko, and Armin Mester. 1997. Sympathy Theory and German Truncations. *University of Maryland Working Papers in Linguistics* 5:117–138.

LaMontagne, Greg, and Keren Rice. 1995. A Correspondence Account of Coalescence. *University of Massachusetts Occasional Papers* 18:249–384.

Legendre, Geraldine, William Raymond, and Paul Smolensky. 1993. An Optimality-Theoretic Typology of Case and Grammatical Voice Systems. In *Proceedings of the 19th Annual Meeting of the Berkeley Linguistic Society*, pp. 464–478.

Lombardi, Linda. 1991. Laryngeal Features and Laryngeal Neutralization. PhD dissertation, University of Massachusetts, Amherst. Published by Garland, 1994.

Lombardi, Linda. 1994. Postlexical Rules and the Status of Privative Features. *Phonology* 13:1–38.

Lombardi, Linda. 1995a. Laryngeal Neutralization and Syllable Wellformedness. *Natural Language and Linguistic Theory* 13:39–74.

Lombardi, Linda. 1995b. Laryngeal Features and Privativity. *The Linguistic Review* 12:355–359.

Lombardi, Linda. 1997. Coronal Sonorants and Markedness. *Maryland Working Papers in Linguistics* 5:156–175.

Lombardi, Linda. 1999. Positional Faithfulness and the Phonology of Voicing in Optimality Theory. *Natural Language and Linguistic Theory* 17:267–302.

McCarthy, John J. 1989. Guttural Phonology. Ms., University of Massachusetts, Amherst.

McCarthy, John J. 1993. The Parallel Advantage: Containment, Consistency, and Alignment. Handout of talk presented at Rutgers Optimality Workshop 1.

McCarthy, John J. 1994a. The Phonetics and Phonology of Semitic Pharyngeals. In *Phonological Structure and Phonetic Form: Papers in Laboratory Phonology III*, ed. P. Keating, pp. 191–233. Cambridge: Cambridge University Press.

McCarthy, John J. 1994b. On [Coronal] "Transparency." Handout of talk presented at TREND-2.

McCarthy, John J., and Alan Prince. 1995. Faithfulness and Reduplicative Identity. In *University of Massachusetts Occasional Papers in Linguistics 18: Papers in Optimality Theory*, pp. 249–384. Amherst, MA: GLSA. ROA 60-0000, http://ruccs.rutgers.edu/roa.html.

Maryott, Kenneth. 1961. The Phonology and Morphophonemics of Tabukang Sangir. *Philippine Social Science and Humanities Review* 26:111–126.

Mester, Armin, and Junko Ito. 1989. Feature Predictability and Underspecification: Palatal Prosody in Japanese Mimetics. *Language* 65:259–293.

Mills, Roger. 1975. Proto South Sulawesi and Proto Austronesian Phonology. PhD dissertation, University of Michigan.

Mithun, M., and H. Basri. 1986. The Phonology of Selayarese. *Oceanic Linguistics* 24:210–254.

Mohanan, K. P. 1992. The Emergence of Complexity in Phonological Development. In *Phonological Development: Models, Research, Implications*, ed. Charles Ferguson et al., pp. 635–662. Timonium, MD: York Press.

Nicholson, Ruth and Ray. 1962. Fore Phonemes and Their Interpretation. *Studies in New Guinea Linguistics, Oceanic Linguistics Monographs* 6:128–148.

Okell, John. 1969. *A Reference Grammar of Colloquial Burmese*. London: Oxford University Press.

Padgett, Jaye. 1995a. Partial Class Behavior and Nasal Place Assimilation. In *Proceedings of the Southwestern Optimality Theory Workshop*, pp. 145–183. Tucson, AZ: University of Arizona Department of Linguistics Coyote Working Papers.

Padgett, Jaye. 1995b. Feature Classes. *University of Massachusetts Occasional Papers* 18:385–420.

Pater, Joe. 1995. Austronesian Nasal Substitution and Other NC Effects. In *The Prosody-Morphology Interface*, ed. R. Kager, H. van der Hulst, and W. Zonneveld, pp. 310–343. Cambridge: Cambridge University Press.

Payne, David L. 1981. *The Phonology and Morphology of Axininca Campa*. Austin, TX: Summer Institute of Linguistics.

Prince, Alan, and Paul Smolensky. 1993. Optimality Theory: Constraint Interaction in Generative Grammar. To appear, MIT press.

Rehg, Kenneth L. 1984. Nasal Substitution Rules in Ponapean. In *Studies in Micronesian linguistics*. ed. B. W. Bender, pp. 317–337. Pacific Linguistics Series C, no. 80.

Rehg, Kenneth L., and Damian G. Sohl. 1981. *Ponapean Reference Grammar*. Honolulu, HI: University of Hawaii Press.

Rice, Keren. 1995. The Representation of the Perfective Suffix in the Athabaskan Language Family. *International Journal of American Linguistics* 61:1–37.

Rice, Keren. 1989. *A Grammar of Slave*. Berlin: Mouton de Gruyter.

Sapir, J. David. 1965. *A Grammar of Diola-Fogny*. Cambridge: Cambridge University Press.

Smolensky, Paul. 1993. Harmony, Markedness, and Phonological Activity. Paper presented at Rutgers Optimality Workshop 1 and revised handout.

Schachter, Paul, and Victoria Fromkin. 1968. A Phonology of Akan: Akuapem, Asante, Fante. UCLA *Working Papers in Phonetics* 9.

Steriade, Donca. 1982. Greek Prosodies and the Nature of Syllabification. PhD dissertation, MIT.

Steriade, Donca. 1987. Locality Conditions and Feature Geometry. In *Proceedings of NELS 17*, pp. 595–618. Amherst, MA: GLSA.

Teoh, Boon Seong. 1988. Aspects of Malay Phonology Revisited, A Non-Linear Approach. PhD dissertation, University of Illinois.

Walker, Rachel. 1997. Faith and Markedness in Esimbi Feature Transfer. *Phonology at Santa Cruz* 5:103–115.

Waltz, Nathan and Carolyn. 1967. Guanano Phonemics. In *Phonemic Systems of Columbian Languages*, ed. Viola Waterhouse, pp. 25–36. Norman, OK: Summer Institute of Linguistics.

Weinberger, Steven H. 1994. Functional and Phonetic Constraints on Second Language Phonology. In *First and Second Language Phonology*, ed. Mehmet Yavas, pp. 283–302. San Diego, CA: Singular Publishing.

Weinberger, Steven H. 1987. The Influence of Linguistic Context on Syllable Simplification. In *Interlanguage Phonology: The Acquisition of a Second*

Language Sound System, ed. Georgette Ioup and Steven Weinberger, pp. 401–417. Cambridge, MA: Newbury House Publishers.

West, Birdie, and Betty Welch. 1967. Phonemic System of Tucana. In *Phonemic Systems of Columbian Languages*, ed. Viola Waterhouse, pp. 11–24. Norman, OK: Summer Institute of Linguistics.

Young, Rosemary. 1962. The Phonemes of Kanite, Kamano, Benabena and Gahuku. *Studies in New Guinea Linguistics, Oceanic Linguistics Monographs* 6:90–110.

2

Constraints and Representation in Subsegmental Phonology

CHERYL ZOLL

1. Introduction

Autosegmental phonology relies almost exclusively on representational distinctions to characterize the diverse patterns of behavior of phonological elements. One important contrast, for example, is between full vowels and the so-called latent vowel in Yawelmani (1). The latent vowels are parsed only when necessary to ensure parsing of an adjacent consonant. In (1a), the final vowel is required to facilitate syllabification of the suffixal *m*. In (1b), on the other hand, this *m* becomes the coda of the preceding open syllable. No syllable structure constraint prohibits vowel parsing here, but as it is not required for any other reason it does not materialize.

(1)   Vowel/ø alternation:

Latent vowels surface only when they are necessary

-m(i) *precative*   (Data from Newman 1944: 135)

a.   /amic-m(i)/   amic-mi   *amic-m   *having approached*

b.   /panaa-m(i)/   panam   *panaa-mi   *having arrived*

Crucially, this is not a consequence of general vowel deletion, since it is not the case that all expendable final vowels are deleted (Noske 1984). As shown in (2), for example, the indirect object suffix *ni* holds on to its final vowel even though suffixed to a vowel-final root.

(2)   Not Final Vowel Deletion:

Compare *ni*   ' indirect object '   (Newman 1944: 201)

a.   /talaap-ni/   talapni   *bow-IO*

b.   /xataa-ni/   xataani   *xatan   *food-IO*

Traditionally a latent segment is given a diacritical representation to mark it as either defective or extrametrical (Clements and Keyser 1983; Hyman 1985; Kenstowicz and Rubach 1987; Clements 1990; Archangeli 1991; Szpyra 1992; Rubach 1993).[1] Syllabification ignores elements thus marked, resulting in the distinction between full and latent segments.

In this chapter I review and augment the evidence supporting the contention of Zoll (1996/1998) that the apparent need for a special diacritic results from the mischaracterization of latent segments as distinct from other kinds of subsegments, such as floating features. The traditional class of floating features includes patterns like that of the Inor labialization shown in (3). Here the masculine morpheme is represented as the floating [+round]. It appears as labialization on the rightmost labial or velar consonant of the root, but never as an independent segment.

(3)   Inor

a.   kəf^{w}əj-u-m   'they (m.) opened'

b.   nək^{w}əš-u-m   'they (m.) bit'

c.   dənəg^w-u-m   'they (m.) hit'

d.   səp^{w}ə-m   'they (m.) broke'

This chapter demonstrates that latent segments can be seen as a species of floating feature (4), distinguished from full segments by the absence of a root node. This eliminates the need for special diacritical distinctions for the latent segment, while capturing generalizations uniting all subsegments that were accidental coincidences in previous approaches.

(4)   *Full Segment*   *Latent Segment &*
                                               Floating Features

               Root

               |

               features   features

This representational distinction accounts for the primary difference between segmental and subsegmental units: namely, that segments are immediately syllabifiable while subsegments require the addition of a root node in order to be parsed. The differences among subsegments derive from the source of the inserted root node (5). In the case of surface dependent features, an existing segment provides the appropriate anchor, while for latent segments a new root node is epenthesized to host the feature.

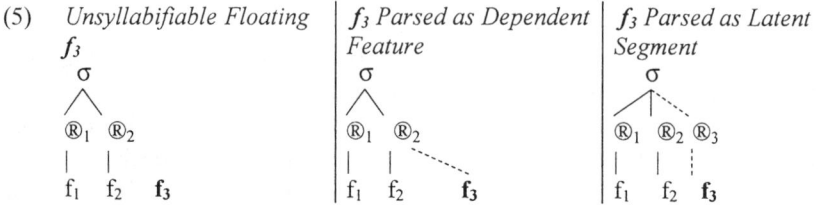

(5)   *Unsyllabifiable Floating* | *f₃ Parsed as Dependent* | *f₃ Parsed as Latent*

(5) *Unsyllabifiable Floating* f_3	*f_3 Parsed as Dependent Feature*	*f_3 Parsed as Latent Segment*
σ	σ	σ
⊕₁ ⊕₂	⊕₁ ⊕₂	⊕₁ ⊕₂ ⊕₃
f_1 f_2 **f_3**	f_1 f_2 **f_3**	f_1 f_2 **f_3**

Utilizing the flexibility of an Optimality Theoretic grammar, I provide an account of subsegmental behavior that generates the variety of surface forms derived from underlying subminimal phonological units and relate the potential mobility of subsegmental elements to the theory of infixation developed by McCarthy and Prince (1993). This work falls together with recent analyses in other areas of phonology that argue for a general move away from representations. These include the reanalysis of autosegmental spreading in terms of constraint-driven harmony domains (Cole and Kisseberth 1994), the recasting of feature geometry as a theory of nonrepresentational feature classes (Padgett 1995), the replacement of underspecification with constraint hierarchies to capture relative markedness (Smolensky 1993; Ito, Mester, and Padgett 1995; Hammond 1997), and more radical nonrepresentational views (Russell 1995; Hammond 1995; Golston 1996), but it differs from these in that it stops short of dispensing with all such distinctions.

2. The Limits of Representation

This section reviews the properties often assumed to be correlated with particular representations – an element's mobility and surface form – and shows that the only reliable diagnostic distinguishing between input segments on the one hand and floating features on the other is their visibility to regular syllable parsing. This has important consequences for a viable theory of subsegmental representations, because it makes it evident that there is no principled basis for an underlying structural distinction between subsegmental elements such as latent segments and floating feature.

2.1. Mobility and Segmenthood Are Not Correlated

Consider first a prototypical floating feature. In Chaha, for example, the third person singular object is indicated by labialization on the verb (6–7). The object affix has been analyzed as a floating [+round] feature (McCarthy 1983; Rose 1997). Because it lacks a root node, the floating feature must dock onto a segment in order to be realized. As shown in (7a–c), here it associates to the rightmost labializable segment, either a labial or a dorsal consonant. If there is no such consonant, [round] cannot dock. Consequently, it does not belong to any segment and fails to appear in the output (7d).

(6)   Chaha object labialization morpheme

          [+round]

(7)   Chaha object labialization   (McCarthy 1983: 179)

		no object	*with object*	
a.	final	dænæg	dænæg^w	*hit*
		nækæb	nækæb^w	*find*
b.	medial	mækær	mæk^{w}ær	*burn*
		s^{y}æfær	s^{y}æf^{w}ær	*cover*
c.	initial	qætær	q^{w}ætær	*kill*
		mæsær	m^{w}æsær	*seem*
d.	none	sædæd	sædæd	*chase*

Chaha labialization exhibits the properties typically associated with the classic subsegment or floating feature (8).

(8)   Ostensible differences between segments and subsegments

underlying representation:	*floating feature*	*segment*
Visible to syllable	no	yes
Surface Form	dependent	independent
Mobile	yes	no

Lacking an underlying root node, [round] does not surface independently (e.g., as a round vowel). Rather, its access to the syllable depends
on its association with the root node of a full segment in the verb, so this
underlying floating feature is ultimately parasitic on an existing segment.
In addition, the floating feature is mobile. That is, it does not have a fixed
position with respect to the segmental string (9).

(9)   Floating features are *mobile*

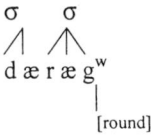

Host is final   *Host is medial*   *Host is initial*

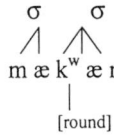

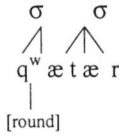

```
 σ    σ                     σ    σ                     σ    σ
 ⋀   ⋀                     ⋀   ⋀                     ⋀   ⋀
 d æ r æ g ʷ               m æ kʷ æ r                 qʷ æ t æ r
        |                        |                         |
     [round]                  [round]                   [round]
```

The floating [round], unencumbered by its own root node, is free to dock
wherever it finds a compatible root.

By contrast, most segmental affixes have a fixed position either to the
left or the right of their host. Compare the floating [round] above to the
prefix *ag-* "present tense" in Ilokano in (10), for example. The affix always
surfaces as a string of fully independent segments and thus presumably
consists underlyingly of the bisegmental sequence /ag/.

(10)   Ilokano Prefix *ag-* (Vanoverbergh 1955)

	Root	**-ag-**	present	
a.	isem	ag-ísem	*(actually) smiles*	132
b.	kagat	ag-kagát	*(actually) bites*	137

Restrained in position by the presence of its own root nodes, it does not
have the freedom to stray from the leftmost edge of the verb in the same
way that the floating morpheme does (11).

(11)   ® = root node

```
        a    g   -   k    a    g    a    t
        ®    ®       ®    ®    ®    ®    ®
        |    |       |    |    |    |    |
        f    f       f    f    f    f    f
```

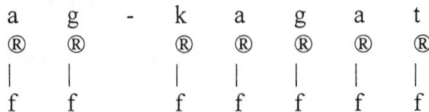

If the properties in (8) were correlated with the presence or absence
of an underlying root node, as exemplified by the differences between

Chaha [round] and Ilokano *ag-*, we expect to find only immobile segments and mobile floating features crosslinguistically (12).

(12)

	Surface Segment	Mobile	Example
A	no	yes	*Chaha labialization*
B	no	no	
C	yes	yes	
D	yes	no	*Ilokano ag-prefix*

However, this is clearly the wrong conclusion. Floating features may or may not have the freedom to stray from an edge (see Archangeli and Pulleyblank 1994), and infixation and metathesis commonly show the potential mobility of full segments. (13) lists some examples.

(13) Every combination attested

	Surface Segment	Mobile	Example
A	no	yes	*Chaha/Inor labialization*
B	no	no	*Inor palatalization*
C	yes	yes	*Ilokano metathetic ni- prefix*
D	yes	no	*Ilokano ag-prefix*

First, metathesis and infixation involve the movement of undiminished consonants and vowels, so we cannot rely on the root node to keep a phonological element in its place. Infixation in Tagalog, for example, involves the movement of an entire affix (14). The prefix *um-* is pronounced at the beginning of vowel-initial verbs (14a), but appears after the entire onset in verbs that are consonant-initial (14b–c).

(14) Tagalog -um- Infixation   (McCarthy and Prince 1993: 19)

	Root	*-um-*	
a.	aral	um-aral	'teach'
b.	sulat	s-um-ulat	'write'
c.	gradwet	gr-um-adwet	'graduate'

Likewise Ilokano contains affixes whose position is not fixed (Vanoverbergh 1955). The past tense *in-*, for example, is pronounced word-initially before vowel-initial verbs (15a), but follows the onset in consonant-initial ones (15b). This affix has even greater flexibility than the Tagalog *um-*. In words that begin with sonorant coronal consonants, metathesis of the affixal segments themselves may take place instead of infixation (15c), yielding *ni-* at the beginning of the word instead.

(15) Ilokano in- Infixation and Metathesis   (Vanoverbergh 1955)

	Root	-in-		PAST TENSE
a.	aso	in-áso	*got*	147
b.	dañgaw	d-in-añgaw	*devastated*	147
c.	lukatán	ni-lukatán ≈ l-in-ukatán	*opened*	40

Moreover, it is not always the case that elements restricted to a single position will be independently visible to syllabification. For example, Inor (Western Gurage) (16–17) has mobile labialization that patterns like that of Chaha (Rose 1994). In addition, certain plural verb forms in Inor are marked by a palatalizing autosegment that can only dock at the right edge (17a–b). If the final consonant is not a coronal obstruent, palatalization fails to occur (17c–d). This subsegmental morpheme is restricted to an edge, but never materializes as its own segment.

(16) Two floating feature morphemes in Inor

    Masculine: *[round]*

    Plural: *[-back]*

(17) Inor Verb Forms (Rose 1994)

    Masculine: Labialize *rightmost* velar or labial

    Plural: Palatalize root *final* consonant if coronal obstruent

		3masc. pl.	3fem.pl.	
a.	√kfd	kəf^{w}əj-u-m	kəfəj-a-m	'they opened'

b. √nks nək^wəš-u-m nəkəš-a-m 'they bit'

c. √drg dənəg^w-u-m dənəg-a-m 'they hit'

d. √sbr səp^wə-m səpər-a-m 'they broke'

No generalization with respect to underlying structure and mobility emerges from this brief survey of the variety of possible patterns. Mobility, or the lack thereof, cannot therefore be used as a diagnostic for the underlying presence or absence of a root node. Whatever the underlying structure of a melodic element is, its potential mobility must be determined by its interaction with a particular grammar. It is necessary to look to other criteria, such as those in (18), to reliably determine underlying representation.[2]

(18)   Ostensible differences II

underlying representation:	*floating feature*	*segment*
Visible to syllable	no	yes
Surface Form	dependent	independent

2.2. Quasi-Segments

A second problem with the traditional representational distinction between floating features and latent segments is that some elements appear on the surface either as a dependent feature or as an independent segment, depending on context. I refer to these as "quasi-segments." This pattern of surface alternation between an independent segment and dependent feature, also known as stability, is widely attested (Goldsmith 1976) and calls for a unified representational approach. The suffix-induced glottalization in Yawelmani in (19) is a classic example of this. Glottalization floats from the suffix into the verb and surfaces on a postvocalic sonorant (19a–b). If there is no such target in a tri-consonantal root, glottalization does not occur (19c). Thus far the glottal looks simply like a well-behaved floating feature. However, in a biconsonantal root that contains no glottalizable sonorants, glottalization emerges as an independent suffix-initial glottal stop (19d), with subsequent shortening of the vowel in the now closed syllable that precedes it (Newman 1944; Archangeli 1983; Noske 1984; Zoll, to appear).

(19)   Glottal quasi-segments in Yawelmani (Archangeli and Pulleyblank 1994)

($^{?}$)aa   *durative*:   ($^{?}$) = [constricted glottis]

a.   glottalize *rightmost post-vocalic sonorant*

/caaw-($^{?}$)aa/   caaw$^{?}$aa-   *shout*

/ʔiilk-($^{?}$)aa/   ʔel$^{?}$kaa-   *sing*

b.   otherwise full glottal root finally if σ structure permits

/maax- ($^{?}$)aa/   maxʔaa-   *procure*

c.   otherwise fail to surface (*CCC)

/hogn- ($^{?}$)aa/   hognaa-   *float*

A less well-known example of this type is the Amharic instrumental
suffix (20–21). On verb roots ending in a coronal consonant, the instrumental is marked by palatalization of the final segment (20).

(20) Palatalization of final consonant, no vowel   (Leslau 1995: 413ff)

			Instrumental	
a.	hedä	'?'	mäheǧa	'means for going somewhere, place where one walks'
b.	käffätä	'open'	mäkfäča	'key'
c.	wäggäzä	'excommunicate'	mäwäggaža	'means for authority to excommunicate'
d.	därräsä	'arrive'	mädräša	'arrival, time or place of arrival'
e.	käddänä	'cover'	mäkdäňňa	'lid'
f.	näqqälä	'pull out'	mänqäya	'instrument for pulling things out'

However, when the final consonant is not a legitimate host for palatalization, the suffix appears as the full vowel, *-i* (21).

(21)   No palatalization, full vowel surfaces   (Leslau 1995: 413ff)

			Instrumental	
a.	t'ärrägä	'sweep'	mät'räg-iya³	'broom'
b.	s'afä	'write'	mäs'af-iya	'writing material'
c.	ğämmärä	'begin'	mäğämmär-iya	'beginning'
d.	däbbäqä	'hide'	mädäbbäq-iya	'hiding place'
e.	marräkä	'take prisoners'	mämaräk-iya	'means, place, or time of taking prisoners'
f.	galläbä	'gallop'	mägaläb-iya	'means for galloping, place where galloping is done'

This phenomenon further belies the ostensible differences between segments and subsegments outlined in (8). Since a single phonological element can appear as either a dependent feature or as an independent segment, surface manifestation is not (wholly) determined by the presence or absence of an underlying root node. Whether or not an element appears as a surface segment does not constitute a reliable diagnostic for underlying representation. Only one structural diagnostic remains: namely, whether or not a phonological element exhibits exceptionality of some kind with regard to syllabification (22).

(22)   ***underlying representation:***   ***floating feature***   ***segment***

       Visible to syllable   no   yes

If this is the case, then all latent segments, quasi-segments and dependent features, which share some kind of invisibility to normal syllabification, should be represented uniformly as floating features that lack a root note (23). The burden of explanation with respect to the manner in which a floating feature manifests itself, including when it may surface as an independent segment, must fall on the grammar. Therefore, the usual representational distinction between latent segments, as in Yawelmani, and floating features, as in Inor, is neither necessary nor does it accurately characterize the variety of phenomena associated with defective parsing in phonology.

(23)   Single representational distinction between full segments vs. *all*
subsegments

> surface: full segments   Latent segments,
>   Quasi-segments &
>   Dependent features
>
>   Root
> |
> underlying: features   features

3. Infixation: Segmental and Subsegmental

Section 2 showed that potential mobility and surface form could not be
reliably predicted from underlying representation. These characteristics
of a phonological element are determined rather from the interaction of
an underlying representation with a particular grammar. This section
extends the analysis of infixation developed by McCarthy and Prince
(1993) to the mobility of dependent features. Section 4 then develops an
account of the variety of possible surface forms that can result from an
underlying floating feature.

3.1. Segmental Infixation

As we saw, floating features and full segments may surface in a position
removed from the edge. (24) presents another example of a fully
segmental infix in Ilokano. Like Tagalog, Ilokano's *um-* affix appears
inside the word in verbs that are consonant-initial (24b).

(24)   Ilokano -*um*- Infixation   (Vanoverbergh 1955: 137)

        (same phenomenon as Tagalog in McCarthy and Prince 1993: 19)

	Root	-*um*-	PRESENT TENSE
a.	isem	um-ísem	*(threatens to) smile*
b.	kagat	k-um-agát	*(threatens to) bite*

Compare the Ilokano affix *ag-*, 'present tense', repeated here in (25).
The *ag*-prefix appears word-initially no matter what form the verb takes.
On both vowel-initial (25a) and consonant-initial roots (25b), the affix
always stays at the left edge of the word.

(25)   Comparison with Ilokano Prefix *ag-* (Vanoverbergh 1955)

	Root	-ag-	PRESENT	
a.	isem	ag-ísem	*(actually) smiles*	132
b.	kagat	ag-kagát	*(actually) bites*	137

Prince and Smolensky (1993) and McCarthy and Prince (1993) argue that infixes such as the Tagalog and Ilokano -*um*- do not constitute a distinct third class of affixes. Rather, they differ from fixed affixes only in that prosodic constraints outweigh the infix's own imperative to align with the left (or right) edge of the stem. In this case, McCarthy and Prince (1993) propose that it is the interaction of the familiar No-Coda constraint (26a) with an alignment constraint (26b) that determines the position of *um*-. Because *um*- is essentially a prefix, the ALIGN constraint specifies the left edge of the stem.

(26)   Constraints   (after McCarthy and Prince 1993: 20)

a.   No-Coda   'A syllable has no coda'

b.   ALIGN(*um*-, L, stem, L)

'Nothing intervenes between the affix *um* and the left edge of a stem'

c.   Ranking: No-Coda » ALIGN-*um*

Rationale: ALIGN will be violated to avoid additional coda

violations

To see how the ALIGN constraint works, consider the tableau in (27). Here (27b) is more harmonic than (27c) because fewer segments intervene between the edge of the stem and the affix.

(27)

	Candidates	ALIGN-um	*comment*
a.	[**um**kagat		nothing intervenes between the affix and the left edge of the stem
b.	[k**um**agat	*	*k* intervenes between the affix and the left edge of the stem
c.	[kag**um**at	***	*k,a,g* intervene between the affix and the left edge of the stem

ALIGN penalizes each segment of the root that precedes *um-* in the stem. Since this constraint ranks below NO-CODA, as shown by the tableau in (28), the optimal candidate (28b) violates ALIGN, but it does so minimally since only one segment intervenes between the affix and the left edge of the word.[4]

(28)   NO-CODA » ALIGN (*um*; L), from /*um, kagat*/Stem

	Candidates	NO-CODA	ALIGN	COMMENTS
a.	[**um**-kagat	**!		
b.☞	[k-**um**-agat	*	*	*k* intervenes
c.	[kag-**um**-at	*	***!	*k,a,g* intervene

Contrast this result with that of prefixation of *ag-* in (29). Here the difference between infixing *-um-* and prefixing *-ag-* follows from the relative ranking of their ALIGN constraints with respect to NO-CODA. The constraint that governs the placement of *ag-* (29) must dominate the NO-CODA constraint since additional coda violations will be tolerated in order to maintain perfect prefixation. As shown by the tableau in (30), in the optimal form the affix appears stem-initially (30a).

(29)   ALIGN(*ag-*, L, stem, L)

      'Nothing intervenes between the affix *ag* and the left edge of a stem'

(30)   ALIGN(*ag-*; L) » NO-CODA, from {*ag, kagat*}Stem

	Candidates	ALIGN(*ag-*; L)	NO-CODA	COMMENTS
a.☞	[**ag**-kagat		**	
b.	[k-**ag**-agat	*!	*	*k* intervenes
c.	[kag-**ag**-at	***!	*	*k,a,g* intervene

These two examples yield the mini-grammar for Ilokano shown in (31). The varied behavior of the two different affixes follows directly from the ranking of their respective ALIGN constraints vis-à-vis NO-CODA. The ranking of ALIGN-*um* below the markedness constraint NO-CODA permits infixation. Since ALIGN-*ag* is ranked above NO-CODA, on the other hand, *um*- is restricted to the left edge.

(31)   ALIGN-*ag* » NO-CODA » ALIGN -*um*

3.2. Subsegmental Infixation

In the cases discussed in Prince and Smolensky (1993) and McCarthy and Prince (1993), the crucial interaction leading to infixation is between the alignment of segmental morphemes and the demands of syllable structure constraints, but their account, adapted with ALIGN, extends easily to floating features. Subsegmental behavior can likewise be accounted for as the result of a conflict between morpheme-specific edge orientation and more general phonological constraints in the grammar.

Recall that in Inor, the third (past and nonpast) and the second (nonpast) person plural forms of verbs (32) are marked by palatalization of the final coronal obstruent (Rose 1994). In addition, masculine is indicated by labialization of the rightmost velar or labial. Thus, in a single form, we find examples of both mobile and edge-bound subsegmental morphemes.

(32)   Inor Plural Verb Forms (Rose 1994)

	Plural ([+ high])		Palatalize *final* consonant if coronal
	Masculine ([+ round])		Labialize *rightmost* labial or velar
	3masc. pl.	3fem.pl.	
√kfd	kəfʷəj-u-m	kəfəj-a-m	'they opened'
√nks	nəkʷəš-u-m	nəkəš-a-m	'they bit'
√drg	dənəgʷ-u-m	dənəg-a-m	'they hit'
√sbr	səpʷə-m	səpər-a-m	'they broke'

The difference between labialization and palatalization here can be derived from the position of their respective precedence constraints with respect to faithfulness constraints. Specifically, it depends on the relative ranking of ALIGN vis-a-vis MAX(Subseg), a constraint that assesses whether or not subsegmental input elements have a correspondent in the output (33).[5]

(33)   MAX(Subseg)

'Every subsegment in the input has a correspondent in the output'

Before illustrating the operation of MAX(Subseg) it is necessary to define the term "subsegment." (34) provides a working definition. In feature geometric terms, a full segment consists of a root node and the F-elements it dominates, where F-elements include class nodes and features (Archangeli and Pulleyblank 1994). A subsegment, therefore, is an undominated F-element. Some examples are given in (35). Note that F-elements joined in a single hierarchy (such as PLACE dominating [coronal] dominating [anterior]) constitute a single subsegment. Conversely, unrelated F-elements (such as floating PLACE and floating LARYNGEAL nodes) are considered to be independent subsegments.

(34)   SUBSEGMENT: an undominated F-element

    (i)   Floating Class nodes

    (ii)   Floating features

(35)

Segment	*Some Subsegments*			
Root	PLACE	LAR		
|	|	|		
[features]	[coronal]	[spread glottis]	[nasal]	H
	|			
	[anterior]			

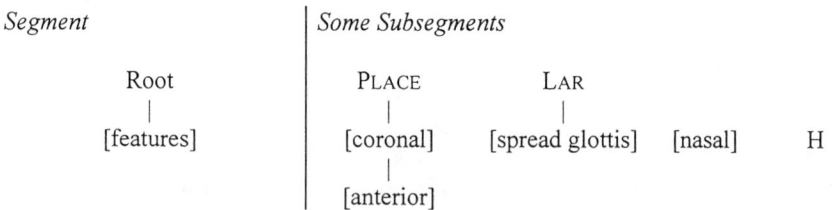

The correspondence relation evaluated by MAX(Subseg) is illustrated by the tableau in (36). I assume that the index of an input subsegment percolates up to the root node of its host and thus can be said to correspond to that segment in the output.[6] Candidate (36a) satisfies MAX(Subseg) because the floating [round] is parsed in the output, so input [round] has an output correspondent. On the other hand, no consonant in (36b) has been rounded, so the constraint assesses one mark for this form.

(36)	/kəf₁əd, [round]₂/	Max(Subseg)	Comments
a. ☞	kəf^{w}₁,₂əd		*ʃ^w corresponds to [round]$_{masc}$*
b.	kəf₁əd	*!	*[round]$_{masc}$ has no output correspondent*

Max(Subseg) is used here rather than Max(Feature) in order to make explicit the different faithfulness conditions that govern floating features as opposed to features that already belong to a segment in the input (37). Under this view, the failure to parse a floating feature results in a Max(Subseg) violation (37a), while a change in feature value for a segment (37b) violates IDENT (McCarthy and Prince 1995).[7] Following Orgun (1996) and Zoll (1996/1998), I assume in addition that feature addition (37c), such as that involved in the change from a plain to a labialized consonant, violates neither of these faithfulness constraints.

(37)		Max(Subseg)	Ident(Segment)
a.	Failure to Parse Floating F-element	*	
b.	Feature Changing (e.g., s → z)		*
c.	Feature Addition (e.g., f → f^w)		

Returning now to the question of mobility, where Max(Subseg) dominates Align, the latent feature will move from the edge in order to find a suitable target if necessary. This is the ranking that governs the masculine labialization in Inor. On the other hand, when Align dominates Max(Subseg), it is more harmonic not to parse the feature at all unless it can dock at the edge specified by the Align constraint. In this case the feature will be restricted to the edge. This ranking regulates the pattern of Inor palatalization for the plural verb forms under consideration. Example (38) shows the two rankings.

(38)   Factorial Typology: Infixation and suffixation/prefixation

a.   MAX(Subseg) » Align   mobile feature   (infix)

b.   Align » MAX(Subseg)   edge-bound feature   (prefix/suffix)

This faithfulness constraint comes into conflict with the precedence constraint for the masculine suffix (39). Because the affix is the subsegment [round] in the input, ALIGN must concern itself with the position of the host segment that has inherited its index in the output, not directly with the feature itself. Evaluation entails identifying the segment that dominates the floating morpheme and determining its degree of displacement from the end of the word.

(39)   ALIGNR(C$^{[round]masc}$, stem)

       'Masculine labialization targets the rightmost stem C'

In Inor, labialization of coronals is prohibited by a high-ranking markedness constraint, *T^w. In the tableau in (40), the possible labialized candidates include only the ones shown in (40b) and (40c). These necessarily both violate ALIGNR(C$^{[round]masc}$) since the final consonant, *d*, is neither labial nor velar and so cannot be labialized. Candidate (40a) has fewer violations of this constraint, since the labialized consonant is followed by only two base segments. Labialization of the initial *k* constitutes a more serious breach of the constraint (40b). In (40c), the subsegmental affix is not realized, since no output segment dominates the affixal floating feature. Since there is thus no *x* that stands between a segment that dominates the affix and the right edge of the stem ALIGNR(C$^{[round]masc}$) is trivially satisfied.

(40)		ALIGNR(C$^{[round]masc}$)
d.	kəfə d]	
e.	kəf^{w}ə d]	**
f.	k^{w}əfə d]	****

Now we are in a position to account for the potential mobility of a latent feature in its quest for a target through the relative rankings of MAX(Subseg) and ALIGN. Since the labialization is mobile, MAX(Subseg) must dominate the morpheme-specific ALIGN (41).

(41)   Inor Labialization

   Ranking: MAX(SUBSEG) » ALIGNR(C$^{[round]masc}$)

   Rationale: Labialization not limited to the final consonant

Consider the tableau in (42). Both labials and velars constitute licit targets for the masculine labialization, but the rightmost consonant, a coronal, does not. Since MAX(Subseg) sits as the top of the hierarchy, the faithfulness-violating (42c) loses out to other candidates that violate only the lower-ranked ALIGNR(C$^{[round]masc}$). Of the others, (42a) is more harmonic than (42b) because *kəf^{w}əd* violates the lower-ranked constraint fewer times.

(42)   k^{w}əfəd from /kəfəd, [round]$_{masc}$/

	Candidates	MAX(SUBSEG)	ALIGNR(C$^{[round]masc}$)
a. ☞	kəf^{w}əd]		**
b.	k^{w}əfəd]		****!
c.	kəfəd]	*!	

Palatalization differs from labialization in that it only appears if it can do so on the rightmost consonant. This is achieved by domination of ALIGNR(C$^{[-back]plural}$) by the MAX(Subseg) constraint (43–44).

(43)   **ALIGNR(C$^{[-back]plural}$)**   '*[-back]$_{plural}$* targets the rightmost stem C'

(44)   *Ranking*:   ALIGNR(C$^{[-back]plural}$) » MAX(SUBSEG)

   Rationale: Floating feature fails to surface rather than violate

   precedence constraint

The tableau in (45) illustrates the implementation of this ranking. Because plural palatalization targets only coronal obstruents, indicating high-ranking markedness constraints, *P^y and *K^y, which prohibit palatalized labials and velars, respectively, the only possible target is the verb-initial *d*(45a). Since here MAX(Subseg) ranks below the precedence constraint, this candidate, which violates AlignR(C$^{[-back]plural}$), is less harmonic than (45b), where the affix does not appear in the output at all. Therefore, in the absence of a suitable word-final target, the feature fails to surface.

(45)   dǝnǝg from / dǝnǝg , *[-back]$_{plural}$* /

		AlignR(C$^{[-back]}$plural)	Max(Subseg)
a.	dǝnǝg		*
b.	jǝnǝg	****!	

The different relationship of Align to Max(Subseg) accounts for both suffixation and infixation of the subsegmental affixes. Together these rankings yield the hierarchy in (46a) for Inor. Although infixation is driven by faithfulness rather than by markedness in Inor, the hierarchy is parallel to the one that distinguished between the segmental prefix and infix in Ilokano (46b). The relative ranking of morpheme-specific Align determines whether a phonological element is able to move from its underlying position. Potential mobility is not a characteristic of any particular phonological representation.

(46)   Infixing and non-infixing affixes

Inor: AlignR(C$^{[-back]plural}$) » Max(Subseg)» AlignR(C$^{[round]masc}$)

Ilokano: AlignL-*ag* » No-Coda » AlignL-*um*

4. A Feature Is a Segment

Traditional literature on floating features usually considers only phenomena like the Chaha and Inor facts discussed earlier, where input features incorporate into the syllable by docking onto an existing segment. Section 2 demonstrated that invisibility to the syllable, which results in some form of exceptional parsing, constitutes the only automatic consequence of representing a phonological element as a floating feature. According to this criterion, latent segments should also be represented as floating features, since they may fail to syllabify even in contexts where regular segments are fully parsed.

If latent segments are represented underlyingly as subsegmental F-elements, how do we derive the surface distinctions between these and the traditional floating feature? The source of the difference is the availability of a potential host. In Inor, for example, high-ranking segment structure constraints disallowed [-back] on labials and velars, but permitted palatalization of coronals. A latent segment results from more extreme segment structure and markedness conditions, where no segment constitutes a licit host for the feature. Latent segments differ from prototypical floating features, therefore, only in that their host must be an inserted root node rather than a consonant or vowel present elsewhere in the string. In this section, I show how a grammar consisting of a hierarchy of ranked and violable constraints can account for the variety of surface forms derivable from an underlying floating feature, here [-back], beginning with quasi-segments (47).

(47)   Exceptional parsing⇒ No root node

surface:	full segments	quasi-segments, latent segments, & floating features
underlying:	Root ... [-back] ...	[-back]

4.1. Palatal Quasi-Segments in Amharic

One important consequence of this proposal for the theory of subsegmental phonology is that it eliminates an awkward indeterminacy that arises if latent segments and floating features have distinct underlying representations. Consider again the instrumental quasi-segment in Amharic, a few forms of which are repeated here in (48). The instrumental is marked by palatalization of the final coronal obstruent, if there is one (48a). Otherwise the suffix is the full vowel -*i* (48b–c). The presence of the glide *y* in the nonpalatalized case is the result of a general process of glide insertion between vowels in Amharic (Leslau 1995:37).

(48)   Amharic instrumental   (Leslau 1995: 413ff)

Instrumental

a.   hedä   '?'   mä-heǧ-a   'means for going somewhere, place

where one walks'

b.   gallAbA   'gallop' mAgalAb-i-ya   'means for galloping, place where

galloping is done'

c.   däbbäqä   'hide'   mädäbbäq-i-ya   'hiding place'

Because the instrumental affix surfaces as either an independent
segment or as a dependent feature (depending on context), there has
been no obvious way to choose a unique underlying representation for
it. In the current framework, however, the theory unequivocally posits
a floating feature as the only possible underlying representation.[8] I
analyze the quasi-segmental portion of the suffix as the floating feature
[-back]. The analysis relies on the same families of constraints discussed
earlier: the segment structure constraints $*K^y$, $*P^y$ (49a) that disallow
palatalized velars and labials, a lower-ranking constraint against palatalized coronals, $*T^y$ (49b), MAX(Subseg), and ALIGNR (49c). The only new
constraint is DEP(Root), assumed earlier but made explicit here (49d),
which penalizes the insertion of a new root node to host the input floating feature.[9] When DEP(Root) is high ranking, it prevents an input floating feature from surfacing as an independent segment in the output.

(49)   a. $*K^y$, $*P^y$ 'a velar is not palatalized, a labial is not palatalized'

b. $*T^y$ 'a coronal is not palatalized'

c. ALIGNR($C^{[-back]inst}$, root)

'Nothing intervenes between [-back]$_{inst}$ and the right edge of a root'

d. DEP(Root)   'an output root node has an input correspondent'

The necessary ranking of the constraints is summarized in (50). The
analysis is illustrated by the following tableaux.

(50)   Ranking: $*K^y$, $*P^y$, ALIGN, MAX(Subseg) » DEP(Root) » $*T^y$

First consider a case where the final consonant is not a legitimate host for [-back] (51). Since candidate (51c), with a full vowel, is optimal, it must be the case that MAX(Subseg) outranks DEP(Root). DEP(Root) is violated here because the presence of a full suffix vowel entails the insertion of a new root node to host the floating feature. Likewise, $*P^y$, $*K^y$ must also rank above DEP(Root), since insertion of a root node is preferable to palatalization of a labial (51b).

(51)	/mägaläb, [-back]/	$*P^y$, $*K^y$	MAX(Subseg)	DEP(Root)
a.	mägaläb-		*!	
b.	mägaläb^y-	*!		
c. ☞	mägaläb-i-			*

The force of ALIGN is visible when some consonant other than the root-final one is a coronal, and thus a potential host for [-back]. As illustrated by the tableau in (52), *mä-däbbäq-i-*, with an inserted root node to host the input floating feature (52d), outperforms the possible but ill-formed **mä-ğäbbäq-*, with initial palatalization (52c), since this fatally violates ALIGN.

(52)	/mä-däbbäq, [-back]/	$*P^y$, $*K^y$	MAX (Subseg)	ALIGNR	DEP(Root)
a.	mä-däbbäq^y-	*!			
b.	mä-däbbäq-		*!		
c.	mä-ğäbbäq-			*****!	
d. ☞	mä-däbbäq-i-				*

Finally, (53) presents a case where the final consonant, a coronal, is a legitimate host for palatalization. Here DEP(Root) crucially eliminates candidate (53b), with a full vowel suffix, since palatalization is possible (53c) without violating ALIGN.

(53) Dep(Root) » *T^y

	/mähed, [-back]/	*P^y, *K^y	Max(Subseg)	Dep(Root)	*T^y
a.	mähed-		*!		
b.	mähedi-			*!	
c. ☞	mäheǧ-				*

To summarize, the case of the Amharic instrumental quasi-segment illustrates how an input floating feature can give rise either to a dependent feature or to an independent segment in the output. In this case, the set of possible hosts for the floating feature [-back] is constrained both by high-ranking segment structure constraints, *P^y and *K^y, and by alignment. These restrict potential hosts to either a final coronal or an epenthetic root node. An epenthetic root is allowed in this case since Max(Subseg) outranks Dep(Root), but palatalization of a final coronal is preferable where possible, since this violates only the lowest-ranking segment structure constraint, *T^y.

4.2. Default Features

Section 4.1 introduced the constraints that may force a floating feature in the input to appear as an independent segment in the output. When this occurs, the remaining features must be supplied by the grammar. Therefore, we expect that the fixed markedness hierarchies that determine the quality of an epenthetic segment (Smolensky 1993), or that apply in any other contexts subject to reduction, such as in reduplicative reduction (TETU) (McCarthy and Prince 1994; Alderete et al. 1999) will likewise be responsible for filling out latent segments and quasi-segments. The requisite markedness hierarchies for the input [-back] are shown in (54).

(54) Fixed markedness rankings

MARKEDNESS HIERARCHIES		RESULT
* +consonantal | VPlace	» *-consonantal | VPlace	[-back] → [-consonantal]
* -sonorant | VPlace	» * +sonorant | VPlace	[-back] → [+sonorant]
* +sonorant | -voice	» * +sonorant | +voice	[-back] → [+voice]
* Vplace | [-high]	» * Vplace | [+high]	[-back] → [+high]
* [-back] [+round]	» * [-back] [-round]	[-back] → [-round]

In this case, then, the segmental outcome of [-back], shown in (55), corresponds to what was previously considered to be the underspecified, and hence "least marked" vowel, [i]. A strong prediction of the proposal that all subsegments are represented underlyingly as subsegmental F-elements is that all quasi-segments and latent segments should be the least marked members of their class.[10]

(55) The outcome:

[-back] → [-consonantal], [+sonorant], [+voice], [+high], [-round] , [-back] → [i]

4.3. Typology

To summarize, the proposed analysis of the instrumental palatal quasi-segment in Amharic straightforwardly derives its two possible output forms – palatalization of an existing consonant or as an independent segment – from an input floating feature. Palatalization is possible only when there is a potential host in the right position, as determined by the ranking of the segment structure constraints and ALIGN with respect to faithfulness and other constraints. Reranking these constraints results in a typology of possible outputs given an underlying floating feature.[11] As shown in (56), the resulting typology predicts that an input floating feature can result in either an output quasi-segment, latent segment, or dependent feature. When DEP(Root) outranks $*T^y$, but both rank below MAX(Subseg), as in the Amharic instrumental (56a), the output pattern is quasi-segmental. Sections 4.4 and 4.5 illustrate how hierarchy (56d) derives dependent palatalization in Inor and how (56e–f) derive the high front latent vowel in Yawelmani.

(56)   Typology

a.	$*P^y$, $*K^y$	MAX(Subseg)	Dep(Root)	$*T^y$	quasi-segment
b.	$*P^y$, $*K^y$	MAX(Subseg)	$*T^y$	Dep(Root)	latent segment
c.	$*P^y$, $*K^y$	$*T^y$	MAX(Subseg)	Dep(Root)	latent segment
d.	$*P^y$, $*K^y$	Dep(Root)	MAX(Subseg)	$*T^y$	dependent feature
e.	$*P^y$, $*K^y$	Dep(Root)	$*T^y$	MAX(Subseg)	subseg doesn't surface unless forced to by higher ranking constraints
f.	$*P^y$, $*K^y$	$*T^y$	Dep(Root)	MAX(Subseg)	subseg doesn't surface unless forced to by higher ranking constraints

4.4. Palatalization in Inor

This section returns to Inor, where the feminine plural form of the verb is marked by a palatalizing autosegment that targets final coronals (57a). In the absence of a final coronal, the affix has no output correspondent (57b).

(57)   Inor again

                   3fem.pl.

a.   √kfd   kəfəj-a-m   'they opened'

b.   √drg   dənəg-a-m   'they hit'

Assuming again the floating feature [-back] as input, the hierarchy in (58) insures that [-back] appears only as a dependent feature in the output.

(58) $*P^y$, $*K^y$, Dep(Root) » MAX(Subseg) »$*T^y$

The tableau in (59) presents a form with a final coronal consonant. As in Amharic, palatalization (59b) is preferable to a full vowel (59c) because palatalization violates only the lowest-ranking markedness constraint. Since $*T^y$ ranks below MAX(Subseg), the optimal output is one with final palatalization.

(59)	/ kəfəd, [-back]/	$*P^y$, $*K^y$	DEP(Root)	MAX(Subseg)	$*T^y$
a.	kəfəd-			*!	
b. ☞	kəfəj-				*
c.	kəfəd-i		*!		

Recall from Section 3.2 that the ranking ALIGN » MAX(Subseg) restricts possible hosts to the final consonant. In the form in (60), the final consonant is not palatalizable since it violates the highest-ranking segment structure constraint (60b). In a similar situation in Amharic, the feature would project its own root node to surface as an independent vowel (60c). Since that does not occur here, DEP(Root) must outrank MAX(Subseg). The optimal candidate (60a) therefore has no overt plural marking.

(60)	/ dənəg, [-back]/	$*P^y$, $*K^y$	DEP(Root)	MAX(Subseg)	$*T^y$
a. ☞	dənəg-			*	
b.	dənəg^y-	*!			
c.	dənəg-i-		*!		

From this it is clear that the surface difference between the Amharic quasi-segment and the Inor dependent feature does not entail an underlying representational difference. Rather, while both allow the palatalization of coronals, only Amharic permits the insertion of an epenthetic root node when no other docking site is available. Section 4.5 shows how from the same underlying representation it is also possible to derive the Yawelmani latent high front vowel.

4.5. *The Latent Vowel in Yawelmani*

Palatalization in Inor makes an apt contrast with the latent vowel *i* in
Yawelmani. Recall that in Yawelmani, latent vowels are parsed only
when necessary. In (1a), repeated here as (61a), the final vowel is
required to facilitate syllabification of the suffixal *m*. In (1b), on the other
hand, repeated as (61b), this *m* becomes the coda of the preceding open
syllable. Syllable structure consideration would permit parsing of the
vowel, but since it is not required, the vowel does not appear.

(61)   Vowel/ø alternation:

   -m(i)   *precative*   (Data from Newman 1944: 135)

a.   /amic-m(i)/   amic-mi   *amic-m•   *having approached*

b.   /panaa-m(i)/   panam•   *panaa-mi   *having arrived*

The first task is to account for the fact that full vowels do not delete
in contexts where the latent vowel does. This follows from the proposed
difference in their representations, where the latent vowel is underlyingly
a subsegmental F-element, or floating feature (62).

(62)   Full Segment   ‖ Latent Segment
   ──
                   Root   ‖
                    | ‖
                 [-back]   ‖   [-back]

The correspondence constraints that make the necessary distinctions
between floating features and full segments are Max(Seg) (McCarthy
and Prince 1995) and Max(Subseg) (63).

(63)   a. Max (Seg)

        'Every *segment* in the input has a correspondent in the output'

        b. Max (Subseg)

        'Every subsegment in the input has a correspondent in the output'

The floating feature is not always parsed. Because the latent vowel
fails to appear in some contexts it must be the case that Dep(Root) outranks Max(Subseg).[12] No Dep(Root) violation is necessary in parsing a

full segment, on the other hand, since it comes equipped with its own root node, so we expect regular segments to be fully syllabified in the same contexts (64).

(64)	/panaa-m[-back]/	DEP(Root)	MAX(Subseg)
a.	panaa-mi	*!	
b. ☞	pana-m		*

This ranking allows the latent vowel to elude syllabification, but two important questions remain. First, why does the underlying [-back] never appear as palatalization in the output? It might be expected to palatalize an existing segment since this would satisfy MAX(Subseg) without violating DEP(Root). I show later on that this follows from a general ban on palatalization in Yawelmani. Second, if DEP(Root) outranks MAX(Subseg), and if palatalization is not allowed, how is it possible for the floating feature to ever appear in the output? Section 4.5.2 demonstrates that this is the result of the independently necessary ranking of MAX(Seg) over DEP(Root). The latent vowel appears only when it is necessary to facilitate syllabification of an adjacent consonant.

4.5.1. No palatalization. The ranking of DEP(Root) over MAX(Subseg) is the same as the ranking for Inor, yet in Yawelmani the floating feature never surfaces as palatalization. This has been a major motivation for distinguishing the two representationally. However, to do so misses the real issue, which is the difference between the set of possible segments in Inor (and Amharic) on the one hand and Yawelmani on the other. There are no palatalized consonants in Yawelmani, so the only possible host for [-back] is an epenthetic root node. No underlying representational distinction is necessary.

The absence of palatalized consonants in Yawelmani reflects the ranking of all three markedness constraints, $*P^y$, $*K^y$, *and* $*T^y$ above MAX(Subseg). In the tableau in (65), palatalization of any consonant fatally violates the high-ranking markedness constraints (65a–b). The input floating feature is also blocked from projecting its own root node (65c), however, due to the ranking of DEP(Root) over MAX(Subseg). In the optimal candidate, [-back] has no output correspondent (65d). With this ranking, palatalization will never occur.

(65) $*P^y$, $*K^y$, $*T^y$ » Max(Subseg)

	/panaa-m[-back]/	$*P^y$, $*K^y$, $*T^y$	DEP(ROOT)	MAX(Subseg)
a.	pana-m^y	*!		
b.	pan^{y}a-m	*!		
c.	pana-mi		*!	
d. ☞	pana-m			*

4.5.2. Root node insertion. It remains now to account for the fact
that the latent vowel is sometimes syllabified despite the fact that
DEP(ROOT) ranks above MAX(Subseg). For this to occur, it must be the
case that some other constraint outranks DEP(ROOT) that can force
DEP(ROOT) to be violated. It has been shown independently that
MAX(Seg) must outrank DEP(ROOT) in Yawelmani (Zoll 1996/1998, to
appear), because in contexts without latent vowel, epenthesis occurs
where necessary to facilitate parsing of an input segment that belongs to
an oversized cluster (Newman 1944; Kuroda 1967; Kisseberth 1970;
Archangeli 1983, 1984, 1991; Noske 1984; Archangeli and Pulleyblank
1994). Since vowel epenthesis necessarily violates DEP(ROOT),
MAX(Segment) must be located above it in the hierarchy. Consider the
form in (66), which contains an illicit triconsonantal sequence in the
input. There is no evidence for a latent vowel here, but an epenthetic
vowel is present in the output. In the tableau in (66), (66a) is optimal
because it best satisfies MAX(Seg). It outdoes (66b) despite the violation
of the lower-ranking DEP(ROOT).

(66)   /wo?y-hin/ → wo. ?uy. hin   sleep (PASSIVE AORIST)

	Candidates	MAX(SEG)	DEP(ROOT)	COMMENTS
a. ☞	wo. ?uy. hin		*	*u* epenthesized
b.	woy. hin	*!		? deleted

The resulting hierarchy, shown in (67), promotes parsing of full
segments, but restricts the syllabification of underlying subsegmental

elements. The need to parse a full segment can force insertion of epenthetic material, including a root node, to create a well-formed syllable. Therefore, it is the high-ranking MAX(Seg) constraint that forces violation of the lower ranking DEP(Root). This compels the floating feature to surface in the output.

(67)   MAX(Seg) » DEP(Root) » MAX(Subseg)

(68)	/amic-m [-back]/	MAX(Seg)	DEP(Root)	MAX(Subseg)
a.	amic	*! (m)		*
b. ☞	amic-mi		*	

The proposed hierarchy captures the fact that the latent vowel, underlyingly the subsegmental F-element [-back], is parsed only when necessary to facilitate the syllabification of otherwise stray consonants. When it does appear, the remaining features are filled according to the feature markedness hierarchies discussed in Section 4.2.

5. Conclusion

It has been demonstrated that neither potential mobility nor the ability of an underlying set of features to manifest itself as an independent segment can be used as a diagnostic for the presence or absence of an underlying root node. Rather, a hierarchy of ranked and violable constraints including ALIGN, MAX(Subseg), DEP(Root), and a variety of segment structure constraints, governs where and how latent features manifest themselves on the surface. The discussion of Amharic, Inor, and Yawelmani has illustrated how a single input representation can give rise to a multiplicity of outputs depending on the ranking of the constraints to which it is subject. These include dependent features, quasi-segments, and full segments. Since the grammar can determine surface position and potential independence of underlying floating features, it obviates the need for an underlying representational distinction between even prototypical cases of latent segments and floating features.

Notes

I am grateful to Linda Lombardi and Sam Rosenthal for their comments, suggestions, and friendly encouragement. Neither is responsible for the outcome.

1. See Tranel (1995) and Zoll (1996/1998) for further discussion.
2. Banksira (1997) and Rose (1997) suggest that the need to establish linear order between elements underlyingly is another indication that an element is an underlying segment.
3. The form *mät'rägya* is also possible here.
4. See Orgun and Sprouse (1999) for important limitations on the allowable degree of misalignment.
5. For a broadly similar approach to the one taken here, see Akinlabi (1996).
6. Struijke (2000) employs a similar definition of correspondence for cases where features of an input segment are split between different segments in an output.
7. But see Lombardi (this volume) for a different view.
8. Rose (1997) discusses other palatalizing affixes in Amharic and related languages that are marked with both a full vowel and palatalization. She asserts correctly, following the criteria outlined here and in Zoll (1996/1998), that those patterns should be represented as full segments underlyingly, since the segment itself is always parsed as such.
9. An alternative to DEP(Root) is a general constraint against syllable structure, *Struc(σ). See Zoll (1996/1998) for discussion.
10. See Zoll (1996/1998) for more on this point.
11. ALIGN further limits the set of possible hosts by restricting an input feature to an edge. The inclusion of ALIGN in the factorial typology refines the predictions further.
12. The constraint violated by vowel shortening, IDENT (Weight) is obviously ranked low enough not to interfere (Zoll, to appear).

References

Akinlabi, A. 1996. Featural Affixation. *Journal of Linguistics* 32:239–289.

Alderete, J., J. Beckman, L. Benua, A. Gnanadesikan, J. McCarthy, and S. Urbanczyk. 1999. Reduplication with Fixed Segmentalism. *Linguistic Inquiry* 30:327–364.

Archangeli, D. 1983. The Root CV-Template as a Property of the Affix: Evidence from Yawelmani. *Natural Language and Linguistic Theory* 1:348–384.

Archangeli, D. 1984. *Underspecification in Yawelmani Phonology and Morphology*. New York, Garland Press.

Archangeli, D. 1991. Syllabification and Prosodic Templates in Yawelmani. *Natural Language and Linguistic Theory* 9:231–284.

Archangeli, D., and D. Pulleyblank. 1994. *Grounded Phonology*. Cambridge, MA: MIT Press.

Banksira, D. P. 1997. The Sound System of Chaha. PhD dissertation, University of Québec at Montréal.

Clements, G. N. 1990. The Role of the Sonority Cycle in Core Syllabification. In *Papers in Laboratory Phonology I: Between the Grammar and Physics of*

Speech, ed. J. Kingston and M. Beckman, pp. 283–333. New York: Cambridge University Press.

Clements, G. N., and J. Keyser. 1983. *CV Phonology: A Generative Theory of the Syllable*. Cambridge, MA: MIT Press.

Cole, J., and C. Kisseberth. 1994. An Optimal Domains Theory of Harmony. *Studies in the Linguistic Sciences* 24:101–114.

Goldsmith, J. 1976. Autosegmental Phonology. PhD dissertation, MIT.

Golston, C. 1996. Direct Optimality Theory: Representation as Pure Markedness. *Language* 72:713–748.

Hammond, M. 1995. There is No Lexicon! ROA-43, University of Arizona.

Hammond, M. 1997. Underlying Representations in Optimality Theory. In *Constraints and Derivations in Phonology*, ed. I. Roca, pp. 349–365. Oxford: Clarendon.

Hyman, L. M. 1985. *A Theory of Phonological Weight*. Dordrecht: Foris.

Ito, J., A. Mester, and J. Padgett. 1995. Licensing and Underspecification in Optimality Theory. *Linguistic Inquiry* 26:571–613.

Kenstowicz, M., and J. Rubach. 1987. The Phonology of Syllable Nuclei in Slovak. *Lauguage* 63:463–497.

Kisseberth, C. W. 1970. On the Functional Unity of Phonological Words. *Linguistic Inquiry* 1:291–306.

Kuroda, S. Y. 1967. *Yawelmani Phonology*. Cambridge, MA: MIT Press.

Leslau, W. 1995. *Reference Grammar of Amharic*. Wiesbaden: Harrassowitz.

McCarthy, J. 1983. Consonantal Morphology in the Chaha Verb. In *Proceedings of WCCFL 2*, ed. M. Barlow, D. Flickinger, and M. Wescoat, pp. 176–188. Stanford, CA: Stanford Linguistics Association.

McCarthy, J., and A. Prince. 1993. Generalized Alignment. Ms., University of Massachusetts, Amherst, and Rutgers University.

McCarthy, J., and A. Prince. 1994. The Emergence of the Unmarked. In *Proceedings of NELS 24*, ed. M. González, pp. 333–379. Amherst, MA: GLSA.

McCarthy, J., and A. Prince. 1995. Faithfulness and Reduplicative Identity. In *University of Massachusetts Occasional Papers in Linguistics 18: Papers in Optimality Theory*, pp. 249–384. Amherst, MA: GLSA. ROA 60, http://ruccs.rutgers.edu/roa.html.

Newman, S. 1944. *Yokuts Language of California*. New York: Viking Fund Publications.

Noske, R. 1984. Syllabification and Syllable Changing Processes in Yawelmani. In *Advances in Nonlinear Phonology*, ed. H. van der Hulst and N. Smith, pp. 335–362. Dordrecht: Foris.

Orgun, C. O. 1996. Sign-Based Morphology and Phonology: With Special Attention to Optimality Theory. Ph.D dissertation, University of California, Berkeley.

Orgun, C. O., and R. Sprouse. 1999. From MParse to Control: Deriving Ungrammaticality. *Phonology* 16:191–224.

Padgett, J. 1995. Partial Class Behavior and Nasal Place Assimilation. In *Proceedings of the South Western Optimality Theory Workshop*. pp. 145–183. Tucson, AZ: University of Arizona Department of Linguistics Coyote Working Papers.

Prince, A., and P. Smolensky. 1993. Optimality Theory: Constraint Interaction in Generative Grammar. To appear, MIT Press.

Rose, S. 1994. The Historical Development of Secondary Articulation in Gurage. In *Proceedings of the Twentieth Annual Meeting of the Berkeley Linguistics Society: Special Session on Historical Issues in African Linguistics*, ed. K. E. Moore, D. A. Peterson, and C. Wentum, pp. 112–124. Berkeley, CA: Berkeley Linguistics Society.

Rose, S. 1997. Theoretical Issues in Comparative Ethio-Semitic Phonology and Morphology. Ph.D dissertation, McGill University.

Rubach, J. 1993. Skeletal vs. Moraic Representations in Slovak. *Natural Language and Linguistic Theory* 11:625–654.

Russell, K. 1995. Morphemes and Candidates in Optimality Theory. ROA 44-0195, http://ruccs.rutgers.edu/roa.html.

Smolensky, P. 1993. Harmony, Markedness, and Phonological Activity. Paper presented at Rutgers Optimality Workshop 1.

Struijke, Caro. 2000. Reduplication, Feature Displacement and Existential Faithfulness. PhD dissertation, University of Maryland, College Park.

Szpyra, J. 1992. Ghost Segments in Nonlinear Phonology: Polish Yers. *Language* 68:277–312.

Tranel, B. 1995. French Final Consonants and Nonlinear Phonology. *Lingua* 95:131–167.

Vanoverbergh, M. 1995. *Iloko Grammar.* Manila: Advocate Book Supply.

Zoll, C. 1996/1998. *Parsing Below the Segment in a Constraint Based Framework.* Stanford, CA: CSLI.

Zoll, C. To appear. Segmental Phonology in Yawelmani. In *Festschrift for Ken Hale*, ed. M. Kenstowicz. Cambridge, MA: MIT Press.

3

Phonological Contrast and Articulatory Effort

ROBERT KIRCHNER

Phonological theory has long been guided by the assumption that the representational elements consist of a limited inventory of distinctive features. Ostensibly, this assumption is motivated by the limited range of contrasts observed in sound systems. For example, segments are standardly categorized, for purposes of phonological analysis, as either [+nasal] or [−nasal]; further phonetic details (e.g., the precise area of the velo-pharyngeal port) are excluded from the representational inventory. The theory thus rules out unattested sound systems in which, for example, unnasalized, slightly nasalized, moderately nasalized, and heavily nasalized vowels all behave as separate phonemes.

In this chapter, I will argue against this representational assumption. In Section 1, I demonstrate that the assumption is superfluous to an adequate treatment of phonological contrast. Rather, within the framework of Optimality Theory (Prince and Smolensky 1993), the contrastive status of a featural distinction [F] within a sound system falls out from the ranking of the corresponding input-output (IO) faithfulness constraint. Under the further assumption that, for some [F], the universal constraint set lacks a corresponding IO faithfulness constraint, it follows that [F] cannot have contrastive status under any constraint ranking. It is thus possible to include the full range of phonetic detail in phonological representations, without thereby predicting spurious contrasts.

I then argue, in Section 2, that phonetic enrichment of phonological representations is crucial to an adequate characterization of phonological phenomena. As a case in point, I focus on the class of lenition processes, which, I contend, motivate direct reference to a universally noncontrastive phonetic property, namely the articulatory effort (qua biomechanical energy) expended in realizing particular segments. An effort-based Optimality Theoretic approach to lenition is proposed, and this approach is illustrated with an analysis of voicing, spirantization, flapping, and elision in Tümpisa Shoshone in Section 3.

1. Contrastiveness and Faithfulness

To begin, I will assume a set of featural faithfulness constraints, of the form PRESERVE(F). PRES(F) is violated just in case [F] is inserted or deleted, or the value of [F] changes, in mapping from input to output.[1]

1.1. Language-Specific Predictable Status

To illustrate the connection between PRES(F) and the predictability or contrastiveness of [F] in a sound system, let us consider predictable aspiration of stops in English. For descriptive purposes, we can encapsulate the conditions governing the distribution of aspiration in terms of the constraint in (1).

(1)   ASPIRATE: A stop is [+aspirated] iff it is [-voiced], occurring in initial

position in a stressed or word-initial syllable.

The English pattern is obtained under the ranking in the tableaux in (2).

(2)		ASPIRATE	PRES(asp)
a.	pɪl → ˈpɪl	*!	
☞	pɪl → ˈpʰɪl		*
b.	pʰɪl → ˈpɪl	*!	*
☞	pʰɪl → ˈpʰɪl		
c. ☞	spɪl → ˈspɪl		
	spɪl → ˈspʰɪl	*!	*
d. ☞	spʰɪl → ˈspɪl		*
	spʰɪl → ˈspʰɪl	*!	

(I assume that PRES(voi), the stress assignment constraints, and so on all dominate PRES(asp), and that therefore candidates ['bɪl], [pɪl] (unstressed), and so on are ruled out.) Tableaux (2a) and (2b) show that, regardless of underlying specification for [asp], a voiceless stop in initial position within a stressed syllable is aspirated on the surface. Tableaux (2c) and (2d) show that, regardless of underlying specification for [asp], a voiceless stop in any other environment is realized as unaspirated. Under this ranking then, for any underlying stops that differ with respect to [asp], the surface form neutralizes to a particular value of [asp]: [+asp] in the aspiration environment, and [−asp] elsewhere. Therefore, stop aspiration is not contrastive under this grammar.

If, however, ASPIRATE is ranked below PRES(asp) (and there is no other higher-ranking constraint on the distribution of [asp] in voiceless stops in this context), then [asp] is contrastive in stops, as shown in (3) for Hindi.

(3)

		PRES(asp)	ASPIRATE
☞	pi → 'pi		*
	pi → 'pʰi	*!	
	pʰi → 'pi	*!	*
☞	pʰi → 'pʰi		

That is, an underlying distinction in [asp] is maintained on the surface (/pi/ → [pi] and /pʰi/ → [pʰi]) under this ranking.

To summarize, within the OT framework, the predictable versus contrastive status of stop aspiration in English and Hindi, respectively, in no way depends upon the absence of [aspirated] specifications from any level of representation. Rather, it depends upon the ranking of faithfulness to this feature relative to constraints on this feature's surface distribution. Indeed, this understanding of contrastiveness, first observed by Smolensky (1993), now appears to be standard in OT (e.g., Kager 1999, ch. 1).

1.2. Universal Predictable Status

Phonetically, of course, aspiration is not a zero-sum thing, but a continuous dimension. The degree of stop aspiration actually varies gradiently, in English and other languages, depending on the stress level and the phrasal position of the relevant syllable (see, e.g., Pierrehumbert and Talkin 1992). I will now show that the surface gradiency of the aspiration pattern can be handled in terms of the same sort of formalism – with constraints on surface distribution interacting with faithfulness constraints – without thereby predicting spurious contrasts involving intermediate degrees of aspiration. We simply recognize the continuous aspiration dimension in the representation, and adopt a gradient version of the ASPIRATE constraint as in (4).[2]

(4)   ASPIRATE (gradient): A voiceless stop in initial position in a degree n stressed

     syllable, or in a degree n prosodic constituent, is realized with degree n

     aspiration.

The faithfulness constraint, PRES(asp), however, still imposes a binary distinction, no aspiration (= [–asp]) versus some positive degree of aspiration (= [+asp]). That is, any treatment of contrastiveness must capture the fact that phonological systems impose categories on the raw phonetic signal; but the source of this categorization is shifted from the representational theory to the set of faithfulness constraints.[3] Other distinctions in aspiration, such as [± degree 33 aspiration], are assumed to lack corresponding faithfulness constraints. This stipulation is simply the analogue, in this approach, of the standard stipulation that only a binary aspiration distinction is represented in the phonology.

Now, just as in the previous tableaux, if the ASPIRATE constraint dominates PRES(asp), aspiration is predictable (albeit now gradiently assigned, depending on the prosodic prominence of the context). PRES(asp) remains completely inactive. On the other hand, if PRES(asp) dominates ASPIRATE, an underlyingly unaspirated stop maintains its lack of aspiration on the surface, regardless of context, while a stop that is underlyingly specified for some positive degree of aspiration is realized with degree n aspiration, in accordance with the gradient ASPIRATE constraint, so long as $n > 0$. This is shown in (5). Crucially, however, since there are, by hypothesis, no faithfulness constraints on intermediate degrees of aspiration (PRES(degree m aspiration)), an underlying distinction between degree *m* aspirated stops and other aspirated stops is not maintained on the surface: a stop with some particular positive degree of aspiration can only map to the positive surface aspiration value that best satisfies the ASPIRATE constraint. Thus, just as in the previous section, regardless of the ranking of the relevant constraints, distinctions among intermediate degrees of aspiration have no contrastive status – notwithstanding the introduction of a continuous aspiration dimension in the representation.

(5)

	PRES(asp)	ASPIRATE (gradient)
☞ stop with degree 0 aspiration → degree 0 aspiration (in context for degree *n* aspiration), $n > 0$		*
stop with degree 0 aspiration → degree *n* aspiration (in context for degree *n* aspiration), $n > 0$	*!	
stop with degree *m* aspiration → degree 0 aspiration (in context for degree *n* aspiration), $m,n > 0$	*!	*
☞ stop with degree *m* aspiration → degree *n* aspiration (in context for degree *n* aspiration), $m,n > 0$		
stop with degree *m* aspiration → degree *m* aspiration (in context for degree *n* aspiration), $m,n > 0$		*!

1.3. Discussion

Note that the foregoing result does not translate elegantly into a rule-based framework. In the absence of representational restrictions, we would have to stipulate that every language has a rule or set of rules that neutralize gradient and other universally noncontrastive distinctions in all contexts, but that the specific rules achieving this outcome differ from language to language. For example, the distinction between released and unreleased stops is universally noncontrastive, though stop release is phonologically relevant in licensing contour segments (partially nasalized or affricated) (Steriade 1993a). Nevertheless, this feature neutralizes (prepausally) to [+released] in French and [−released] in Korean, and it is in free variation in English. In a rule-based framework, we would have to posit three distinct neutralizing rules for the three languages; thus, there is no unified formal expression of the feature's universal noncontrastiveness. In the OT formalism, however, what unifies the three cases is the universal absence of a PRES(released) constraint, and what distinguishes them is the ranking of conflicting constraints on the surface value of [released], such as "Stops must be released" versus "Coda stops must be unreleased."

This approach should also be contrasted with an OT framework using a more standard (i.e., restrictive) theory of representations. To reiterate, my point is that the general notion of interaction between faithfulness and markedness constraints, which already constitutes a part of virtually all conceptions of OT, renders such representational restrictions and the attendant distinction between phonological and phonetic levels of representation superfluous.

Further note that the OT device of constraint ranking permits us to appeal to a *potential contrastiveness hierarchy*. Intuitively, the position of PRES(F) in the constraint hierarchy of a grammar for a given speaker corresponds to the degree to which the speaker attends to feature [F] in the mapping between input and output. Thus, for example, speakers of Hindi attend to stop aspiration distinctions in a way that English speakers do not. Although constraint ranking is generally a language-specific matter, it must be recognized that certain featural distinctions are inherently more salient than others – for instance, [consonantal] (characterized by abrupt, large-scale changes in amplitude) versus [longitudinal vocal fold tension] (principally cued by subtle F0 perturbations in the beginning of a following vowel), which is contrastive only in Musey (Shryock 1995). The notion of potential contrastiveness, or inherent salience, can thus be formalized in terms of a set of universal stochastic ranking conditions: if feature [F] is inherently more salient than feature G, then PRES(F) has a correspondingly high probability of outranking PRES(G) (cf. Jun 1995 for a deterministic treatment of such ranking conditions; see generally Boersma 1998, ch. 15, for discussion of stochastic ranking). In sum, features that are inherently highly salient have corresponding faithfulness constraints that are universally highly ranked; while inherently subtler features have lower-ranked faithfulness constraints. And, as discussed earlier, universally noncontrastive features lack faithfulness constraints altogether – or, equivalently, they are universally so low ranked that their probability of being active in any grammar approaches zero.

Moreover, this approach potentially captures the connection between the frequent noncontrastiveness of some feature and its usual restriction to narrow environments in languages where it is contrastive. For example, Kaun (1994) observes that most languages do not permit a contrast in [round] independent of [back], but in those languages that do (e.g., Turkish), contrastive rounding is typically subject to vowel harmony – that is, surface restrictions on the vowels that can occur with it (within some domain). The lower the ranking of PRES(F), the more constraints on the distribution of [F] that may dominate PRES(F), hence the narrower the contexts in which [F] is contrastive, and the greater the likelihood that [F] will not be contrastive in any context at all.

The traditional representational treatment of contrastiveness, on the other hand, is all or nothing. If a phonetic property is admitted to the pantheon of phonological features, it is formally equal to all other features in its potential for signaling contrasts, and no distinction can then be drawn between features that are frequently contrastive and those that are rarely contrastive, crosslinguistically. Similarly, if a feature is contrastive in a given language, it must be present underlyingly, and no distinction can then be drawn between features that are contrastive in a broad array of contexts and contrasts that surface only in narrow contexts. The representational treatment thus fails to capture the notion of a potential contrastiveness hierarchy as well as the connection between potential contrastiveness and contextual restrictions on contrast.

For further discussion of this approach, including a formal proof of the relation between contrastiveness and ranking of faithfulness constraints, see Kirchner (1997). A more richly articulated system of OT constraints for handling gradient variation (albeit following the same general approach to contrastiveness) is proposed in Boersma (1998). Alternatively, Flemming (1995) rejects IO faithfulness constraints in favor of constraints that refer directly to the maintenance of contrast over sets of possible forms, but his proposal is in accord with Kirchner's and Boersma's to the extent that he handles phonological contrast in terms of the constraint system, rather than in terms of representational abstraction.

2. An Effort-Based Approach to Lenition

We have seen in Section 1, that a restrictive feature inventory is super-fluous to an adequate treatment of contrastiveness, and that by dis-pensing with this assumption – thereby allowing rich phonetic detail in phonological representation – phonological theory can take on the problem of gradient variation. I will now argue that this move is motivated as well by phenomena from the phonological "heartland," focusing on the class of processes generally referred to as lenition, or weakening. These traditionally include:

- *degemination*, i.e., reduction of a long (geminate) to a short (sin-gleton) consonant (e.g., tː → t);
- *voicing* (e.g., t → d);
- *flapping*, i.e., reduction of a stop to a flap (e.g., t → ɾ);
- *spirantization*, i.e., reduction from a stop (or affricate) to a fricative or approximant continuant (e.g., t → {θ, θ̞});
- reduction of other consonants to approximants (e.g., r → ɹ, s → s̞);
- *debuccalization*, i.e., reduction to a laryngeal consonant (e.g., t → ʔ, s → h);
- and, at its most extreme, complete *elision* (e.g., t → Ø).

2.1. Previous Approaches to Lenition

As a threshold matter, we must ask why this set of processes should be regarded as a unified phenomenon. First, lenition processes have a unified phonetic characterization: they all involve reduction of the mag-nitude or duration of articulatory gestures.[4] Second, these processes occur in substantially the same set of contexts crosslinguistically (most typically intervocalic and coda positions). Indeed, sometimes we find lenitional chain shifts in a single context within a given language (e.g., Danish t → d → ð, Bauer et al. 1980), or lenition patterns whereby con-sonants display more extreme lenition in faster/more casual speech (e.g., Florentine Italian t → {θ, θ̞, ð, or Ø} depending on rate/register of speech;

see Giannelli and Savoia 1979). Clearly, then, an approach which treated lenition as a collection of unrelated processes would be missing significant generalizations.

Nevertheless, previous treatments of lenition have failed to offer an (empirically adequate) unified formal characterization of lenition or to account for the contexts in which lenition typically occurs. Let us briefly consider the two most standard approaches. First, autosegmental feature-spreading treatments have been proposed (e.g., Harris 1984, who handles Spanish spirantization as [+continuant] spreading, cf. Mascaró 1983, Jacobs and Wetzels 1988; and see Selkirk 1980, Mascaró 1987, Cho 1990, and Lombardi 1991 for treatments of voicing assimilation as autosegmental spreading). But feature spreading cannot be extended to lenition generally, for degemination, debuccalization, and elision can only be expressed in autosegmental theory as deletion or delinking of phonological material. Moreover, this approach fails to give a natural account of the most typical lenition context, namely, intervocalic position: it suffices to spread the relevant feature from either adjacent vowel, and so the role of the other vowel in conditioning the lenition is unexplained.

An alternative approach, often tentatively suggested (e.g., Foley 1977; Churma 1988; Clements 1990; Hock 1991; NíChiosáin 1991; Elmedlaoui 1993; Lavoie 1996), but rarely fleshed out in explicit analyses, is the notion of lenition as sonority promotion. But if we take the sonority scale (e.g., stops > voiceless fricatives > voiced fricatives > nasals > liquids > high vowels/glides > low vowels (Dell and Elmedlaoui 1985)) seriously as a characterization of lenition, we incorrectly predict that fricatives ought to be able to lenite to nasals. Moreover, vowel reduction, which would appear to be the vocalic counterpart of consonant lenition, typically involves raising (and centralization) – e.g., a → ə (see Crosswhite, to appear); but the higher the vowel, the less sonorous it is. Finally, the sonority promotion proposal says nothing, per se, about the contexts and conditions under which lenition naturally occurs.

2.2. A Unified, Effort-Based Approach

In contrast to the approaches just discussed, I propose that lenition is driven by the phonetic imperative in (6).

(6)   LAZY: Minimize articulatory effort (i.e. biomechanical energy).

I assume, following Flemming (1995), that a phonological representation consists of parallel perceptual and articulatory representations, the latter in the form of a gestural score (e.g., Browman and Goldstein 1990). The perceptual side of the representation should, in principle, be viewed as an (auditorily transformed) spectrogram (cf. Boersma 1998), but for reasons of expository convenience, I will continue to refer to binary-valued features of the familiar sort in the discussion to follow. This approach thus crucially presupposes that phonological representations include universally predictable phonetic properties – in particular, the *effort cost* associated with, and computable from, a given set of articulatory gestures. The biomechanical energy required for a set of gestures, is, of course, an empirical question, to be addressed through phonetic experimentation and articulatory modeling (see generally Lindblom 1983, Boersma 1998), but we can go a long way towards an analysis of consonant lenition patterns relying merely on the general inference that, all else being equal, a consonant constriction gesture involving greater displacement of the articulator requires more energy than a gesture of lesser displacement.

Language-specific lenition patterns arise from LAZY, interacting with faithfulness constraints, within an Optimality Theoretic grammar. Spirantization, for example, is analyzed in terms of rankings where LAZY dominates PRES(continuant) (7a). Under the opposite ranking (b), spirantization is blocked.

(7) a.

/d/	LAZY	PRES(cont)
d	**!	
☞ ð	*	*

b.

/d/	PRES(cont)	LAZY
☞ d		**
ð	*!	*

The treatment of spirantization in (7), in terms of conflict between LAZY and faithfulness, can trivially be extended to all manner of lenition phenomena. The type of structural change occurring in a given language depends upon which of the lenition-blocking constraints, if any, are ranked below LAZY. If PRES(length), then degemination; if PRES(voiced), then voicing; if PRES(sonorant), then reduction of an obstruent to an approximant; if PRES(place features), then debuccalization; if PRES(consonant), then elision; if no PRESERVE constraint, then no lenition at all. Lenition thus receives a unified characterization, under this approach, in terms of the ranking schema: LAZY » faithfulness.[5]

2.3. Contexts

In the simple case of LAZY outranking some faithfulness constraint, such as PRES(cont), the result is context-free lenition, as in Berber (Saib 1977), where all singleton obstruents are realized as fricatives, in all contexts. However, with a few enrichments, the theory can capture context-sensitive lenition patterns as well in terms of the same basic ranking schema. First, restriction of lenition to coda and word-final position can be understood in terms of the impoverished perceptual cues to a consonant's identity in phonotactic positions where it lacks an audible release; see Steriade (1993b, 1995, 2000) and Jun (1995). The greater perceptibility of consonants in positions where their release is audible can be formally expressed by breaking up faithfulness constraints according to context: the more salient position corresponds to a universally higher-ranked faithfulness constraint, thus PRES(F/released position) » PRES(F), as motivated by Jun (1995), cf. Beckman (1997). Coda and word-final lenition can then be obtained by ranking LAZY between these, as in (8). Intuitively speaking, this treatment captures the insight that there is greater impetus to lenite in contexts where there is relatively little perceptual "bang" for the articulatory "buck."

(8)

	PRES(cont/ released)	LAZY	PRES(cont)
ak' → ak'		**!	
☞ ak' → ax		*	*
ak'ta → ak'ta		**!	
☞ ak'ta → axta		*	*
☞ aka → aka		**	
aka → axa	*!	*	*

Restriction of lenition to particular places of articulation may similarly be obtained in terms of context-sensitive faithfulness constraints: specifically, the operative context refers to specific place features. For example, the ranking in (9) results in spirantization of coda dorsal consonants, but not coronals or labials, as in Quechua.[6]

(9)

	PRES(cont/ released)	PRES(cont/ lab)	PRES(cont/ cor)	LAZY	PRES(cont /dors)
Coda position: ak˺ → ak˺				**!	
☞ ak˺ → ax				*	*
ap˺ → ap˺				**	
☞ ap˺ → aɸ		*!		*	*
at˺ → at˺				**	
☞ at˺ → aθ			*!	*	*
Onset position: ☞ pa, ta, ka → pa, ta, ka				**	
pa, ta, ka → ɸa, θa, xa	*!	*	*	*	*

Furthermore, intervocalic lenition receives a straightforward effort-based treatment. Ceteris paribus, the more open (i.e., unconstricted) the flanking segments, the greater the displacement (hence effort) required to achieve a given degree of consonantal constriction. The primacy of intervocalic position as a context for lenition thus falls out from the natural assumption that the impetus to lenite more effortful gestures is stronger than the impetus to lenite easier gestures. The correctness of this displacement-based understanding of intervocalic position is supported by the existence of the following related contexts.

Case 1: triggers include open Cs as well as Vs, as in (10).

(10)   Shina (Rajapurohit 1983)

   a.   *Voiced stops spirantize in /V__V position:*

      baβo   'father'   səði: 'monkey'   muɣuɾ 'bowl'

   b.   *and when flanked by liquids or vowels, i.e. /ɾ__V position:*

      daɾβak 'race'   parða: 'veil'   gurɣuɾ 'churning rod'

   c.   *but not elsewhere (e.g., preceded by another stop):*

      ekbo   'alone'   səkdər   'file (tool)'

Case 2: triggers restricted to low Vs, as in (11).

(11)   Middle Italian (Central dialects) (Grammont 1933)

   a.   *k > g /V__V when either flanking vowel was low:*

      laku > lago 'lake'   mika > miga 'crumb'

   b.   *but not elsewhere:*

      amiku > amiko 'friend'   kaeku > tʃieko 'blind'

A formal treatment of intervocalic and other displacement-based lenition contexts, simply requires decomposition of LAZY into a family of binary effort thresholds, with a fixed internal ranking from higher to lower thresholds, as in (12). Cf. Prince and Smolensky's (1993) similar binarization of the scalar HNUC into a family of "peak affinity" constraints, with a fixed internal ranking corresponding to the sonority hierarchy. The intervocalic lenition context (and variations thereon) can now be obtained by interleaving PRES(cont) (or other lenition-blocking constraints) at particular points within the LAZY series, as shown in Figure 3.1.

(12)   <u>LAZY "binarized"</u>:

   ... $LAZY_{n+1}$ » $LAZY_n$ » $LAZY_{n-1}$ ... (where $LAZY_n$ ="Do not expend

   effort $\geq n$")

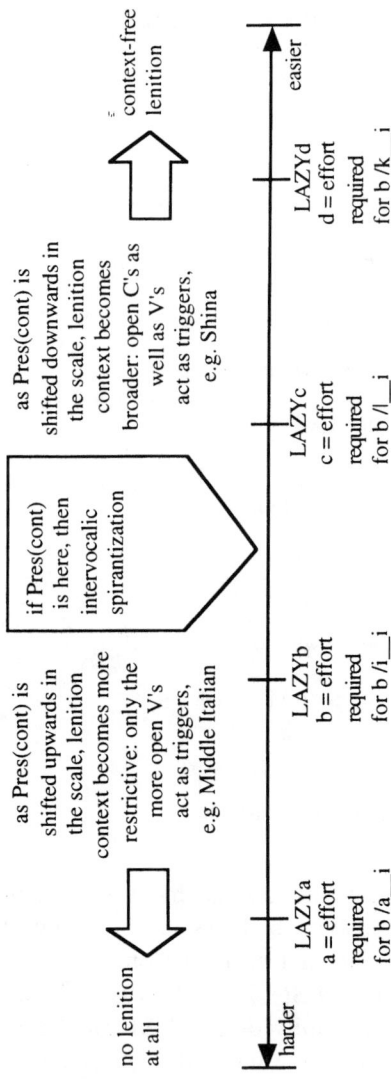

Figure 3.1. Intervocalic (and similar) lenition contexts obtained by interleaving the relevant faithfulness constraint(s) within the LAZY hierarchy.

2.4. Fortition Constraints

Note, however, that for cases of complementary distribution (e.g., no word-initial fricatives and no noninitial stops), the use of faithfulness constraints as lenition blockers is insufficient. This is illustrated in (13).

(13)

		PRES(cont/#__)	LAZY	PRES(cont)
☞	a. #ka → #ka		**	
	#ka → #xa	*!	*	*
☞	b. #aka → #aka		**!	
	#aka → #axa		*	*
	c. #xa → #ka	*!	**	*
	#xa → #xa		*	
	d. #axa → #aka		**!	*
☞	#axa → #axa		*	

If, as in (13c), some word-initial obstruent is underlyingly [+cont] (and the OT tenet of Richness of the Base (Prince and Smolensky 1993, ch. 9) prevents us from excluding such an input), both faithfulness and LAZY favor the fricative candidate. Thus, it is impossible to rule out word-initial fricatives. An additional class of lenition-blocking constraints is therefore required. These must not only block lenition, but actively induce fortition, for instance, requiring word-initial obstruents to be realized as stops (*[+cont,−son]/#__).[7] It seems plausible that these fortition constraints are, like the context-sensitive faithfulness constraints, grounded in perceptual considerations. For example, the release burst of a stop contains salient place of articulation (e.g., Wright 1996). Thus, by militating in favor of consonants with a release burst, this constraint can be viewed as enhancing the perceptibility of the consonant, and the allocation of more robust cues to word-initial position may be viewed as reflecting the greater importance of word-initial consonants in lexical access. More generally, I will assume that the fortition constraints that we appeal to, for purposes of lenition typology, are of the form $*\alpha F/[_{D\_}$, where D is some prosodic or morphological domain (including a stressed syllable), and [αF] refers to some feature specification that is less perceptually salient in the context /[$_{D\_}$ than is [-αF].[8]

2.5. Further Generalizations

The effort-based approach to lenition straightforwardly accounts for a number of additional generalizations concerning lenition typology.

- Synchronic spirantization processes never convert a stop to a sibilant or other strongly fricated continuant; rather, spirantization typically results in weak fricatives or approximants, such as [ð] or [ð̞]. This result is surprising, given the general observation that [s] and other stridents are the unmarked fricatives. Strident fricatives require a sustained interval of precise, close constriction: this is more effortful than a stop. Hence stop → strident fricative constitutes a net increase in effort, whereas stop → non-strident fricative involves a change to a less effortful, imprecise, acoustically weak partial constriction.

- Geminates never lenite, unless they concomitantly degeminate. (The phenomenon of geminate "inalterability" (cf. Guerssel 1977; Hayes 1986; Schein and Steriade 1986), reduces to this generalization, to the extent that it does not reduce to language-specific blocking effects.) Geminate continuants require an even longer interval of precise, close constriction; a fortiori, therefore, they are more effortful than a geminate stop. Voiced (obstruent) geminates are more effortful for aerodynamic reasons, cf. Ohala (1983). Consequently, geminate spirantization or voicing would constitute an increase in effort; since lenition is, by hypothesis, driven by effort minimization, such geminate lenition processes are ruled out universally.

- All else being equal, the faster or more casual the speech style, the more likely a given consonant is to undergo lenition. Greater effort (qua velocity) is required to achieve a given constriction in a shorter amount of time, so there is greater impetus to lenite in fast speech. Register sensitivity can be captured in similar terms, using a register-adjusted effort cost. That is, a numerical index, inversely proportional to register, is added to the raw effort cost. Thus, a gesture that counts as sufficiently cost-effective in formal speech may be evaluated as too costly in casual speech, resulting in lenition.

For documentation and fuller discussion of these generalizations and my account of them, and for fuller discussion of the effort-based approach to lenition generally, see Kirchner (1998).

3. A Case Study: Lenition in Tümpisa Shoshone

To exemplify the effort-based approach to lenition in greater depth, we now examine the sound system of Tümpisa Shoshone, which includes spirantization, voicing, nasal weakening, and elision processes.

3.1. Data

The data for this case study are drawn from Dayley's (1989) grammar of the Tümpisa (also known as Panamint) dialect of Shoshone, a Uto-Aztecan language spoken in the region of the California–Nevada border. As a frame of reference, I present the chart of consonant "phonemes" for Tümpisa Shoshone (TS) in (14). Note that here and throughout the description of consonant variation, my use of phonemic terminology and notation (e.g., voiceless stop phonemes realized as voiced fricative allophones) is purely descriptive; it does not imply the assumption that the surface fricatives are uniformly stops in underlying representation. Syllables are maximally CVVC, and the only permissible clusters are full geminates and homorganic nasal + stop clusters. All words end in vowels on the surface, though Dayley posits some underlying instances of word-final /h/ and /n/.

(14)

labial	coronal	dorsal	labio-dorsal	laryngeal
p	t	k	k^w	ʔ
pp	tt	kk	kk^w	
	ts			
	tts			
	s			h
m	n	ŋ	$ŋ^w$	
mm	nn			

3.1.1. Spirantization. In TS, stops occur in initial position (15a), as geminates (15b), and following a homorganic nasal (15c). Flaps (15b) and nonstrident fricatives (15a) occur elsewhere.[9] That is, [p,k,k^w] are in complementary distribution with [β,ɣ,$ɣ^w$], as [t] is with [ð] (after a front vowel) and with [ɾ] (after a back vowel or /h/, the latter context illustrated by /tɨkkappih tukk^{w}an/ → [tɨkkappi̥ ɾukk^{w}an] "under the food"). "Initial position" in Dayley's description appears to mean utterance-initial, since spirantization applies across word boundaries, as illustrated in (16).

(15) a.   puhayãnṭi   'shaman'

            taβettʃi   'sun'

            tuyʷãnni   'night'

            tsiðoohį   'push'

            kĩmmãyĩnn̥a   'to come here'

            kʷĩjãã   'eagle'

      b.   paɾiasippi   'ice'

            uttũnn̥a   'to give'

            taβettʃi   'sun'

            pũnĩkkḁ   'see, look at'

            ukkʷḁ   'when, if'

      c.   taziũmbi   'star'

            indãw̃ĩʔi   'your little brother'

            tippiʃiɸũŋki   'stinkbug'

(16)   pie ðuyʷãnni jããyĩnn̥a   'it's already getting dark'

The distribution of sibilants is somewhat more complicated. On the
one hand, the affricate /ts/ spirantizes (to [z]), except in initial position
and in full or partial geminates, just like the stops, as in /motso/ → [mõzõ]
"whiskers". But unlike the other fricatives, [s] can occur in initial
(17a) as well as medial (17b) position.

(17) a.   suɾĩmmı̥   'those'

      b.   paɾiasippi   'ice'

Nor is there a contrast between geminate and singleton [s], as there is in
the stop and affricate series.

3.1.2. Voicing and devoicing. The distribution of voicing is also predictable. Stops are voiced following a nasal (15c); in initial position, and

in geminates, however, they are voiceless (15a,b). The fricatives resulting from spirantization are voiced in most contexts. However, the underlying fricative /s/ (i.e., /s/ that does not derive by spirantization from /ts/)
is realized as voiceless in all contexts. Moreover, utterance-final vowels
are optionally devoiced, in which case the preceding consonant (18a) (or
the second half of a geminate nasal, as in (17a)) is devoiced as well.[10]
Furthermore, /h/ + obstruent clusters coalesce to voiceless obstruents
(18b). In these noninitial singleton obstruents that surface as voiceless,
either due to final devoicing, or due to underlying /h/, spirantization is
optional, whereas flapping (18c) is obligatory, as is spirantization in the
non-devoiced case (15a).[11]

(18) a.   tahaβi ~ (ɸ/p)i̥   'snow'

            huβiariɣi ~ ...(x/k)i̥   'sing'

            peði ~ ...(θ/t)i̥   'daughter'

            mõzõ ~ ...(z̥/ts)o̥   'whiskers'

      b.   /ohpimpi/ → o(ɸ/p)ïmbi   'mesquite tree'

            /iattiah ka/ → iattia(x/k)a   (no gloss)

      c.   /tikkappih tukkʷan/ → tikkappi̥rukkʷan   'under the food'

Note that the devoiced sibilant fricative [z̥], derived from /ts/, does not
neutralize with /s/: Dayley describes [z̥] as more "lenis," presumably
meaning shorter, than [s].

3.1.3. Nasal weakening. The spirantization pattern of obstruents is partially paralleled by nasals: a noninitial singleton labial is realized as [w̃]
(19a), and a noninitial singleton coronal nasal as [j̃] after a front vowel
(19b).

(19) a.   si̇̃w̃õõri   'ten'

      b.   sẽj̃ū   'therefore'

      c.   ji̥βãni   'autumn'

After a back vowel, Dayley transcribes the coronal nasal as [n],
apparently without weakening (19c). The velar nasal [ŋ] likewise is

not described as weakening (20a). Labiovelar [ŋʷ] does not weaken after a front vowel; however, after back vowels [ŋʷ] occurs in free variation with [w̃] (20b). Note that there are no geminate velar or labiovelar nasals, unlike the labial and coronal nasals. Also note that vowels are nasalized before and (to a lesser extent) after a nasal consonant.

(20)   a.   pãŋe   'up'

        b.   sɔ̃(ŋʷ/w̃)ɔ̃   'lungs'

3.1.4. Elision of laryngeal consonants. Dayley further describes an optional process of elision of intervocalic /h/ and /ʔ/, as in [po(ʔ)ittʃi] "path", [ta(h)aβi] "snow". However, as /ʔ/ is restricted to intervocalic word-medial position to begin with, the /ʔ/ elision can alternatively be viewed as context-free. The distribution of /h/ is somewhat broader. It can occur initially, as in [huβiarɨ̵i] "sing", and before a following glide, as in [tɨkkappi̥h ȷ̃ãã] "on the food". As noted in Section 3.1.2, /h/ + obstruent clusters coalesce to a devoiced fricative or stop (or a devoiced flap, in the case of coronal stops). Thus, /h/ elision is restricted to intervocalic and pre-obstruent position.

3.2. Analysis of Spirantization and Flapping

3.2.1. Basic spirantization pattern. In accordance with the effort-based approach to lenition outlined in Section 2, the basic TS pattern of context-free spirantization at all places of articulation, subject to blocking in utterance-initial position, follows from the ranking in (21).[12]

(21)

non-initial:	*[+cont,-strid,+cons]/[__...]Utt	Lazy	Pres(cont)
tapettʃi̥		**!	
☞ taβettʃi̥		*	*
tsitoohi̥		**!	
☞ tsiðoohi̥		*	*
puhakã̃nti̥		**!	
☞ puhaɣã̃nti̥		*	*
tukʷã̃nni		**!	
☞ tuɣʷã̃nni		*	*
initial:			
☞ puhaɣã̃nti̥		**	*
βuhaɣã̃nti̥	*!	*	
☞ tuɣʷã̃nni		**	*
ðuɣʷã̃nni	*!	*	
☞ k̃ĩmmã̃ɣĩnn̥a		**	*
ɣĩmmã̃ɣĩnn̥a	*!	*	
☞ kʷĩ̃jã̃ã̃		**	*
ɣʷĩ̃jã̃ã̃	*!	*	

(Here, and in tableaux later on where the lenition-blocking constraints
need not be interleaved within the Lazy series, I present Lazy as a single
scalar constraint (with greater or lesser violations). As discussed in
Section 1, since continuancy is allophonic in these obstruents, it is the
constraint system that determines the surface value; even if we assume
that the underlying specification is contrary to the surface value (as indicated in the tableaux in (21) by assuming Pres(cont) violations even in

the winning candidates), the noninitial singletons surface as continuants. The failure of these consonants to lenite further is captured by ranking faithfulness with respect to other features above LAZY, such as PRES(cons), as shown in (22). Moreover, the failure of /t/ to spirantize to [s] and the blocking of spirantization in geminates and homorganic nasal + stop clusters (i.e., partial geminates) instantiate crosslinguistic generalizations, which follow from the effort-based approach, as mentioned in Section 2.5.

(22)

		PRES(cons)	LAZY
☞	p → β		*
	p → Ø	*!	

3.2.2. Sibilants. The sibilant fricative /s/ occurs in initial position, and hence the utterance-initial fortition constraint in (21) does not prohibit strident continuants; but under the constraint hierarchy in (21), we incorrectly fail to block spriantization of initial /ts/. I assume that the general property distinguishing /s/ from /ts/ and its allophones [ts,z,z̥,ʒ,ʒ̊] is the shorter duration of strident energy in the latter. This seems plausible in light of the general observation that voiced fricatives are typically shorter than voiceless (e.g., Nartey 1982), and of Dayley's comment that [z̥,ʒ̊] are more "lenis" than [s,ʃ]; moreover, I observe in spectrograms of my own speech that the fricated portion of a sibilant affricate (or /t + s/ cluster) is typically shorter than that of a fricative, presumably due to the more gradual onset of strident energy in the latter. Furthermore, a short strident fricative (with gradual onset of strident friction) is presumably perceptually weaker than an affricate (with abrupt onset of full-strength stridency, due to the sudden release of the preceding stop closure), or than a longer strident fricative. I therefore posit a binary feature, [long stridency], which distinguishes the fortis strident fricative [s] ([+long strid]) from the lenis strident fricative [z] or [z̥], and the strident affricate [ts] ([–long strid]), as well as the palatalized variants of all of the above (nonstridents are unspecified for this feature). The TS sibilant pattern now follows from undominated ranking of PRES(long strid), in combination with another utterance-initial fortition constraint, *[–long strid,+cont]/[__ ...]$_{Utterance}$, grounded in the relative perceptual weakness of the shorter nonaffricate sibilants, as summarized in (23). These constraints block initial /ts/ from spirantizing, but do not block spirantization of medial /ts/ and permit /s/ to surface unchanged both initially and medially.

(23)

initial:	PRES(long strid)	*[-long strid, +cont] /[__...]Utt	LAZY
☞ tsitoohi → tsiðoohį̌			***
tsitoohi → siðoohį̌	*!		**
tsitoohi → z̥iðoohį̌		*!	*
senu → tsẽ̌jũ	*!		***
☞ senu → sẽ̌jũ			**
senu → z̥ẽ̌jũ	*!		*
non-initial:			
motso → mõtsõ			**!*
motso → mõsõ	*!		**
☞ motso → mõz̥õ			*
patɨasɨppɨ → parɨatsɨppɨ			***!
☞ patɨasɨppɨ → parɨasɨppɨ			**
patɨasɨppɨ → parɨaz̥ippį̌	*!		*

Finally, note that the absence of a geminate fricative [ss] reflects the higher effort cost, hence markedness, of geminate fricatives relative to stops (Section 2.5) and follows from subordination of PRES(cont) to LAZY (24). Thus, even if an input contains a geminate sibilant fricative, it will neutralize to an affricate in all contexts (degeminated and deaffricated outputs are presumably ruled out by ranking of PRES(length) and PRES(strid) above LAZY).

(24)

	LAZY	PRES(cont)
ss → ss	**!	
☞ ss → tts	*	*

3.2.3. Variation with flapping. A minor elaboration of this analysis further captures the variation between [ð] and [ɾ] as lenited allophones of /t/. Relative to a stop, a flap involves a reduction in magnitude, such that the active articulator makes the briefest of contacts with the passive articulator, while still maintaining noncontinuancy (see generally Inouye 1995). Presumably, coronal (specifically, apical) flaps are common, whereas noncoronal flaps are rare or unattested,[13] because of the greater stiffness of the coronal articulator, which allows it to reach its closure target and release the closure relatively quickly, without additional expenditure of energy (see (25)).

(25)		Lazy	Pres(son)
☞	p, k	**	
	ɓ, ǧ (extra-short)	***!	*
	t	**!	
☞	ɾ	*	*

I further hypothesize that in TS, the distribution of [ɾ] (after back vowels) versus [ð] (after front vowels) is due to (Lazy-driven) coarticulation involving the tongue body. That is, in contexts where the noncontinuant ([ɾ]) can be achieved without significant tongue body displacement, namely following a back vowel (see Figure 3.2b), this is done. However, in a front vowel context, the tongue tip is closer to the dental region (Figure 3.2a). To achieve a flap, therefore, the tongue tip must either be dramatically retroflexed, or the tongue body must be retracted before the flap is produced. (A dental flap is presumably not generally feasible, due to typical leakage of airflow through the teeth.) Hence, I assume that a flap is slightly more effortful following a front vowel than following a back vowel. Specifically, let x denote the minimum of effort required to achieve a flap following a front vowel, and y following a back vowel. Then, for the foregoing phonetic reasons, $x > y$. The TS allophonic flapping pattern now follows from interleaving of a spirantization-blocking fortition constraint, *[+cont,–strid,+cons], between these effort thresholds, as in (26). Analysis of (devoiced) flapping from coalescence of /h + t/ is deferred until after the general account of voicing and devoicing in Section 3.3.

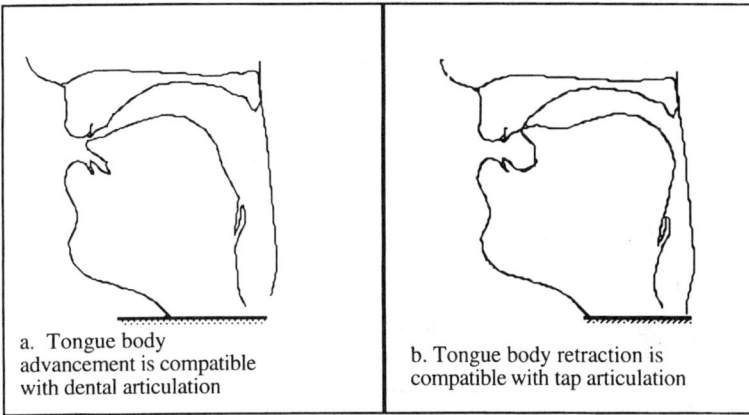

| a. Tongue body advancement is compatible with dental articulation | b. Tongue body retraction is compatible with tap articulation |

Figure 3.2. Flapping as coarticulatory retraction of the tongue tip.

(26)

	LAZY$_x$	*[+cont,-strid,+cons]	LAZY$_y$
at	*!		*
☞ aɾ			*
að		*!	*
it	*!		*
iɾ	*!		*
☞ ið		*	*

3.3. Analysis of (De)voicing

3.3.1. Basic pattern. The TS context-free devoicing of (full) geminate obstruents reflects a crosslinguistic markedness generalization and
follows from the general effort-based aerodynamic account of geminate
devoicing/blocking of voicing alluded to in Section 2.5. TS utterance-
initial obstruent devoicing and voicing in most other contexts likewise
follow from aerodynamic considerations. Obstruents passively devoice
in utterance-initial position (Westbury and Keating 1986). Of course, as
in the aerodynamic account of geminate devoicing, this aerodynamic
state of affairs may be overcome by intercostal contraction (raising subglottal pressure) or by various oral cavity expansion gestures, such as
larynx lowering and pharynx expansion (lowering oral pressure), but
these additional voicing-enabling gestures carry some additional effort

cost (27). Moreover, in utterance-medial position, (singleton) obstruents are passively voiced (Westbury and Keating 1986) (28). TS voicing allophony now follows from the ranking in (29).

(27)   Utterance-initial voiced obstruent >effort Utterance-initial voiceless obstruent

(28)   Utterance-medial voiceless obstruent >effort Utterance-medial voiced obstruent

(29)

medial:	Lazy	Pres(voi)
taɸettʃi̥	**!	
☞ taβettʃi̥	*	*
tsiθoohi̥	**!	
☞ tsiðoohi̥	*	*
puhaxãnti̥	**!	
☞ puhaɣãnti̥	*	*
tuxʷãnni	**!	
☞ tuɣʷãnni	*	*
initial:		
☞ puhaɣãnti̥	*	*
buhaɣãnti̥	**!	
☞ tuɣʷãnni	*	*
duɣʷãnni	**!	
☞ kĩmmãɣĩnn̥a	*	*
gĩmmãɣĩnn̥a	**!	
☞ kʷĩjãã	*	*
gʷĩjãã	**!	

3.3.2. /h/ + obstruent coalescence/devoicing. The coalescence/devoicing resulting from /h/ + obstruent clusters can be obtained by local conjunction of PRES(–voi) and PRES(asp). The resulting composite constraint, PRES(–voi)&PRES(asp) is violated if and only if both component constraints are violated (Smolensky 1995; Kirchner 1996). Elision of the /h/ then follows from ranking LAZY between this conjoined constraint and plain PRES(asp) (30). That is, the [ɸ] candidate satisfies the locally conjoined constraint, even though the aspiration noise is lost, because the voicelessness of the /h/ is preserved by being shifted onto the following obstruent, thereby satisfying PRES(–voi), whereas the [β] candidate violates both conjuncts.

(30)		PRES(-voi)&PRES(asp)	LAZY	PRES(asp)
	...hɸ...		***!	
☞	...ɸ...		**	*
	...β...	*!	*	*

3.3.3. Final devoicing. Finally, TS devoicing of utterance-final syllables may be attributed to abduction of the vocal folds, or increase in inspiratory force (causing subglottal pressure to drop off) (Westbury and Keating 1986), in anticipation of post-utterance breathing. Variable timing of these respiratory gestures relative to the end of the utterance is sufficient to account for the optionality of this process.

3.3.4. Interaction with spirantization and flapping. Recall that spirantization is optionally blocked in devoiced obstruents. I attribute this blocking to a fortition constraint, *[+cont,–voi,{–stridˇ–long strid}]. This constraint is presumably grounded in the observation (cf. Silverman 1995) that lack of modal voicing tends to obscure the formant transitions associated with these continuants, which are relatively acoustically weak, either because they lack strong friction, as in the nonstridents [ɸ,θ,x], or because the duration of this friction is brief, as in [z̥]. The TS optional blocking of spirantization now follows from free ranking of this constraint with LAZY (31).

(31)

		*[+cont,-voi,{-stridv-long strid}]	Lazy
☞	tahap̥i̥		**
☞	tahaɸ̥i̥	*	*
☞	huβiarɨ̥k̥i̥		**
☞	huβiarɨ̥x̥i̥	*	*
☞	mõts̥o̥		**
☞	mõz̥o̥	*	*

An additional aspect of the post-/h/ context is that coronals lenite to a voiceless flap, rather than to [ð] or [θ], even following a front vowel (cf. Section 3.2.3). Presumably, the loss of the /h/ in this context results in some phonetic compensatory lengthening of the transition from the preceding vowel into the consonant, preserving something of the duration of the original /hC/ cluster. As a consequence, the tongue tip/tongue body ensemble have a longer time to achieve a noncontinuant target.

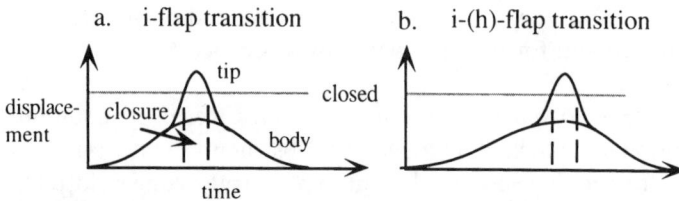

Figure 3.3. Schemata of tongue tip/tongue body ensemble displacement vs. time, without and with compensatorily attenuated transition.

Because the consonant gesture does not require as great a velocity to reach closure (Figure 3.3b) as it would in the nonattenuated case (3.3a), less effort is required in (b) than in (a). Thus, if the effort required to achieve a flap in Figure 3.3a = x (as assumed in example (26)), the effort required in Figure 3.3b (call it w) is somewhat less than x. Under the same ranking as posited in (26), with the additional assumption that *[+cont,−strid,+cons] » Lazy$_w$, we obtain the result that the coronal stop lenites to a flap, rather than a continuant, in the post-

/h/ context (32a), whereas it otherwise lenites to [ð] following a front vowel (32b).

(32)		PRES(cluster duration)	LAZY$_X$	*[+cont,-strid,+cons]	LAZY$_W$
a.	it → iɾ		*!		*
☞	it → ið			*	
b. ☞	iht → i·ɾ̥				*
	iht → i·θ			*!	
	iht → iθ	*!			

3.4. Analysis of Nasal Weakening

3.4.1. Basic pattern. The foregoing analysis of spirantization can be extended to the nasal weakening facts with minimal elaboration. Indeed, the general ranking LAZY » PRES(cont), motivated earlier for TS, results in spirantization of obstruents and nasals alike.[14] TS differs from most other languages (e.g., Spanish (Harris 1969)), in which spirantization is restricted to oral noncontinuants, in that TS further subordinates the nasal fortition constraint, *[+nas,+cont], to LAZY (33). The blocking of weakening in full and partial geminate nasals follows from the same considerations as does the blocking of spirantization in geminate obstruents. Moreover, utterance-initial nasal weakening is blocked by the same fortition constraint that blocks obstruent spirantization (34).

(33)		LAZY	*[+nas,+cont]	PRES(cont)
☞	kʷĩnãã	**!		
	kʷĩjãã	*	*	*
	sïïmɔ̃ɔ̃ɾɨ	**!		
☞	sïïwɔ̃ɔ̃ɾɨ	*	*	*

(34)

		*[+cont,-strid,+cons]/[__...]Utt	Lazy
☞	mõtso̩		**
	w̃õtso̩	*!	*

3.4.2. Voicing. The failure of the nasals to devoice initially, as the obstruents do, is attributable to nasal venting of airflow, which prevents significant buildup of oral pressure; hence, initiation of voicing in nasals does not present the same aerodynamic problems as in oral stops. Nasals are therefore passively voiced in all contexts, modulo optional utterance-final devoicing due to anticipatory glottal abduction, as discussed in Section 3.3.3.

3.4.3. Apparent place restrictions on nasal weakening. Two facts remain to be explained. First, according to Dayley's transcription, the coronal nasal surfaces as [n] after a back vowel, apparently failing to lenite. Given the reduction of the oral coronal stop to a flap in this context, and in light of the generally parallel behavior of obstruent spirantization and nasal weakening in TS, we would expect /n/ to reduce to a nasalized flap, [ɾ̃] in this context. However, without instrumental measurements of duration, it is difficult to distinguish [n] from [ɾ̃], since the other acoustic cues to the stop/flap distinction (e.g., presence of a burst) are absent in nasals.[15] It therefore seems plausible that these coronal nasals are actually flaps. Assuming this to be the case, the variation between [j̃] and what Dayley transcribes as [n] follows on a par with the variation between coronal fricatives and flaps from the analysis in Section 3.2.3 (35).

(35)

		Lazy$_x$	*[+cont,-strid,+cons]	Lazy$_y$
	an	*!		*
☞	aɾ̃			*
	aj̃		*!	*
	in	*!		*
	ĩɾ̃	*!		*
☞	ĩj̃		*	*

Second, according to Dayley, the velar nasal /ŋ/ never weakens, though velar stops spirantize. This fact might be attributed to the lowering of the velum during nasalization, decreasing the distance that the tongue body must travel to achieve full closure. Blocking of /ŋ/ weakening would then follow from an interleaved ranking as in (36), where u denotes the effort required for [ŋ], and v denotes the (greater) effort required for a non-velar nasal.[16]

(36)

		LAZY$_v$	*[+cont,-strid,+cons]	LAZY$_u$
☞	ŋ			*
	ũɰ̃		*!	
	m	*!		*
☞	w̃		*	

However, the presence or absence of complete closure in a velar nasal is a subtle cue. Ohala (1975: 297) observes that [ŋ] is acoustically quite close to nasalized vocoids.

[T]he velar nasal has primarily just a single resonating cavity with a small, perhaps negligible side-cavity, unlike other nasals, and thus negligible anti-resonances with large bandwidths and is more like that of a nasalized vowel than are those of any other nasal.

It is therefore plausible (again, notwithstanding Dayley's transcription) that these velar nasals are, at least in some cases, a nasalized vocoid (presumably a nasalized dorsal glide, [ũɰ̃]) rather than a noncontinuant (cf. Trigo 1988 on the "placeless" behavior of many nasals that have been transcribed as [ŋ]).

In fact, the variable weakening of the labiovelar nasal ([ŋʷ] ~ [w̃]) suggests that both scenarios occur in TS. When complete velar closure is achieved, the nasal does not appear to weaken. Hence, /ŋ/ and /ŋʷ/ can surface unlenited. But when velar closure does not occur, due to contextual or pragmatic conditions that raise the effort cost of velar closure in a nasal (recall the discussion of register-adjusted effort cost in Section 2.5), the resulting continuants are heard (by Dayley) as [ŋ] in the case of the plain velar (due to its confusibility with [ũɰ̃]), and as [w̃] in the case of the labiovelar. Indeed the notion of contextual raising of the effort cost of velar closure allows us to understand why the variation in the realization of /ŋʷ/ appears to be limited to the context /V$_{+back}$__. Presumably, it is easier to achieve closure with the tongue body against the velum when the tongue body is already retracted due to the preceding vowel.

3.5. Analysis of Laryngeal Elision

We have already accounted for obligatory elision of /h/ in pre-obstruent position (Section 3.3.4). To account for its optional elision in intervocalic position, we simply need a context-sensitive version of the blocking constraint, PRES(asp): specifically, higher ranking for preservation of aspiration noise in contexts where it is followed by a more sonorous segment (see Bladon 1986 and Silverman 1995 for the auditory basis for greater salience of quiet–loud vs. loud–quiet transition). Moreover, the variability of /h/ elision in intervocalic position, versus nonelision in preglide position, follows from interleaving of the context-sensitive faithfulness constraint within the LAZY series (37): specifically, between effort thresholds s (corresponding to [h] in preglide position) and t (corresponding to [h] in prevocalic position). Because high tongue body position tends, for aerodynamic reasons, to facilitate friction (see Ohala 1983), $s > t$.

(37)

	LAZY$_s$	PRES(asp/__[-cons])	LAZY$_t$	PRES(asp)
...hφ...			*!	
☞ ...φ...				*
☞ ...VhV...	*		*	
☞ ...VV...		*		*
☞ ...Vhw...			*	
...Vw...		*!		*

Finally, context-free optional elision of /ʔ/ follows from free ranking of PRES(glottalization) relative to LAZY (38).

(38)

	LAZY	PRES(glottalization)
☞ ʔ → ʔ	*	
☞ ʔ → Ø		*

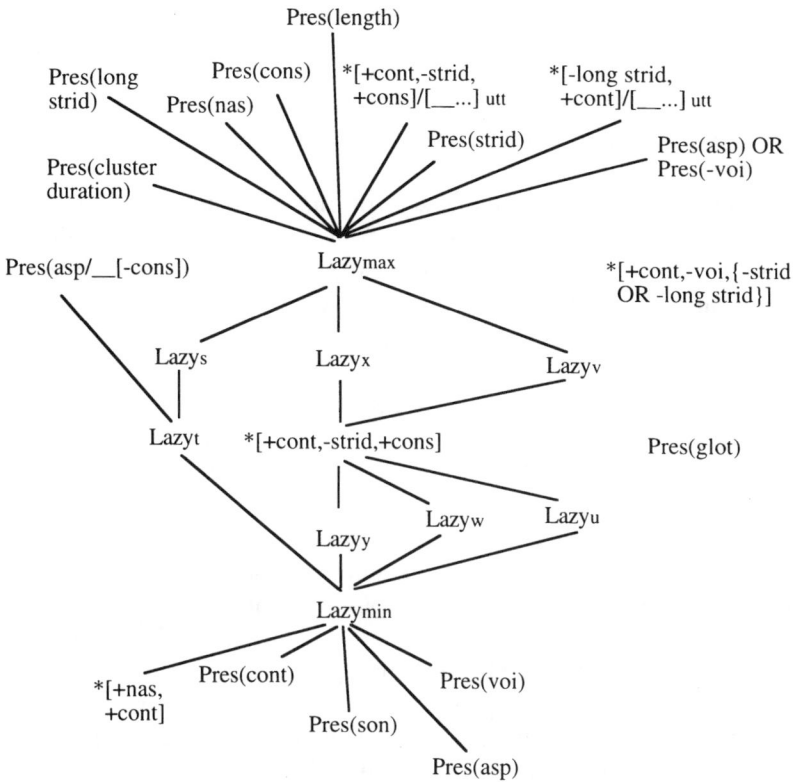

Figure 3.4. Diagram of partial constraint hierarchy for Tümpisa Shoshone lenition patterns.

3.6. Summary

The TS lenition facts can thus be accounted for in terms of the partial constraint hierarchy in Figure 3.4. LAZY$_{max}$ and LAZY$_{min}$ in Figure 3.4 refer to the highest and lowest effort threshold, respectively, within the LAZY series. This corresponds to ranking in previous tableaux where LAZY (i.e., the whole series) either dominates or is dominated by some lenition-blocking constraint. Constraints not connected to the lattice in Figure 3.4 are freely ranked with respect to the other constraints.

It is worthwhile to contrast this analysis with conceivable rule-based alternatives, which permit no unified expression of the spirantization operation ([–cont] → [+cont], i.e., constriction reduction) and the flapping operation ([–son] → [+son], i.e., temporal reduction).[17] The effort-based analysis, on the other hand, is unified in the sense that both the flapping process and the spirantization process (as well as all the other lenition processes in this language) are driven by the same constraint, LAZY (or particular thresholds thereof). The choice between the spirantized and flapped outputs thus follows from a single, consistent constraint hierarchy.

We may further contrast this sort of analysis with an OT account that does not refer to articulatory effort. Rather, lenition might be attributed to a set of atomized markedness constraints, such as *[−cont], *[−voi], and so on. But such an approach gives up on a unified treatment of lenition, which is, as argued in Section 2.2, abundantly motivated. Alternatively, one might appeal to a scalar REDUCE constraint, favoring reduction of constriction degree (e.g., approximant < fricative < stop), homologous to LAZY, but without explicitly referring to effort. But neither this REDUCE approach nor the atomized markedness approach captures the typological generalizations identified in Section 2.5: the nonstridency of spirantization outputs, geminate resistance to lenition, and rate and register sensitivity of lenition. For example, one might attempt to analyze the blocking of spirantization of the geminates in TS as a consequence of the ranking *[+cont,+long] (i.e., geminate fricatives are marked) » *[−cont], or *[+cont,+long] » REDUCE. But such an analysis predicts languages with the opposite ranking as well, in the absence of a stipulation that this ranking is universal. Under the effort-based approach to lenition, however, no such stipulation is required.

4. Conclusion

In the foregoing chapter, I have argued that, contrary to standard assumptions, an adequate formal treatment of phonological contrast within the OT framework does not require a restrictive inventory of distinctive features. Rather, phonological representation can include the entire sea of predictable or freely varying phonetic detail, including articulatory effort cost. Furthermore, by including effort cost in the representation, and allowing a set of phonological constraints that refer to effort cost, namely the LAZY series, we can devise a unified approach to lenition that captures a number of typological generalizations without further stipulation. Moreover, the foregoing analysis of Tümpisa Shoshone demonstrates that this effort-based approach is not only capable of accounting for isolated typological generalizations, but can also offer a coherent and comprehensive analysis of the detailed lenition patterns of a particular language.

Notes

I wish to express thanks to Linda Lombardi and Armin Mester for their helpful comments. Additionally, the acknowledgments in my dissertation are hereby incorporated by reference. All errors are, of course, my sole responsibility.

1. The featural PRESERVE constraints differ from the homologous IDENT constraints of standard correspondence theory (McCarthy and Prince 1995) in that PRES(F) cannot be satisfied by deleting (or inserting) the segment in which feature F occurs (in standard correspondence theory, this would involve a MAX or DEP violation, but no IDENT(F) violation). That is, PRES(F) evaluates whether a given input specification for F has a correspondent F specification in the output, and vice versa, without requiring a prior determination that these feature specifications belong to correspondent segments. Furthermore, the PRESERVE constraints are symmetric: no distinction is drawn between insertion and deletion (i.e., DEP(F) vs. MAX(F)), whether that specification is +F or −F. For further explication and motivation, see Kirchner (1997).

2. This assumes some function, the details of which do not concern us here, for relating degree n in the stress dimension or prosodic hierarchy to degree n in the aspiration dimension.

3. This move thus precisely parallels the shift in the locus of markedness observations in OT from representations (as in underspecification theory or particle theoretic treatments of markedness, as in Schane 1984 or van der Hulst 1991) to the system of markedness constraints.

4. Voicing lenition might appear to involve adjustment of laryngeal specification rather than reduction. Nevertheless, upon a closer phonetic examination, voicing in fact conforms to the gestural reduction characterization. First, voiced obstruents are typically realized with a more reduced oral constriction than their voiceless counterparts, and second, voicing lenition typically occurs in medial position, where reduction of an active devoicing (glottal abduction) gesture results in passive voicing (Westbury and Keating 1986).

5. In Section 2.4, I introduce an additional class of constraints, fortition constraints, which may also function as lenition blockers.

6. Alternatively, such patterns may be obtained by allowing place-specific LAZY constraints: the ranking {LAZY$_{cor}$, LAZY$_{lab}$} » IDENT(cont) » LAZY$_{dors}$ yields the same pattern. It is not clear to me that any empirical difference follows from this place-specific LAZY proposal. I am inclined to favor the context-sensitive faithfulness proposal, however, based on the intuition that effort is an indivisible notion, and that it therefore does not make sense to suppose that languages might arbitrarily disfavor effort involving some particular articulator, whereas it does make sense to suppose that speakers of languages differentially attend to particular auditory cues (see Section 1.3).

7. The ASPIRATE constraint introduced in Section 1 falls into this fortition class.

8. I thus follow Zoll (1999) in assuming context-sensitive markedness constraints (i.e., the fortition constraints) as well as context-sensitive faithful-

ness constraints. The LAZY family also, of course, belongs in the general class of markedness constraints, though the context-sensitive or context-free effect of a particular LAZY threshold depends upon specific consequences of the phonetic context for effort cost and upon the context-sensitivity of the lenition-blocking constraints with which it interacts.

9. Dayley characterizes the spirantization/flapping environment as "intervocalic" (or more precisely, /V(h)___V). However, as the language's phonotactics permit no consonant clusters other than geminates, homorganic nasal + stop clusters, and (rarely) [hC] clusters, the spirantization context reduces to the context-free characterization, subject to blocking in initial position and in full and partial geminates.

10. This utterance-final devoicing optionally takes the form of glottalization of the final vowel, described by Dayley as insertion of [ʔ] plus a voiceless echo vowel. Dayley notes that this devoicing by glottalization is most common in uninflected nouns (in final position) and speculates that it may function as an allomorph of the absolutive suffix.

11. In addition, /h + k$^{(w)}$/ sequences can debuccalize to [h$^{(w)}$], but this outcome is restricted to particular suffixes.

12. Voicing and devoicing of the outputs is addressed in Section 2.2.

13. Margi presents the only known case of labial flaps (see Ladefoged and Maddieson 1996). Dorsal flaps are unattested.

14. Loss of closure in a nasal results in a nasalized approximant rather than in a fricative (in the absence of dramatically increased subglottal pressure), due to the inhibiting effect of nasal venting on oral pressure, which is necessary to generate fricated airflow.

15. The difficulty is aggravated by the nonphonemic character of the [n/ř] distinction in English, Dayley's native language.

16. This ranking is consistent with the previous tableaux, provided that $v > y$ and $x > u$.

17. See generally Inouye (1995) for a review of the phonetic and phonological arguments against treatment of flaps as continuants (though Inouye does propose that flaps are [+cont] at their edges – i.e., tripartite contour segments).

References

Bauer, L., J. Dienhart, H. Hartvigson, and L. Jakobsen. 1980. *American English Pronunciation: Supplement, Comparison with Danish.* Copenhagen: Gyldendalsk Boghandel.

Beckman, J. 1997. Positional Faithfulness. PhD dissertation, University of Massachusetts at Amherst. ROA 234-1297, http://ruccs.rutgers.edu/roa.html.

Bladon, A. 1986. *Phonetics for Hearers.* In *Language for Hearers,* ed. G. McGregor, pp. 1–24. Oxford: Pergamon.

Boersma, P. 1988. Functional Phonology. PhD dissertation, University of Amsterdam.

Browman, C., and L. Goldstein. 1990. Tiers in Articulatory Phonology, with Some Implications for Casual Speech. In *Papers in Laboratory Phonology I,* ed.

J. Kingston and M. Beckman, pp. 341–376. London: Cambridge University Press.

Cho, Y. 1990. Parameters of Consonantal Assimilation. PhD dissertation, Stanford University.

Churma, D. 1998. On "On Geminates". Ms., SUNY Buffalo.

Clements, G. N. 1990. The Role of the Sonority Cycle in Core Syllabification. In *Papers in Laboratory Phonology I*, ed. J. Kingston and M. Beckman, pp. 283–333. London: Cambridge University Press.

Crosswhite, K. To appear. Vowel Reduction. In *Phonetically-Driven Phonology*, ed. B. Hayes, R. Kirchner, and D. Steriade. London: Cambridge University Press.

Dayley, J. 1989. *Tümpisa (Panamint) Shoshone Grammar*. University of California Publications in Linguistics, vol. 115. Berkeley, CA: University of California Press.

Dell, F., and M. Elmedlaoui. 1985. Syllabic Consonants and Syllabification in Imdlawn Tashlhiyt Berber. *Journal of African Languages and Linguistics* 7:105–130.

Elmedlaoui, M. 1993. Gemination and Spirantization in Hebrew, Berber, and Tigrinya: A Fortis-Lenis Module Analysis. *Linguistica Communicatio* 5:121–176.

Flemming, E. 1995. Auditory Features in Phonology. PhD dissertation, UCLA.

Foley, J. 1977. *Foundations of Theoretical Phonology*. London: Cambridge University Press.

Giannelli, L., and L. Savoia. 1979. Indebolimento Consonantico in Toscana. *Revista Italiana di Dialettologia* 2:23–58.

Grammont, M. 1933. *Traité de Phonétique*. Paris: Delgrave.

Guerssel, M. 1977. Constraints on Phonological Rules. *Linguistic Analysis* 3:267–305.

Harris, J. 1969. *Spanish Phonology*. Cambridge, MA: MIT Press.

Harris, J. 1984. La espirantización en castellano y su representación fonológica autosegmental. In *Estudis Grammaticals*, ed. J. Mascaró et al., pp. 149–167. Bellaterra: Universitat Autònoma de Barcelona.

Hayes, B. 1986. Inalterability in CV Phonology. *Language* 62:321–352.

Hock, H. 1991. *Principles of Historical Linguistics* (2nd ed.). Berlin: Mouton de Gruyter.

Hulst, H. van der. 1991. The Molecular Structure of Segments [The Book of Segments]. Ms., University of Leiden.

Inouye, S. 1995. Trills, Taps and Stops in Contrast and Variation. PhD dissertation, UCLA.

Jacobs, H., and L. Wetzels. 1988. Early French Lenition: A Formal Account of an Integrated Sound Change. In *Features, Segmental Structures and Harmony Processes*, ed. H. van der Hulst and N. Smith, pp. 105–129. Dordrecht: Foris.

Jun, J. 1995. Perceptual and Articulatory Factors in Place Assimilation: An Optimality Theoretic Approach. PhD dissertation, UCLA.

Kager, R. 1999. *Optimality Theory*. London: Cambridge University Press.

Kaun, A. 1994. The Typology of Rounding Harmony. PhD dissertation, UCLA. ROA 227-1097, http://ruccs.rutgers.edu/roa.html.

Kirchner, R. 1996. Synchronic Chain Shifts in Optimality Theory. *Linguistic Inquiry* 27:341–350.

Kirchner, R. 1997. Contrastiveness and Faithfulness. *Phonology* 14:83–111.

Kirchner, R. 1998. An Effort-Based Approach to Consonant Lenition. PhD dissertation, UCLA. ROA 276-0898, http://ruccs.rutgers.edu/roa.html.

Ladefoged, P., and I. Maddieson. 1996. *The Sounds of the World's Languages*. London: Blackwell.

Lavoie, L. 1996. Consonant Strength: Results of a Data Base Development Project. *Working Papers of the Cornell Phonetics Laboratory* 11:269–316.

Lindblom, B. 1983. Economy of Speech Gestures. In *Speech Production*, ed. P. MacNeilage, pp. 217–245. New York, Springer.

Lombardi, L. 1991. Laryngeal Features and Laryngeal Neutralization. PhD dissertation, University of Massachusetts at Amherst.

Mascaró, J. 1983. Continuant Spreading in Basque, Catalan, and Spanish. In *Language Sound Structure*, ed. M. Aronoff and R. Oehrle, pp. 287–298. Cambridge, MA: MIT Press.

Mascaró, J. 1987. A Reduction and Spreading Theory of Voicing and Other Sound Effects. Ms., Universitat Autònoma de Barcelona.

McCarthy, J., and A Prince. 1995. Faithfulness and Reduplicative Identity. In *University of Massachusetts Occasional Papers in Linguistics 18: Papers in Optimality Theory*, pp. 249–384. Amherst, MA: GLSA. ROA 60-0000, http://ruccs.rutgers.edu/roa.html.

Nartey, J. 1982. On Fricative Phones and Phonemes: Measuring the Phonetic Differences Within and Between Languages. *UCLA Working Papers in Phonetics* 55.

NíChiosáin, M. 1991. Topics in the Phonology of Irish. PhD dissertation, University of Massachusetts at Amherst.

Ohala, J. 1975. Phonetic Explanations for Nasal Sound Patterns. In *Nasalfest: Papers from a Symposium on Nasals and Nasalization*, ed. C. Ferguson, L. Hyman, and J. Ohala, pp. 289–316. Stanford, CA: Language Universals Project.

Ohala, J. 1983. The Origin of Sound Patterns in Vocal Tract Constraints. In *The Production of Speech*, ed. P. MacNeilage, pp. 189–216. New York: Springer.

Pierrehumbert, J., and D. Talkin. 1992. Lenition of /h/ and Glottal Stop. In *Papers in Laboratory Phonology II: Gesture, Segment, Prosody*, ed. G. Docherty and A. Ladd, pp. 90–117. London: Cambridge University Press.

Prince, A., and P. Smolensky. 1993. Optimality Theory: Constraint Interaction in Generative Grammar. To appear, MIT Press.

Rajapurohit, B. 1983. *Shina Phonetic Reader*. Mysore: Central Institute of Indian Languages.

Saib, J. 1977. A Phonological Study of Tamazight Berber: Dialect of the Ayt Ndhir. PhD dissertation, UCLA.

Schane, S. 1984. The Fundamentals of Particle Phonology. *Phonology* 1:129–155.

Schein, B., and D. Steriade. 1986. On Geminates. *Linguistic Inquiry* 17:691–744.

Selkirk, E. 1980. Prosodic Domains in Phonology: Sanskrit Revisited. In *Juncture*, ed. M. Aronoff and M.-L. Kean, pp. 107–129. Saratoga, CA: Anma Libri.

Shryock, A. 1995. Investigating Laryngeal Contrasts: An Acoustic Study of the Consonants of Musey. PhD dissertation, UCLA.

Silverman, D. 1995. Phasing and Recoverability. PhD dissertation, UCLA.

Smolensky, P. 1993. Harmony, Markedness, and Phonological Activity. Paper presented at Rutgers Optimality Workshop 1.

Smolensky, P. 1995. On the Structure of the Constraint Component Con of UG. Paper presented at UCLA Colloquium, April 1995. ROA 86-0000, http://ruccs.rutgers.edu/roa.html.

Steriade, D. 1993a. Closure, Release, and Nasal Contours. *Phonetics and Phonology* 5:401–470.

Steriade, D. 1993b. Positional Neutralization. Ms., UCLA.

Steriade, D. 1995. Neutralization and the Expression of Contrast. Ms., UCLA.

Steriade, D. 2000. Paradigm Uniformity and the Phonetics-Phonology Boundary. In *Papers in Laboratory Phonology 5*, ed. M. Broe and J. Pierrehumbert, pp. 313–335. London: Cambridge University Press.

Trigo, L. 1988. On the Phonological Derivation and Behavior of Nasal Glides. PhD dissertation, MIT.

Westbury, J., and P. Keating. 1986. On the Naturalness of Stop Consonant Voicing. *Journal of Linguistics* 22:145–166.

Wright, R. 1996. Consonant Clusters and Cue Preservation in Tsou. PhD dissertation, UCLA.

Zoll, C. 1999. Positional Asymmetries and Licensing. Ms., MIT. ROA 282-0998, http://ruccs.rutgers.edu/roa.html.

4

Markedness, Segment Realization, and Locality in Spreading

MÁIRE NÍCHIOSÁIN AND JAYE PADGETT

1. Introduction

An important goal of phonological theory has been the elucidation of "action at a distance." This term refers to processes, such as assimilations or dissimilations, in which the trigger segment and affected segment are not string-adjacent; there are segments that intervene, yet seem not to participate in the process. Transparency of this sort raises questions. How and why does it occur? What determines which segments, if any, will be transparent for a given process? The search for answers to such questions has been one of the important forces driving the elaboration of metrical and autosegmental representations.

Consider the case of long-distance feature spreading, or harmony. It is well known that segments within a spreading domain may appear to be nonparticipants, transparent to the harmony process. Various strategies have been proposed to account for such cases of transparency. Within nonlinear phonological frameworks, a property that many approaches have in common is the preservation of locality by relativizing it to what might very generally be called a legitimate target: some notion of "anchor," "projection," or "feature-bearing unit." Locality is obeyed so long as spreading does not skip such a legitimate target. Notable examples of this line of thinking include Goldsmith (1976) and Clements (1980) on the notion "feature-bearing unit," Halle and Vergnaud (1978) on "projections" of features, Kiparsky (1981) on the notion " harmonic vowel," and Archangeli and Pulleyblank (1987, 1994) and Anderson and Ewen (1987) on the relativization of adjacency to prosodically or geometrically defined anchors.[1] The basic idea is depicted in (1), where a feature F is linked to the elements T_1 and T_2, legitimate targets in some respect. Locality is not violated by the skipping of intervening α, since α lacks whatever property it is that grants legitimacy (e.g., it is not F-bearing, has the wrong prosodic status, or lacks a certain feature geometric node; see the references cited earlier). Equivalently, the elements T_1 and T_2 are adjacent for the purposes of F-spreading.

(1)   Local linkage (relativized to legitimate targets T)

$$T_1 \ \alpha \ T_2$$
$$\backslash \quad /$$
$$F$$

The above approaches are sometimes combined with assumptions about underspecification: the intervening segment α might be transparent because it is unspecified for either F, or whatever feature/node makes α a legitimate target (see for example Paradis and Prunet 1989 and Shaw 1991 on [coronal] transparency).

In a series of recent works, an alternative view of locality in spreading is considered, in which spreading is seen as strictly, segmentally local (McCarthy 1994; Flemming 1995a; Padgett 1995; Gafos 1996; Gafos and Lombardi, in press; NíChiosáin and Padgett 1997; Walker 1998). According to this view, all segments in a spreading domain are necessarily participants. The goal of this chapter is to further motivate this view of locality in spreading. We assume that locality holds strictly, in two senses of "strict." First, spreading respects segmental adjacency, as proposed by the references just mentioned. An essential result of this view is that segments are either blockers or participants in spreading; there is no transparency or skipping. Second, segmentally strict locality is inviolable; in Optimality Theoretic terms, Gen does not produce structures in which segments are skipped in a spreading domain.

In an obvious sense, it is a simpler and more restrictive theory that countenances only blockers and participants in spreading, compared to one that includes a third class of transparent segments. This point can be compelling, however, only given a convincing alternative account of seemingly transparent segments. The main work of this chapter is to motivate such an account for one class of cases, and to show thereby that strict locality is indeed possible for such cases. The argument focuses on consonantal transparency in vowel harmony, examining the case of Turkish.

Strictly local spreading for such cases becomes possible once we reconsider some fundamental assumptions about markedness and segment realization in phonology, a move that is independently necessary. The general ideas we will pursue could be formalized and understood variously, but the framework we adopt for these purposes is Dispersion Theory (Flemming 1995b), an instantiation of the Theory of Adaptive Dispersion (Liljencrants and Lindblom 1972; Lindblom 1986, 1990), implemented within Optimality Theory (OT) (Prince and Smolensky, in press). Dispersion Theory motivates an essentially bidimensional understanding of markedness and contrast: segment well-formedness depends on constraints phonetically grounded in articulatory complexity on the one hand and others grounded in the needs of perceptual contrast on the other. Flemming (1995b) argues this point in considerable detail, and here we extend the theory to show that the same ideas make sense of one kind of apparent transparency in a striking way.[2]

The analyses and general thinking of this paper are in good part propelled by the central tenets of constraint ranking and violability of Optimality Theory (Prince and Smolensky, in press). A related property of this chapter is the reduced role given to explanation in terms of the formal properties of a nonlinear representation, counter to tradition in the area of locality. Rather, locality issues are understood by means of the interplay of substantive, typically phonetically grounded constraints in an Optimality Theoretic hierarchy of violability. For arguments and analyses underpinning this general view of explanation in phonology, we refer the reader to Prince and Smolensky (in press), Smolensky (1993), Cole and Kisseberth (1994, 1995), Padgett (1995), Gafos (1996), Zoll (1996), and Walker (1998).

The chapter is organized as follows. Section 2 discusses the empirical evidence for strictly local spreading in Turkish vowel harmony and considers the place of that evidence in phonological theory. In addition, our representational assumptions are presented. Section 3 introduces Dispersion Theory. Section 4 applies this theory to the domain of consonantal backness contrasts, a prerequisite to the locality demonstration. Section 5 shows how the theory makes strictly local spreading possible for Turkish vowel harmony. Section 6 is the conclusion.

2. Background and Assumptions

2.1. Segment Skipping Is Theory-Dependent

What facts are at stake when we weigh strict locality against relativized locality? We think that this question is more complicated than has been realized. On the one hand, the evidence for segment skipping in spreading seems compelling: in many cases of long-distance spreading, there are intervening segments that in one way or another do not seem to realize the spreading feature. On the other hand, it turns out that a great deal can depend on what is meant by "realize the spreading feature." In fact, in some (and possibly most) cases of apparent transparency, the relevant segment is affected by spreading. How or even whether this fact is taken to bear on the transparency question depends on deeply held assumptions about markedness and segment realization, assumptions centering around contrast in particular. Here we demonstrate this point with respect to the case of spreading in Turkish vowel harmony, with some of the discussion covering vowel harmony more generally.

Turkish presents a well-known instance of vowel harmony involving both backness (or palatality) and roundness. Spreading is rightward, so that the initial vowels in forms such as *son-un* 'end gen.' and *ip-in* 'rope gen.' determine the values for backness and roundness of the second vowel (two alternants of the genitive suffix *-In* are seen here). In the work of generative phonologists, the spreading posited is from vowel to vowel, the intervening consonant being skipped. This is true of both earlier linear work (see for example Lightner 1972, who treats intervening C_0 as part of the structural condition of Turkish harmony, rather than a target), and of later nonlinear work (Clements and Sezer 1982, and much subsequent work). This assumption is applied to other vowel harmonies as well. What is the empirical basis for this claim?

Many works outside of generative phonology have made quite the contrary claim, finding clear evidence of participation by the intervening consonant. A notable precedent to our general locality claim is found in works of Firthian Prosodic Phonology, with its notion of "prosody" (see for example Allen 1951; Ogden and Local 1994; among others). Working within the Firthian framework, Waterson (1956) posits uninterrupted vowel backness and roundness prosodies in Turkish, having the entire syllable or word as domain. (Also arguing for a kind of strict locality, Gafos (1996) notes the significance of the Waterson study, and of that by Boyce (1990).) Waterson's notation for vowel prosodies is intended to highlight the equal participation of consonants and vowels. As evidence that consonants do indeed vary in the backness dimension, she provides palatograms of six Turkish word pairs (implied to be representative of an extensive study), e.g., *ün* 'voice' versus *un* 'flour'. The consonants involved include the velars and the lateral, with [k,g,l] in back words and palatal [c,ɟ,lʲ] in front words, respectively. These are well-known alternations, but differences also hold for the rest of the consonants shown (*r, n, z, tʃ*, and *ʃ*), and Waterson transcribes them as palatalized in front words. In such words most of these consonants are distinguished by wider tongue contact along the sides of the teeth, as well as more contact in the postalveolar area, consistent with a more palatal tongue body position. Only *tʃ* and *ʃ* do not differ in this way, possibly because these sounds make inherent demands on the tongue body, but they show slightly more contact further forward in the alveolar zone in front words, consistent with a fronted tongue body.

As Waterson (1956: 579, fn. 4) points out, these differences have not generally been taken into account in Western linguistics. On the other hand, there is a rich tradition among Soviet phonologists and Turkologists, extending to the Prague School, of regarding consonants as participants in Turkic vowel harmonies. Indeed, a precursor to Waterson is Sharaf (1927), a palatographic study of (Volga) Tatar, another Turkic language. Sharaf finds systematic differences between Tatar consonants in front versus back harmonic words, which he transcribes and refers to as "soft" versus "hard" consonants respectively (palatalized and non-palatalized). The results broadly resemble Waterson's: consonants in front harmonic words generally show more contact along the sides of the teeth and contact in the dental to postalveolar region that is both fronter and greater in area. Sharaf states that based on his observations similar results hold for other Turkic languages (including Kirgiz and Bashkir), and he is led by these results to agree with the principle of synharmonism, which states that all segments in Turkic words agree in backness. The idea of synharmonism is reasserted in Jakobson (1962), Trubetzkoy (1969), and many other works relating to the phonology of particular Turkic languages.[3]

Turning to roundness, Waterson's observations on this point are impressionistic. She states that all segments in a syllable with a round vowel are round, as in *kol* 'arm', in which "there is lip rounding throughout the articulation of *k, o, l*" (Waterson 1956: 579). More recently, Boyce (1990), has undertaken a study of lip protrusion and EMG patterns in Turkish and English, and finds that lip rounding gestures in nonsense words like *kuktuk* are maintained in a more or less uniform "plateau" across the consonants in Turkish, while in English there are two gestures clearly distinguished with a period of diminished rounding, a "trough," during the consonants. Boyce suggests that Turkish speakers employ an articulation strategy different from that employed by English speakers, because the existence of rounding harmony in Turkish "provides ideal conditions for articulatory look-ahead" (1990: 2594). We do not know of any similar studies on other Turkic languages.[4]

The notion that vocalic gestures can overlap consonantal ones, significantly affecting them in both articulation and resultant auditory properties, is very well motivated. A large number of studies of articulatory dynamics (or their acoustic consequences) from diverse languages support the general view that for any language, vocalic place gestures in a string VC_0V are articulatorily contiguous (at least to the extent that intervening consonants are not specified themselves for the relevant vocalic properties, whether contrastively or not, see note 4). Even when consonantal place gestures seem to intervene, they are in fact superimposed on these vocalic gestures, with the latter functioning as though on their own independent "channel." To put it more commonly, consonant and vowel places are coarticulated (Öhman 1966; Carney and Moll 1971; Fowler 1983; Browman and Goldstein 1990; Choi and Keating 1991; Farnetani 1997; and references therein). Gafos (1996) discusses the implications of this fact for phonology, coming to conclusions broadly consistent with those of this paper and providing much further motivation. The coarticulation is best illustrated with a diagram, as in (2). This diagram renders a gestural score for the English utterance [pis 'plats] (treated as two words), and is based on Figures 19.5 and 19.7 of Browman and Goldstein (1990) and the accompanying discussion. Browman and Goldstein's figures are themselves based on articulatory data. In this example and others like it (within or across words), the transition in tongue backness from [i] to [a] proceeds through the intervening consonants.

(2) Contiguous vocalic gestures in VC_0V ([pis # 'plats])

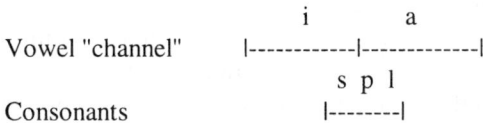

```
                          i          a
Vowel "channel"     |------------|-------------|
                              s p l
Consonants                |--------|
```

More generally, the observation of Browman and Goldstein for English is that a vowel place gesture overlaps the place gestures of tautosyllabic consonants. Putting tautosyllabicity aside, however, consider just the environment VC_0V relevant to the transparency question. Languages might vary in the details of the relative timing of consonant and vowel place gestures (see the references cited earlier); however, where vowel harmony holds, the two vowels agree in the harmonizing feature, and so C_0 will be coarticulated with this feature under any scenario, given V-V contiguity. We assume that the results of Sharaf, Waterson, and others represent cases of such coarticulation.

Returning to the question posed at the outset, if the empirical claim implicit in the skipping of consonants by vowel harmony, for Turkish and similar languages, were that those consonants are not affected by the spreading feature, then this claim would certainly be incorrect. However, this claim most likely should not be attributed to generative analyses. Rather, the implicit claim is that consonants are not affected enough to matter to phonology, the issue being instead the responsibility of phonetics. Generative phonology is rooted in distinctive feature theory; a central tenet of that theory is that any posited feature must be motivated by contrast in some language(s). Distinctive features are also employed to account for predictable properties in language, but precisely because it is distinctive features that are employed in these accounts, these features therefore must be contrastive by definition in some language. For example, though *l*-velarization in English or backness in Turkish suffixes are predictable, it is equally true that velarization and backness can be contrastive sometimes. Given distinctive feature theory, in other words, the only phonetic properties visible to phonology are those with contrast potential, and the segmental realizations entertained by phonologists are identified with contrastive realizations, whether they act as contrastive in a particular scenario or not. The effects of vowel harmony on intervening consonants in Turkish do not generally meet the distinctive feature criterion of contrast potential: though consonants in front harmonic words are more palatal than those in back words, they are not palatal enough to elicit transcriptions such as [ipʲinʲ] for *ipin*, where the offglide realization is understood as having contrast potential for palatalization. Similar remarks hold for roundness: *sonun* is not [sʷonʷunʷ]. The genuine *coarticulatory* distinctions discussed earlier therefore fall outside of the purview of phonology.

Summing up, the claim of transparency for Turkish and similar cases does not follow from a trivial factual observation, but involves interpretation of the facts within distinctive feature theory. In other, nongenerative frameworks, the coarticulatory realizations of consonants within vowel harmony domains are very much part of the phonological analysis. In this paper we reconsider the distinctive feature position and suggest that phonology should indeed embrace a range of segment types or realizations that may or may not form the basis of contrast (including the coarticulatory realizations discussed earlier). This conclusion is shared in other recent work, including Steriade (1994), Flemming (1995c), Kirchner (1997, this volume), and references therein, for reasons independent of locality concerns. With this shift in perspective, there is no longer any reason to posit skipping in cases such as Turkish. In fact we are compelled not to, because this "transparency" can be understood in terms of an independently motivated theory of markedness and segment realization. Locality-specific stipulations are not required.

2.2. *More on Turkish*

With the preceding in mind, more discussion of the empirical claims here is in order. We take consonants within spans of rounding harmony to be round, those in front harmonic spans to be front, and so on. The consonants of Turkish participate in harmony if we understand this statement to mean that the consonants of *sonun* are coarticulated with vocalic lip rounding, and those of *ipin* with tongue fronting, having the properties we would expect of them if some amount of these vocalic properties were maintained throughout the word, and nothing more. Since we identify these realizations with the well-known finding of vowel-to-vowel coarticulation across consonants, and since the body of phonetic evidence suggests that such coarticulation occurs quite generally and regardless of the language (modulo interfering specifications on the consonants), we rely on these findings as support for the claim about Turkish in particular. However, as we saw earlier, there is also evidence that is specific to Turkish.

In the case of rounding, Boyce (1990) demonstrates that [k,t,l] are roughly as round articulatorily as the vowels that flank them in Turkish. This finding might suggest the strong claim that in order to consider consonants participants in a vowel harmony domain we must see the relevant gesture continuing from vowel to vowel through the consonant with unabated intensity, the plateau found by Boyce. Though this indeed occurs in many cases, judging from studies of coarticulation – even in languages that lack harmony – the worry for such a claim is that there is reason to believe that vowel harmony spans need not be phonetically completely uniform. For example, the degree of lip protrusion in round vowels depends on other properties of the vowel such as height and backness (Linker 1982) and so might vary even from vowel to vowel in vowel harmony spans. More generally, the phonetic correlates of phonological features are far from precisely uniform across segment types.

The more reasonable claim is simply that for consonants to be considered round (or front, etc.), they should be round (or front) to some degree, and in this way reliably distinct from consonants that are unround (or back) in similar contexts. In order to further test the claim for Turkish, we examined the spectra of the fricatives [ʃ,s] in round and unround harmony spans. The fricatives occurred finally in actual Turkish roots, with a suffix vowel occurring to the right, as in *iʃ-i, kiʃ-i*. A strategy that we assumed for motivating hypothesized phonetic correlates of a phonological feature (see Stevens and Blumstein 1981 for a well-known example) involves stating a quantitative procedure for classifying the spectral representations of tokens, subjecting a sample of tokens to the procedure, and reporting on the success rate at classification. Given the problem of variation across speakers, utterances and phonetic contexts, this is a persistently daunting task even for phonologically contrastive features. We chose fricatives because it is possible to examine their acoustic properties at their midpoint, unlike the case of plosives for instance, allowing us to obtain stronger evidence about the extent of coarticulation. We examined 48 tokens of [ʃ]; these tokens came from 12 words, each spoken twice, by two native speakers, one male, one female. The same holds of [s]. For both sounds, the 12 words represented every possible vocalic environment allowed by Turkish that is harmonic (where the flanking vowels are both round or unround).[5]

In the case of [ʃ], a very simple procedure correctly classified 100% of the tokens into round versus unround categories. Specifically, if a spectrum had a peak in the 3,200–4,500 Hz range that was higher than any peak in the range 5,000 Hz and above, then it was classified as unround; otherwise it was round. For [s], a different but equally simple procedure correctly classified 94% of the tokens (45/48). In both cases, the procedure gauged the gross shape of the spectrum in such a way as to identify frequency regions that for round tokens were relatively low in energy compared to another region. We assume that this difference is due to a shift in the shape of the resonant cavity between the constriction site for the fricative and the lips, giving a lower-frequency auditory impression in the case of the round tokens (for relevant discussion of the spectral properties of fricatives, see Hughes and Halle 1956). We conclude that there is justification for attributing (un)roundness to these consonants.

We do not expect to find acoustic evidence as easily in the case of backness. This is because the acoustic properties of frication depend virtually entirely on the properties of the oral cavity in front of the place constriction. Since lip rounding does not correlate with backness in Turkish, and given previous evidence that tongue body position has little effect on the place of constriction of coronal sounds (Carney and Moll 1971; Farnetani, Vagges, and Magno-Caldognette 1985), we expect little systematic variation in the shape of this cavity due to shifts in tongue body backness. Indeed, it was much more difficult to distinguish among spectra of [ʃ,s] according to backness than according to roundness. However, upon examining more closely the spectra of [s] in unround words of one speaker, we were able to find a somewhat more complex quantitative procedure which, though it classified less well than was seen in the case of rounding, indicated a difference between unround back and front [s] that was statistically significant ($p < .01$ in a t-test), and we take this as some support.[6] It is important to bear in mind that there is no requirement that the distinctions we are considering be auditorily robust or even audible, since they need not have contrast potential. The criterion is simply that there be a systematic articulatory difference. Waterson's palatographic data show for a range of consonants in Turkish that there is.

2.3. The Statement of Strict Locality

Consider the formulation of locality given in (3) (Kiparsky 1981; Lever-good 1984; Archangeli and Pulleyblank 1994; Pulleyblank 1996; cf. Smolensky 1993). In contrast to the works cited, we take α, β, γ to be segments; that is, every segment is a legitimate target, so that locality is not achieved by relativizing adjacency to any notion of tier, projection, anchor, or the like.

(3) $*\alpha\ \beta\ \gamma$
    \ /   where F is any feature, and α,β,γ are segments
    F

Various works have attempted to elucidate the intuition underlying (3) and to explicate more fully the formal assumptions behind it, often in relation to the No Crossing Constraint (see Sagey 1988; Hammond 1988; Bird and Klein 1990; Scobbie 1991; Archangeli and Pulleyblank 1994; see Coleman and Local 1991 for more general relevant discussion). As some of these authors note, it seems desirable to understand the restriction by reducing it to an issue of linear precedence relations. Assume, for instance, that the association lines in (3) mean that F overlaps α, while also overlapping γ (Sagey 1988). Since β is ordered between α and γ, F necessarily overlaps β as well. However, this conclusion follows only if F is taken to be a "continuous, uninterrupted, unitary" entity (Scobbie 1991:64), and if some formal rigor is given to this notion. To this end, Bird and Klein (1990:41) provide a definition of a convex phonological event (the term is borrowed from van Benthem 1983:68), which we adapt in (4) (cf. Scobbie 1991).

(4) A featural event F is convex iff it satisfies the following condition:

For all segments α, β, γ, if α precedes β, β precedes γ, α overlaps F and γ

overlaps F, then β overlaps F.

This definition is not reduced in comparison to (3). It is a necessary axiom, however, a rigorous statement of what it means for a gesture to be continuous, uninterrupted, and unitary. (These properties are plausible attributes of phonetic gestures, as Scobbie notes. They are entailed by the dynamical conception of a gesture in Articulatory Phonology; see Browman and Goldstein 1986, 1990.) We take convexity in the sense of (4) as our phonological locality statement, and we assume it holds of phonological representations without exception: in Optimality Theoretic terms, it constrains the candidate set that Gen produces.

2.4. Coarticulation

We adopt from Smolensky (1993) and Cole and Kisseberth (1994, 1995) the convention of indicating feature association by means of labeled bracketing. Thus [ipin]$_{Fr}$ indicates a word with Front spread throughout (we assume single-valued features and focus only on the those relevant to Turkish vowel harmony: Back, Front, and Round). [[p]$_{Bk}$]$_{Rd}$ is p with associated backing and rounding, as in *upun*, and so on. We transcribe the effects of coarticulation with a superscripted segment, so that p^i indicates p coarticulated with the vowel i, and so on.

Consider the difference between a palatalized p as in p^ju and a plain p as in *pu*. From a phonetic point of view we can actually distinguish even among "plain" consonants, given the discussion of coarticulation in Section 2.1: a plain consonant generally shares the vowel place properties of a neighboring vowel. For instance, p bears the backness and rounding properties of u in *pu*. The p in *pa* likewise shares the backness of a. Speaking generally, there are as many kinds of p as there are vowels with which p can be coarticulated. Focusing only on the common five vowels, this gives the five kinds of p illustrated in (5), with the feature specifications of interest shown on the right. Similar variants exist for other consonants. We propose to expand the number of segments that phonology can entertain along these lines.

(5) p^i, p^e [p]$_{Fr}$

    p^a [p]$_{Bk}$

    p^u, p^o [[p]$_{Bk}$]$_{Rd}$

In this context, consider the representation of palatalization, velarization, and rounding on consonants. Since the plain consonants shown in (5) are specified for vocalic place features due to coarticulation, how are we to distinguish them from consonants with secondary articulations? If we take our cue from the transcriptions p^j, p^γ, and p^w, we can reduce this to the question, how do we distinguish high vowels from glides? According to Ladefoged and Maddieson (1996:323), glides across languages are produced with a narrower constriction of the vocal cavity compared to their vocalic counterparts (they are classified as approximants by Ladefoged 1993 and Catford 1988). Similarly, a difference conventionally transcribed as [pi] versus [p^{j}i] (in our terms p^ji versus p^ji) must imply a greater degree of constriction for the high front tongue body during the consonantal release of the latter. We assume that this difference between vowels and glides is encoded featurally.

To be concrete, suppose we assume a feature [vocalic], such that vowels are [+vocalic, −consonantal], while glides are [−vocalic, −consonantal]. Though vowels and glides were similarly distinguished in Chomsky and Halle (1968) (by means of the feature [syllabic], a term that would be inappropriate in the current context), it was subsequently widely accepted that high vowels and glides are identical in featural makeup (Kaye and Lowenstamm 1984; Selkirk 1984; Levin 1985). The basis of the latter view, however, is that vowels and glides cannot contrast. In Dispersion Theory, such facts fall out from output constraints regulating the goodness of contrast directly, as shown in Section 3. As we have already noted, having such constraints removes the most compelling reason to limit the representational distinctions of phonology.

In fact, there are well-known instances in which glides contrast with vowels – for example, Berber (Guerssel 1986). For the great majority of languages in which they do not contrast, we can simply assume that vocoids are redundantly [+vocalic] in a syllable nucleus, and [−vocalic] otherwise. Such a featural distinction can be motivated on independent grounds. For example, there are languages in which nasal harmony is blocked by glides but not vowels, such as Sundanese (Cohn 1989).

The discussion here presupposes that the strictural specifications of both the primary and secondary articulations of consonants like p^i and p^j, which are a species of complex segment, can be independently given. There are a number of ways to accomplish this, including adopting the articulator group of Padgett (1991), or separate closure and release representations for consonants, following Steriade (1994). Assuming the latter, representations for hypothetical $ip^i i$ and $ip^j i$, assuming one harmony span of Front for each, are given in (6). X stands for whatever representational entity denotes segmenthood, e.g., the Root node of feature geometry, or "aperture" node of Steriade; C, G, and V are abbreviations for the stricture specifications of consonants, glides, and vowels, respectively.

(6) a. $\quad$ i p ^{i} i $\qquad$ b. $\quad$ i p ^{j} i
$\quad\quad\quad [X_V\ X_C\ X_V\ X_V]_{Fr} \qquad\qquad [X_V\ X_C\ X_G\ X_V]_{Fr}$

3. Dispersion Theory in OT

Underlying the problem of segment realization are very general issues of markedness and contrast. Within one line of work in generative phonology, markedness and contrast are intrinsically linked via constraints on feature cooccurrence: a segment is marked to some degree if it violates a constraint of the form *[F, G, . . . , Z], and the activity of such a constraint in the phonology can suppress a potential contrast (Kiparsky 1981, 1985; Archangeli and Pulleyblank 1986, 1994). In Optimality Theoretic terms, Prince and Smolensky (in press) recast this idea in the following way: if a constraint *[F, G, . . . , Z], which for convenience can be abbreviated *S, where S is the relevant (class of) segment(s), dominates the relevant faithfulness constraints, then a contrast will be suppressed; otherwise, it will emerge.

Take as an example three kinds of consonant: plain, palatalized, and velarized. On typological grounds we might posit the following universal ranking of constraints: $*C^j$, $*C^\gamma$ » $*C$ (we do not argue for a ranking between the first two constraints; nothing here depends on it). The hypothesized ranking, immutable, is intended to express a typological generalization: plain consonants occur more often in inventories. Further, a language that has C^j or C^γ must have C according to this hierarchy. To see this, we must consider what happens when faithfulness is included in the hierarchy. To simplify the discussion, we assume one general constraint IDENT requiring identity of feature content between input and output (McCarthy and Prince 1995); this constraint ensures that a posited contrast will surface if the relevant markedness constraints are lower ranked. As Prince and Smolensky (in press) argue, markedness hierarchies coupled with faithfulness provide an appealingly direct and elegant account of markedness implications and contrast. An important result of the Optimality Theoretic account, in addition, is that contrast is an emergent output property, following entirely from the ranking of constraints in the grammar; see (7).

(7)   Typological predictions of markedness and faithfulness

	Ranking	*Result*
a.	IDENT >> $*C^j$, $*C^\gamma$ >> $*C$	C^j, C^γ, C surface
b.	$*C^\gamma$ >> IDENT >> $*C^j$, C	C^j, C surface (*alternatively*, C^γ, C)
c.	$*C^j$, $*C^\gamma$ >> IDENT, $*C$	C surfaces

This Optimality Theoretic account for the consonantal typology shares an important drawback with all phonological approaches to markedness known to us. On the one hand, cases such as (7a) are attested. For example, there are languages with a contrast among plain, palatalized, and velarized laterals, including Bernera Scots Gaelic (Lade-foged and Ladefoged 1997) and Marshallese (Bender 1969; Choi 1992). (7c) is also uncontroversially attested. On the other hand, the prediction entailed by (7b) is too strong: in languages with a palatalization contrast, the opposing plain consonants are frequently velarized. This is true of Irish (to be discussed), of Russian (Trubetzkoy 1969; Reformatskii 1958; Fant 1960; Padgett, in press), and of Marshallese (outside of laterals). The hierarchy in (7) specifying plain C as the inevitable best is fatally inca-pable of capturing this fact. The facts present a markedness paradox for the theory, and this problem is general to any theory that uniformly favors C over C^j and C^γ.

Flemming (1995b) raises other markedness paradoxes with similar properties. For example, while languages with two vowels overwhelm-ingly prefer *i* and *u* (compare palatalized versus velarized consonants), those with only one high vowel select *i* (compare plain consonants). The "linear" vowel systems of the languages of the Caucasus such as Abkhaz and Kabardian provide well-known examples of the latter (Trubetzkoy 1969; see Ladefoged and Maddieson 1996:286–287 and Flemming 1995b for other examples).

Flemming shows how such facts argue for Dispersion Theory (hence-forth DT). In a more general form this argument is due to the work of Lindblom and precursors, and DT adapts the well-known phonetic explanation for such markedness dichotomies from the Theory of Adap-tive Dispersion (Lindblom 1986, 1990). According to that theory, inven-tories strike a balance between two often contradictory needs. There is a tendency to maximize the perceptual distinctiveness (dispersion) of contrasts; however, there is also a need for articulations to be minimally complex. Given two high vowels in a language, perceptual considerations demand that they be *i* and *u*, since these are highly distinct, but achiev-ing this distinction comes at the cost of articulating these particular vowels. On the other hand, a language with no high vowel contrast by definition makes no demands of distinctiveness or dispersion in the front-back dimension. In such a language, articulatory concerns carry the day, and the result is *i*. This vowel is articulatorily simpler, involving the least displacement of the vocal tract configuration from the neutral position of ə. These points extend in a straightforward way to the case of plain, palatalized, and velarized consonants, where the perceptual and articulatory considerations are roughly the same.[7]

In the context of OT, the drawback of the approach to markedness exemplified in (7) is its unidimensionality: segments are ranked along one universal scale of markedness, such that C^j and C^γ are invariably more marked than C. DT is instead bidimensional, in the sense that there are separate families of constraints regulating articulatory simplicity on the one hand and the perceptual distinctiveness of contrast on the other, and these constraints often conflict. Thus C can be disfavored in comparison to C^j and C^γ precisely when there is contrast involving palatalization/velarization, because a contrast between C^j and C^γ is more perceptually distinct.

To capture the articulatory markedness facts, we simply carry over the constraints and rankings seen already: *C^j, *C^γ » *C.[8] Consider then the perceptual markedness relations. These are illustrated by the hypothetical segment spacings shown in (8a), each distinguished by how much of the available perceptual space is given to every segment (we make the idealizing assumption that the perceptual space is divided into equal intervals, with a segment located in the center of each). Obviously the more contrasting segments, the less the perceptual space for each. We posit a family of SPACE constraints, (8b), assumed to be indexed by type of contrast, here consonantal backness. The relevant acoustic correlate is roughly the second formant value at the release of the consonant (see Ladefoged and Maddieson 1996). We also assume a universal ranking among them, (8c), from which it follows that more spacing between contrasting segments is preferred, all else equal.[9]

(8)   Space constraints for consonantal backness (C-F2)

a.   Spacing: |....C^j....|....C....|.....C^γ....| Each segment gets 1/3 of the

perceptual space

|.......C^j.......|.......C^γ.......| Each segment gets 1/2 of the

perceptual space

|...............C...............| Each segment gets 1/1 of the

perceptual space

b.   SPACE$_{C\text{-}F2}$≥ 1/N: For every pair of words differing only in the F2 value of one

consonant, the contrasting consonants differ by at least

1/nth of the full F2 range[10]

c.   Space$_{C\text{-}F2}$≥ 1/3 >> Space$_{C\text{-}F2}$≥ 1/2 >> Space$_{C\text{-}F2}$≥ 1

The number of space constraints required in the theory depends on the type of contrast. In the case of consonantal backness, we find at most a three-way contrast in languages (as in the examples mentioned earlier). We account for this by assuming that $\text{SPACE}_{\text{C-F2}} \geq 1/3$ is in Gen (this does the work of distinctive feature theory's stipulation that there is only one [back] feature, or privative Front versus Back). Hence only the two remaining constraints can be ranked in a constraint hierarchy.

To understand space constraints, we must posit a third family of constraints, following Flemming (1995b), that favor maximizing the number of contrasts. This third constraint family is necessary, since constraints punishing both articulatory effort and spacing needs could always be vacuously satisfied by having no contrasts at all. However, we depart from Flemming in our formulation of these constraints. Flemming (1995b) largely considers only inventories of segments. In order to fully integrate the ideas of DT into phonology, we must be able to evaluate entire words – otherwise there is no way to consider most phonological processes, such as stress, assimilation, final devoicing, and so on, simultaneously with matters of contrast. Indeed, contrast can be context-sensitive or positional, as is well known. The constraint family in (9a) therefore considers not the number of contrasting segments, but of contrasting words. We assume that two words contrast if they differ by any feature specification. It should be borne in mind that it is the job of the SPACE constraints, and not of these constraints, to ensure that a contrast is perceptually well formed.

(9) NWord constraints

    a.   NWORDS: A language must have at least *n* contrasting words

    b.   1WORD >> 2WORDS >> ... >> N-1WORDS >> NWORDS

Tied up with these proposals is the question of what candidates are in DT, and how they are to be evaluated by these constraints. Following Flemming (1999), we take candidates to be languages. In generative phonology, a language can be understood as the set of forms generated by a grammar (Halle 1962). (Of these forms, only some need be actually occuring forms. For instance, [tɪg] is a grammatical, but not actual, word of English. It will be useful to keep this idea in mind later, when we include both actual and merely possible words in our tableaux.) Though the idea of candidates as languages seems daunting, we propose to manage the task by means of severe idealization. In approaching the problem in this way, we differ from Flemming (1999). Consider, for example, the following idealization: assume that a language can have words of the form $C^{(j/\gamma)}a$ only. That is, the only possible words are Ca, $C^j a$ and $C^\gamma a$, and the nature of C is irrelevant. Given this idealization, a language can have at most three words. Therefore, we need only rely on the NWORD constraints 2WORDS and 3WORDS. Violations of 1WORD will not be of interest to us, and we assume this constraint is in Gen.

Tableau (10) illustrates how all of this works. Each candidate should be regarded as a possible language, within the idealization. For example, (10a) is a language having a three-way backness contrast in consonants, and (10e) is one having only palatalized consonants. The ranking here selects (10f) as optimal, a language with a two-way backness contrast that is maximally dispersed. The NWORD constraints simply count the number of words in a candidate language, and disfavor languages with fewer than n words. The SPACE constraints evaluate a candidate language in the following way: each (unordered) pairing of words is checked once, and a violation is recorded for each such pair violating the required spacing. For example, there are three words in candidate (10a); for three words there are three possible pairings – namely, $C^j a$–Ca, Ca–$C^\gamma a$, and $C^j a$–$C^\gamma a$. Since these all differ only in consonantal backness, SPACE$_{\text{C-F2}} \geq 1/2$ requires that each such pair differs by one-half of the total perceptual space (recall (8a)). The candidate receives two violation marks since only one of these pairs – the third – respects this requirement. (We group together the constraints $*C^j$ and $*C^\gamma$ only for expository convenience. Also, candidates are arranged so as to suggest the relative positioning of words in the perceptual space.)

(10) Contrast can force articulatorily marked realizations

	2Words	Space≥1/2	3Words	Space≥1	$*C^{\gamma/j}$
a. $\ C^j a \ \ Ca \ \ C^\gamma a$		*!*		***	**
b. $\ C^j a \ \ Ca$		*!	*	*	*
c. $\quad\quad Ca \ \ C^\gamma a$		*!	*	*	*
d.☞$C^j a \quad\quad C^\gamma a$			*	*	**
e. $\ C^j a$	*!		*		*
f. $\quad\quad Ca$	*!		*		
g. $\quad\quad\quad\quad C^\gamma a$	*!		*		*

(10) shows how NWord and Space constraints work together to force a maximally dispersed contrast (the high vowels *i* and *u* would be selected in the same way). This perceptually motivated contrast comes at the cost of extra articulatory markedness (and violates the lowest ranking but demanding Space constraint also). One the other hand, when contrast is suppressed for any reason, articulatory constraints make the selection, since Space constraints are vacuously satisfied. This is shown in (11). Here the Space constraints are undominated; this ranking entails that no amount of perceptual spacing is good enough for a contrast, hence the neutralization (ɨ would be chosen in this way). This same result would be obtained if one or both of the articulatory markedness constraints themselves were undominated, regardless of the ranking of Space constraints.

(11) Articulatory simplicity wins under neutralization

	Space≥1/2	Space≥1	2Words	3Words	*C$^{γ/j}$
a. Cʲa Ca Cˠa	*!*	***			**
b. Cʲa Ca	*!	*		*	*
c. Ca Cˠa	*!	*		*	*
d. Cʲa Cˠa		*!		*	**
e. Cʲa			*	*	*!
f. ☞ Ca			*	*	
g. Cˠa			*	*	*!

We note that all of these candidates, except for (11e) and (11g), can be chosen as optimal under some ranking of these constraints. This correct prediction differs from that of the unidimensional markedness approach of (7) in only one way: the latter has no way of favoring the maximally dispersed two-way contrast, since plain *C* is regarded as universally the best. As Lyovin (1997) points out, the contrast in Russian between palatalized *lʲ* and velarized *ɫ* (and that of Irish, NíChasaide 1979), therefore presents standard markedness with a problem. The case just outlined exemplifies one class of argument for DT: the markedness of a segment depends both on its inherent properties and on the system of contrasts in which it participates. Flemming (1995b) provides more examples, to which we refer the reader. As we will argue, this markedness pattern is central to an understanding of locality in phonology.

Before moving on, we briefly touch on several fundamental points concerning DT. The first concerns the 'status of faithfulness and of underlying representations in DT. As noted earlier, one of the fundamental roles of faithfulness constraints in OT is to ensure (or dispel) contrast. Yet DT posits constraints that demand contrast directly in the output, entirely taking over this job. Flemming (1995b) in fact argues that faithfulness, along with underlying representations, should be eliminated from the theory. To address the other major role of underlying forms, the encoding of morphological relatedness, he suggests that similarity among morpheme alternants be dealt with exclusively by constraints governing the similarity of surface forms. Similar ideas resonate in an increasing number of works arguing for constraints on the identity of output forms, or other means of maintaining surface similarities (see, e.g., Benua 1995; Buckley 1995; Burzio 1994, 1996; Ito and Mester 1997; Kager 1999; Kenstowicz 1996; McCarthy 1995; cf. Orgun 1994, 1996; Kenstowicz 1995). For the sake of discussion in this paper, we follow Flemming, as well as Burzio (1996), in requiring no underlying representations for the forms we consider, at least as crucial determinants of output well-formedness. For the same reason we employ no faithfulness constraints, instead letting the NWORD constraints do the relevant work. A consequence of this is that lexical entries correspond to surface representations, that is, forms licensed by output-based grammars such as OT.

A second point concerns the apparent "phonetic" nature of DT. The theory might seem especially phonetic compared to other theories of phonology for two reasons. First is the fundamental reliance on constraints based on articulatory simplicity and perceptual distinctiveness. Second is the increased number of segmental representations we entertain, a move that is possible once contrast is regulated separately by output constraints (to be discussed). However, these properties of DT do not make it qualitatively different from other theories of phonology, virtually all of which have relied on constraints with some phonetic grounding, and all of which entail some rather large number of possible segments. In DT phonetic grounding is made especially explicit, and the number of possible representations is larger. Yet as understood here, the theoretical language remains one of constraints that consider a finite number of categorical entities and choose only some as optimal. To be clear, we are claiming neither that phonology and phonetics are "the same," nor that phonology is determined solely by phonetically grounded principles (as opposed to principles grounded in other domains, cognitive or otherwise), nor even that phonology cannot have abstract inclinations of the sort suggested by derivational opacity effects. The idea is simply that a good deal of phonology is determined by phonetic principles.

Finally, an important research goal for DT is to further refine our understanding of constraints on contrast and spacing, the nature of candidates, and the manner in which candidates are evaluated. Though the direct evaluation of contrast requires a kind of globality that might seem daunting at first – since candidates are not simply forms, but (idealized) languages – we take the view eloquently expressed by Prince and Smolensky (in press) that explanatory developments should not be constrained by a priori computational assumptions. This point is all the more forceful when there is clear and wide-ranging empirical support for the relevant ideas, as is the case with DT.

4. More on Consonantal Backness Contrasts: Irish

The argument we make about locality depends on the claim that phonology can distinguish segment types such as C^i versus C^j without overgenerating contrasts.[11] This claim in turn depends on the basic phonological model we assume, DT. It is therefore important to examine the DT account of consonantal backness contrasts against real data involving such contrasts. In addition, it is neccessary to consider distinctions such as C^i versus C^j in more detail in order to follow the discussion of Turkish in Section 5. Here we examine facts of the western dialect of Irish, which reveal ways in which the account proposed earlier for consonantal backness contrasts should be elaborated. As it turns out, the Irish facts provide further support for DT over unidimensional markedness.

The facts of interest involve the realization of a consonantal backness contrast before long vowels (short vowels in Irish acquire their backness specification from neighboring consonants). The contrast is realized as shown in (12): a secondary articulation is pronounced when the consonant is followed by a long vowel that carries the opposite specification for backness, otherwise the consonant is plain. Thus a contrastively Front labial consonant is realized with a palatal offglide preceding a long back vowel, while the corresponding Back labial consonant is realized as plain in the same context, as in (12a–c). On the other hand, a Back consonant is strongly velarized before front vowels, and plain otherwise, as in (12d–e).

The distribution of plain, palatalized, and velarized consonants in Irish therefore depends very much on the vocalic context. An understanding of the pattern begins to emerge when we consider the effect of context on the perceptual spacing of consonantal backness contrasts. (13) shows sequences of a consonant followed by a vowel, arranged in a manner to suggest their relative similarity. The palatalized C before i is perceptually very close in this context to its plain counterpart (the latter is actually coarticulated with the vowel *i*, as discussed in Section 2.1). Both consonants are quite distant from a velarized *C* in this context. The facts are different when the vowel is *u*; now it is the coarticulated and velarized consonants that are very similar (indeed, given the rounding of *u* added in, virtually indistinguishable). The facts are similar in the case of mid and low vowels, though the problem of perceptual similarity is less severe in this case.[12]

(12)   a. f^ju: 'worth'   fu:ə   'hate'

       b. b^jo: 'alive'   bo: 'cow'

       c. $f^jɔ$:n   'skin, flay'   fɔ:n   'straying, wandering'

       d.   bi: 'be (imp.)' $b^ɣi$:   'yellow'

       e.   be:l   'mouth' $b^ɣe$:l/$b^ɣi$:l   'danger'

(13)   Spacing is context-dependent

       $C^ji..C^ji$...........................$C^ɣi$ C^ju......................$C^uu..C^ɣu$

       C^je.....C^ee....................$C^ɣe$ C^jo....................C^oo.....$C^ɣo$

                                                             $C^jɔ$..................$C^ɔɔ$.......$C^ɣɔ$

                          C^ja............C^aa...........$C^ɣa$

This diagram is only schematic, but what matters is that we can infer the following: if the contrast C^ja versus C^aa violates $\text{SPACE}_{\text{C-F2}} \geq 1/2$, as assumed in the last section, then so do the contrasts C^ji versus C^ii, C^je versus C^ee, C^uu versus $C^ɣu$, C^oo versus $C^ɣo$, and $C^oɔ$ versus $C^ɣɔ$. That is, the latter contrasts are as bad as, or worse than, the former (this inference is easily confirmed by spectrographic estimations). We take the remaining spacings shown to pass this constraint (also based on rough acoustic comparisons). Given this state of affairs, the array of realizations found in Irish turns out to be optimal for a consonantal backness contrast, from the bidimensional viewpoint of DT.

The ranking in (14) is identical to that of (10). In (14), however, we replace the vowel *a* with *u* in our idealized languages. Both (14a) and (14c) include the problematic contrast C^uu versus C^ju, which falls short of the spacing requirement of $\text{SPACE}_{\text{C-F2}} \geq 1/2$. The two remaining candidates pass this constraint, and the choice between them is made on the basis of articulatory difficulty alone. Of these, (14b) maintains a contrast while involving the least articulatory effort. Thus preceding a back vowel, the optimal contrast is a palatalized–plain one (we omit single-word candidates here, which are trivially eliminated by 2WORDS, as shown in Section 3.)

(14) Before back vowels: "plain" vs. palatalized

		2Words	Space≥ 1/2	3Words	Space≥ 1	$*C^{ɣ/j}$
a. C^{j}u	Cu C^{ɣ}u		*!		***	**
b.☞C^{j}u	Cu			*	*	*
c.	Cu C^{ɣ}u		*!	*	*	*
d. C^{j}u	C^{ɣ}u			*	*	**!

Preceding a front vowel, on the other hand, the optimal contrast is a velarized–plain one, as seen in (15).

(15) Before front vowels: "plain" vs. velarized

		2Words	Space≥1/2	3Words	Space≥ 1	$*C^{ɣ/j}$
a. C^{j}i Ci	C^{ɣ}i		*!		***	**
b. C^{j}i Ci			*!	*	*	*
c. ☞ Ci	C^{ɣ}i			*	*	*
d. C^{j}i	C^{ɣ}i			*	*	**!

We do not have "idealized Irish," strictly speaking, until we combine these two analyses. Suppose we allow words of the form $C^{(j/ɣ)}V$ in a new idealization now, where V is either i or u. There are then six possible words, rather than three, and four words to be chosen as optimal, rather than two. An expansion of the idealization of this kind requires that we consider higher NWORD constraints in order to achieve the desired result. That is, where 2WORDS is undominated in the above tableaux, 4WORDS must be in this new idealization. This is shown in (16). Again, the SPACE constraints consider every logically possible pair of words in a candidate language and record a violation for every pair that fails for the relevant amount of spacing. The statement of these constraints (see (8b)) requires that the words compared be identical except for a difference in backness for one consonant. This is in order not to penalize pairs such as $C^j i$ versus $C^j u$, as in (16a), for failing to differ in consonantal backness, since this contrast is borne by their respective vowels. Hence there are only two pairs violating SPACE$_{C\text{-}F2}$ ≥ 1/2 in (16a), and so on for the other candidates (some logically possible candidates are omitted).

(16) Idealized Irish

		4Words	Space≥1/2	5Words	Space≥1	*C^{γ/j}
a.	$C^j i$ Ci　　$C^γ i$ $C^j u$　　Cu $C^γ u$		*!*		******	****
b.	$C^j i$ Ci 　　　Cu $C^γ u$		*!*	*	**	**
c. ☞	Ci　　$C^γ i$ $C^j u$　　Cu			*	**	**
d.	$C^j i$　　$C^γ i$ $C^j u$　　$C^γ u$			*	**	**!**
e.	Ci 　　　Cu	*!		*		

As these tableaux show, DT's bidimensional approach to markedness predicts exactly the kind of variability in realization seen in the Irish case: articulatory complexity is forced where necessary to fulfill the spacing requirement on contrast, giving one of C^j or $C^γ$, depending on the vocalic context. Articulatory simplicity determines the remaining realization.[13] The Irish case is not unique: the distribution of consonantal backness before vowels in Russian is remarkably similar (see Padgett, in press). The explanatory intuition here is not available to traditional distinctive feature theory, which makes no reference to the output well-formedness of contrast. In that theory, though one can posit that some consonants are palatalized and others are not (or are velarized), the shift in the actual realization of this contrast will remain entirely unrelated to this fact, having nothing to do with contrast preservation.[14]

5. Markedness, Segment Realization, and Permeability in Spreading: Turkish

The previous discussion paves the way for a return to Turkish vowel harmony and the issue of locality. An important result above is that plain consonants like C^i and C^u can be posited without overgenerating contrasts. In fact, such consonants actually participate in backness contrasts in certain contexts, as we saw. The emergence of the coarticulated realization of consonants in these contexts, it turns out, is mirrored by what is found in vowel harmony domains: once the needs of contrast are met or rendered irrelevant, segment realization is determined by articulatory constraints alone. The goal of this section is to demonstrate that, given Turkish vowel harmony, consonantal participation follows automatically from assumptions already laid out.

Vowels in Turkish agree in backness with the preceding vowel, and a high vowel in addition agrees in roundness, as illustrated in (17). For an understanding of the Turkish facts we rely on Lewis (1967), Underhill (1976), Clements and Sezer (1982), van der Hulst and van de Weijer (1991), Kirchner (1993), Orgun (1996), and references therein (root–suffix morpheme boundaries are indicated).

(17)   [Round]

[Back]	son-un	'end gen.'	kɨz-ɨn	'girl gen.'
	kol-u	'arm acc.'	sabɨr-ɨ	'patience acc.'
	pul-un	'stamp gen.'	sap-ɨn	'stalk gen.'
	kurd-u	'worm poss.'	at-ɨ	'horse poss.'
[Front]	köy-ün	'village gen.'	el-in	'hand gen.'
	göz-ü	'eye acc.'	dere-si	'river poss.'[15]
	yüz-ün	'face gen.'	ip-in	'rope gen.'
	ütü-sü	'iron poss.'	it-i	'dog acc.'

There is some controversy over whether vowel harmony holds within roots, given the existence of many disharmonic roots such as *politika* "politics", which are largely due to borrowings from other languages (compare Clements and Sezer 1982 and van der Hulst and van de Weijer

1991, who differ greatly in approaching this issue). Since our claims here concern only consonants in a vowel harmony domain, we focus on cases of unambiguous spreading, such as those in (17) (and many others), in which suffixes are involved. In addition, for the sake of brevity we analyze only backness harmony among high vowels. As should be clear, the ideas extend in a straightforward way to predict consonant participation in vowel harmony generally.

In most work within OT, feature spreading is compelled by constraints requiring that a feature align with either a left or a right word edge; in conjunction with locality constraints, satisfaction of alignment often results in long-distance feature spreading (see for example Kirchner 1993, Smolensky 1993, Pulleyblank 1993, Cole and Kisseberth 1994, and Akinlabi 1997 on alignment for this purpose, and McCarthy and Prince 1993 on the general notion of alignment). To effect harmony in Turkish, we assume the alignment constraint shown in (18). This formulation follows Zoll (1996) and Walker (1998) in making certain aspects of featural alignment more precise. The rightward direction mimics the rightward spreading posited in many analyses of Turkish (see Anderson 1980 for arguments in favor of rightward spreading in Turkish). Less formally stated, for every instance of Front or Back in a prosodic word, if that feature is dominated by any segment, it is dominated by all segments to the right of that segment. Alignment is generally taken to be gradiently violable (see the references cited earlier). Though we assume this is correct, the analysis below does not require that we consider gradience of violation, since ALIGN-R is undominated, and so we will simply distinguish candidates that fully satisfy alignment from those that do not.

(18) ALIGN-R(BACKNESS, PWD), where *Backness* = {Front, Back}

Let f be a variable ranging over occurrences of any feature specification $F \in$

Backness, S be the string of segments $s_1...s_n$ in the prosodic word domain, and

$s_i \delta f$ mean that f is dominated by s_i. Then $\forall s_i, f [s_i \delta f \rightarrow \forall s_j [s_j \delta f]]$, where $j > i$.

Consider as our idealization languages having words of the form $Ip^{(i/\gamma)}In$, where *I* is either *i* or *ɨ*. An occurring Turkish word of this form is *ipin* 'rope gen.'. As promised earlier this idealization limits us to an examination of backness harmony among high vowels. Suppose in addition we do not consider words that violate ALIGN-R, except by virtue of having a conflicting secondary articulation on p. The reason for this is that we are interested only in the fate of consonants in harmony domains, and the role that secondary articulations on such consonants can have assuming harmony. Given these assumptions, all of the possible words occurring in any of these idealized languages are given in (19).

(19) Possible words under current idealization

    a.   [ipin]$_{Fr}$ d.   [ɨpɨn]$_{Bk}$

    b.   [ipʲin]$_{Fr}$ e.   [ɨpˠɨn]$_{Bk}$

    c.   [i]$_{Fr}$[pˠɨn]$_{Bk}$ f.   [ɨ]$_{Bk}$[pʲin]$_{Fr}$

As should be clear, strict locality directly entails segments such as [p]$_{Fr}$ and [p]$_{Bk}$ (more fully, p^i and p^i) occurring in forms such as (19a) and (19d). These are the coarticulated segments seen earlier. Yet phonologists have generally assumed that consonants are not participants in vowel harmony. Taking up our discussion from Section 2.1, this is because to conclude the opposite – that consonants are participants – leads to a paradox within distinctive feature theory, where representational distinctions are generally identified with contrastive distinctions. Given distinctive feature theory, the expectation derived from observations of realizations in contrast (as in Irish or Russian) is that Front harmony in a form like *ipin* 'rope gen.', together with strict locality, should entail [ipʲinʲ], since there is no other notion of frontness in a consonant available to the theory. Similarly, Round harmony in *sonun* 'end gen.' should give something like [sʷonʷunʷ]. Since the Turkish forms do not actually elicit transcriptions of this sort, the conclusion is that consonants do not acquire these spreading features and thus cannot be considered participants.

The issue can be approached from another angle by granting first that locality is segmentally strict. Then consonants participate in vowel harmony, and segments like p^i must be rather unmarked, since this kind of participation is almost ubiquitous, and indeed p^i occurs throughout languages by coarticulation. But if p^i is unmarked (or even exists), why does it not occur contrastively, e.g., p^i versus p^i? From the perspective of OT with unidimensional markedness, for example, contrastiveness should arise straightforwardly from a constraint ranking such as that in (20).[16]

(20) Unmarked → contrastive for unidimensional markedness

   IDENT >> *p^j >> *p^i *p^j versus p^i is contrastive*

Approached from either direction, the source of the problem lies in the assumption that potentially contrastive distinctions are the only distinctions known to phonology. Our approach instead is to give up identifying the two, and to acknowledge the extra realizational possibilities that this move provides. Within DT it is possible to embrace strict locality while avoiding the problems caused for distinctive feature theory. It does not follow from the occurrence of p^i and so on in harmony spans that this segment should also freely contrast with other segments. This is because contrast is directly limited by output constraints in DT. As we saw in the case of Irish, DT actually makes predictions in this area that are correct and somewhat intricate. Further, with contrast aside, given the choice of either p^i or p^j in a harmony domain, all else equal, the former will always be favored in DT, since it is less marked articulatorily. Analogous reasoning holds for p^u versus p^w and for many similar cases. To see this, consider the tableau in (21).

(21) Consonant permeability in vowel harmony

	2Words	Space≥1/2	Align-R	3Words	*$C^{\gamma/j}$
a. [ipin]$_{Fr}$	*!			*	
b.☞ [ipin]$_{Fr}$ [ɨpɨn]$_{Bk}$				*	
c. [ipʲin]$_{Fr}$ [ɨpˠɨn]$_{Bk}$				*	*!*
d. [i]$_{Fr}$[pˠɨn]$_{Bk}$ [ɨ]$_{Bk}$[pʲin]$_{Fr}$			*!	*	**
e. [ipin]$_{Fr}$ [ɨpɨn]$_{Bk}$ [ipʲin]$_{Fr}$ [ɨpˠɨn]$_{Bk}$		*!*			**
f. [ipin]$_{Fr}$ [ɨpɨn]$_{Bk}$ [ipʲin]$_{Fr}$ [ɨpˠɨn]$_{Bk}$ [i]$_{Fr}$[pˠɨn]$_{Bk}$ [ɨ]$_{Bk}$[pʲin]$_{Fr}$		*!*	*!		****

(21a) is a language that fully obeys backness harmony; however, it is possible to be such a language and still respect 2WORDS (i.e., have more contrasts), as (21b) does. This second candidate is our idealized Turkish. (21c) also respects harmony and 2WORDS. In this language, the secondary articulations on *p* are consistent with the Front or Back harmony spans of words. Yet they also represent gratuitous violations of articulatory markedness, since the secondary articulations achieve nothing in the way of contrast or harmony. In fact, the violations incurred by such a candidate are a superset of those incurred by (21b), and so such a candidate can never win. (21d) is even worse, since the secondary articulations on *p* are not consistent with vowel harmony (velarization is Back, palatalization Front), and so ALIGN-R is violated (since our goal is to consider consonants in harmony spans, Align-R is undominated by assumption). The backness specification on $p^{j/\gamma}$ blocks the spreading of Front/Back from the root vowel, and itself spreads due to ALIGN-R. (21e) is an interesting attempt to respect harmony while increasing contrast, maintaining a contrast in consonantal backness as well as initial vowel backness. As we saw in the discussion of Irish, however, a contrast such as *ipin* versus *ip^jin* fails badly in the area of perceptual salience, as does *ipin* versus $ip^\gamma i\,n$, and so this candidate incurs two violations of SPACE$_{C-F2}$ ≥ 1/2. (Recall that this constraint records a violation only for a pair of words that are identical except for the backness specification of one consonant. Therefore the other pairings seen in this candidate do not violate it.) Finally, (21f) (which inclues all possible words under our idealization) has the same fatal faults as (21d–e) and so loses as well.

To summarize the implications of (21), the existence of vowel harmony implies that consonants in the harmony domain bear the harmonizing feature, given the assumption of strict locality. This does not entail secondary articulations as in p^j or p^γ, for two reasons. On the one hand, a contrast based on such articulations, in a language with vowel harmony, violates an independently motivated constraint on the perceptual well-formedness of contrast, as in (21e). On the other hand, secondary articulations not motivated by contrast, as in (21c), violate articulatory markedness with no redeeming gain. For the purposes of this demonstration we assumed that the constraints on articulatory markedness, $*C^{\gamma/j}$, are low ranked. The same result would be achieved under any ranking of these constraints, as the reader can verify.[17]

While (21c) is not optimal in the analysis given, it does not follow that it could never be. Indeed, we would not want this to follow, since the Turkish consonants *k*, *g*, and *l* are in fact allophonically palatalized in Front harmonic words (see the references on Turkish cited earlier). Allophonic palatalization of these segments is not uncommon across languages, implying that there are constraints (other than those governing a consonantal backness contrast) that favor palatalization and therefore articulatorily marked C^j. For example, if we were to include in the tableau in (21) undominated constraints requiring that velars and laterals be palatalized in a front vowel context, this would force realizations such as [ik^{j}in] for just these segments.

The conclusion we are led to here is rather that harmony in itself does not imply secondary articulations on consonants, even under strict locality, and that indeed secondary articulations under harmony are disfavored by basic constraints on both articulatory and perceptual well-formedness. As should be clear, similar reasoning holds for consonants in harmonic words with nonhigh vowels and for those bearing other harmonic features, say, consonants like p^w in words with rounding harmony.

We see here another example of the markedness pattern predicted by DT: a segment p^i that is marked for the purposes of contrast due to spacing requirements is unmarked when contrast is irrelevant; what determines the consonantal realization here is articulatory complexity alone, and so coarticulation holds. The situation here fully parallels that concerning the facts of C^j, C, C^y discussed earlier: a unidimensional markedness paradox resolves itself once the two genuine dimensions of markedness are recognized. Stepping back, we have the larger conclusion: namely, that segment skipping in cases such as this can be viewed as an artifact of a particular approach to markedness, distinctive feature theory. Given another markedness theory, the issue of locality disappears.

6. Conclusion

As we have shown, once markedness is factored into independent components with articulatory and perceptual underpinnings respectively, with the well-formedness of contrast regulated by output constraints, a seemingly obvious example of transparency in spreading can be eliminated, reduced to a more basic issue of markedness and segment realization. We have argued this for Turkish only, but current work by us and others suggests that the same principles apply to a significant range of phenomena, including consonants in other vowel harmonies, and consonantal harmonies. The hope is that this approach can help bring increased explanatory unity to these phenomena, and more significantly, unify these locality facts with the fundamental facts of markedness. Apart from the prohibition on segment skipping itself, the account we have presented makes no mention at all of locality or locality-specific notions.

There are of course other kinds of apparent transparency in spreading that present different challenges to the notion of strict locality – for example, transparent vowels in vowel harmony or transparent obstruents in nasal harmony. Walker (1998) argues that even such cases are best handled by independently required theoretical notions requiring no segment skipping or locality-specific statements. Similarly, recent work by Gafos (1996) makes a persuasive case that templatic effects of Semitic, and other similar facts, require neither planar C–V segregation nor the concomitant crossvowel spreading of consonants in words (as in McCarthy 1979). Instead these facts are subsumed under the independently necessary realm of reduplicative effects. Walker (2000, in press) similarly analyzes certain spectacular examples of alleged long-distance spreading as involving consonantal correspondence instead and provides forceful arguments for this point of view. Though much investigation remains to be done in this area, we consider the question of transparency in spreading to be very much an open one.

What of phenomena other than spreading that seem to require "action at a distance"? Obligatory Contour (dissimilatory) effects can involve apparent action at a distance, as when consonants in a CVC form must not be of identical place (see McCarthy 1986; Mester 1986; Yip 1989; Padgett 1991; and for new perspectives Pierrehumbert 1993; Frisch 1996; Alderete 1997; Ito and Mester, in press). Since the reasons for the existence of OCP effects have not been made clear, it is not at all obvious that they can be considered action at a distance in the sense that alleged transparency in spreading is action at a distance. What *is* clear is that the locality-related facts in the two areas are not the same. For instance, while the place features [labial], [coronal], and [dorsal] famously dissimilate long-distance, they do not spread long-distance (see Gafos 1996, Flemming 1995a, and NíChiosáin and Padgett 1997 for arguments that this is true even of [coronal]). These considerations suggest that, rather than seek a unified theory of locality, it is more promising to derive seeming transparency effects from a better understanding of the specific phenomena involved. This has been our goal here.

Notes

We would like to thank Jill Beckman, Diamandis Gafos, Bruce Hayes, René Kager, Geoffrey Pullum, Paul Smolensky, Laura Walsh, Mark Verhijde, and members of classes at the LOT Winter School in Nijmegen (January 1996) and at the University of California, Santa Cruz (spring 1998), whose ideas and feedback have contributed significantly to this chapter. We especially thank Junko Ito, Linda Lombardi, Armin Mester, Rachel Walker, and Cheryl

Zoll, who provided detailed commentary leading to many improvements. We also thank audiences at the Trilateral Phonology Weekend (Stanford, 1996), HILP3 (Amsterdam, 1997), SWOT4 (University of Arizona, 1998), and a Stanford phonology workshop. This work was supported by faculty research funds granted by the University of California, Santa Cruz, and University College Dublin.

1. See Odden (1994) for a recent example of this strategy and a review of the area. For long-distance spreading in the Sound Pattern of English framework, see especially Chomsky and Halle (1968), Johnson (1972), Howard (1973), Anderson (1974), Jensen and Strong-Jensen (1976), Ringen (1976), Vago (1976), and Kenstowicz and Kisseberth (1977).

2. Some other recent works arguably advocating a kind of strict (nonrelativized) locality are Smolensky (1993) and Cole and Kisseberth (1994, 1995), though these works pursue the locality and segment realization issues in a very different way.

3. Jakobson (1962:173–174) states (our translation), ". . . vowel harmony is indissolubly connected to consonantal harmony: some words consist of soft consonants and soft vowels, others of hard consonants and hard vowels." Trubetzkoy (1969:285) says similarly, "Synharmonism can be compared to tonality in music. In a 'synharmonic' language each word is like a string of sounds moving within a particular key." As an intriguing aside, Sharaf (1927:98) mentions that the alphabet employed in the Yenisey-Orkhon runic inscriptions attesting Old Turkic (approximately 700 CE, Comrie 1981), is "built on the foundation of pairings of consonants" (in frontness vs. backness), a point made to us also by Vügar Sultanov (p.c.).

4. The trough seen in English uC_ou has been observed in Swedish, French, and Spanish as well, and it is not fully understood. One class of coarticulation theories ("look-ahead") predicts that the consonants should be fully rounded even in these languages, and another ("coproduction") at least allows for some overlap of the consonants by rounding, assuming there are no contrary forces at work. There is some evidence that certain consonants have some phonetic specification for lip protrusion/retraction even though this property is not phonemic, a fact that might be responsible for certain troughs. See the references and discussion in Boyce (1990) and Perkell (1986). Given the complexity of the issue, and the general possibility of coarticulation (to be discussed), it seems unsafe to conclude that languages without vowel harmony should always exhibit troughs.

5. We thank Sibel Bargu and Orhan Orgun for volunteering as speakers. We especially thank Orhan Orgun for devising the extremely helpful list of Turkish forms. The forms were recorded by a Walkman Professional and analyzed on a Kay Elemetrics CSL 4300. They were digitized at 20,000 Hz (and automatically low-pass filtered). For each fricative, we examined LPC-derived spectra, using a 20-ms window around the fricative's midpoint, a filter order of 20, and full pre-emphasis. The authors can provide more details on the materials and methodology upon request.

6. The procedure was the following: find the ratio P1/P2, where P1 is the

highest peak (in decibels) in the 3–6 KHz range, and P2 is the highest peak above 6 KHz. The values were generally higher for [s] in front contexts.

7. Throughout the paper we make the simplifying assumption that articulatory simplicity is computed for a segment in isolation. In truth it is context-dependent. For example, ə is not favored reduced vowel in some contexts, as in English *dish[ɪ]s*, where the surrounding consonants have some effect. Similarly, Kabardian /ɨ/ has realizations ranging from [i] to [u] when following a consonant with tongue body or round specifications, but is [ɨ] otherwise (Choi 1991). In the same way, though we speak of plain consonants, the realization of a consonant can vary according to language and context.

8. Though interpreting these particular constraints as articulatory gives us the rankings that would be assumed on typological grounds, the same is not true of the similar example involving vowels, where articulatory considerations give us *i, *u » *ɨ.

9. These constraints and rankings are modeled after the "Minimal Distance" constraints of Flemming 1995b, but avoid some artifacts of the latter (see Padgett 1997, note 4).

10. Several issues for future research are raised by this formulation. To mention just one, it is important that differences are gauged along the perceptual dimension (couched crudely here as consonantal F2), and not in terms of articulatory specifications. This ensures that, say, $p^j i$ and $p^j i$ differ in just the same way that $p^j i$ and $p^{\gamma} i$ do (though to a lesser degree), and only in that way. Hence these two word pairs fall under the same spacing requirement. On the articulatory side these contrasts cannot be characterized in a uniform way, since the first pair differs in a strictural specification at the consonantal release (as discussed in Section 2.4), the second in Front/Back specifications.

11. Recall that contrasts are not overgenerated because Gen is assumed to put a lower limit on the spacing of contrasts. For example, we assumed earlier that the constraint $\text{SPACE}_{\text{C-F2}} \geq 1/3$ is in Gen.

12. It is important to note that the discussion here is based only on the secondary offglides transcribed (with roughly F2 location as the acoustic correlate), perhaps along with the slight frication that can typically accompany them, especially for C^j. It is well known that palatalization can lead to full-fledged affrication, especially for coronals, as in $t\int^j d\mathfrak{z}$. In such cases the distance between $C^j i$ and Ci can be much greater than suggested here. This degree of affrication does not occur in the dialect of Irish described here.

13. It is conceivable that C^i occurs with even greater frequency under palatalization contrasts than our account suggests. Though we assume the optimal contrast $C^j u$ versus Cu, the contrast $C^i u$ versus Cu might satisfy spacing requirements too, and would then be preferred on the grounds of articulatory simplicity. That is, what is called palatalization might involve a lesser degree of offglide constriction than C^j implies.

14. Probably the best account for these facts within distinctive feature theory

appeals to the Obligatory Contour Principle. See Padgett (in press) for arguments against such an alternative.

15. The nonpossessed form is *dere*. The *s* in *deresi* is inserted by a regular morphophonemic alternation. The same is true of *ütü* 'iron'.

16. Assuming that there are no constraints of the form $*p^V$, where V stands for
any coarticulated vocalic features, would also predict that such segments are
unmarked, but would still predict contrastiveness. All languages would have
segments like p^i, and those with the ranking Ident » $*p^j$ would contrast them
with p^j.

17. On the other hand, given the ranking 3Words » Space$_{C-F2}$ ≥ 1/2 we would
derive (21e) as optimal. In the discussion of Irish we left open the question
whether contrasts such as p^ji versus pi should be universally ruled out – that
is, whether they violate Space ≥ 1/3, assumed to be in Gen. We are not aware
of a clear case of contrast involving plain versus palatalized consonants
before phonetic [i] (assuming C is not affricated or spirantized). It does not
occur in either Irish or Russian. Nyangumarda contrasts "Ci" versus "Cyi."
However "i" is described by Hoard and O'Grady (1976) as lax [ɪ], so we
actually have [Cɪ] versus [Cʲɪ].

References

Akinlabi, Akinbiyi. 1997. Kalabari Vowel Harmony. *The Linguistic Review*
14:97–138.

Alderete, John. 1997. Dissimilation as Local Conjunction. In *Proceedings of
NELS 27*, pp. 17–32. Amherst, MA: GLSA.

Allen, W. 1951. Some Prosodic Aspects of Retroflexion and Aspiration in
Sanskrit. *Bulletin of the School of Oriental and African Studies* 13:939–
946.

Anderson, John, and Colin Ewen. 1987. *Principles of Dependency Phonology*.
Cambridge: Cambridge University Press.

Anderson, Stephen R. 1974. *The Organization of Phonology*. New York:
Academic.

Anderson, Stephen R. 1980. Problems and Perspectives in the Description
of Vowel Harmony. In *Issues in Vowel Harmony*, ed. R. Vago, pp. 1–48.
Amsterdam: Benjamins.

Archangeli, Diana, and Douglas Pulleyblank. 1986. The Content and Structure
of Phonological Representations. Ms., University of Arizona and University
of British Columbia.

Archangeli, Diana, and Douglas Pulleyblank. 1987. Minimal and Maximal Rules:
Effects of Tier Scansion. In *Proceedings of NELS 17*, pp. 16–35. Amherst,
MA: GLSA.

Archangeli, Diana, and Douglas Pulleyblank. 1994. *Grounded Phonology*.
Cambridge, MA: MIT Press.

Bender, Byron W. 1969. *Spoken Marshallese*. Honolulu, HI: University of Hawaii
Press.

Benthem, Johan van. 1983. *The Logic of Time – a Model-Theoretic Investigation* into the Varieties of Temporal Ontology and Temporal Discourse. Dordrecht: Reidel.

Benua, Laura. 1995. Identity Effects in Morphological Truncation. In *University of Massachusetts Occasional Papers in Linguistics 18: Papers in Optimality Theory*, pp. 77–136. Amherst, MA: GLSA.

Bird, Steven, and Ewan Klein. 1990. Phonological Events. *Journal of Linguistics* 26:33–56.

Boyce, S. 1990. Coarticulatory Organization for Lip Rounding in Turkish and English. *Journal of the Acoustical Society of America* 88:2584–2595.

Browman, Catherine, and Louis Goldstein. 1986. Towards an Articulatory Phonology. *Phonology Yearbook* 3:219–252.

Browman, Catherine, and Louis Goldstein. 1990. Tiers in Articulatory Phonology, with some Implications for Casual Speech. In *Papers in Laboratory Phonology I: Between the Grammar and Physics of Speech*, ed. Mary Beckman and John Kingston, pp. 341–397. Cambridge: Cambridge University Press.

Buckley, Eugene. 1995. Cyclicity as Correspondence. Ms., University of Pennsylvania. ROA 93c-0000, http://ruccs.rutgers.edu/roa.html.

Burzio, Luigi. 1994. *Principles of English Stress*. Cambridge: Cambridge University Press.

Burzio, Luigi. 1996. Surface Constraints versus Underlying Representations. In *Current Trends in Phonology: Models and Methods*, vol. 1, ed. Jacques Durand and Bernard Laks, pp. 123–141. Salford, Manchester: European Studies Research Institute.

Carney, P. J., and K. L. Moll. 1971. A Cinefluorographic Investigation of Fricative Consonant-Vowel Coarticulation. *Phonetica* 23:193–202.

Catford, J. C. 1988. *A Practical Introduction to Phonetics*. Oxford: Clarendon Press.

Choi, John D. 1991. An Acoustic Study of Kabardian Vowels. *Journal of the International Phonetic Association* 21:4–12.

Choi, John. 1992. Phonetic Underspecification and Target-Interpolation: An Acoustic Study of Marshallese Vowel Allophony. PhD dissertation, UCLA.

Choi, John, and Patricia Keating. 1991. Vowel-to-Vowel Coarticulation in Three Slavic Languages. *UCLA Working Papers in Phonetics* 78:78–86.

Chomsky, Noam, and Morris Halle. 1968. *The Sound Pattern of English*. New York: Harper & Row.

Clements, G. N. 1980. *Vowel Harmony in Nonlinear Generative Phonology: An Autosegmental Model*. Bloomington, IN: Indiana University Linguistics Club.

Clements, G. N., and Engin Sezer. 1982. Vowel and Consonant Disharmony in Turkish. In *The Structure of Phonological Representations*, vol. 1, ed. Harry van der Hulst and Norval Smith, pp. 213–255. Dordrecht: Foris.

Cohn, Abigail. 1989. Phonetic Evidence for Configuration Constraints. In *Proceedings of NELS 19*, pp. 63–77. Amherst, MA: GLSA.

Cole, Jennifer, and Charles Kisseberth. 1994. An Optimal Domains Theory of Harmony. Urbana-Champaign, IL: Cognitive Science Technical Report UIUC-BI-CS-94-02, University of Illinois.

Cole, Jennifer, and Charles Kisseberth. 1995. Nasal Harmony in Optimal Domains Theory. Urbana-Champaign, IL: Cognitive Science Technical Report UIUC-BI-CS-95-02, University of Illinois.

Coleman, John, and John Local. 1991. The "No Crossing Constraint" in Autosegmental Phonology. *Linguistics and Philosophy* 14:295–338.

Comrie, Bernard. 1981. *The Languages of the Soviet Union*. Cambridge: Cambridge University Press.

Fant, Gunnar. 1960. *Acoustic Theory of Speech Production*. The Hague: Mouton.

Farnetani, Edda. 1997. Coarticulation and Connected Speech Processes. In *The Handbook of Phonetic Sciences*, ed. William J. Hardcastle and John Laver, pp. 371–404. Cambridge, MA: Blackwell.

Farnetani, Edda, Kyriaki Vagges, and Emanuela Magno-Caldognetto. 1985. Coarticulation in Italian /VtV/ Sequences: A Palatographic Study. *Phonetica* 42:78–99.

Flemming, Edward. 1995a. Vowels Undergo Consonant Harmony. Paper presented at the Trilateral Phonology Weekend, Stanford University.

Flemming, Edward. 1995b. Auditory Representations in Phonology. PhD Dissertation, UCLA.

Flemming, Edward. 1995c. Phonetic Detail in Phonology: Evidence from Assimilation and Coarticulation. In *Proceedings of South Western Optimality Theory Workshop 1995 (Arizona Phonology Conference, vol. 5)*, ed. Keiichiro Suzuki and Dirk Elzinga, pp. 39–50. Tucson, AZ: University of Arizona, Department of Linguistics.

Flemming, Edward. 1999. How to Formalize Constraints on Perceptual Distinctiveness. Handout of paper presented at ICPhS San Francisco, CA.

Fowler, C. A. 1983. Converging Sources of Evidence on Spoken and Perceived Rhythms of Speech: Cyclic Production of Vowels in Sequences of Monosyllabic Stress Feet. *Journal of Experimental Psychology: General* 112:386–412.

Frisch, Stefan. 1996. Similarity and Frequency in Phonology. PhD dissertation, Northwestern University.

Gafos, Adamantios. 1996. The Articulatory Basis of Locality in Phonology. PhD dissertation, Johns Hopkins University.

Gafos, Adamantios, and Linda Lombardi. In press. Consonant Transparency and Vowel Echo. In *Proceedings of NELS 29*, vol. 2, 81–95. Amherst, MA: GLSA.

Goldsmith, John. 1976. Autosegmental Phonology. PhD dissertation, MIT. 1979. New York: Garland.

Guerssel, Mohammed. 1986. Glides in Berber and Syllabicity. *Linguistic Inquiry* 17:1–12.

Halle, Morris. 1962. Phonology in Generative Grammar. *Word* 18:54–72.

Halle, Morris, and Jean-Roger Vergnaud. 1978. Metrical Structures in Phonology. Ms., MIT.

Hammond, Michael. 1988. On Deriving the Well-Formedness Condition. *Linguistic Inquiry* 19:319–325.

Hoard, James, and G. N. O'Grady. 1976. Nyangumarda Phonology, a Preliminary Report. In *Grammatical Categories in Australian Languages*, ed. Robert Dixon, pp. 51–77. Canberra: Australian Institute of Aboriginal Studies.

Howard, Irwin. 1973. A Directional Theory of Rule Application in Phonology. PhD dissertation, MIT.

Hughes, George W., and Morris Halle. 1956. Spectral Properties of Fricative Consonants. *Journal of the Acoustical Society of America* 28:303–310.

Hulst, Harry van der, and Jeroen van de Weijer. 1991. Topics in Turkish Phonology. In *Turkish Linguistics Today*, ed. H. Boeschoten and L. Verhoeven, pp. 11–59. Kinderhook, NY: E. J. Brill.

Ito, Junko, and Armin Mester. 1997. Correspondence and Compositionality: The Ga-Gyo Variation in Japanese Phonology. In *Derivations and Constraints in Phonology*, ed. I. Roca, pp. 419–462. Oxford: Oxford University Press.

Ito, Junko, and Armin Mester. In press. Markedness and Word structure: OCP effects in Japanese. Cambridge, MA: MIT Press.

Jakobson, Roman. 1962. K Xarakteristike Evrazijskogo Jazykovogo Sojuza. In *Roman Jakobson: Selected Writings*, vol. 1, pp. 144–201. 'S-Gravenhage: Mouton.

Jensen, John T, and Margaret Stong-Jensen. 1976. Ordering and Directionality of Iterative Rules. In *The Application and Ordering of Grammatical Rules*, ed. Andreas Koutsoudas, pp. 104–121. The Hague: Mouton.

Johnson, C. Douglas. 1972. *Formal Aspects of Phonological Description.* The Hague: Mouton.

Kager, René. 1999. Surface Opacity of Metrical Structure in Optimality Theory. In *The Derivational Residue in Phonological Optimality Theory*, ed. B. Hermans and M. van Dostendorp, pp. 207–245. Philadelphia: Benjamins.

Kaye, Jonathan, and Jean Lowenstamm. 1984. De la Syllabicité. In *Forme Sonore du Language: Structure des Représentations en Phonologie*, ed. Francois Dell, D. Hirst, and Jean-Roger Vergnaud, pp. 123–159. Paris: Hermann.

Kenstowicz, Michael. 1995. Cyclic vs. Non-Cyclic Constraint Evaluation. *Phonology* 12:397–436.

Kenstowicz, Michael. 1996. Base Identity and Uniform Exponence: Alternatives to Cyclicity. In *Current Trends in Phonology: Models and Methods*, vol. 1, ed. Jacques Durand, and Bernard Laks, pp. 363–393. Salford, Manchester: European Studies Research Institute.

Kenstowicz, Michael, and Charles Kisseberth. 1977. *Topics in Phonological Theory.* New York: Academic.

Kiparsky, Paul. 1981. Vowel Harmony. Ms., MIT.

Kiparsky, Paul. 1985. Some Consequences of Lexical Phonology. *Phonology* 2:85–138.

Kirchner, Robert. 1993. Round and Back Vowel Harmony and Disharmony: An Optimality Theoretic Account. Ms., UCLA.

Kirchner, Robert. 1997. Contrastiveness and Faithfulness. *Phonology* 14:83–111.

Ladefoged, Peter. 1993. *A Course in Phonetics.* Fort Worth: Harcourt Brace Jovanovich.

Ladefoged, Peter, and Jenny Ladefoged. 1997. Phonetic Structures of Scottish Gaelic. *UCLA Working Papers in Phonetics* 95:144–153.

Ladefoged, Peter, and Ian Maddieson. 1996. *The Sounds of the World's Languages.* Cambridge, MA: Blackwell.

Levergood, Barbara. 1984. Rule Governed Vowel Harmony and the Strict Cycle. In *Proceedings of NELS 14*, pp. 275–293. Amherst, MA: GLSA.

Levin, Juliette. 1985. A Metrical Theory of Syllabicity. PhD dissertation, MIT.

Lewis, G. L. 1967. *Turkish Grammar.* Oxford: Clarendon.

Lightner, Theodore. 1972. *Problems in the Theory of Phonology, Vol. 1: Russian Phonology and Turkish Phonology.* Edmonton: Linguistic Research, Inc.

Liljencrants, Johan, and Björn Lindblom. 1972. Numerical Simulation of Vowel Quality Systems: The Role of Perceptual Contrast. *Language* 48:839–862.

Lindblom, Björn. 1986. Phonetic Universals in Vowel Systems. In *Experimental Phonology*, ed. John J. Ohala and Jeri Jaeger, pp. 13–44. Orlando, FL: Academic.

Lindblom, Björn. 1990. On the Notion "Possible Speech Sound." *Journal of Phonetics* 18:135–152.

Linker, Wendy. 1982. Articulatory and Acoustic Correlates of Labial Activity in Vowels: A Cross-linguistic Study. *UCLA Working Papers in Phonetics* 56.

Lyovin, Anatole V. 1997. *An Introduction to the Languages of the World.* Oxford: Oxford University Press.

McCarthy, John J. 1979. Formal Problems in Semitic Phonology and Morphology. PhD dissertation, MIT.

McCarthy, John J. 1986. OCP Effects: Gemination and Antigemination. *Linguistic Inquiry* 17:207–263.

McCarthy, John J. 1994. On Coronal "Transparency." Paper presented at the Annual Trilateral Phonology Weekend, University of California, Santa Cruz.

McCarthy, John J. 1995. Extensions of Faithfulness: Rotuman Revisited. Ms., University of Massachusetts, Amherst.

McCarthy, John J., and Alan Prince. 1993. Generalized Alignment. In *Yearbook of Morphology*, pp. 79–153.

McCarthy, John J., and Alan S. Prince. 1995. Faithfulness and Reduplicative Identity. In *University of Massachusetts Occasional Papers in Linguistics 18: Papers in Optimality Theory*, pp. 249–384. Amherst, MA: GLSA.

Mester, Armin. 1986. Studies in Tier Structure. PhD dissertation, University of Massachusetts, Amherst.

NíChasaide, Ailbhe. 1979. Laterals of Gaoth-Dobhair Irish and of Hiberno English. In *Occasional Papers in Linguistics and Language Learning 6, Papers in Celtic Phonology*, ed. D. P. Ó Baoill, pp. 54–78. Ulster: The New University of Ulster.

NíChiosáin, Máire, and Jaye Padgett. 1997. Markedness, Segment Realization, and Locality in Spreading. Report No. LRC-97-01, Linguistics Research Center, University of California, Santa Cruz.

Odden, David. 1994. Adjacency Parameters in Phonology. *Language* 70:289–330.

Ogden, Richard, and John Local. 1994. Disentangling Autosegments from Prosodies: A Note on the Misrepresentation of a Research Tradition in Phonology. *Journal of Linguistics* 30:477–498.

Öhman, S. E. G. 1966. Coarticulation in VCV Utterances: Spectrographic Measurements. *Journal of the Acoustical Society of America* 39:151–168.

Orgun, Orhan. 1994. Monotonic Cyclicity and Optimality Theory. In *Proceedings of NELS 24*, pp. 461–474. Amherst, MA: GLSA.

Orgun, Orhan. 1996. Sign-based Morphology and Phonology. PhD dissertation, University of California, Berkeley.

Padgett, Jaye. 1991. Stricture in Feature Geometry. PhD dissertation, University of Massachusetts, Amherst. Revised version 1995. Stanford, CA: CSLI Press.

Padgett, Jaye. 1995. Feature Classes. In *University of Massachusetts Occasional Papers in Linguistics 18: Papers in Optimality Theory*, pp. 385–420. Amherst, MA: GLSA.

Padgett, Jaye. 1997. Perceptual Distance of Contrast: Vowel Height and Nasality. In *Phonology at Santa Cruz*, Vol. 5, ed. Rachel Walker, Motoko Katayama, and Daniel Karvonen, pp. 63–78. Santa Cruz, CA: Linguistics Research Center, University of California.

Padgett, Jaye. In press. Contrast Dispersion and Russian Palatalization. In *The Role of Speech Perception Phenomena in Phonology*, ed. Elizabeth Hume and Keith Johnson. San Diego, CA: Academic.

Paradis, Carole, and Jean-François Prunet. 1989. On Coronal Transparency. *Phonology* 6:317–348.

Perkell, Joseph S. 1986. Coarticulation Strategies: Preliminary Implications of a Detailed Analysis of Lower Lip Protrusion Movements. *Speech Communication* 5:47–68.

Pierrehumbert, Janet. 1993. Dissimilarity in the Arabic Verbal Roots. In *Proceedings of NELS 23*, pp. 367–381. Amherst, MA: GLSA.

Prince, Alan, and Paul Smolensky. In press. *Optimality Theory: Constraint Interaction in Generative Grammar*. Cambridge, MA: MIT Press.

Pulleyblank, Douglas. 1993. Vowel Harmony and Optimality Theory. In *Proceedings of the Workshop on Phonology*, pp. 1–18. Coimbra: Assoçião Portugesa de Linguística.

Pulleyblank, Douglas. 1996. Neutral Vowels in Optimality Theory: A Comparison of Yoruba and Wolof. *Canadian Journal of Linguistics* 41:295–347.

Reformatskii, Aleksandr Aleksandrovich. 1958. O Korrelatsii "Tverdykh" i "Miagkikh" Soglasnykh (v Sovremennom Russkom Literaturnom Iazyke). In *Mélanges Linguistiques Offerts à Emil Petrovici par ses Amis Étrangers a l'Occasion de son Soixantième Anniversaire*, pp. 494–499. Bucarest: Editura Academiei Republicii Populare Romine.

Ringen, Catherine O. 1976. Vacuous Application, Iterative Application, Reapplication, and the Unordered Rule Hypothesis. In *The Application and Ordering of Grammatical Rules*, ed. Andreas Koutsoudas, pp. 55–75. The Hague: Mouton.

Sagey, Elizabeth. 1988. On the Ill-Formedness of Crossing Association Lines. *Linguistic Inquiry* 19:109–118.

Scobbie, James. 1991. Attribute Value Phonology. PhD dissertation, University of Edinburgh.

Selkirk, Elizabeth. 1984. On the Major Class Features and Syllable Theory. In *Language Sound Structures*, ed. Mark Aronoff and Richard T. Oehrle, pp. 107–136. Cambridge, MA: MIT Press.

Sharaf, G. 1927. Paljatogrammy Zvukov Tatarskogo Jazyka Sravnitel'no s Russkimi. *Vestnik Nauchnogo Obshchestva Tatarovedenija* 7:65–102.

Shaw, Patricia. 1991. Consonant Harmony Systems: The Special Status of Coronal Harmony. In *The Special Status of Coronals*, ed. Carole Paradis and Jean-Francois Prunet, pp. 125–157. New York: Academic.

Smolensky, Paul. 1993. Optimality, Markedness, and Underspecification. Paper presented at the Rutgers University Optimality Workshop.

Steriade, Donca. 1994. Complex Onsets as Single Segments: The Mazateco Pattern. In *Perspectives in Phonology*, ed. Jennifer Cole and Charles Kisseberth, pp. 203–291. Stanford, CA: CSLI Publications.

Stevens, Kenneth N., and Sheila E. Blumstein. 1981. The Search for Invariant Acoustic Correlates of Phonetic Features. In *Perspectives on the Study of Speech*, ed. J. Miller and P. Eimas, pp. 1–38. Hillsdale, NJ: Erlbaum.

Trubetzkoy, Nikolai. 1969. *Principles of Phonology*. Berkeley, CA: University of California Press.

Underhill, Robert. 1976. *Turkish Grammar*. Cambridge, MA: MIT Press.

Vago, Robert. 1976. Theoretical Implications of Hungarian Vowel Harmony. *Linguistic Inquiry* 7:242–263.

Walker, Rachel. 1998. Nasalization, Neutral Segments, and Opacity Effects. PhD dissertation, University of California, Santa Cruz.

Walker, Rachel. In Press. Consonantal Correspondence. In *Proceedings of the Workshop on the Lexicon in Phonetics and Phonology: Papers in Experimental and Theoretical Linguistics 6*. Edmonton: University of Alberta.

Walker, Rachel. 2000. Long-Distance Consonantal Identity Effects. In *Proceedings of WCCFL 19*, pp. 532–545.

Waterson, Natalie. 1956. Some Aspects of the Phonology of the Nominal Forms of the Turkish Word, *Bulletin of the School of Oriental and African Studies* 18:578–591.

Yip, Moira. 1989. Feature Geometry and Cooccurrence Restrictions. *Phonology* 6:349–374.

Zoll, Cheryl. 1996. Parsing Below the Segment in a Constraint-Based Framework. PhD dissertation, University of California, Berkeley.

PART II

THE CONTENT OF CONSTRAINTS

5

Austronesian Nasal Substitution Revisited: What's Wrong with *NC̥ (and What's Not)

JOE PATER

Introduction

In Indonesian, the voicing of the root-initial obstruent determines the outcome of /məŋ-/ prefixation. When that consonant is voiceless, it coalesces with the prefix-final nasal to produce a nasal with the same place of articulation as the obstruent, in a process referred to as nasal substitution (e.g., /məŋ+paksa/ → [məmaksa] 'to force'). When the root-initial obstruent is voiced, though, simple place assimilation results (/məŋ+buat/ → [məmbuat] 'to make/do').

In traditional analyses of nasal substitution, the limitation to voiceless consonants is expressed as a featural restriction on the scope of the relevant rule. No attempt is made to derive this restriction from principles active elsewhere in Indonesian, or in other languages. Pater (1999) points out that Indonesian is far from alone in its avoidance of nasal–voiceless obstruent clusters and invokes a substantive output constraint against these clusters, *NC̥, as the formal driving force behind processes like nasal substitution, postnasal voicing, nasal deletion, and denasalization. The Optimality Theoretic ranking between *NC̥ and faithfulness constraints determines which of these routes a language chooses to take to eliminate nasal–voiceless obstruent clusters.

Despite the relative success of the *NC̥ account in formally connecting nasal substitution to a crosslinguistic range of phonological processes, in this chapter I will argue for a reanalysis, based on evidence from other Austronesian languages as well as Indonesian itself. Muna nasal substitution (van den Berg 1989) parallels Indonesian in targeting only voiceless obstruents, but differs in that coalescence arises from the avoidance of multiple labials in a word rather than from the avoidance of NC̥ clusters. To deal with the Muna case, it is necessary to posit a constraint that specifically blocks coalescence between a nasal and a voiced obstruent, which is argued to be one that forces preservation of an obstruent-specific voice feature, Pharyngeal Expansion (IDENTPHAREXP; cf. Trigo 1991; Steriade 1995).

Adoption of this constraint pays off in the context of Indonesian by permitting a more principled account of the restriction of nasal substitution to root-initial position (e.g., [əmpat] 'four', /məŋ+pər+besar/ → [məmpərbesar] 'to enlarge'). While this morphological restriction was handled only awkwardly in the *NC̥ analysis, here the limited scope of nasal substitution is explained by relating it to other phonological processes that treat the left edge of the root as special (Cohn and McCarthy 1994). Along with Cohn and McCarthy's (1994) ALIGN-WD constraint, crucial use is made of Ito and Mester's (1999a) related CRISPEDGE. Through factorial typology, this reanalysis extends to other cases of Austronesian nasal substitution that are clearly out of the reach of *NC̥, in which voiced obstruents are targeted along with voiceless ones.

In the first section of the chapter, I review the *NC̥ analysis of nasal substitution, demonstrating how it succeeds in relating the asymmetric coalescence behavior of voiceless stops to other crosslinguistically common processes. Section 2 introduces the Muna data, showing why they are problematic for that approach to Austronesian nasal substitution. This will then lead to the reanalysis of Indonesian, followed by some discussion of factorial typology. In the concluding section, I discuss whether this reanalysis of Austronesian nasal substitution, or that of Archangeli, Moll, and Ohno (1998), threatens the general viability of *NC̥ as a constraint.

1. Austronesian Nasal Substitution as a *NC̥ Effect

As mentioned in the introduction, nasal substitution is only one of a number of phonological processes that serve to eliminate nasal–voiceless obstruent sequences. The table in (1) provides schematic descriptions of some others, using T and D to stand for voiceless and voiced obstruents and N for nasals, as well as a few illustrative languages (see Pater 1996, 1999 for references and further language examples).

(1)   Post-nasal voicing   NT → ND   (Japanese, Puyo Pungo Quechua)
      Nasal deletion   NT → T   (Kelanatan Malay, Swahili)
      Denasalization   NT → TT   (Toba Batak, Kaingang)

The goal of the analysis in Pater (1996, 1999) is to provide a unified account for these processes, without generating unattested ones, such as prenasal voicing. A set of conspiracies (cf. Kisseberth 1970), in which two processes cooperate to rid a language of NC̥ clusters, provides strong support for the need for an analysis that generalizes across these cases; see (2).

(2) **NC̥ conspiracies**

Modern Greek:	NT → ND	MPS → PS	*post-nasal voicing and deletion*
Karpathos Greek:	NT → ND	N#T → T#T	*post-nasal voicing and denasalization*
OshiKwanyama:	NT → ND	N#T → N	*post-nasal voicing and nasal substitution*
Kihehe:	NT → N	NS → S	*nasal substitution and deletion*

In Optimality Theory, this goal can be met straightforwardly due to the theory's reliance on substantive output constraints to drive phonological phenomena. In the present instance, an output constraint against nasal–voiceless obstruent clusters (*NC̥) can be justified in terms of the articulatory difficulty of the quick velum raising needed to produce a voiceless obstruent following a nasal (see also Hayes 1999; cf. Hyman 1998). If *NC̥ outranks a faithfulness constraint against segmental fusion, or coalescence (e.g., UNIFORMITY; McCarthy and Prince 1999), the result is nasal substitution, as shown in the tableaux in (3). Subscripted numbers are used to indicate the correspondence relation between segments (see McCarthy and Prince 1999); fusion is interpreted as a two-to-one mapping between input and output that incurs a UNIFORMITY violation.

(3) Nasal substitution: *NC̥ >> UNIFORM(ITY)

Input: məŋ₁+p₂aksa	*NC̥	UNIFORM
☞ məm₁,₂aksa		*
məm₁p₂aksa	* !	

Input: məŋ₁+b₂uat	*NC̥	UNIFORM
məm₁,₂uat		* !
☞ məm₁b₂uat		

To account for the blocking of nasal substitution within roots, Pater (1999) appeals to a root-specific instantiation of an antifusion constraint; this blocks coalescence between pairs of root segments (see also McCarthy and Prince 1994, Urbanczyk 1996, and Beckman 1997 on root-specific faithfulness). With this constraint ranked above *NC̥, nasal substitution continues to apply at the prefix-root boundary, but not within roots, as shown in (4).

(4) UNIFORM(ITY)^{RT} >> *NC̥ >> UNIFORM(ITY)

Input: əm$_1$p$_2$at	UNI-FORM^{RT}	*NC̥	UNI-FORM
əm$_{12}$at	*!		
☞ əm$_1$p$_2$at		*!	*

Input: məŋ$_1$+p$_2$aksa	UNI-FORM^{RT}	*NC̥	UNI-FORM
☞ məm$_{1,2}$aksa			*
məm$_1$p$_2$aksa		*!	

Constraint reranking generates the other NC̥ effects. For instance, if a constraint demanding a match between input and output voice specification (IDENT[VOICE]: "correspondent segments are identical in voice")[1] falls beneath *NC̥, the result is postnasal voicing, as shown in (5).

(5) Postnasal voicing: *NC̥ >> IDENT[VOICE]

Input: NT	*NC̥	IDENT [VOICE]
☞ ND		*
NT	*!	

A conspiracy can be produced if *NC̥ dominates two relevant faithfulness constraints. While the ranking between these two constraints will generally determine the outcome, violation of the higher-ranked one can be forced if violation of the lower-ranked one is disallowed in a particular morphological or phonological environment. The makings of such a situation are present in (4), where nasal substitution is blocked root-internally. If IDENT[VOICE] falls between *NC̥ and UNIFORMITY, then the OshiKwanyama conspiracy between nasal substitution and postnasal voicing occurs. The tableau in (6) shows that postnasal voicing occurs root-medially. Root-initially, nasal substitution continues to apply as in (4), due to the ranking of IDENT[VOICE] above UNIFORMITY.

(6) UNIFORM(ITY)^{RT}, *NC̥ >> IDENT[VOICE] >> UNIFORM(ITY)

Input: N$_1$T$_2$	UNIFORM^{RT}	*NC̥	IDENT [VOICE]	UNIFORM
☞ N$_1$D$_2$			*	
N$_1$T$_2$		*!		
N$_{1,2}$	*!			*

2. Muna Morphophonemics

Data from Muna, a Western Austronesian language spoken on an island off the southeast coast of Sulawesi, Indonesia (van den Berg 1989), present what seems to be an insurmountable challenge for the *NC̥ analysis of nasal substitution. Austronesian nasal substitution is most commonly associated with prefixation of an affix similar to Indonesian *məŋ-* (e.g., *man-* both in Chamorro (Topping 1973) and Malagasy (Dziwirek 1989)). In Muna, however, it occurs in the contest of *-um-* affixation, which marks the irrealis form of verbs. Before proceeding to nasal substitution and the challenge it poses, there are a relatively large number of preliminaries to be dealt with. Section 2.1 presents the basic pattern of infixation and prefixation displayed by *-um-*, with Section 2.2 focusing on the special behavior of labials in *-um-* affixation, and related root internal phonotactics. Finally, in Section 2.3 we return to the main issue at hand: nasal substitution.

2.1. Onset-Driven Infixation

The data in (7) display two of the realizations of *-um-*.

(7)
a.	/um+dadi/	[dumadi]	'live'
b.	/um+gaa/	[gumaa]	'marry'
c.	/um+rende/	[rumende]	'alight'
d.	/um+solo/	[sumolo]	'flow'
e.	/um+ala/	[mala]	'take'
f.	/um+ere/	[mere]	'stand up'
g.	/um+uta/	[muta]	'pick fruit'

As illustrated by (7a–d), *-um-* appears as an infix with consonant-initial roots. When the root is vowel-initial, as in (7e–g), the vowel of *-um-* deletes. Both infixation and vowel deletion can be understood as ways of satisfying a constraint against onsetless syllables, ONSET. As (8) shows, infixation occurs at the cost of a violation of ALIGNLEFT, which demands that *-um-* occur at the left edge of the output word (see McCarthy and Prince's 1993 analysis of Tagalog infixation).

(8) ONSET >> ALIGNLEFT

Input: um+dadi	ONSET	ALIGN LEFT
☞ dumadi		*
umdadi	* !	

Deletion violates Max, as shown in (9).[2]

(9) ONSET >> MAX

Input: um+ala	ONSET	MAX
☞ mala		*
umala	* !	

Making the simplifying assumption that Max applies to both consonants
and vowels (cf. McCarthy and Prince 1999:294), it would need to dominate AlignLeft to block the alternative of deletion of the entire affix (as
long as this vacuously satisfies AlignLeft), as in (10).

(10) ONSET >> MAX >> ALIGNLEFT

Input: um+dadi	ONSET	MAX	ALIGN LEFT
☞ dumadi			*
dadi		**!	
umdadi	* !		

2.2. *Labial-Initial Roots*

Roots beginning with labials form a set of systematic exceptions to the
pattern of infixation with consonant-initial roots.[3] As the examples in
(11) show, both the vowel and the nasal are deleted when the root begins
with a voiced (11a) or implosive (11b) labial. When the root-initial labial
is voiceless, we find deletion of the vowel, accompanied by nasal substitution (11c,d). Finally, roots beginning with a bilabial approximant can
induce either nasal substitution (11e) or deletion (11f), with a majority
in the latter category. The question to be addressed in this subsection
is what is responsible for the blocking of the infixation pattern with this
set of roots. The answer appears to lie in the general phonotactics of the
language.

(11) a. /um+baru/   [baru]   'happy'
      b. /um+ɓala/   [ɓala]   'big'
      c. /um+pili/   [mili]   'choose'
      d. /um+futaa/   [mutaa]   'laugh'
      e. /um+waa/   [maa]   'give'
      f. /um+wanu/   [wanu]   'get up'

Following Uhlenbeck's (1949) study of root constraints in Javanese, van den Berg (1989) examined the cooccurrence patterns between consonants in the 1,100 CVCV roots in his database. In terms of restrictions between homorganic consonants, van den Berg (1989:30–31) makes the observations in (12).

(12)   "Obstruents and prenasalized consonants do not co-occur with homorganic nasals . . .
Initial plosives do not co-occur with contra-voiced homorganic plosives"

One might wonder whether these cooccurrence constraints are symptomatic of a wider ban on homorganic consonants, of the type found in Javanese (Uhlenbeck 1949) or Semitic (Greenberg 1950).

The data in (13) support this conjecture. Root types are organized according to the initial consonant, which is listed in the first row under "C1". The pairs of consonants in the following columns refer to the initial and medial consonants of the CVCV roots. Whether or not a particular root type occurs is indicated by whether it falls into the "Occurring," "Non-occurring," or "Marginal" column, the categories that van den Berg (1989) uses. Unfortunately van den Berg (1989) does not provide the raw data (i.e., the number of instances of occurring root types) that would be required for a proper statistical treatment. However, to give some impression of the relative robustness of the cooccurrence patterns for each initial consonant, the total number of roots starting with that consonant in the database is given in the final row.[4] For the labial and dorsal initial roots, we find much the same pattern as in Javanese and Semitic: nonidentical homorganic consonants are not permitted to cooccur. Exceptions to this generalization are highlighted in boldface in the table, and there are very few of them among the labials and dorsals. However, unlike the root constraints first documented in Uhlenbeck (1949) and Greenberg (1950), in Muna we find that coronals cooccur freely (see McCarthy 1988 and Frisch, Broe, and Pierrhumbert 1997 on the more limited cooccurrence allowed between coronals in Arabic).

(13) Muna homorganic consonant co-occurrence patterns

C1	Occurring (n≥2)	Non-occurring (n=0)	Marginal (n=1)	Total
p-	p-p	p-b, p-ɓ, p-f, p-w, p-m		84
b-	b-b	b-p, b-ɓ, b-f, b-w, b-m		50
ɓ-	ɓ-ɓ, **ɓ-w**	ɓ-p, ɓ-b, ɓ-f, ɓ-m		73
f-	f-f, **f-p**	f-b, f-ɓ, f-w, f-m		17
w-	w-w	w-p, w-b, w-f, w-m	w-ɓ	59
m-	m-m	m-p, m-b, m-ɓ	m-f, m-w	44
k-		k-k, k-g, k-ʁ, k-ŋ		86
g-	g-g	g-k, g-ʁ, g-ŋ		46
ʁ-	ʁ-ʁ	ʁ-k, ʁ-g, ʁ-ŋ		62
ŋ-		ŋ-ŋ, ŋ-k, ŋ-ʁ, ŋ-g		5
t-	**t-t, t-d, t-s, t-l, t-r, t-n**			127
d-	**d-d, d-t, d-l, d-n**		d-s, d-r	50
s-	**s-s, s-d, s-l, s-r**	s-t, s-n		89
l-	**l-l, l-t, l-d, l-s, l-n**		l-r	97
r-	**r-r, r-t, r-d, r-s, r-n**	r-l		72
n-	**n-t, n-d, n-l**		n-s, n-n, n-r	20

It seems likely that the blocking of *-um-* infixation with initial labials is a morphophonemic response to the same phonotactic constraint that bans multiple labials in a root. A number of proposals have surfaced in the recent literature for how to formalize such dissimilatory constraints, which following McCarthy (1986, 1988) are usually assumed to be the result of the OCP (Leben 1973). These include Ito and Mester (1996), Alderete (1997), Frisch et al. (1997), MacEachern (1997), and Suzuki (1998). Here I will follow Alderete's (1997) suggestion that dissimilation results from local self-conjunction (cf. Smolensky 1995) of markedness constraints (see also Ito and Mester 1996).

Of particular relevance is Alderete's analysis of a morphophonemic pattern in Tashlhiyt Berber, which like the Muna root restriction eliminates multiple labials, but tolerates multiple coronals. To account for this, he suggests that the constraints in Prince and Smolensky's (1993) place markedness hierarchy be self-conjoined, preserving the fixed rankings in the original hierarchy. As illustrated in (14), Prince and Smolensky's hierarchy fixes the rank of constraints against labial and dorsal place of articulation above coronal, yielding the general unmarkedness of coronal place.

(14)   *PL/LAB, *PL/DORS >> *PL/COR

Local self-conjunction of a constraint results in a new constraint that penalizes forms that contain two violations of the original constraint, within a particular domain. The self-conjoined place markedness hierarchy appears in (15). With an appropriate faithfulness constraint intervening between the noncoronal and the coronal markedness constraints, multiple instances of homorganic noncoronals, but not coronals, will be eliminated, just as the Muna root constraints require.

(15)   *PL/LAB^2, *PL/DORS^2 >> *PL/COR^2

Returning to -*um*- affixation, a ranking of *PL/LAB^2 above MAX will produce deletion of the affix's nasal when it is added to labial initial roots (recall that ONSET forces deletion of the vowel), as shown in (16).[5]

(16) *PL/LAB^2 >> MAX

Input: um$_1$+b$_2$aru	*PL/LAB^2	MAX
a. b$_2$um$_1$aru	* !	
☞ b$_2$aru		**

2.3. Nasal Substitution

We are now finally in a position to deal with the Muna nasal substitution pattern. Under the assumption that nasal substitution results from fusion of the nasal and the root-initial consonant, it produces no violation of MAX. MAX requires that Input segments have Output correspondents; in fusion, both segments share a single Output correspondent. As fusion does violate UNIFORMITY, MAX must rank above that constraint to produce fusion rather than simple deletion, as in (17).

(17) *PL/LAB^2 >> MAX >> UNIFORM(ITY)

Input: um$_1$+p$_2$ili	*PL/LAB^2	MAX	UNIFORM
p$_2$um$_1$ili	* !		
p$_2$ili		* !	
☞ m$_{1,2}$ili			*

Here we see a classic case of a conspiracy: $*\text{PL/LAB}^2$ is satisfied by either deletion or fusion, depending on the voicing of the initial consonant. To complete our account of it, we must explain why fusion is blocked in the case of voiced consonants, but not of voiceless ones. More specifically, there must be some constraint that militates against satisfaction of $*\text{PL/LAB}^2$ by fusion between a nasal and voiced obstruent, and this constraint must be ranked above MAX, as shown in (18).

(18) $*\text{PL/LAB}^2$, CON(X) >> MAX >> UNIFORM(ITY)

Input: um₁+b₂aru	$*\text{PL/LAB}^2$	CON (X)	MAX	UNIFORM
b₂um₁aru	* !			
☞ b₂aru			*	
m₁,₂aru		* !		*

Fusion is often blocked by featural incompatibility between participants. For example, Pater (1999) points out that in the nasal substitution patterns observed in many African languages, fricatives fail to undergo fusion, with the nasal deleting instead. Since incompatibility between nasality and frication is phonetically and phonologically well documented (Cohn 1993a; Padgett 1994), such a pattern is to be expected, assuming an imperative to preserve underlying continuancy. However, expectations in the present case are not so clear. In fact, voicing would seem to make a consonant more amenable to fusion with a nasal, since this results in no perturbation of underlying [voice] specification. The figure in (19) schematizes fusional relationships between nasals and obstruents specified underlyingly as voiced and voiceless, showing that only the latter violates IDENT[VOICE]. For Faithfulness to block fusion between voiced obstruents and nasals, voiced obstruents must bear a feature that is shared by neither nasals nor voiceless obstruents.[6]

(19) a. N₁D₂   →   N₁,₂   ✓ IDENT[VOICE]
[+nas, +vce][-nas, **+vce**]   [+nas, **+vce**]

     b. N₁T₂   →   N₁,₂   * IDENT[VOICE]
[+nas, +vce][-nas, **-vce**]   [+nas, **+vce**]

Trigo (1991) provides evidence for exactly such a feature. She points out that in Madurese (Stevens 1968), vowel height is conditioned by the preceding consonant. Following Cohn (1993b), I will use the feature [+/−high] to label the distinction between the two sets of vowels. The [+high] vowels occur after voiced obstruent stops, and after what are referred to as heavy aspirated stops, with the [−high] vowels appearing elsewhere, as shown in (20).

(20) a. [+high] vowels: i   ɨ   u
                                   ɤ

      b. [-high] vowels: ɛ   ə̱   ɔ

Trigo argues that the feature spread from the voiced and heavy aspirated stops to following vowels is a pharyngeal feature, either Lowered Larynx or Advanced Tongue Root (see Cohn 1993b for arguments against the latter). I adopt Steriade's (1995) label Pharyngeal Expansion for this feature. Of particular interest in the present context is that nasals and voiceless stops pattern together as blockers of this harmony pattern (21a), with liquids and glides being transparent (21b).

(21) a.   abɤssɔ 'wash'   bɤtɔ 'stone'   kʰɤman 'weapon'
      b.   bɤrɤs 'health'   buwɤ 'fruit'   diyɤ 'here'

In (21a), a [+high] vowel appears only immediately following a voiced or heavy aspirated stop, with [−high] vowels surfacing to the right of the blocking segments. In (21b), on the other hand, harmony affects both the immediately adjacent vowel and the one following a subsequent liquid or glide. Blocking, claims Trigo, is due to incompatibility between the spreading feature, on the one hand, nasals and voiceless obstruents, on the other. On the obstruents pharyngeal expansion would induce voicing, while nasality appears to be perceptually and articulatorily linked with pharyngeal constriction.

The spreading and blocking pattern in Madurese provides an especially strong argument for adding a feature separating voiced obstruents from nasals and voiceless obstruents to the traditional feature set. Steriade (1995) also points out that the adoption of an obstruent-specific voicing feature allows one to analyze cases of voice assimilation and dissimilation in which only voicing of obstruents assimilates (e.g., Russian) or dissimilates (Japanese), without the need to invoke underspecification. For cases in which sonorants and obstruents do interact, the traditional [voice] feature (relabeled Vibrating Vocal cords by Steriade) is retained.

As (22) demonstrates, preservation of such a Pharyngeal Expansion feature ([PharExp]) can be invoked to account for the blocking of fusion between nasals and voiced obstruents.

(22)   a. N_1T_2 → $N_{1,2}$ ┌────────────────────┐
       [+nas, -PE][-nas, -PE]   [+nas, -PE]   │ ✓ IDENT[PHAREXP] │
                                                                        └────────────────────┘

       b. N_1D_2 → $N_{1,2}$ ┌────────────────────┐
       [+nas, +vce][-nas, +PE]   [+nas, -PE]   │ * IDENT[PHAREXP] │
                                                                        └────────────────────┘

With IDENT[PHAREXP] taking the place of CONX, we now have an account of the conspiracy between nasal substitution and deletion in *PL/LAB^2 satisfaction; see (23).

(23) *PL/LAB^2, IDENT[PHAREXP] >> MAX >> UNIFORM(ITY)

Input: um_1+b_2aru	*PL/LAB^2	IDENT [PHAREXP]	MAX	UNIFORM
b_2um_1aru	* !			
☞ b_2aru			*	
$m_{1,2}aru$		* !		*

As implosives are also produced with an articulatory gesture of pharyngeal expansion (forceful larynx lowering), they would pattern with the voiced stops in this analysis, as the data require (e.g., /um+ɓala/ → [ɓala] 'big'). Since neither nasals nor voiceless stops are pharyngeally expanded, IDENT(PHAREXP) is satisfied when they are coalesced, so that the MAX violation that would be incurred by deletion becomes fatal, as shown in (24).

(24) *PL/LAB^2, IDENT(PHAREXP) >> MAX >> UNIFORM(ITY)

Input: um_1+p_2ili	*PL/LAB^2	IDENT (PHAREXP)	MAX	UNIFORM
p_2um_1ili	* !			
p_2ili			* !	
☞ $m_{1,2}ili$				*

This account would also predict nasal substitution with /w/, as does in fact occur in some cases (e.g., /um+waa/ → [maa] 'give'). For the blocking pattern observed with other roots (e.g., /um+wanu/ → [wanu] 'get up'), it would seem to be necessary to invoke a lexically specific faithfulness constraint forcing preservation of approximant features in that subset of the lexicon (cf. Pater 1995; Ito and Mester 1999b).

In Muna, then, we have a case of Austronesian nasal substitution that as in Indonesian, targets voiceless but not voiced obstruents. Unlike Indonesian, however, *NC̥ cannot be invoked as either the driving constraint behind fusion, or the motivation for the voiced/voiceless asymmetry, since clusters are not produced at all in -*um*- affixation. I have suggested that fusion in Muna -*um*- affixation is a response to a general constraint in the language against multiple labials, and that it is blocked in voiced obstruents by a constraint forcing the preservation of a Pharyngeal Expansion feature. In Section 3, I argue that this account of voiced/voiceless asymmetry can be usefully generalized to the Indonesian case, suggesting that Indonesian nasal substitution is in fact not an effect of *NC̥ either.

3. A Reanalysis of Indonesian Nasal Substitution

In Section 1, we noted that NC̥ clusters are permitted root-internally, a fact that Pater (1999) attributes to the activity of a root-specific faithfulness constraint. However, these clusters are also found between morphemes, even when the same *məŋ*- prefix that triggers nasal substitution at the prefix-root boundary appears before the prefix *pər*- (Lapoliwa 1981:49, 51, 106), as shown in (25).

(25)　/məŋ+pər+besar/　　　　　　məmpərbesar　　　'to enlarge'

　　　/məŋ+pər+tuɳdʒuk+kan/　　məmpərtuɳdʒukan　'to show'

　　　/məŋ+pər+timbaŋ+kan+ɲa/　məmpərtimbaŋkanɲa 'to consider it'

In (25c), there are in fact three NC̥ clusters: between the prefixes, root-internally, and at the root-suffix boundary. While Pater (1999:fn. 7) suggests that fusion might be blocked between morphemes by DISJOINTNESS constraints (McCarthy and Prince 1995), the need to invoke this device along with root faithfulness just to limit nasal substitution to the prefix-root boundary is surely a deficit of this analysis. Ideally, an account of Indonesian nasal substitution would instead derive the morphological restriction on nasal substitution from constraints observably active elsewhere in the language. This is the aim of the following reanalysis.

3.1. CRISPEDGE *in Indonesian*

Cohn (1989) and Cohn and McCarthy (1994) discuss a number of phenomena related to stress and syllabification in Indonesian that require reference to the left edge of the root. One of these is the choice between glide formation and glottal stop epenthesis in the resolution of hiatus.

Glide formation occurs both root internally and at the root-suffix boundary. A glide agreeing in backness with the preceding vowel is inserted
between a high vowel and a following nonidentical vowel. Examples of
glide insertion following high front vowels are provided in (26).

(26)   a. /diam/   [dijam]   'quiet'
       b. /siap/   [sijap]   'ready'
       c. /hari+an/   [harijan]   'daily'
       d. /udʒi+an/   [udʒijan]   'exam'

Root-initially, however, glide formation is blocked, and instead a glottal
stop is inserted, even when the phonological environment is identical
(i__a), as shown in (27).

(27)   a. /di+ambil/   [diʔambil]   'taken'
       b. /di+adʒari/   [diʔadʒari]   'taught'

Cohn and McCarthy's (1994) account of this relies on the ALIGN-WD
constraint in (28).

(28) ALIGN-WD

       Align(Root, Left; PrWd, Left)
       'The left edge of each root coincides with the left edge of some PrWd'

Cohn and McCarthy initially invoke this constraint to deal with stress
facts: that prefixes lie outside the domain of stress assignment, and that
root compounds and reduplicated roots are parsed into two separate
prosodic words. They argue, however, that Root-to-Prosodic Word alignment also has consequences further down the prosodic hierarchy. One
of these consequences is the blocking of glide formation at the left edge
of the root.

   The figure in (29) (Cohn and McCarthy's Figure (92)) provides an
illustration of how glide formation would violate ALIGN-WD.

(29) Misalignment by glide formation

Glide formation is formalized as the spreading of the vowel's features into onset position, thereby creating an approximant (see Rosenthall 1994). ALIGN-WD is violated because the left edge of the root does not match up with the left edge of the Prosodic Word. In Cohn and McCarthy's account, ranking of ALIGN-WD above ONSET renders the above structure ill-formed. Satisfaction of ONSET yields glide formation in a form like [harijan] (from /hari+an/), but when the higher-ranked ALIGN-WD is at stake, ONSET must be violated, as shown in (30).

(30) ALIGN-WD >> ONSET

Input: hari+an	ALIGN-WD	ONSET
☞ harijan		
harian		* !

Input: di+ambil	ALIGN-WD	ONSET
dijambil	* !	
☞ diambil		*

A significant complication arises because the optimal candidate [diambil] does not correspond to the actual surface form [diʔambil], which has an intervocalic epenthetic glottal stop. As (31) illustrates, the glottal stop also interferes with alignment.

(31) Misalignment by epenthesis

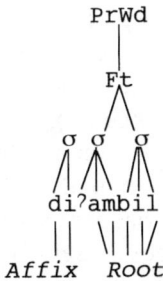

Cohn and McCarthy's solution to this problem is to place glottal stop insertion into the postlexical phonology. The output of the lexical phonology permits onsetless syllables initially in the Prosodic Word, which are then repaired postlexically, where ALIGN-WD is demoted beneath ONSET (and presumably, faithfulness constraints deciding between glide formation and glottal insertion are reranked).

An alternative solution that does not require serialism can be achieved by appealing to what Ito and Mester (1999a) refer to as edge "crispness" (cf. McCarthy and Prince 1993 for another analysis). One difference between the structures created by glottal stop insertion and glide formation is that only the latter has segmental content shared across the left edge of the prosodic word; that is, glottal stop insertion yields a crisp edge. The relevant constraint can be stated as in (32) (see Ito and Mester (1999a:208) for a more careful formulation).

(32) CRISPEDGE[PRWD]

No element belonging to a Prosodic Word may be linked to a prosodic category external to that Prosodic Word

Since suffixes, unlike prefixes, are incorporated into the Prosodic Word, there is no need to relativize this constraint to a particular edge. For present purposes, I will label the constraint that leads to a general preference for glide formation over glottal insertion as "*?". The tableaux in (33) show how the ranking of CRISPEDGE[PRWD] above this constraint yields glottal insertion in Prosodic Word–initial position.

(33) CRISPEDGE[PRWD] >> *?

Input: hari+an	CRISPEDGE [PRWD]	*?
☞ harijan		
hari?an		* !

Input: di+ambil	CRISPEDGE [PRWD]	*?
dijambil	* !	
☞ di?ambil		*

ALIGN-WD retains a key role in this analysis, as it must place the left edge of the Prosodic Word in the correct position for CRISPEDGE to have the desired effect. To do this, ALIGN-WD requires a gradient, rather than a categorical interpretation (see McCarthy and Prince 1993:133), so as to prefer the minimal misalignment caused by epenthesis over the more drastic divergence of category boundaries that would be caused by incorporating the prefix into the Prosodic Word. Assuming that each segment intervening between the root and Prosodic Word edges causes a violation of ALIGN-WD, the tableau in (34) shows that the correct placement of the left edge of the Prosodic Word is achieved ('l' marks root edges, with square brackets showing Prosodic Word edges).[7]

(34) Gradient ALIGN-WD

Input: di+ambil	ALIGN-WD
[dilambill]	*** !
☞ di[?lambill]	*

3.2. *Nasal Substitution and* CRISPEDGE

CRISPEDGE[PRWD] does admit violations, in one particular situation. As we have seen, the *məŋ*-prefix assimilates to a root-initial voiced consonant. With the usual assumption that place assimilation involves the spreading of a feature or gesture, this will disrupt the integrity of the left edge of the Prosodic Word, as illustrated in (35).

(35) /məŋ+bəli/   məm[bəli]
                        V
                      [LAB]

Indonesian has a general requirement that nasals must be homorganic with following consonants; this is true of all root-internal NC clusters, with the exception of a few loan words, and -*ŋs*-clusters (Hardjadibrata 1978; Lapoliwa 1981).[8] I will assume the simplified constraint in (36) (cf. Jun 1995; Padgett 1995; Boersma 1998).

(36) NASASSIM

    A nasal must share place features with a following consonant

Ranked above CRISPEDGE[PRWD], this constraint, shown in (37), explains the permissibility of the structure in (35).

(37) NASASSIM >> CRISPEDGE[PRWD]

Input: Məŋ+bəli	NAS ASSIM	CRISPEDGE [PRWD]
☞ məmbəli		*
məŋbəli	* !	

We now have a motivation for nasal substitution in Prosodic Word–initial position: it satisfies both NASASSIM and CRISPEDGE[PRWD]. With these constraints dominating UNIFORMITY, nasal substitution emerges as optimal, as shown in (38).

(38) NASASSIM >> CRISPEDGE[PRWD] >> UNIFORM(ITY)

Input: /məŋ$_1$+p$_2$ilih/	NAS ASSIM	CRISPEDGE [PRWD]	UNIFORM
☞ məm$_{1,2}$ilih			*
məm$_1$p$_2$ilih		* !	
məŋ$_1$p$_2$ilih	* !		

As it stands, there is nothing to stop voiced obstruents from undergoing nasal substitution as well. To prohibit this, we can make use of the same constraint that served this purpose in the analysis of Muna: IDENT[PHAREXP]. As the tableaux in (39) show, ranking this constraint above CRISPEDGE[PRWD] limits nasal substitution to voiceless obstruents.

(39) IDENT[PHAREXP] >> CRISPEDGE[PRWD]

Input: Məŋ₁+b₂əli	IDENT [PHAREXP]	CRISPEDGE [PRWD]	Input: məŋ₁+p₂ilih	IDENT [PHAREXP]	CRISPEDGE [PRWD]
☞ məm₁b₂əli		*	☞ məm₁,₂ilih		
Məm₁,₂əli	* !		məm₁p₂ ilih		* !

One advantage of using IDENT[PHAREXP] rather than *NC̥ to explain the voiced/voiceless asymmetry is that simple reranking of these two constraints produces a pattern of nasal substitution in which both voiced and voiceless obstruents are subject to fusion, as seen in (40).

(40) CRISPEDGE[PRWD] >> IDENT[PHAREXP]

Input: N₁+B₂	CRISPEDGE [PRWD]	IDENT [PHAREXP]	Input: N₁+P₂	CRISPEDGE [PRWD]	IDENT [PHAREXP]
☞ M₁,₂		*	☞ M₁,₂		
M₁B₂	* !		M₁P₂	* !	

Newman (1984: Figure 22) provides the typology of productive nasal substitution in Austronesian shown in (41).

(41)   Consonants replaced by nasals

	p	t,s	k	b	d	g
Malay type	+	+	+	−	−	−
Sama Badjao (Sulu Archipelago, northern Borneo) type	+	+	+	+	−	−
Cebuano	+	+	+	+	+	−
Kalinga (northern Luzon)	+	+	+	+	+	+

Languages like Kalinga instantiate the ranking in (40).[9] The intermediate cases, in which replacement of voiced obstruents is limited to labials, or labials and coronals, might also be accounted for in this way, given an appropriate constraint to block velars (and coronals) from undergoing the process (see Zuraw 2000, where a similar place effect is observed in frequency distributions in Tagalog nasal substitution).

Clearly, these instances of nasal substitution are beyond the reach of *NC̥. The other benefit of this reanalysis is that the problem of picking out the prefix-root boundary as the locus for this process is resolved by relying on CRISPEDGE[PRWD]. Between prefixes (and root-internally) CRISPEDGE[PRWD] is vacuously satisfied and NASASSIM is fulfilled by simple assimilation. Since assimilation results in a change of the underlying place specification of the nasal, a faithfulness constraint on place identity is violated, and must be ranked beneath constraints favoring other outcomes, as shown in (42). To sum up then, in this analysis nasal substitution is driven by the need to satisfy two constraints, CRISPEDGE[PRWD] and NASASSIM, both independently motivated in the phonology of Indonesian, while the limitation to voiceless obstruents is explained by the activity of IDENT[PHAREXP], a constraint postulated for a similar limitation in Muna.

(42)   NASASSIM >> CRISPEDGE[PRWD] >> UNIFORM(ITY)>> IDENT[PLACE]

Input: /məŋ$_1$+p$_2$ər+besar/	NAS ASSIM	CRISPEDGE [PRWD]	UNIFORM (ITY)	IDENT [PLACE]
məm$_{1,2}$ərbesar			* !	
☞ məm$_1$p$_2$ərbesar				*
məŋ$_1$p$_2$ərbesar	* !			

4. Conclusions

The *NC̥ analysis of Indonesian nasal substitution sought to explain the asymmetry between voiced and voiceless consonants by drawing a formal connection between nasal substitution and other processes affecting NC̥ clusters. The evidence from Muna -*um*- affixation discussed in Section 2, however, shows that *NC̥ fails in this capacity, since even though nasal obstruent clusters are not at issue, we see the same voicing asymmetry. In Section 3 another deficiency of the *NC̥ approach was highlighted: the difficulty of limiting it to the correct root-initial morphological environment. This led to a reanalysis of the voicing asymmetry in terms of a constraint on faithfulness to obstruent voicing, IDENT(PHAREXP), which in turn opened the door to a reinterpretation of Indonesian nasal substitution as being driven by constraints on morphological and prosodic structure, thus explaining its morphologically restricted nature.

Though it may be obvious, it is worth emphasizing that the analysis of nasal substitution posited here will not contribute further to the recasting of NC̥ effects; it has nothing to say about postnasal voicing, nasal deletion, or denasalization before voiceless consonants. The position taken here is that while Austronesian nasal substitution is best analyzed in other terms, a constraint like *NC̥ is still required to deal with the broader range of NC̥ effects. Specifically, it appears that no other analysis succeeds in generalizing to all of these processes, without generating unattested phenomena. While the constraint is unabashedly formally stipulative, this weakness is mitigated considerably by its phonetic grounding (see especially Hayes 1999).

Archangeli et al. (1998) provide an analysis of Indonesian nasal substitution that does aim to completely supplant *NC̥. It derives fusion of NC sequences from the interaction of a general constraint against clusters (*CC) with a constraint forcing the preservation of nasality (MaxNasal). However, as it stands, this analysis does not provide an account for the voicing asymmetry that *NC̥ was designed to cope with. Furthermore, it is far from obvious whether it will be capable of meeting the twin goals of generality and restrictiveness that the NC̥ account sets. Therefore, although the *NC̥ analysis of Austronesian nasal substitution may be fatally flawed, the use of this constraint to account for the broader range of NC̥ effects in Hayes (1999) and Pater (1996, 1999) seems to remain well motivated.

Notes

Portions of this chapter were presented at the Utrecht Workshop on Typology and Acquisition, at the University of Calgary, and at the University of Massachusetts, Amherst. I would like to thank the members of those audiences for discussion, especially John Archibald, Michael Dobrovolsky, Bruce Hayes, René Kager, John Kingston, John McCarthy, Lisa Selkirk, and Wim Zonneveld. I am also grateful to Bruce Hayes, Donca Steriade, and Cheryl Zoll for their comments on a handout, to David Mead for correspondence on the phonology of languages of Sulawesi, and to Linda Lombardi and Robert Kirchner for their helpful reviews of the chapter. This work was supported by SSHRCC research grant 410-98-1595, as well as a grant from the NWO, which supported a stay at Universiteit Utrecht in the fall of 1999, when this paper was written.

1. More properly, this constraint must be specific to obstruent voicing, so that it does not rule out fusion, in which a voiceless obstruent stands in correspondence with a nasal (see Pater 1999:324; see also Section 2.3 of this chapter).

2. To capture the fact that onsetless roots, and other vowel-initial prefixes survive intact, one could either relativize Max to -*um*- or adopt an allo-

morphic approach, in which the choice between underlying /-um-/ and /m-/ is determined by output constraints (see, e.g., Kager 1996; Mester 1994).

3. The other exceptions are roots beginning with nasals and prenasalized stops, which also trigger deletion. I will not deal with those cases here, except to note that while this is also perhaps driven by a dissimilatory constraint, root-internally nasals are allowed to cooccur with nonhomorganic nasals and prenasalized stops. Therefore, one would have to treat the activity of this constraint as an instance of the emergence of the unmarked.

4. Van den Berg provides a percentage representing the relative occurrence in initial position of each consonant. The totals were arrived at by multiplying that percentage by 1,100 (the corpus includes just over 1,100 roots).

5. That *PL/LAB^2 has effects in affixation requires that its domain be larger than the root itself. Definition of this domain, though, is far from straightforward. Affixes other than -*um*- contain labials, and hence seem immune to the effects of the constraint. Simply placing them outside its domain, however, is rendered problematic by the fact that -*um*- can be affixed to certain prefix-root combinations, with the normal rules of allomorphy applying (e.g., [no-fo-ada-e] 'he borrows it (realis)' vs. [no-mo-ada-e] 'he borrows it (irrealis)').

6. A puzzle here is that in the nasal harmony systems of Amazonian languages there are cases in which voiced stops undergo harmony and are nasalized, while voiceless stops are transparent and fail to be nasalized (see Piggott 1992; Walker 1998, to appear). The harmony facts and the fusion facts are difficult to reconcile, but it may be relevant that the languages with this harmony pattern lack an oral/nasal contrast.

7. While adopting a gradient ALIGN-WD constraint does depart from Cohn and McCarthy (1994:48), it should be noted that the evidence supporting the categorical interpretation comes from right edge alignment, and that even there, questions of the robustness of the data remain (Cohn and McCarthy 1994:fn. 31). There remains an interesting question about how the violation of ALIGN-WD in the optimal candidate in (34) is to be compelled. In the dialect that Cohn (1989) and Cohn and McCarthy (1994) discuss (cf. Cohn and McCarthy 1994:fn. 29), glottal stops appear only in hiatus; the onsetless syllables that arise because of a lack of resyllabification across the left edge of the Prosodic Word are tolerated. Therefore, it would appear that the ONSET constraint forcing the appearance of glottal stop would have to be specific to the V__V environment (see Cohn 1989:192).

8. At the root-suffix juncture, heterorganic NC clusters do occur, perhaps due to positional faithfulness or paradigm uniformity.

9. There is some evidence of a similar typological reranking in -*um*- nasal substitution, resulting in both voiced and voiceless obstruents participating in coalescence. David Mead (p.c.) points to the following observation of Wolff (1973:83–84):

> There was a rule in the protolanguage [Proto-Austronesian – JP] that when *-um-
> was added to a base beginning *p or a *b [sic], the *p or *b was changed to an m and
> no other changes were made. Mongondow, a language of the Celebes, retains this rule
> intact.

References

Alderete, John. 1997. Dissimilation as Local Conjunction. In *Proceedings of the North East Linguistics Society 27*, ed. K. Kusumoto, pp. 17–32. Amherst, MA: GLSA.

Archangeli, Diana, Laura Moll, and Kazutoshi Ohno. 1998. Why not *NC̦. In *Proceedings from the Main Session of the Chicago Linguistics Society's Thirty-fourth Meeting*, pp. 1–26.

Beckman, Jill. 1997. Positional Faithfulness. PhD dissertation, University of Massachusetts, Amherst, MA.

Berg, René van den. 1989. *A Grammar of the Muna Language*. Dordrecht: Foris.

Boersma, Paul. 1998. Typology and Acquisition in Functional and Arbitrary Phonology. Ms., University of Amsterdam.

Cohn, Abigail C. 1989. Stress in Indonesian and Bracketing Paradoxes. *Natural Language and Linguistic Theory* 7:167–216.

Cohn, Abigail C. 1993a. The Status of Nasalized Continuants. In *Phonetics and Phonology 5: Nasals, Nasalization, and the Velum*, ed. M. Huffman and R. Krakow, pp. 329–367. San Diego, CA: Academic.

Cohn, Abigail C. 1993b. Voicing and Vowel Height in Madurese: A Preliminary Report. In *Tonality in Austronesian Languages*, ed. J. E. Edmonson and K. J. Gregerson, pp. 107–121. Oceanic Linguistics Special Publications 24.

Cohn, Abigail C., and John J. McCarthy. 1994. Alignment and Parallelism in Indonesian Phonology. Ms., Cornell University and University of Massachusetts, Amherst.

Dziwirek, Katarzyna. 1989. Malagasy Phonology and Morphology. *Linguistics Notes from La Jolla* 15:1–30.

Frisch, Stefan, Michael Broe, and Janet Pierrehumbert. 1997. Similarity and Phonotactics in Arabic. Ms., Indiana University.

Greenberg, Joseph. 1950. The Patterning of Root Morphemes in Semitic. *Word* 6:162–181.

Hardjadibrata, R. 1978. Consonant Clusters in Indonesian. In *Proceedings of the Second International Conference on Austronesian Linguistics*, ed. S. A. Wurm and L. Carrington, pp. 165–179. Canberra: Pacific Linguistics.

Hayes, Bruce. 1999. Phonetically-Driven Phonology: The Role of Optimality Theory and Inductive Grounding. In *Functionalism and Formalism in Linguistics, Volume I: General Papers*, M. Darnell, E. Moravscik, M. Noonan, F. Newmeyer, and K. Wheatley, pp. 243–285. Amsterdam: Benjamins.

Hyman, Larry. 1998. The Limits of Phonetic Determinism in Phonology: *NC Revisited. Ms., University of California, Berkeley.

Ito, Junko, and Armin Mester. 1996. Rendaku I: Constraint Conjunction and the OCP. Handout to a lecture delivered at the Kobe Phonology Forum.

Ito, Junko, and Armin Mester. 1999a. Realignment. In *The Prosody Morphology Interface*, ed. R. Kager, H. van der Hulst, and W. Zonneveld, pp. 188–217. Cambridge: Cambridge University Pess.

Ito, Junko, and Armin Mester. 1999b. The Phonological Lexicon. In *The Handbook of Japanese Linguistics*, ed. N. Tsujimura, pp. 62–100. Oxford: Blackwell.

Jun, Jongho. 1995. Place Assimilation as the Result of Conflicting Perceptual and Articulatory Constraints. In *Proceedings of the Fourteenth West Coast Conference on Formal Linguistics*, pp. 221–237. Stanford, CA: Linguistics Department, Stanford University.

Kager, René. 1996. On Affix Allomorphy and Syllable Counting. In *Interfaces in Phonology*, ed. U. Kleinhenz, pp. 155–171. Studia Grammatica 41. Berlin: Akademie Verlag.

Kisseberth, Charles. 1970. On the Functional Unity of Phonological Rules. *Linguistic Inquiry* 1:291–306.

Lapoliwa, Hans. 1981. *A Generative Approach to the Phonology of Bahasa Indonesia*. Canberra: Pacific Linguistics D 34.

Leben, William. 1973. Suprasegmental phonology. PhD dissertation, MIT.

MacEachern, Margaret. 1997. Laryngeal Cooccurrence Constraints. PhD dissertation, UCLA.

McCarthy, John J. 1986. OCP Effects: Gemination and Antigemination. *Linguistic Inquiry* 17:207–263.

McCarthy, John J. 1988. Feature Geometry and Dependency: A Review. *Phonetica* 43:84–108.

McCarthy, John J., and Alan S. Prince. 1993. Generalized Alignment. In *Yearbook of Morphology 1993*, ed. G. E. Booij and J. van der Marle, pp. 79–153. Dordrecht: Kluwer.

McCarthy, John J., and Alan S. Prince. 1994. Prosodic Morphology: An Overview. Paper presented at the Workshop on Prosodic Morphology, University of Utrecht, June 1994.

McCarthy, John J., and Alan S. Prince. 1995. Faithfulness and Reduplicative Identity. In *University of Massachusetts Occasional Papers 18: Papers in Optimality Theory*, pp. 249–384. Amherst, MA: GLSA.

McCarthy, John J., and Alan S. Prince. 1999. Faithfulness and Identity in Prosodic Morphology. In *The Prosody Morphology Interface*, ed. R. Kager, H. van der Hulst, and W. Zonneveld, pp. 218–309. Cambridge: Cambridge University Press.

Mester, Armin. 1994. The Quantitative Trochee in Latin. *Natural Language and Linguistic Theory* 12:1–61.

Newman, John. 1984. Nasal Replacement in Western Austronesian: An Overview. *Philippine Journal of Linguistics* 15:1–17.

Padgett, Jaye. 1994. Stricture and Nasal Place Assimilation. *Natural Language and Linguistic Theory* 12:465–513.

Padgett, Jaye. 1995. Partial Class Behavior and Nasal Place Assimilation. *Proceedings of the Arizona Phonology Conference: Workshop on Features in Optimality Theory. Coyote Working Papers*, pp. 145–183. Tucson, AZ: University of Arizona Department of Linguistics.

Pater, Joe. 1995. On the Nonuniformity of Weight-to-Stress and Stress Preservation Effects in English. Ms., McGill University.

Pater, Joe. 1996. *NC̥. Proceedings of the North East Linguistics Society* 26:227–239. Amherst, MA: GLSA.

Pater, Joe. 1999. Austronesian Nasal Substitution and Other NC̥ Effects. In *The Prosody Morphology Interface*, ed. R. Kager, H. van der Hulst, and W. Zonneveld, pp. 310–343. Cambridge: Cambridge University Press.

Piggott, Glyne. 1992. Variability in Feature Dependency: The Case of Nasality. *Natural Language and Linguistic Theory*, 10:33–78.

Prince, Alan, and Paul Smolensky. 1993. *Optimality Theory: Constraint Interaction in Generative Grammar*. To appear, MIT Press.

Rosenthall, Samuel. 1994. Vowel/Glide Alternations in a Theory of Constraint Interaction. PhD dissertation, University of Massachusetts, Amherst.

Smolensky, Paul. 1995. On the Internal Structure of the Constraint Component Con of UG. Handout to a talk presented at UCLA.

Steriade, Donca. 1995. Underspecification and Markedness. In *A Handbook of Phonological Theory*, ed. J. Goldsmith, pp. 114–174. Cambridge, MA: Blackwell.

Stevens, Alan M. 1968. *Madurese Phonology and Morphology*. American Oriental Series 52. New Haven, CT: American Oriental Series.

Suzuki, Keichiro. 1998. A Typological Investigation of Dissimilation. PhD dissertation, University of Arizona, Tucson.

Topping, Donald M. 1973. *Chamorro Reference Grammar*. Honolulu, HI: University of Hawaii Press.

Trigo, Loren. 1991. On Pharynx-Larynx Interactions. *Phonology* 8:113–136.

Uhlenbeck, E. M. 1949. *De Structuur van het Javaanse Morpheem*. Bandung: Nix.

Urbanczyk, Suzanne. 1996. *Patterns of Reduplication in Lushootseed*. PhD dissertation, University of Massachusetts, Amherst.

Walker, Rachel. 1998. *Nasalization, Neutral Segments, and Opacity Effects*. PhD dissertation, University of California, Santa Cruz.

Walker, Rachel. To appear. Reinterpreting Transparency in Nasal Harmony. In *HIL Phonology Papers IV*. Amsterdam: Benjamins. ROA 306-0399, http://ruccs.rutgers.edu/roa.html.

Wolff, J. U. 1973. Verbal Inflection in Proto-Austronesian. *Parangal kay Cecilio Lopez: Essays in Honor of Cecilio Lopez on his Seventy-Fifth Birthday*, ed. A. B. Gonzalez, pp. 71–94. Philippine Journal of Linguistics special monograph issue 4.

Zuraw, Kie. 2000. Patterned Exceptions in Phonology. PhD dissertation, UCLA.

6

A Critical View of Licensing by Cue: Codas and Obstruents in Eastern Andalusian Spanish

CHIP GERFEN

1. Introduction

The confluence of two interconnected yet independent research programs underlies this chapter. One regards the issue of language-particular phonetics, while the other concerns the emergence of Optimality Theory as the dominant paradigm in contemporary phonology. Regarding the first, research over the past twenty years has clearly shown that at least part of phonetic implementation must be viewed as falling within the purview of the linguistic grammar (see, for example, Pierrehumbert 1980; Pierrehumbert and Beckman 1988; Keating 1988; Cohn 1990; Huffman 1989). An interesting consequence of this is that language-particular phonetics raises difficult questions regarding the objects and nature of phonological inquiry. These questions pertain, for example, to whether certain phenomena are phonological or phonetic, to where and/or how the line should be drawn between phonetics and phonology (e.g., Keating 1990; Huffman 1993; Pierrehumbert 1991; Cohn 1993, 1999; Zsiga 1997; Kingston and Diehl 1994; Myers 1999; Gerfen 1999), and to whether any line should be drawn at all (Ohala 1990).

Secondly, Optimality Theory (Prince and Smolensky 1993, hereafter OT) does not constitute a theory of possible linguistic constraints per se. Rather it provides an architecture for evaluating input/output pairings in terms of a set of (partially) rank-ordered constraints. Insofar as it is a theory of how constraints interact, nothing in the architecture of the theory itself dictates the nature of the constraints invoked. In fact, given that a fundamental axiom of OT is that all constraints are violable, OT actually affords the opportunity to construct grammars from universal phonetic principles. This has traditionally been somewhat problematic for phonological theory, in that it has been difficult to reconcile the putative universality of phonetically based principles with language-particular counterexamples to the generalizations that give rise to those very same principles.[1] In OT, by contrast, we expect to find constraint violations. That is, violations do not falsify the universality of phonetically motivated principles. Rather, violations account for why such principles constitute tendencies rather than absolutes.[2]

The combination of an architecture that does not inherently restrict the nature of what can be a constraint with the ability to express phonetic universals in a violable fashion has given rise to a proliferation of constraints in the literature. Thus, constraints have been proposed that take as their arguments an ever-growing range of elements. Many refer to familiar categorical features. Constraints governing feature co-occurrence, such as ATR/HI (Archangeli and Pulleyblank 1994), are an example. Other constraints refer to the alignment of morphological and/or phonological structures (McCarthy and Prince 1993) or to privileged positions within morphemes (Beckman 1997a). Of particular relevance here is that numerous constraints have been employed that reference syllable structure. For example, Onset and *Complex (see Prince and Smolensky 1993) militate for syllables with onsets while constraining possible syllable margins, respectively. Beckman (1997b) makes use of Faithfulness in Onset position. Ito, Mester, and Padgett (1995) and Ito and Mester (1994) employ Coda Conditions (CodaCond) to account for featural licensing or nonlicensing, as does Lombardi (1999, this volume), who also employs a positional licensing constraint that presupposes syllable structure.[3]

At the same time, numerous constraints have been proposed that refer to phenomena outside of the traditional purview of work in generative phonology. Such constraints reference gradient phonetic properties such as duration or f0 (Kirchner 1997), general functional principles regarding minimal effort or maximal clarity, such as Lazy (Kirchner 1997, this volume), Maintain and Mindist (Flemming 1995), perceptual Space constraints (NíChosáin and Padgett, this volume), or phonetic contexts directly (Steriade 1997). In short, if research in phonetics and phonology has called attention to the role that phonetics must play in the grammar and, as a consequence, to the difficulty of distinguishing between the phonetic and the phonological, OT has made it easy, formally, to eradicate the line between the two.

Within this context, the broad issue under consideration here is the licensing of segmental contrast, with a specific focus on the role of phonetic cues in determining contrast distribution. In particular, I examine recent claims that contrast licensing is best viewed as being directly driven by the presence or absence of phonetic cues (cf. Steriade 1997), rather than by constraints that call upon familiar phonological entities such as syllable onsets and/or codas. Anticipating my conclusions, I will argue that while cue-based accounts are attractive and often highly insightful, they fail to eliminate the need for more traditional constraints in the phonological grammar.

As a point of departure, in Section 2 I discuss Steriade's (1997) notion of licensing by cue as representative of direct phonetic licensing. In so doing, I review two cases that appear to motivate the superiority of cue licensing both in terms of empirical coverage and explanatory depth. In Section 3, I turn to the problem of obstruent licensing (or, alternatively, obstruent neutralization) in coda position in Eastern Andalusian Spanish. Here, I argue that the best account of obstruent licensing in Eastern Andalusian resides in a more traditional, syllable-based analysis. Finally, I present my conclusions in Section 4, advocating a view in which both phonetic cues and traditional structures have an active role to play in phonology.

2. Direct Phonetic Licensing

Steriade's (1997) recent discussion of licensing by cue provides a clear example of a directly phonetic approach to accounting for phonotactic constraints on contrast licensing. A simple example is her discussion of the distribution of apical stops in Gujarati (with data from Dave 1977), which contrasts the plain alveolar [t] with its retroflex counterpart [ʈ]. Steriade notes that, phonetically, what most clearly differentiates these stops is the presence of VC, but not CV, formant transitions. In Steriade's terms, the VC context supplies the richest acoustic cues for implementing the distinction, and Steriade argues that this phonetic generalization has two direct consequences for phonological markedness. One is that if a language loses the contrast between [t] and [ʈ], it will do so first in word-initial or postconsonantal position – that is, in a position lacking VC transitions. The other is that if a language possesses this contrast, it will have it postvocalically. Importantly, neither of the relevant contexts, postvocalic and non-postvocalic, translates into a single syllable position. For example, although word-initial consonants will be onsets, postconsonantal consonants can either be onsets or codas, depending on the preceding segmental material and the syllabification pattern of the language. Steriade concludes that it is thus not syllable position per se that licenses contrast and drives markedness in this case. Rather, it is the presence of a phonetic environment that is cue-rich – that is, a phonetic environment that renders the contrast easier to implement.

A second illustrative case discussed by Steriade involves the licensing (or neutralization) of laryngeal features in Klamath. Building on Blevins (1993), Steriade notes that Klamath has contrastive aspiration and ejection on obstruents, but that these contrasts are positionally conditioned. Specifically, laryngeal contrasts are neutralized in two contexts: before another obstruent and word-finally. At first glance, this appears to make Klamath a prototypical case of laryngeal neutralization in coda position (cf. Lombardi 1991, 1995), given that pre-obstruent and word-final positions are generally subsumable under the category of syllable coda. However, for Klamath this approach quickly runs into trouble.

The problem stems from the fact that aspirates and ejectives are licensed in Klamath before plain sonorant consonants and that all VCCV sequences in Klamath must be syllabified VC.CV. Thus, even if a CC cluster consists of an obstruent followed by a plain sonorant, as in /pʰet'-wa/ 'floats in water', the surface syllabification is [pʰet'.wa], a form in which ejection is licensed in coda position.[4] Clearly, then, one cannot trivially argue that syllable position is responsible for the licensing/neutralization of contrastive ejection and aspiration in obstruents in Klamath. Instead, Steriade claims that the situation is better understood in terms of the phonetic context in which the laryngeal features are licensed – that is, that laryngealization is licensed in an environment sufficiently rich in phonetic cues.

What are the relevant cues? For obstruent aspiration and ejection, Steriade argues that they are burst properties and VOT, both of which require a "right-hand modal sonorant context" (1997:94) to be felicitously implemented. Under this view, the modal voicing of a plain sonorant consonant provides the necessary context, regardless of whether that sonorant is an onset or a coda. In broad strokes, then, Steriade's arguments really amount to two fundamental claims. First, we should look to what have traditionally been viewed by phonologists as low-level phonetic (i.e., nonphonological) contextual properties such as CV transitions, presence or absence of burst, f0 excursions, duration, and so forth, for explanations regarding where phonological contrasts are licensed/neutralized. Secondly, the formal encoding of these patterns in the grammar should be accomplished by direct reference to these phonetic properties rather than through more traditional phonological constraints. That is, *EJECTION IN CUE-IMPOVERISHED CONTEXTS* – contexts that are decomposed into harmonic scales and that project a range of constraints – rather than *EJECTION IN CODA*. That this is not an oversimplification of Steriade's position is evidenced by the following strong claim: "More generally, it remains to be seen whether the syllable as a constituent is at all a relevant factor in controlling phonotactic possibilities" (1997:99).

In the remainder of this chapter, I discuss data that challenge this view by militating for a case of syllable-based rather than direct phonetic licensing of contrast. In particular, I examine the licensing of obstruents in coda position in Eastern Andalusian Spanish (EAS).

3. Obstruent Licensing in Eastern Andalusian

In this section I examine the phenomenon of obstruent licensing in Eastern Andalusian. Section 3.1 provides the necessary background, with a brief discussion of coda phonotactics in Standard Peninsular Spanish (SPS). I then turn in Section 3.2 to a description of the relevant EAS facts and to the arguments for why syllable position, and not simply phonetic context, is crucial to understanding the EAS patterns. In Section 3.3, I briefly sketch how a syllable-based account would proceed in OT.

3.1. *Standard Peninsular Spanish and Obstruent Codas*

As is well known, /s/ is by far the most common coda obstruent in Spanish. This is exemplified in forms such as [kas.ko] 'helmet' and [ga.fas] 'eyeglasses'.[5] Other obstruents also surface as codas, although these almost always appear word-internally.[6] Relevant here is that word-internal coda obstruents are contrastive for both place and voice features in SPS. The range of data is given in (1) and (2).

1) Voiced and voiceless coda obstruents before voiceless onsets

    a) [ab.sur.do] 'absurd', [sub.sis.tir] 'subsist', [ob.tu.so] 'obtuse',

        [ob.θe.no] 'obscene', [sub.ko.mi.sjon] 'subcommission',

        [ab.sen.tis.mo] 'absenteeism', [ad.sor.ber] 'absorb', [ad.ki.rir]

        'acquire', [ad.xun.to] 'adjunct', [ob.te.ner] 'obtain'

    b) [kap.tar] 'capture', [ap.to] 'apt', [kap.su.la] 'capsule', [klep.to.ma.no]

        'kleptomaniac', [et.θe.te.ra] 'etcetera', [pak.to] 'pact', [ak. θe.so]

        'access', [ek.si.lio] 'exile', [ak.tor] 'actor', [de.fek.to] 'defect',

        [in.fek.tar] 'infect', [fak.tor] 'factor'

In (1a), voiced obstruent codas surface before voiceless onsets. Note that these consonants need not share place or manner features (e.g., [ad.xun.to]). In (1b), we have cases in which voiceless obstruent codas are followed by voiceless onsets, which, again, need not share their place and manner features with the preceding coda (e.g., [ak.θe.so] 'access').

By contrast, (2a) and (2b), respectively, provide examples in which voiced and voiceless codas precede a following onset that is phonetically voiced. Again, there is no obligatory sharing of place and manner features between the coda and the following onset (e.g., [mag.da.le.na] 'cupcake' and [tek.ni.ko] 'technical').

2) Voiced and voiceless obstruents before phonetically voiced onsets

  a) [ab.di.kar] 'abdicate', [sub.di.to] 'subject', [ab.ne.gar] 'renounce',

      [ad.mi.rar] 'admire', [e.nig.ma] 'enigma', [ag.nos.ti.ko] 'agnostic',

      [sig.no] 'sign', [pug.nar] 'bid', [dig.no] 'dignified', [mag.da.le.na]

      'cupcake', [ig.no.ran.te] 'ignorant', [dog.ma.ti.ko] 'dogmatic'

  b) [ip.no.sis] 'hypnosis', [et.na] 'Etna', [a.rak.ni.do] 'arachnid', [fut.bol]

      'soccer', [et.ni.ko] 'ethnic', [ak.ne] 'acne', [ak.me] 'acme', [ap.nea]

      'apnea', [tek.ni.co] 'technical', [rit.mo] 'rhythm', [a.rit.me.ti.ka]

      'arithmetic'

Note that while this does not pretend to exhaust the generalizations regarding syllable contact in Spanish, such forms do indicate that we cannot globally attribute the voicing, place, or manner of coda obstruents to those of a following onset. In SPS, these features can be licensed on their own. These observations lead us to the case of Eastern Andalusian.

3.2. *Obstruent Codas and EAS*

One of the best-known features of EAS is the phenomenon of s-aspiration, which is most commonly discussed as involving the "deletion" of word-final /s/ and the concomitant aspiration and sometimes lengthening of the preceding vowel (see, for example, Zamora Vicente 1969; Rodríguez Castellano and Palacio 1948; Alarcos Llorach 1958; Goldsmith 1981; Zamora Munné and Guitart 1982; Guitart 1985; Hualde

1987). This is illustrated in forms such as /ganas/, 'desire', which are real-ized in EAS as [ga.naʰ]. Less discussion, however, has focused on the fact that s-aspiration is not limited to word-final tokens of /s/ (see, for example, Romero 1995; Gerfen and Piñar 1999).[7] These word-internal cases of s-aspiration result in the lengthening (i.e., gemination) of the following consonant. This can be seen in the words in (3), which contrast EAS realizations with their SPS counterparts.

(3) SPS   EAS   gloss

   [boṣ.ke]   [boʰk.ke]   forest

   [eṣ.la.βo]   [eʰl.la.βo]   Slavic

For purposes of illustration, we can see that gemination is clearly visible in the representative spectrograms in Figures 6.1 and 6.2 for a native EAS speaker (S1). Figure 6.1 shows the singleton /l/ of [alero] 'eaves of a roof', while Figure 6.2 provides an example of the geminate in [eʰl.la.βo] 'Slavic'.

Descriptively, the simplest characterization of both word-internal and word-final s-aspiration is that they occur in coda position. This becomes clear when we consider the general behavior of [sC] clusters across all dialects of Spanish. As is well known, [sC] clusters (where C is any obstruent, liquid, or nasal) are banned in onsets in Spanish. That [sC] clusters must be heterosyllabic can be demonstrated by garden-variety distributional arguments. Thus, while forms such as [es.ta.do] 'state' abound, Spanish lacks any forms such as *[sta.do]. Additionally, bor-rowed forms beginning with [sC] clusters are phonologized via the epenthesis of a word-initial [e], as in [es.ki] 'ski', and, similarly, the so-called foreign accent syndrome, exemplified by the production of [es.kul] for English [skul] 'school', also provides evidence for the impossibility of tautosyllabic [sC] clusters in Spanish.

Arguably, in and of itself this constitutes evidence that syllable structure plays a role in general Spanish phonotactics. That is, it is impor-tant to recognize that Spanish does not ban [sC] sequences. Rather, [sC] sequences are only prohibited in a particular syllable position, namely, in the onset. If we abandon the notion of the syllable in accounting for the behavior of /s/ in /sC/ clusters, one might attempt to claim that /s/ is licensed only when adjacent to a preceding or following vowel. However, such an approach quickly runs into problems because of forms such as [abs.trak.to] 'abstract', in which /s/ is both preceded and followed by a consonant. In addition, it is unclear why such a condition should be

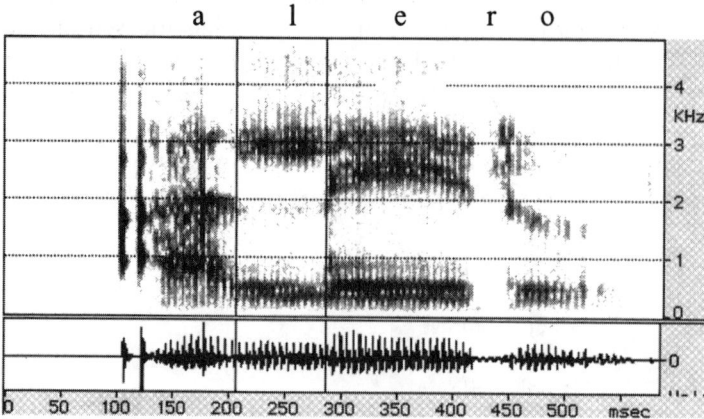

Figure 6.1. /alero/ 'eaves of a roof'.

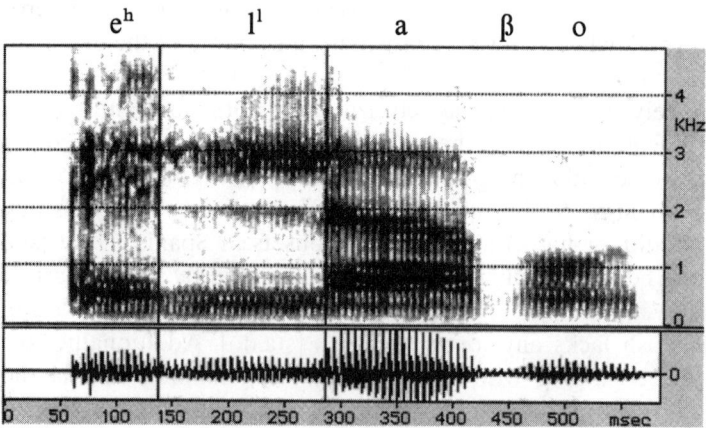

Figure 6.2. /es.la.ßo/ 'Slavic'.

imposed at all, given that the strongest cues for place are found in VC and CV transitions. That is, it is unclear why VC or CV contexts should be a requisite for cueing /s/ in particular, a sibilant whose most salient cues are internal to the segment (more on this later). Crucially, then, the generalization that [sC] clusters are banned in onset raises serious challenges to anyone seeking to abandon the syllable in favor of constraints that govern segmental licensing via direct reference to phonetic cues.

Returning to the issue of s-aspiration in EAS, we see that all of the word-internal cases of s-aspiration thus correspond to forms in which /s/

would surface as a coda in SPS. The length distinction illustrated in the spectrograms in Figures 6.1 and 6.2 is highly robust.[8] To confirm this, I ran a small experiment, in which I recorded two female native speakers of EAS (S1 and S2), both from the city of Granada, Spain. The speakers recorded a set of eight words ([es.la.βo] 'Slavic' appeared twice on the list), each of which was written on a single note card in Spanish orthography. The list is provided in (4).

(4) Experimental list

orthography	gloss	phonemic representation
eslavo	'Slavic'	/eslabo/
Atlanta	'Atlanta'	/atlanta/
atleta	'athlete'	/atleta/
aclara	's/he/it clears up'	/aklara/
aclama	's/he acclaims'	/aklama/
alaba	's/he praised'	/alaba/
alero	'eaves of a roof'	/alero/

Speakers were instructed to produce each word in the frame sentence *La palabra es* _____, *tío* 'the word is _____, pal'. The note cards were randomized by shuffling after each pass through the list, and each was read multiple times by each speaker (speaker S1 = 21 repetitions per word; speaker S2 = 12 repetitions per word). The readings were done in a quiet room and recorded on a Marantz PMD 222 professional cassette recorder with a Shure SM10A-CM close-talking, unidirectional microphone. Speakers were informed that they were participating in a study of how people from Granada speak and that they should speak in a natural and relaxed fashion, as if they were at home with family. These instructions were aimed at mitigating the chances that the standard orthography would induce a formal reading register – that is, that speakers would fail to produce forms with their normal s-aspiration. Additionally, the frame itself is highly informal in tone in order to induce speakers to speak naturally. During the task, neither speaker had any difficulty producing typical EAS forms.

The data were digitized at 22 kHz with 16-bit sampling and analyzed in SoundScope on a Power Macintosh computer. For each word, the

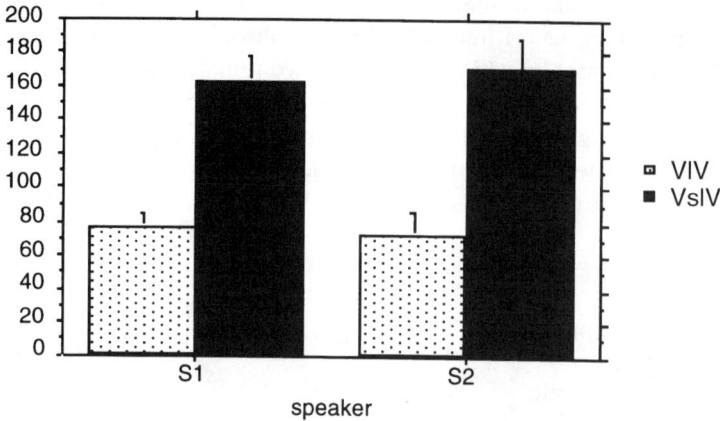

Figure 6.3. /l/ durations in msec by speaker and context.

duration of /l/ was measured by hand. The onset of /l/ was determined
by locating the amplitude drop in the waveform and the offset of F2 of
the preceding vowel. The offset of /l/ was determined by locating the rise
in amplitude of the waveform and the onset of F2 in the following vowel.
After measuring the data, I first compared the duration of the geminate
[lː] in the s-aspirated context (/es.la.bo/ 'Slavic') with that of the singleton [l] in the words /a.le.ro/ 'eaves' and /a.la.ba/ 's/he praises'. That is, I
compared the duration of [l] in the underlying /VslV/ context with that
of the /VlV/ context. The robustness of the distinction is shown in (5),
where the mean duration of geminated [l] in the s-aspirated forms is
more than twice that of the singleton [l] for both speakers. Figure 6.3
provides a bar graph of the mean [l] durations and standard deviations
by context for each speaker. Not surprisingly, a two-factor ANOVA with
context (/VlV/ vs. /VslV/) as the first factor and speaker as the second
shows that the difference in [l] duration is highly significant by context
($p = .0001$).

(5) Mean /l/ durations

speaker	[l] duration in /VlV/ in msec.	st. dev.	[l] duration in /VslV/ in msec.	st. dev.
S1	76.936	(8.012)	162.843	(14.989)
S2	72.302	(13.260)	171.5	(17.706)

Comparing Eastern Andalusian to Standard Peninsular Spanish, we thus see that in SPS all [sC] clusters must be heterosyllabic, while EAS bans /s/ from appearing in coda position. In word-final position in EAS, /s/ is deleted, but word-internally, the coda position is maintained via gemination of the following onset. This is summarized in (6).

(6) Comparison of SPS and EAS

Context	SPS	EAS
$_\sigma$[sC	no	no
s]$_\sigma$#	yes	no
s]$_\sigma$[C	yes	no, but syllable is closed via gemination

How might this scenario be accounted for under a phonetic cues approach? If we abandon syllable structure as the driving force behind the distributional facts, it is reasonable to assume that we would be led to claim that EAS requires [sV] contexts for the licensing of [s]. That is, [s] is only licensed in contexts in which there is a transition to a following vowel. Our contextual constraints would thus be ordered such that [s] is banned in contexts lacking this transition.

One objection to this approach, however, is that unlike laryngeal features in stops, the most salient cues for fricatives lie largely within the fricatives themselves. In the case of sibilants such as /s/, high-frequency noise is generated as a result of channel turbulence at the point of constriction, as well as by the noise resulting from airflow hitting the teeth in front of the constriction (see, for example, Shadle 1997; Johnson 1997; Stevens 1998). In Steriade's terms, sibilants can be said to have strong internal cues, rather than relying heavily on contextual cues, as stops must. A priori, we should thus expect contexts such as [CV] transitions to play a far less significant role in licensing fricatives than in the licensing of laryngeal features in stops.

Further objections to a phonetic cues approach emerge when we consider the behavior of other obstruents in Eastern Andalusian. As noted earlier, relatively little attention has been paid to the fact that all obstruent codas are aspirated, in that all word-internal codas that would surface as obstruents in SPS trigger the gemination of the following onset in EAS. Examples are given in (7).[9,10]

(7) Aspiration of all obstruent codas in EAS

SPS	EAS	Gloss
[ap.to]	[aʰt.to]	'apt'
[piθ.ka]	[piʰk.ka]	'pinch, small amount'
[ak.θjon]	[aʰθ.θjon] ([aʰs.sjon])	'action'
[ob.tu.so]	[oʰt.tu.so]	'obtuse'

Of particular interest here is the behavior of stop + liquid clusters. As the data in (8) show, these are not globally banned as onsets in EAS (or any other dialect of Spanish).

(8) Initial stop+liquid clusters

a) [k̲l̲aro]   'clear'   c) [p̲l̲ano]   'flat'

b) [g̲r̲ado]   'grade'   d) [t̲r̲apo]   'rag'

Word-internally in EAS, the clusters in (8) do not trigger the gemination of the following liquid, as seen in (9). Put in simple terms, the obstruents appear to be patterning as part of the onset.

(9) Word-internal obstruent+liquid clusters

a) [a.k̲l̲ara]   's/he/it clears up'   c) [a.p̲l̲ika]   's/he/it applies'

b) [a.g̲r̲ada]   's/he/it pleases'   d) [a.t̲r̲apa]   's/he/it traps'

However, such forms might equally look like an argument in favor of the cue licensing approach. Specifically, the distinctive voicing and place features for obstruent stops can be viewed as banned when the following C is an obstruent. Thus, underlying /apto/ 'apt' is realized in EAS as [aʰtto] because the underlying obstruent + obstruent contexts are cue-impoverished relative to the expression of voicing and place on C1. By contrast, the modal voicing of the following liquid in forms such as [aplika] 's/he applies' presumably provides a sufficiently rich context for the expression of the cues for voicing and place at the release of the stop.

Though I have no disagreement with the reasoning behind such a story, serious problems arise regarding its adequacy in accounting for the

a   k   l   a   r   a

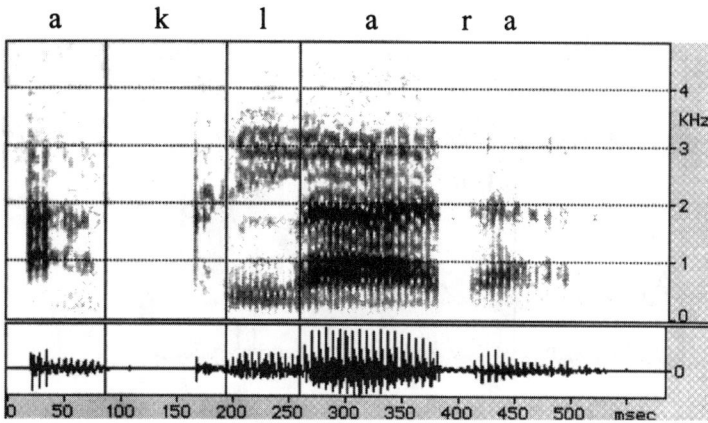

Figure 6.4. /aklara/ 's/he clears up'.

data directly. First, the problem of /sl/ clusters remains unresolved. That is, why should medial [kl] and [pl] be licit clusters, while /sl/ triggers s-aspiration? Secondly, we miss a broader generalization that becomes evident upon consideration of the behavior of /tl/ clusters in EAS. Interestingly, these behave phonetically like /sl/ clusters, rather than like their /pl/ and /kl/ counterparts. That is, input /tl/ clusters pattern as though the underlying /t/ must be syllabified as a coda, thus conditioning the gemination of the following /l/.

Note that the syllabification of /tl/ clusters is variable across Spanish dialects (see Harris 1983). In Mexico, they can be onsets, as evidenced by the word-initial /tl/ clusters incorporated into Mexican Spanish from contact with indigenous American languages; see (10). Though initial /tl/ clusters are vanishingly rare at best in peninsular Spanish dialects, we do find common forms such as /atlas/ 'atlas', /atlantico/ 'Atlantic', /atleta/ 'athlete', or /atlanta/ 'Atlanta', all of which contain medial /tl/ clusters. Of particular importance here is that their phonetic implementation makes it clear that EAS treats the /t/ of underlying word-internal /VtlV/ sequences as it does all other obstruent codas. Consider, for example, the spectrograms in Figures 6.4 and 6.5, which contrast /aklara/ 's/he makes clear' with /atleta/ 'athlete', respectively, for S1.

(10) /tl/ onsets in Mexican Spanish

a) [tla.pa.ne.co] 'Tlapaneco (language)'

b) [wau.tla] 'Huautla (name of a town)'

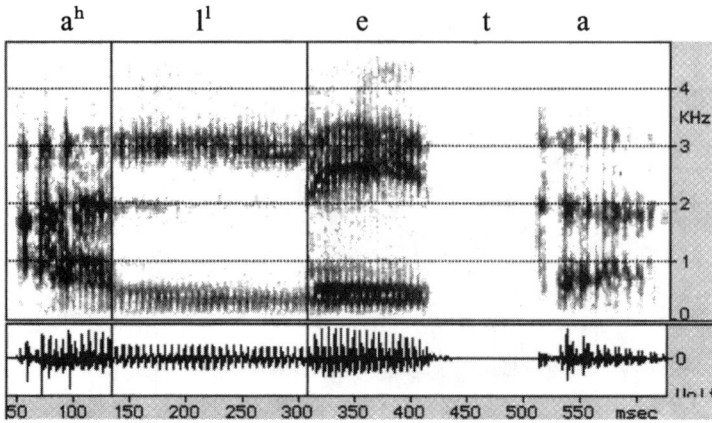

Figure 6.5. /atleta/ 'athlete'.

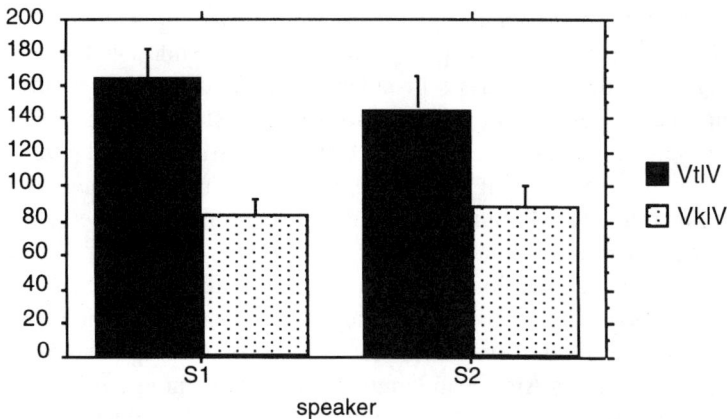

Figure 6.6. [l] in /VtlV/ vs. /VklV/.

In /aklara/, there is full stop closure for [k] followed by the liquid [l].
By contrast, /atleta/ lacks any stop closure for the first /t/. Rather, /atleta/
is phonetically realized as [aʰlleta], with [l] gemination of the type that
we saw above in [eʰllaßo] from underlying /eslabo/ 'Slavic'. Phonetically,
then, /t/ in /tl/ clusters is behaving in the same way that all other
obstruent codas behave in EAS. This can be seen by comparing average
[l] durations in underlying /VtlV/ contexts with /VklV/ contexts
in Figure 6.6. Again, a two-factor ANOVA of /l/ duration by context
(/VklV/ vs. /VtlV/) and speaker reveals context to be highly significant
($p = .0001$).

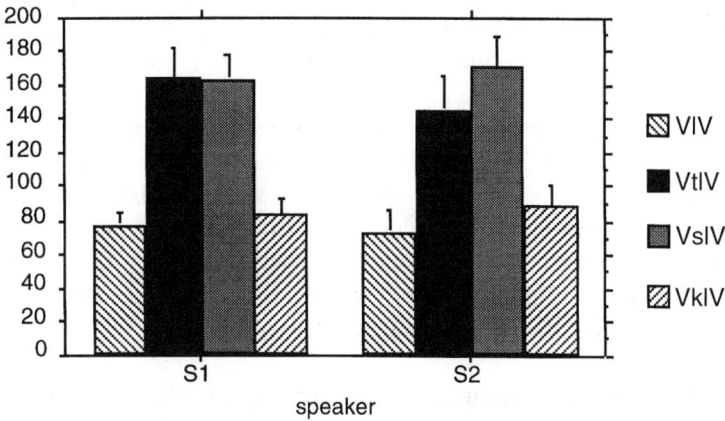

Figure 6.7. /l/ duration in all contexts by speaker.

The bar graph in Figure 6.7 shows the full range of data involving all four contexts measured in the words in the experimental list above: /VlV/, /VtlV/, /VslV/, and /VklV/, respectively. Note the clear two-way split for both speakers consisting of [l]-gemination in coda contexts (/VslV/ and /VtlV/) versus the singleton [l] in the onset cluster context /VklV/ and the /VlV/ context. To test this, I recoded the data, creating two categories, coda (pooling the /VtlV/ and /VslV/ conditions) and onset (pooling /VklV/ and /VlV/ conditions). Again, a two-factor ANOVA of [l] duration by context and subject confirms that [l] is significantly longer in the coda context ($p = .0001$).

In sum, phonetic evidence confirms that [kl] patterns as an onset in EAS, while the /t/ of /tl/ clusters patterns identically to underlying /s/ in /sC/ clusters in triggering so-called s-aspiration. Its behavior is entirely consistent with what we know to be the behavior of all obstruent codas in EAS. And this leads us to the larger conclusion that it is syllable position and not simply phonetic context that dictates the licensing of distinctive features in EAS obstruents. In this sense, EAS constitutes an interesting counterpoint to Steriade's Klamath discussion in that EAS can be viewed as an anti-Klamath. It isn't the phonetic sequencing that conditions contrast licensing independent of syllable structure. Rather, it is syllable structure itself that drives licensing.[11]

3.3. Sketching an OT Approach

In OT terms, the most straightforward characterization of the differences in the distributional properties of obstruent contrasts in EAS versus

SPS lie in constraints which invoke syllable structure directly. Though an exhaustive characterization of EAS syllabification is beyond the scope of this paper, the general picture emerges fairly clearly. I first assume that EAS and SPS share the ranking of constraints governing licit onset combinations. The dialects' respective hierarchies thus generate the same set of possible onsets, and, importantly, dictate which segments must be mapped into coda position for any given input string. Of interest here is that the difference between the dialects lies in the treatment of how input obstruents that cannot be mapped into output onsets are realized (or not) as codas. The task of generating the differences between the two dialects thus falls to the relative ranking of coda and faithfulness constraints.

This is the typical scenario in OT, according to which constraint ranking derives typological variation. For its part, SPS must be characterized by a high ranking of faithfulness over coda constraints, thus allowing for the independent licensing of obstruents in coda. In EAS, coda constraints on obstruents will outrank input faithfulness. Of course, coda constraints will not outrank all input-output faithfulness, given that EAS is not driven toward the more unmarked situation in which codas are banned altogether. Thus, EAS does not simply delete word-internal obstruents in coda position. Instead, it geminates the following onset to maintain a closed syllable. (Additionally, sonorant consonants must be allowed to surface as codas, as seen in forms such as [par.ke] 'park' or [al.kal.de] 'mayor'.)

As an illustration of how such an analysis would proceed, let us consider a form such as /kasta/ 'caste', which surfaces as [kat.ta].[12] First, assuming a correspondence-based view of faithfulness (McCarthy and Prince 1995), we might argue that MaxC militates for the preservation of input consonants, while Coda Condition (CodaCond) bans obstruents from coda position. (Note that for simplicity I employ CodaCond here as shorthand for the family of right margin constraints in Prince and Smolensky (1993); I return to this issue.) Simply ordering CodaCond » MaxC alone would produce the effect of deletion, predicting a surface [ka.ta]. Since s-aspiration in EAS preserves syllable weight, a highly-ranked Max constraint for moras, MaxMora (see, for example Broselow, Chen, and Huffman 1997) would appear to be well motivated, as seen in (11).[13]

(11) MaxMora

Input: /kas.ta/	CodaCond	MaxMora	MaxC
a) kas.ta	*!		
b) ka.ta		*!	*
c) ☞ kat.ta			*

Three points are of note regarding candidate (11c). First, while it preserves the moraic structure of the input, one might ask why vowel lengthening does not occur, giving us an optimal output of [kaa.ta]. Formally, this can be accomplished by penalizing surface long vowels more heavily than banning geminate consonants: *V: » *C:. Both of these constraints must be ordered below MaxMora.[14] Secondly, I have assessed a MaxC violation to the winning candidate in (11c) under the assumption that gemination involves the association of a single segment to the coda mora of the first syllable and the onset of the second (see Hayes 1989), as in (12).

(12) Geminate representation

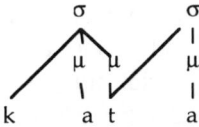

The optimal output in (11) thus violates MaxC for the input /s/. Finally, I have not assessed a CodaCond violation to (11c), even though gemination supplies a coda consonant. In this sense, my use of CodaCond is clearly an oversimplification. A comprehensive analysis would require a more finely grained approach (cf. Ito 1989; Ito et al. 1995; Ito and Mester 1994), in which obstruents cannot be independently licensed in coda position. Specifically, the strategy would entail the argument that the shared association of the geminate segment spares it from violating CodaCond. By contrast, an obstruent uniquely associated to the final mora of the first syllable would violate CodaCond.

Note that the formal possibilities here vary depending on assumptions regarding the representation of geminates and the interpretation of association lines. More importantly, however, the particular articulation of coda constraints is orthogonal to the larger issue under discussion. That is, the range of EAS facts receive the simplest, most unified account in terms of direct reference to syllable structure in the constraint hierarchy rather than in terms of a *F (sans phonetic cues) approach to the data.

4. Conclusions

In this chapter, I have argued against viewing the licensing of contrast strictly in terms of licensing by phonetic cue. In so doing, I have provided evidence from Eastern Andalusian that strongly points towards the necessity of taking syllable structure into account in order to understand where obstruent contrasts can be licensed in this dialect. Though attempting to prove a negative is an inherently dangerous proposition, my analysis argues that phonology cannot reduce to directly referencing cues such as formant transitions, f0 perturbations, duration, and so forth. That is, we cannot (and thus should not) dispense with higher-order categorical categories such as onset and coda, nor with the constraints that refer to them in our OT grammar. In EAS, a highly ranked CodaCond (Ito et al. 1995; Ito and Mester 1994; Lombardi 1999, this volume) drives the surface licensing of contrastive obstruent features; that is, it neutralizes obstruents that are contrastive in coda position in the standard peninsular variety of the language.

I do not, however, wish to claim that the project of direct phonetic licensing is off the mark or that subphonemic phonetic cues have no place in phonological analyses. There are, in fact, good reasons to believe that such approaches provide productive and insightful results. A particularly important aspect of the cue licensing approach is that it attempts to derive phonological patterns from an in-depth consideration of the physiological and physical properties of both speech production and perception (cf. Ohala 1990; Lindblom 1990). The potential benefits are enormous if we consider the circularity in much phonological work. For example, Ohala (1990) discusses the pitfalls of invoking constraints such as *[F] in coda, based on the observation that [F] fails to appear in coda position in language after language. Undeniably, there is a fundamental circularity in using observed patterns of segmental ordering in syllables to derive a sonority hierarchy and subsequently using that same hierarchy to explain the possible orderings of segments within syllables. This is not to say that such a hierarchy fails to make predictions about the likelihood of finding particular syllable types in natural languages, but it offers little in the way of understanding why such patterns arise.[15]

Nevertheless, the EAS data show that it is not clear that the viability of such constraints obviates the need for traditional syllable-based analyses. To the extent that these approaches often afford identical empirical coverage, the situation invites reduction, as seen in Steriade's (1997) questioning of the relevance of syllable structure at all in conditioning segmental phonotactics. At the very least, a phonetic cues approach should shift the burden of proof to traditional approaches like the one I have sketched for EAS. That is, we must ask why one should resort first to explanations that are less directly grounded in articulation and/or acoustics, rather than assuming a priori the adequacy of an account based on higher-level constraints.

At this point, we are only at the initial stages of an exploration of these issues. And, for now, I would advocate a hybrid, and admittedly less restrictive, approach. That is, if it is necessary to recognize that phonetics drives much of phonotactics, we must also countenance the continuing relevance of more abstract phonological structures to our understanding of generalized patterns in the grammar. In simple terms, once such structures are part of the grammar, there is no reason to think that they, themselves, will not make their influence felt within the grammar.

Notes

Many thanks to audiences at the University of Maryland, UNC-Chapel Hill, and WCCFL 18 for their helpful feedback on earlier incarnations of this chapter. Thanks also to Megan Crowhurst and Pilar Piñar for their valuable input and to Linda Lombardi and Jaye Padgett for helpful criticism of this final version. All errors are my own.

1. See, for example, Archangeli and Pulleyblank (1994) for extended discussion of phonetically motivated grounding conditions that function, in essence, as soft universals.
2. I am grateful to Paul Smolensky and Jaye Padgett for feedback on this issue. See Padgett (to appear) for additional discussion.
3. See also Padgett (1995), who proposes a constraint requiring Faithfulness to Release that presupposes syllabification in that consonants can be predicted to be released in part based on their position in the syllable.
4. The Klamath data are actually more complicated than discussed here in that laryngeal contrasts are neutralized not only before obstruents but also before aspirated and glottalized sonorants. See Steriade (1997) and the references therein for more details. The larger point regarding the role or non-role of syllable structure in the licensing of laryngeal contrasts in obstruents is not undermined by the additional data, however.
5. See Harris (1983) for the most complete overview of syllable structure in Spanish in general.

6. In peninsular dialects with phonetic [θ], there are numerous words containing [θ] word-finally, as in [lapiθ] 'stone'. In all American dialects and some peninsular dialects, of course, [θ] has merged with [s]. Some words also have a [d] word-finally (e.g., /bajadolid/ 'Valladolid', /madrid/ 'Madrid'), and other obstruents surface in codas of word-final syllables in borrowed forms such as [klub] 'club' or [biθeps] 'biceps', though these are highly marginal.

7. The lack of focus on word-internal s-aspiration is due to the potential morphological consequences of word-final s-aspiration, given that both familiarity and plurality are expressed by word-final /s/ in Spanish.

8. See also Gerfen and Piñar (1999) for evidence of the robust nature of the gemination process. In that study, ten native speakers of EAS exhibit the same pattern of gemination for /t/ in [kaʰt.ta] (from underlying /kas.ta/ 'caste') that the two speakers here exhibit for /l/.

9. EAS does not ban codas altogether. Nasals and liquids do surface in coda position just as they do in SPS. Examples include forms such as [par.ke] 'park', [pal.ko] 'balcony', and [men.ta] 'mint'.

10. As pointed out in note 4, many Andalusians speak the so-called *seseo* dialect, in which all SPS interdental fricatives are realized as [s]. Thus, [aʰθ.θjon] 'action' in the table is realized as [aʰs.sjon] in the *seseo* dialect.

11. One might argue that a phonetic cues approach to "s-aspiration" in /tl/ contexts resides in the increased difficulty of releasing /t/ into a lateral, as opposed to releasing velar or bilabial stops into a following lateral, as in forms such as [a.kla.ra] in which there is no aspiration. Under such an approach, the aspiration of obstruents in Eastern Andalusian would obtain in the more phonetically driven unreleased contexts, rather than in syllable-final position. The idea merits further investigation, though one would have to quantify more carefully the notion of difficulty. Note, for example, that /t/ does not aspirate before the alveolar tap, as in [a.tra.pa] 's/he traps'. Under the analysis here, this is due to the fact that /tr/ is a licit onset cluster, while /tl/ is not. A larger problem is that this account still fails to account for behavior of /s/, which aspirates before all following consonants. The treatment in the text unifies the explanation under the rubric of the syllable.

12. I abstract away from the issue of aspiration here.

13. Note that, given richness of the base, there is no reason to assume that moraic information must be excluded from input.

14. Word-finally, where there is no following onset available for gemination, at least some degree of vowel lengthening does occur.

15. Jaye Padgett (p.c.) has questioned whether the sonority hierarchy does, in fact, make predictions, given that the predictions are based on observations of the kind of things being predicted. I would argue, in fact, that there are two distinct issues here. The first regards prediction, and the second regards explanatory depth. Clearly, a sonority hierarchy derived from observing segmental ordering with syllables across many languages makes predictions about syllable phonotactics in languages outside the set of languages used to derive the hierarchy. Nevertheless, what is missing is an explanation for why the hierarchy should be structured thus – that is, for why sound A is

more or less sonorous than sound B. Such an explanation cannot be derived from the facts of segmental sequencing.

References

Alarcos Llorach, E. 1958. Fonología y Fonética: A Propósito de las Vocales Andaluzas. *Archivum* 8:191–203.

Archangeli, D., and D. Pulleyblank. 1994. *Grounded Phonology*. Cambridge, MA: MIT Press.

Beckman, J. 1997a. Positional Faithfulness, Positional Neutralisation and Shona Vowel Harmony. *Phonology* 14:1–46.

Beckman, J. 1997b. Positional Faithfulness. PhD dissertation, University of Massachusetts, Amherst.

Blevins, J. 1993. Klamath Laryngeal Phonology. *International Journal of American Linguistics* 59:237–280.

Broselow, E., S-I. Chen, and M. Huffman. 1997. Syllable Weight: Convergence of Phonology and Phonetics. *Phonology* 14:47–82.

Cohn, A. 1990. Phonetic and Phonological Rules of Nasalization. PhD dissertation, UCLA.

Cohn, A. 1993. Nasalization in English: Phonology or Phonetics. *Phonology* 10:43–81.

Cohn, A. 1999. The Phonetics-Phonology Interface Revisited: Where's Phonetics? In *Texas Linguistic Forum 41: Exploring the Boundaries Between Phonetics and Phonology*, ed. A. Doran, T. Majors, C. E. Mauk, and N. M. Goss, pp. 25–40. Austin, TX: University of Texas Department of Linguistics.

Dave, R. 1977. Retroflex and Dental Consonants in Gujarati: A Palatographic and Acoustic Study. *Annual Report of the Institute of Phonetics, University of Copenhagen* 11:27–156.

Flemming, E. 1995. Auditory Representations in Phonology. PhD dissertation, UCLA.

Gerfen, C. 1999. *Phonology and Phonetics in Coatzospan Mixtec*. Dordrecht: Kluwer.

Gerfen, C., and P. Piñar. 1999. Andalusian Codas. Paper presented at the annual meeting of the Linguistic Society of America, Los Angeles, CA.

Goldsmith, J. 1981. Subsegmentals in Spanish Phonology: An Autosegmental Approach. In *Linguistic Symposium on Romance Languages 9*, ed. W. Cressey and D. J. Napoli, pp. 1–16. Washington, DC: Georgetown University Press.

Guitart, J. M. 1985. Variable Rules in Caribbean Spanish and the Organization of Phonology. In *Current Issues in Hispanic Phonology and Morphology*, ed. F. Nuessel, pp. 28–33. Bloomington, IN: Indiana University Linguistics Club.

Harris, J. 1983. *Syllable Structure and Stress in Spanish*. Cambridge, MA: MIT Press.

Hayes, B. 1989. Compensatory Lengthening in Moraic Phonology. *Linguistic Inquiry* 20:253–306.

Hualde, J. I. 1987. Delinking Processes in Romance. In *Studies in Romance Linguistics*, ed. C. Kirschener and J. DeCesaris, pp. 177–193. Philadelphia: Benjamins.

Huffman, M. K. 1989. Implementation of Nasal: Timing and Articulatory Landmarks. PhD dissertation, UCLA.

Huffman, M. K. 1993. Phonetic Patterns of Nasalization and Implications for Feature Specification. In *Phonetics and Phonology 5: Nasals, Nasalization, and the Velum*, ed. M. K. Huffman and R. A. Krakow, pp. 303–327. San Diego, CA: Academic.

Ito, J. 1989. A Prosodic Theory of Epenthesis. *Natural Language and Linguistic Theory* 7:217–259.

Ito, J., and A. Mester. 1994. Reflections on CodaCond and Alignment. In *Phonology at Santa Cruz 3*, ed. R. Walker, J. Padgett, and J. Merchant, pp. 27–46. Santa Cruz, CA: Linguistics Research Center.

Ito, J., A. Mester, and J. Padgett. 1995. NC: Licensing and Underspecification in Optimality Theory. *Linguistic Inquiry* 26:571–613.

Johnson, K. 1997. *Acoustic and Auditory Phonetics*. Oxford: Blackwell.

Keating, P. 1988. Underspecification in Phonetics. *Phonology* 5:275–292.

Keating, P. 1990. Phonetic Representation in a Generative Grammar. *Journal of Phonetics* 18:321–334.

Kingston, J., and R. Diehl. 1994. Phonetic Knowledge. *Language* 70:419–454.

Kirchner, R. 1997. Contrastiveness and Faithfulness. *Phonology* 14:83–111.

Lindblom, B. 1990. On the Notion of "Possible Speech Sound." *Journal of Phonetics* 18:135–152.

Lombardi, L. 1991. Laryngeal Features and Laryngeal Neutralization. PhD dissertation, University of Massachusetts at Amherst.

Lombardi, L. 1995. Laryngeal Neutralization and Syllable Wellformedness. *Natural Language and Linguistic Theory* 13:39–74.

Lombardi, L. 1999. Positional Faithfulness and Voicing Assimilation in Optimality Theory. *Natural Language and Linguistic Theory* 17:267–302.

McCarthy, J., and A. Prince. 1993. Generalized Alignment. In *Yearbook of Morphology 1993*, ed. G. Booij and J. van Marle, pp. 79–153. Dordrecht: Kluwer.

McCarthy, J., and A. Prince. 1995. Faithfulness and Reduplicative Identity. In *University of Massachusetts Occasional Papers in Linguistics 18: Papers in Optimality Theory*, pp. 249–384. Amherst, MA: GLSA. ROA 60-0000, http://ruccs.rutgers.edu/roa.html.

Myers, S. 1999. Surface Underspecification of Tone in Chichewa. In *Texas Linguistic Forum 41: Exploring the Boundaries between Phonetics and Phonology*, ed. A. Doran, T. Majors, C. E. Mauk, and N. M. Goss, pp. 117–132. Austin, TX: University of Texas Department of Linguistics.

Ohala, J. J. 1990. There is No Interface between Phonology and Phonetics: A Personal View. *Journal of Phonetics* 18:153–171.

Padgett, J. 1995. Partial Class Behavior and Nasal Place Assimilation. In *Proceedings of the Southwestern Optimality Theory Workshop*, pp. 145–183. Tucson, AZ: University of Arizona Department of Linguistics Coyote Working Papers.

Padgett, J. To appear. Contrast Dispersion and Russian Palatalization. In *The Role of Speech Perception Phenomena in Phonology*, ed. E. V. Hume and K. Johnson. San Diego, CA: Academic.

Pierrehumbert, J. B. 1980. The Phonetics and Phonology of English Intonation. PhD dissertation, MIT.

Pierrehumbert, J. B. 1991. The Whole Theory of Sound Structure. *Phonetica* 48:223–232.

Pierrehumbert, J. B., and M. E. Beckman. 1988. *Japanese Tone Structure*. Cambridge, MA: MIT Press.

Prince, A., and P. Smolensky. 1993. *Optimality Theory: Constraint Interaction in a Generative Grammar*. To appear, MIT Press.

Rodríguez Castellano, L., and A. Palacio. 1948. El Habla de Cabra. *Revista de dialectología y tradiciones populares* 4:378–418.

Romero, J. 1995. Gestural Organization in Spanish: An Experimental Study of Spirantization and Aspiration. PhD dissertation, University of Connecticut.

Shadle, C. H. 1997. The Aerodynamics of Speech. In *The Handbook of Phonetic Sciences*, ed. W. J. Hardcastle and J. Laver, pp. 33–64. Oxford: Blackwell.

Steriade, D. 1997. Phonetics in Phonology: The Case of Laryngeal Neutralization. Ms., UCLA.

Stevens, K. 1998. *Acoustic Phonetics*. Cambridge, MA: MIT Press.

Zamora Munné, J. C., and M. M. Guitart. 1982. *Dialectología Hispanoamericana: Teoría, Descripción, Historia*. Salamanca: Ediciones Almar.

Zamora Vicente, A. 1969. *Dialectología Española* (2nd ed.). Madrid: Gredos.

Zsiga, E. 1997. Features, Gestures, and Igbo Vowel Assimilation: An Approach to the Phonology/Phonetics Mapping. *Language* 73: 227–275.

7

Segmental Unmarkedness versus Input Preservation in Reduplication

MOIRA YIP

1. Introduction

Reduplication creates new words by affixing a copy of all or part of the base word. This chapter discusses types of reduplication from Chinese languages that differ in two ways from the most familiar and prototypical cases. First, it is not obvious which piece of the output is the base and which is the affixed copy, and instead the outputs look more like compounds of a word with itself. Second, and the focus of this chapter, the copies are imperfect, with various segments from the input being replaced by fixed segments, [l] in onsets, [i] in nuclei, and [ʔ] or [ŋ] in codas. I argue that these segmental replacements are the unmarked segments for these syllabic positions, and that they represent instances of The Emergence of The Unmarked (TETU), as discussed in Alderete et al. (1999).

After a survey of the data, I begin by laying out the basic analysis of reduplication as a response to two constraints, ALLITERATE and RHYME. I then show how the ranking of these with respect to segmental markedness constraints gives rise to the segmental changes. In the next section I discuss the particular choice of unmarked segments, and propose a set of markedness constraints. The final two sections discuss cases where segmental markedness is violated on the surface in that the replacement segments do not appear to be the most unmarked ones. In the first case, a special requirement of secret languages forces an increase in markedness. In the second case, conflicting markedness constraints interact with the secret language constraint to produce surface marked segments.

2. Data

The following sections show four patterns of reduplication: onset change, nucleus and coda change, syllable structure change, and "concealed reduplication."

2.1. Onset Change in Chaoyang Verbal Reduplication

The following data (Zhang 1979a,b, 1980, 1982) contrast two types of morphology. The first set of data (1) shows ordinary compounding and full reduplication, while the second set (2) shows onset-changing reduplication, where the second onset becomes [l], or [n] in the presence of nasality.

(1) *No onset change:*

    a. *non-reduplicative compounding/affixation:*

        teŋ tioʔ   'heavy weight'

    b. *most types of reduplication, including verbal, nominal,*

    adjectival/adverbial, measure word

    hou bui bui 'rain slight'   kuaŋ kuaŋ aŋ   'blush red'

    haŋ toi toi 'alley's end'   zik zik tsiõ paŋ   'everyday go to work'

(2) *Onset change:*

    a. *resultatives:*   kuaʔ   kuaʔ luaʔ tŋ 'cut off'

    b. *directional complements* kiã   kiã niã lai   'walk-come'

    c. *durational complements* paʔ   paʔ laʔ e   'pat once'

These data raise three puzzles: (i) why do onsets change at all, (ii) why do they change to [l] or [n], and (iii) why can only some onsets change? I will propose the following answers: (i) onsets change to reduce markedness, (ii) [l] is chosen because it has the least marked place (Coronal), because it is phonologically [−cont] in Chaoyang, making it a suitably low-sonority segment for an onset, and because it is voiced, which is the preferred laryngeal state in medial position, and (iii) marked onsets resist change if either (a) they are the only surface correspondent of the input onset as is the case in nonreduplicative morphology, or (b) they are initial in the morphological word, or (c) they are final in X″. This chapter will provide detailed support for the answers to (i) and (ii), and for (iiia). On (iiib–c), see Yip (to appear).

The basic facts are given in (3).

(3) a. *Onsets become [l] if original onset and vowel are oral:*

kua? lua? tŋ   'cut off'   pa? la? e   'pat once'

tsuŋ luŋ ta   'twist dry'   tui lui tik   'pull straight'

b. *Onsets become [n] if original onset or nucleus are nasal:*

kiã niã lai   'walk-come'   k'ŋ nŋ muã   'hide things'

kuẽ nuẽ k'u   'close-go'   mue? nue? tiau   'finish up'

ŋaŋ naŋ tiau   'dig out with nails'

c. *Only onset of second syllable changes.*

ts'u lu tik   *lu ts'u tik * lu lu tik

d. *Second syllable must have onset; first syllable may be onsetless*

uãi nuãi tiau 'dig out w. knives'   *uãi uãi tiau,*nuãi nuãi tiau

e. *Nucleus and coda never change/ delete:*

tsuŋ luŋ ta   'twist dry' *tsuŋ lun ta, * tsuŋ lu ta, *tsuŋ liŋ ta

siap liap (siap liap)   'puckery' *siap liat, *siap lia

2.2. Nucleus and Coda Changes: Chaoyang Onomatopoeia

Some further data is of interest here. In onomatopoeia, Chaoyang has two additional reduplicative patterns (4). These show vowel and coda change in both patterns, and onset change in one of the two. The vocoids become [i], and any coda becomes velar, glottal, or deletes. The onset changes are the same as before.

(4)   **Chaoyang onomatopoeia:**

Vocoids change to [i]: Ci(k /ʔ/ŋ) CV(C) kio

kʰi kʰa kio   tik tok kio

First vocoids & third onset change: Ci(k/ʔ/ŋ) CV(C) lV(C) kio:

kʰi kʰa la kio   tsi tsiau liau kio   piŋ paŋ laŋ kio

kik kiak liak kio   ĩ uãĩ nuãĩ kio

Coda change/loss: First coda becomes velar, glottal, or deletes

kʰiŋ kʰom kio   hiʔ hop lop kio   hi hom lom kio

2.3. Syllable Structure Change: Fuzhou Reduplication

A final set of data from the Fuzhou dialect (Zheng 1983) shows identical onset change in the second syllable (although Fuzhou has no morphemic nasality, so the onset is always [l]), but accompanied by simplification of the preceding rhyme to a CGV syllable with one of a reduced set of tones, as shown in (5).

(5)   /pieu/   pie lieu ʒouʔ li   'squirt-come-out'

        /kuŋ/   ku luŋ......   'roll'

        /tau/   ta lau ....   'cover'

        /niaʔ/   nia liaʔ tɔ a   'blink once'

        /loʔ/   lo loʔ ....   'cover, sheath'

        /tʰaiŋ/   tʰa laiŋ lɛ   'stand straight (lit: stick out chest)'

2.4. Concealed Reduplication: Jin Dialects

The data in (6) and (7) from Jin dialects (Sagart 1996; synchronically not productive) do not look like reduplication at all, but infixation. However, I shall argue that this pattern represents an expected outcome from the interaction of markedness and reduplication under the analysis proposed here, involving replacement of the first nucleus and coda with unmarked [əʔ] and of the second onset with the familiar [l].

(6) Yimeng:

pai	'to agitate'	pə(ʔ) lai	'to oscillate'
pən	'to run'	pə(ʔ) lən	'to run on all sides'
xua	'to draw'	xuə(ʔ) la	'to scribble'

(7) Huojia

| paʔ | 'to select, pick' | pə(ʔ) laʔ | 'to manipulate (as an abacus)' |
| phau | 'to dig' | phə(ʔ) lau | 'to dig repeatedly' |

In all four cases discussed in this section, I will argue for a markedness account of these facts.

3. Reduplication as Self-Compounding

I start with the assumption that this type of (near) total reduplication is self-compounding (as suggested in McCarthy and Prince 1986 for English echowords). Since both halves of the output have equal status, no base-affix relationship exists, so FAITH-BR constraints can play no role. Instead, FAITH-IO constraints relate each half to the input (for related proposals that view reduplication in nonaffixal ways, see Sherrard 1997, Raimy and Idsardi 1997, Struijke 2000, and Inkelas and Zoll 1999). Reduplication is forced by constraints that require repetition, but I differ from Yip (1993:8) in subdividing these constraints (there called ECHO or REPEAT) into two that I will call ALLITERATE and RHYME. This proposal immediately captures one obvious generalization missed by the standard base-reduplicant analysis of McCarthy and Prince (1995): namely, that the reduplicant and the copy are always adjacent, resulting in rhyming or alliterating sequences. I suggest that the real core of reduplication is an attempt to produce these sequences, and that rather than involving an abstract affix, reduplication is caused by RHYME and ALLITERATE constraints, where ALLITERATE governs the initial consonant, and RHYME governs the rest of the syllable, including any prenuclear glide, as expressed in (8).[1]

(8)   ALLITERATE: Output must contain at least one pair of adjacent syllables

with identical onsets

RHYME: Output must contain at least one pair of adjacent syllables with

identical rhymes

Under the influence of these constraints, input segments may thus have two output correspondents (violating INTEGRITY); there is no base or affix in the familiar sense. For an input /pati/ there will be two outputs which fully satisfy both RHYME and ALLITERATE, [*pa*-pati] and [pati-*ti*], analogous to Tagalog [pag-*la*-lakad] and Chamorro [bunita-*ta*], respectively.

Note crucially that this analysis does not mean that reduplication necessarily copies syllables, something known to be untrue since Moravcsik (1978) and Marantz (1982). Firstly, markedness considerations such as *COMPLEXONSET or NOCODA can result in "undercopying", as in Tagalog [*ta*-trabaho] or Ponapean [*ke*-kens] 'ulcerate', respectively. Secondly, if the rhyming portion precedes the alliterating portion, the result is a VC copy as in Tzeltal [nit-*it*-an], Oyakangand [*ed*-eder], or Mangarayi [gab-*ab*-uji]. In [nit-it-an], for example, the syllables [ni] and [ti] rhyme, and the syllables [ti] and [ta] alliterate.

To see how this works, consider a simple input /$b_1u_2i_3$/. In the absence of any Markedness constraints, this grammar will produce total reduplication, satisfying all constraints except IO-Integrity, as shown in (9).

(9)

/$b_1u_2i_3$/	MAX-IO	RHYME	ALLITERATE	IO-INTEGRITY
☞ a. $b_1u_2i_3$ $b_1u_2i_3$				***
b. $b_1u_2i_3$ u_2		*!	*!	*
c. b_1u_2 b_1u_2	*!			**

The focus of this chapter, however, is on types of reduplication where segments change, rendering the reduplication less than total, and on the cause and nature of those changes. Alderete et al. (1999) argue that some languages use unmarked segments in reduplication, and attribute it to the ranking of base-reduplicant faithfulness constraints below markedness constraints. The general schema for The Emergence of The Unmarked (TETU) effect is FAITH-IO » MARKEDNESS » FAITH-BR. I adopt this basic idea in this chapter, but elaborate it to account for the differential treatment of different syllabic positions.[2]

In the approach advocated here, if MARKEDNESS » ALLITERATE, onsets will become unmarked, and if MARKEDNESS » RHYME, rhymes will become unmarked. Chaoyang and Fuzhou show a whole collection of patterns illustrating four of these interactions, and the fifth is illustrated by data from Jin. Again, no commitment to a base/affix distinction is needed. In (10), a hypothetical syllable /hop/ is used to illustrate the constraint rankings, which are construction-specific and therefore lexically specified just like an affix would be. The alert reader will notice that patterns 1 and 4 have the same constraint ranking. Both patterns satisfy RHYME (with adjacent instances of [op]) and ALLITERATE (with adjacent instances of [h]), and the difference lies in the number of syllables in the output. I will assume that the trisyllabic pattern must be lexically specified, perhaps as requiring two binary feet in the output: $(\sigma\ \sigma)\ (\sigma\ \text{kio})$.

(10)

	/hop/	Rankings
Pattern 1	hop hop	ALLITERATE, RHYME >> MARKEDNESS
Pattern 2	hop lop (+ suffix)	RHYME >> MARKEDNESS >> ALLITERATE
Pattern 3	hiʔ hop (kio)	ALLITERATE >> MARKEDNESS >> RHYME
Pattern 4	hiʔ hop lop (kio)	ALLITERATE, RHYME >> MARKEDNESS
Pattern 5	həʔ lop	MARKEDNESS >> ALLITERATE, RHYME

I shall now show in more detail how onset change, resulting in less than full reduplication, is caused by markedness pressures. The discussion is presented using data from onset change, but extends straightforwardly to rhyme change. The central idea is that in reduplication each input segment has two output correspondents, each of which incurs a markedness violation. Replacing one correspondent with a less marked segment is thus a way to improve matters with respect to markedness, without violating MAX-IO. I assume that the fixed segment is an introduced segment, in violation of DEP-IO, not a correspondent of an input segment. Consider what happens if we introduce into the above grammar the markedness constraint *LABIAL, ranked above ALLITERATE, as in (11). Note that wholesale loss of /b/, as in candidate (11c), is blocked by MAX-IO, the same constraint which blocks any loss of input segments in nonreduplicative contexts where there is only one output correspondent possible. On the other hand excessive retention of /b/ results in unnecessary violations of *LABIAL, and thus /b/ is replaced by the less marked [l] in the second syllable. Note that a further candidate *[lui bui] is excluded by a prohibition on change to initial consonants, a type of positional faithfulness (see Beckman (1996) and Yip (to appear)).

(11)

/bui/	Max-IO	Rhyme	*Labial	Alliterate
☞ a. bui lui			*	*
b. bui bui			**!	
c. lui lui	*! (b)			

I will now justify the distinction between the two constraints that cause reduplication, Rhyme and Alliterate. The argument rests on the resolution of a potential problem with a markedness account. Unlike marked segments in the onset, marked segments such as velars in the rhyme survive in both correspondents, doubly violating markedness: /siap/ reduplicates as [siap liap], and /ŋaŋ/ reduplicates as [ŋaŋ], not as [ŋaŋ nan] or [ŋaŋ na]. Final coronals are not allowed in Chaoyang, but complete loss of one final coda would remove a marked segment, and a NoCoda violation, without a Max-IO violation, and yet this does not happen. These facts argue strongly for a division of the constraint that produces reduplication into two parts, Rhyme and Alliterate, with Rhyme dominating markedness constraints, which in turn dominate Alliterate. This ranking will force onset change, while preserving rhymes intact. Once this division is made, the relative ranking of each constraint with respect to markedness will determine whether it is onset segments or rhyme segments that move toward unmarkedness, and thus allow us to explain the full range of reduplication patterns laid out in Section 2.

Let us see how this works in the tableau in (12). Note that the constraints are assessed gradiently. For each segment by which input and output differ in the presence or absence of some segment, or in the features of that segment, the candidate incurs one asterisk (but see Section 6 for fine-tuning in connection with the active role played by Alliterate in Kunshan).

(12) Rhyme>> Markedness >> Alliterate

/ŋaŋ/	Rhyme	*Dorsal	Alliterate
☞ a. ŋaŋ naŋ		***	*
b. ŋaŋ na	*!	**	*
c. ŋaŋ ŋaŋ		****!	
d. ŋaŋ ŋa	*!	***	

Candidates (12b) and (12d) have removed the marked Dorsal coda in the second syllable, but this causes a violation of high-ranked Rhyme, so they are ruled out. Candidates (12a) and (12c) now pass down to *DORSAL, which assigns an asterisk for each Dorsal segment. Candidate (12c), with four, loses to candidate (12a), with only three, even though (12a) violates the lower-ranked ALLITERATE.

It is important to note that in the account presented here markedness both causes the loss and picks the best candidate. This was not the case in Yip (1993:8), where a single constraint, *ECHO (or *REPEAT), forced nonidentity, and markedness chose the best candidate from those that satisfied *ECHO. In this paper, there is no need for the negative constraint *ECHO: markedness does all the work. There is good reason to prefer this approach. If markedness, not *ECHO, drives onset change, then inputs with already unmarked /l/ or /n/ onsets will not undergo further change. This is correct, as shown by examples like [lio? lio? e kiã] or [nuã nuã e]. *ECHO would wrongly predict onset change of some kind, even at the expense of a markedness increase. In the next section I turn to why [l] and [n] should be chosen as the unmarked segments, followed finally by a discussion of segmental and structural changes in the rhyme.

4. The Choice of Unmarked Segments

Chaoyang has the segment inventory in (13). Notice importantly that /l/ occupies the inventory slot where /d/ would be expected on both historical and synchronic grounds, and that /l/ is flaplike in most Min dialects. Final consonants may be [m,ŋ,p,k]. Syllables may also end in a glottal stop. There are eight tones. Chaoyang syllables may be open, (C) (G) V (G) (?), or closed, (C) (G) V C. Some examples are given in (14).

(13)   p   t   ts   k   i   u

        p^h t^h ts^h k^h e   o

        b   l   g   a

                   s   h

                   z

        m   n   ŋ

(14)   pou^{11} 'chew' p^haŋ^{33} 'fragrant'   mẽ:^{53} 'fast'

      ŋiam^{55} 'surname'   bi:?^{11} 'hide'   lok^{11} 'shake'

      siap^{11} 'forty'   oi?^{55} 'narrow'   lau?^{11} 'lick'

      iãũ?^{11} 'fold'   tsi:?^{55} 'stone'

4.1. [l] or [n] as the Unmarked Onsets

In this section I justify the choice of Coronal, [+voice], [–cont] [l] as the unmarked onset. I will arrive at a small set of markedness constraints for onset consonants that must dominate ALLITERATE in order for onset change to take place.

The choice of the coronal [l] results from the familiar markedness hierarchy, *LABIAL, *DORSAL » *CORONAL. The preference for a coronal over no onset at all shows that ONSET » *CORONAL (cf. Gafos 1998 on Temiar). Codas, by contrast, can delete (to be discussed). ONSET also forces the addition of an onset to a vowel-initial syllable, as in [uãi nuãi tiau]; this is blocked in word-initial position by positional faithfulness constraints (Beckman 1996).

The [–cont] [l] is preferred to the [+cont] [s] because stops, even the flaplike [l], are the quintessential onsets, providing the sharpest start to the syllable. It is not clear whether stops, especially these flaps, are less sonorous than fricatives; see Clements (1988), Dell and Elmedlaoui (1985), and Prince and Smolensky (1993) for discussion. Certainly calling [l] less sonorous than [s] seems odd, so rather than stating the preference in sonority terms I content myself with assuming that for onsets *[+cont] » *[–cont].

The choice of [l] over [t] suggests that *[–voice] is high-ranked, selecting the only voiced oral Coronal, /l/ in Chaoyang. Ranking *[–voice] » *[+voice] is, however, crosslinguistically rather dubious, given that voiceless stops are usually preferred. Indeed, many languages have no voiced stops at all, and if voice is privative, as suggested by Lombardi (this volume, then) ranking voiceless as more marked than voice is in fact impossible. In most cases, the choice of voiced /l/ could be attributed to intersonorant voicing since the preceding syllable ends in a vocoid or a nasal (see Section 6 on Kunshan), suggesting the constraint INTERSONO-RANT VOICING: *[+son][–voice][+son].[3,4] This leaves unexplained the cases where /l/ follows [ŋ, k]. Jie Zhang (p.c.) has suggested to me that [t] may be avoided in these contexts for a separate reason: it would be hard to detect after an unreleased, glottalized stop.

The tableau in (15) shows how these constraints select [l]. High-ranked *LABIAL, *DORSAL excludes candidate (15e) at once, and ONSET rules out the onset deletion candidate (15d). The choice is now reduced to some sort of coronal onset, and the final two constraints select (15a), which satisfies both INTERSONVOICE and *[+cont].

(15)

/p'oi/	*LABIAL, *DORSAL	ONSET	*CORONAL	INTER SON VOICE	*[+cont]
☞a. p'oi loi	*		*		
b. p'oi zoi	*		*		*!
c. p'oi toi	*		*	*!	
d. p'oi oi	*	*!			
e. p'oi koi	**!			*	

[n] is chosen in the presence of [nasal], in conformity with the general behavior of nasality in Chaoyang. Nasality is specified at the level of the morpheme, and voiced onsets harmonize in nasality with the following vowel in open syllables, so we find [la] and [nã], but not *[lã] or *[na]. Because nasality is morphemic, it is not automatically lost when an onset is lost (see Yip 1994, 1997 for more details, including discussion of the lack of nasal vowels in closed syllables).

4.2. [i] as the Unmarked Vowel

I now turn to vowels. The basic analysis is identical to that for onset change, except that just as markedness dominated ALLITERATE in the case of onset change, it dominates RHYME in the case of rhyme change.

Recall that in onomatopoeia Chaoyang replaces all vocoids by [i], for example [tik tok]. This can be unified with the consonantal explanation if we follow Clements and Hume (1995) in assuming that front vowels are Coronal. Then the ranking *LAB, *DORS » *COR, established for onsets, also covers the vowels. The choice of high [i] over mid [e] may be language-specific. Spanish chooses [e] in epenthesis, and the Jin dialects use [ə].

Just as high-ranked ONSET blocks deletion as a way to reduce markedness, so HNUC, which requires every syllable to have a sufficiently harmonic (i.e., sonorant) nucleus, blocks deletion of the vowel. Non-nuclear vowels and codas may in fact delete: an input /kuai/ becomes [ki], although this would be hard to distinguish from [kiii]! The tableau in (16) illustrates how these constraints interact. RHYME is low ranked and not shown here, whereas ALLITERATE is high ranked and blocks any onset changes.

(16) Tableau for vowel change: (counting only violations involving vowels)

/lom/	HNUC	*LAB, *DORS	*COR
☞li lom		*	*
lo lom		**!	
l lom	*!	*	

4.3. Codas: Deletion, Debuccalization, or Velars

The facts about codas are more complex than they are for onsets or nuclei. First, remember that coda change accompanies nucleus change, not onset change. This is because onset change is the result of RHYME » MARKEDNESS » ALLITERATE, whereas any change in the rhyme, be it nucleus or coda, is the result of ALLITERATE » MARKEDNESS » RHYME. When markedness is reduced in the rhyme, nuclei cannot delete because of HNUC, but there is no such constraint on coda deletion: indeed, crosslinguistically codas are marked, and the constraint NOCODA captures this fact. We would thus expect codas to delete, eliminating both a marked syllable type and the marked features of the coda segment, and this is indeed one option, as shown by forms like [hi hom]. However, codas do not all delete: they may survive as either a glottal stop or as a velar nasal or stop. I attribute this retention to pressure for what I will term structural rhyme, in which the syllables match in syllable type, remaining both CVN [hiŋ-hom] or CVO [hiʔ-hop], where N and O stand for nasal and obstruent, respectively. The difference between CVN and CVO syllables is pervasive in Chinese, and CVO syllables can usually bear only a limited set of mostly level tones. Many dialects have lost them altogether, while preserving CVN syllables. Since this structural rhyme pressure results in retention of codas, it must outrank both featural markedness and NOCODA. I discuss this in detail in the remainder of this section.

First, though, let me deal with the choice of glottal stop or velars for the retained codas. It is frequently observed that glottal stop is characterized by a lack of place features, thus eliminating markedness violations of *LAB, *COR, *DORS.[5] Final stops in Chaoyang are unreleased and glottalized and bear the feature [constricted glottis]. If the pressure for structural rhyme requires the presence of a stop, debuccalization to [ʔ] is the least marked option. For nasals in Chaoyang no such option exists. The language has no placeless nasal glide equivalent to the Japanese moraic nasal, and it can be shown that phonologically final nasals are simply characterized by Place features without the feature [constricted glottis] borne by the stops (see Yip 1994, 1997 for details). Importantly, they do not bear the feature nasal, so their loss does not leave a nasal residue behind. The upshot of all this is that if a final nasal is retained, it must necessarily be as a nasal with some specified oral place of articulation.

In the case of onsets, the least marked place was Coronal, and yet codas survive as velar, not coronal. Chaoyang has only labial and velar codas, for both nasals and stops, so coronal codas are not an option, but why? Trigo (1988) argues that velars are the unmarked consonants in coda position, and one can perhaps understand this as resulting from a preference for moraic consonants to use the tongue body, making them more vowel-like in nature, so I formulate this as $*\mu_C$ = LAB, COR, crucially dominating *LAB, *DORS, *COR. The complete markedness ranking so far is given in (17).

(17) HNUC, ONSET, $*\mu_C$=LAB, COR $>>$ *LAB,*DORS $>>$ *COR

4.4. Codas Continued: Structural Rhyme versus Featural Rhyme

In the last section I introduced the notion of structural rhyme to account for the retention of coda consonants. I will now flesh out this idea, using the syllables /hom/ and /hop/ as schematic examples. I will split RHYME into the pair of constraints given in (18) and (19).

(18) STRUCTRHYME: Output must contain a pair of adjacent structurally

identical syllables, where structurally identical means both CV, both CVN, or

both CVO.

(19) FEATRHYME: Any structurally identical positions (i.e. nuclei, off-glides,

codas) in the two rhymes must match in features.

Syllables may obey any mixture of these constraints, as conveyed in (20). (I give only outputs in which vowel change has taken place.) Moving from left to right across the table, as codas degrade or delete, rhyme deteriorates from perfect to nonexistent, but markedness improves. The tension between these two gives rise to two options in the case of nasals: observe structural rhyme at the expense of markedness [hiŋ hom] or minimize markedness at the expense of rhyme [hi hom]. In the case of obstruents, however, [hiʔ hop] satisfies both, and is therefore always to be preferred. One last empirical complication: although labial stop codas can't become velars, underlying velar codas may sometimes persist, as in [kik kiak liak kio]. Apparently velar codas are not very marked; the perceptual cues for the difference between [kik'] and [kiʔ] are very subtle, since stop codas are unreleased and glottalized anyway.

(20)   Perfect rhyme → structurally good rhyme →   no rhyme

--→

        Most marked   →   least marked

/hom/ *him-hom   **hiŋ-hom**   **hi-hom**

/hop/ *hip-hop   *hik-hop   **hiʔ-hop** *hi-hop

I now give a more formal OT treatment of the account just outlined, beginning with the stop-final case. I give the tableau in (21), showing STRUCTRHYME high ranked (above NOCODA), forcing coda retention. Here and in subsequent tableaux in this section I show only violations for the coda of the first syllable. Note crucially that [hiʔ hop] will win under any ranking of these constraints, since it is perfect.

(21) Tableau for stop coda change: /hop/ > hiʔ hop (lop kio)

/hop/	STRUCTRHYME	$*\mu_C$ = LAB,COR	*LAB, *DORS	*COR
☞ hiʔ hop				
hik hop			*!	
hip hop		*!	*	
hi hop	*!			

When we turn our attention to nasal codas, we have to account for two possible outputs, [hi hom] or [hiŋ hom]. In OT, optionality is usually captured by proposing that constraints are freely ranked with respect to each other (see Clements 1997, among others) and that is the position I shall take here. [hiŋ hom] is the result of low-ranked markedness and high-ranked STRUCTRHYME (as in (21)), and [hi hom] is the result of high-ranked markedness and low-ranked STRUCTRHYME. Stated in this way, the optionality involves the free ranking of STRUCTRHYME with respect to the adjacent block of related markedness constraints, an unsurprising extension of the usual assumption that optionality freely ranks adjacent singleton constraints only.

The tableaux in (22) and (23) tell the tale; I repeat that under either ranking, /hop/ still becomes [hi? hop].

(22) Option one for nasal codas: Tableau for nasal coda change: /lom/ > liŋ

lom (kio)

/lom/	STRUCTRHYME	$*\mu_C$ = LAB,COR	*LAB, DORS	*COR
☞ liŋ lom			*	
lim lom		*!	*	
li lom	*!			

(23) Option two for nasal codas: Tableau for nasal loss: /lom/ > li lom (kio)

/lom/	$*\mu_C$ = LAB,COR	*LAB, DORS	*COR	STRUCTRHYME
☞ li lom				*
liŋ lom		*!		
lim lom	*!	*		

The distinction between STRUCTRHYME and FEATRHYME is not only useful in Chaoyang, where STRUCTRHYME is the higher ranked of the two, but in other dialects where the reverse ranking can be seen. Consider Fuzhou forms like /kuŋ/ > [ku luŋ], where the first syllable keeps its nucleus, so that the nuclei of the two syllables remain identical, satisfying FEATRHYME, but loses its coda, showing that NOCODA » STRUCTRHYME. For completeness, let me also observe that Fuzhou rhymes show a reduction in segmental markedness of one further type: diphthongs are lost. We can therefore conclude that in addition to NOCODA, NODIPHTHONG also outranks STRUCTRHYME.

The various rankings of STRUCTRHYME and FEATRHYME with respect to MARKEDNESS produce a factorial typology shown in (24). For rhyme changes to take place at all, markedness must dominate at least one of the RHYME constraints, as shown by the first three rows in the typology; the fourth row shows the case of no rhyme change (although the onset can of course change independently if ALLITERATE is low ranked).

(24) A typology of Rhyme/Markedness rankings:

(MARKEDNESS here includes *PLACE, NOCODA, NODIPHTH)

Dialect	Typical data	Constraint Ranking
Chaoyang	kiŋ kom	STRUCTRHYME > > MARKEDNESS > > FEATRHYME
Chaoyang	ki kom	MARKEDNESS > > STRUCTRHYME, FEATRHYME
Fuzhou	ko lom	FEATRHYME > > MARKEDNESS > > STRUCTRHYME
Chaoyang	kom lom	FEATRHYME, STRUCTRHYME > > MARKEDNESS

This completes the basic analysis, which in its essentials will extend to the data in the following sections also. I have shown that Chaoyang and Fuzhou offer instances of Alderete et al.'s first type of fixed segmentism, but with the twist that onsets and rhymes behave differently, motivating a richer typology. In (25), I compare their schema with that argued for here: For convenience, I repeat the TETU typology that emerges under an ALLITERATE/RHYME account in (26). One nice result is that Pattern 5, historically related to Patterns 1–4, can be seen to arise out of a simple reranking of the same constraint set. Thus what appears on the surface to be a drastic change – infixation instead of reduplication – is grammatically just a small ranking shift.

(25)   The Emergence of the Unmarked (TETU): (Alderete et al. 1999)

MAX-IO > > MARKEDNESS > > MAX-BR

(26)

	/hop/	Rankings
Pattern 1	hop hop	ALLITERATE, RHYME > > MARKEDNESS
Pattern 2	hop lop (+ suffix)	RHYME > > MARKEDNESS > > ALLITERATE
Pattern 3	hiʔ hop (kio)	ALLITERATE > > MARKEDNESS > > RHYME
Pattern 4	hiʔ hop lop (kio)	ALLITERATE, RHYME > > MARKEDNESS
Pattern 5	həʔ lop	MARKEDNESS > > ALLITERATE, RHYME

The major difference between these two proposals is that only the ALLITERATE/RHYME account directly distinguishes between the different treatment of the same segment in a single language depending on (i) whether that segment is in onset or rhyme, as in /ŋaŋ/ → [ŋaŋ naŋ], and (ii) which type of reduplication it is found in, as in /siap/ → [siap liap], with /p/ unchanged, but /hop/ → [hiʔ hop], with /p/ → [ʔ]. In an account along the lines of Alderete et al., to achieve the change of /ŋ/ → [n] in the onset, we must have *DORSAL » FAITH-BR, but then it should change in the coda too. To distinguish the different treatments of a segment in two types of reduplication, we would have to have two sets of FAITH-BR constraints, one specific to "suffixing reduplication" as in [siap liap] and standing above *LABIAL, and one specific to "prefixing reduplication" as in [hiʔ hop] and standing below. Various fixups are of course possible, but only the ALLITERATE/RHYME account directly captures the observed typology.

5. Markedness Increases

Although markedness is the main determiner of fixed segmentism in this type of reduplication, it can be overruled by higher-ranked constraints. To see this, I now turn to secret languages. I shall argue that the defining characteristic of secret languages is that no output syllable/morpheme may be fully identical to the input syllable/morpheme. This obfuscation is functionally motivated, of course: if it fails, then secrecy is not achieved! In secret languages, the role of markedness is limited to determining the solution: it does not cause the loss. The loss is instead caused by the essential property of these speech games: their secrecy, which I will instantiate as a constraint requiring that O≠I.

Changzhou has a secret language labeled by Chao (1931) as [məŋ-la], after the output from the input /ma/. Data can be found in Chao's paper, and analysis in Yip (1982) and Bao (1990), among others. The syllable is reduplicated, the second onset is replaced by [l], and the first rhyme by [əŋ]. I only discuss the onset change here. As in Chaoyang and Fuzhou, the change can be seen as a response to markedness pressures, but there is a crucial difference. Recall that in Chaoyang and Fuzhou, unmarked inputs undergo no further change. But in the language game that is not the case: even an unmarked input changes, even though any change is in the direction of increasing markedness. /laɣ/ becomes [ləŋ taɣ], not *[ləŋ laɣ]. The reason is clear: if the onset did not change, the second syllable of the output would be entirely identical to the input syllable, sacrificing the very secrecy these games are designed to achieve. The change is minimal: the next least-marked onset, /t/, is chosen instead, so the role of markedness is still clear. The tableau in (27) shows two different inputs to the grammar, /ma/ and /laɣ/, and the role of O≠I in forcing an increase in markedness. This situation in which one default segment is replaced by another slightly more marked one if and only if the output would otherwise contain the input intact is pervasive in secret languages.

(27)

/ma/	O ≠ I	*LABIAL	*CORONAL	*[-voice]
☞ a. məŋ la		*	*	
b. məŋ ta		*	*	*!
c. məŋ ma	*!	**		
/laɣ/				
☞ a. ləŋ taɣ			**	*
b. ləŋ laɣ	*!		**	
c. ləŋ paɣ		*!	*	*

6. Conflicting Markedness Constraints: Markedness Obscured

Markedness is a cover term for a collection of constraints, and they can conflict. For example, we know that voiced consonants are more marked crosslinguistically than voiceless ones, so *[+voice] » *[−voice], assuming binary features. Intervocalically, on the other hand, voiceless consonants may be more marked, so *V[−voice]V. If this outranks *[+voice], then the result is intervocalic voicing. A sufficiently rich interaction of such constraints can obscure the role of markedness in the final output, but it is there nonetheless, as we shall now see.

A particularly interesting secret language is found in Kunshan, a Wu dialect of Kiangsu. It is called the Mo-pa language by Chao. Some data are given in (28); I shall discuss only the onset changes here.

(28) Kunshan Mo pa secret language:

/təw/	to ləw	/vã/	vo pã
/k'ɛ/	k'o ɦɛ	/sya/	so tsya
/d'oŋ/	d'o loŋ	/nəw/	no təw
/tsa/	tso za	/ñən/	ño tɕən

The generalizations are as follows. In the second syllable, stops become voiced continuants, nasals and continuants become voiceless unaspirated stops, and place features are always unchanged. At first glance, this hardly looks like a markedness effect, since the new onset can have either value of the features [voice, cont]. Indeed, Yip (1982) analyzed the changes as dissimilation. I shall show that despite appearances this is also the result of markedness pressures, but here they are not just absolute, but also contextual (Steriade 1995): that is, a set of paradigmatic and syntagmatic markedness constraints. In combination with O≠I, they produce the desired results. An outline of the solution is given in (29); it is the various constraints on voicing and continuancy that select the preferred output. The general idea is that O≠I forces some change, but high-ranked IDENT-IO-PLACE blocks change in Place, leaving Manner as the only possible locus of change. The particular changes in manner are selected by the markedness constraints in conjunction with O≠I. Throughout, I focus on the second syllable, whose rhyme is identical to the input rhyme.

(29) The solution: an outline

Constraints	Effect
O ≠ I	Forces onset change
ONSET	Blocks onset deletion
IDENT-IO PLACE > > *PLACE	Blocks Place change
*MANNER > >IDENT-IO MANNER	Permits Manner change. *Manner is a cover-term for the following three constraints.
*[+vce, -cont]	Voiced stops are marked (Maddieson 1984)
*[+cont]	Stops preferred to fricatives (Maddieson 1984)
INTERSONVOICE: *[+son] [-voice] [+son]	Intervocalic voicing. Onset of second syllable always intervocalic. Stated in terms of [+son] as in Chaoyang.

The resistance of Place features to change is demonstrated in the tableau in (30). Throughout this section I mark only violations for the onset of the second syllable.

(30)

/vã/	O ≠ I	IDENT-PLACE	*LABIAL
☞ a. vo pã			*
b. vo vã	*!		*
c. vo lã		*!	

The tableaux in (31) and (32) show how the grammar selects among various candidates in which Place has been held constant.[6]

(31) Voiced fricative changes to voiceless stop:

/vã/	O ≠ I	*MANNER			IDENT-
		*[+vce, -cont]	INTERSON VOICE	*[+cont]	MANNER
☞ a. vo pã			*		*
b. vo vã	*!			*	
c. vo bã		*!			*
d. vo fã			*	*!	

(32) Voiceless stop/affricate changes to voiced fricative

/tsa/	O ≠ I	*MANNER			IDENT-
		*[+vce, -cont]	INTERSON VOICE	*[+cont]	MANNER
☞ a. tso za				*	*
b. tso tsa	*!		*		
c. tso dza	*!				
d. tso sa			*!	*	*

7. Conclusion

The segmental changes that accompany reduplication have been argued in this chapter to be a response to markedness pressures. Their various manifestations in different syllabic positions and in different types of word formation have been argued to be the result of both morphological pressures, such as O≠I, and conflicting markedness constraints. Finally, reduplication of the Chinese type has been argued to be self-compounding and to be the result of RHYME and ALLITERATE constraints that trigger repetition. Yip (in press) extends these proposals to other languages, pointing out that the reduplicant is nearly always adjacent to its base, so we get *pa-pati* or *pati-ti*, but not *pati-pa*. In Correspondence Theory this requires not only FAITH-BR, but also an anchoring constraint. In contrast, the ALLITERATE/RHYME approach builds adjacency into the constraints from the start. The matching portions may be made larger than a syllable by taking ALLITERATE and RHYME to be a family of constraints requiring rhyming feet as well as syllables. Undercopying can be achieved by ranking syllable structure markedness such as *COM-PLEXONSET, or NOCODA above ALLITERATE and RHYME. VC reduplication, a problem for many past theories, falls out simply as the case where the rhyming portion precedes the alliterating portion, instead of the more usual order. Some problems remain, principally overcopying of the kind that results in a heavy-syllable prefix, as in Ilokano *puspusa*, but the basic approach offers sufficient advantages beyond those laid out in this chapter that it is worth further research.

Notes

The original version of this chapter was written with the generous support of a grant from the Chiang Ching Kuo Foundation. This version was made possible by the hospitality of University College London during the academic years 1998–2000, and particularly of Neil Smith. It has been greatly improved by the comments of two reviewers for this volume, especially the editor, Linda Lombardi. I would also like to thank the organizers of the conference "On the Formal Way to Chinese Languages," Sze-wing Tang and Luther Liu; my research assistants, Li Xiao-guang, Sze-wing Tang, and Di Wu; and all the participants in the conference. This chapter has been greatly improved as a result of comments from the audience, especially Raung-fu Chung and Jie Zhang. All errors are of course my own.

1. In some languages ALLITERATE and RHYME refer to adjacent feet or words, rather than to syllables.
2. Other types of fixed segmentism, including the familiar *table-schmable* formation, are probably affixal. See Alderete et al. 1999 for discussion.
3. Of course, if voice is privative this constraint cannot be stated in this form – a problem I leave for future research!
4. In Taiwanese, a related Min dialect for which phonetic information is available, syllable-final stops voice intervocalically, but syllable-initial ones do not (Hsu 1996).
5. But see Lombardi (this volume) for another proposal.
6. Nothing yet blocks deletion of the second onset, plus epenthesis of an unmarked /l/: MAX-IO only ensures one surviving correspondent, and here we need two. ALLITERATE must be highly ranked and assessed gradiently (one * for each feature that differs), so that it can eliminate even noncorrespondent unmarked segments that do not alliterate in Place, as shown in (i).

(i)

v_1ã	ALLITERATE	IDENT-PLACE	*LABIAL
☞ a. v_1o p_1ã	**		**
b. v_1o t_1ã	***!	*	*
c. v_1o tã	***!		*

References

Alderete, John, Jill Beckman, Laura Benua, Amalia Gnanadesikan, John McCarthy, and Suzanne Urbanczyk. 1999. Reduplication with Fixed Segmentism. *Linguistic Inquiry* 30:327–364.

Bao, Zhi-ming. 1990. Fanqie Languages and Reduplication. *Linguistic Inquiry* 21:317–350.

Beckman, Jill. 1996. Positional Faithfulness and the Distribution of Phonological Features. Ms., University of Massachusetts at Amherst.

Chao, Y-R. 1931. Fanqie yu ba zhong (Eight Varieties of Languages Based on the Principle of Fanqie). *Bulletin of the Institute of History and Philology* (Academia Sinica) 2:320–354.

Clements, George N. 1988. The Role of the Sonority Cycle in Core Syllabification. *Working Papers of the Cornell Phonetics Laboratory* 2:1–68.

Clements, George N. 1997. Berber Syllabification: Derivations or Constraints? In *Derivations and Constraints in Phonology*, ed. I. Roca, pp. 289–330. Cambridge: Cambridge University Press.

Clements, George N., and Elizabeth Hume. 1995. The Internal Organization of Speech Sounds. In *The Handbook of Phonological Theory*, ed. John Goldsmith, pp. 245–306. Oxford: Blackwell.

Dell, Francois, and Mohammed El-Medlaoui. 1985. Syllabic Consonants and Syllabification in Tashlhiyt Berber. *Journal of African Languages and Linguistics* 7:105–130.

Gafos, D. 1998. Eliminating Long-Distance Consonantal Spreading. *Natural Language and Linguistic Theory* 16:223–278.

Hsu, Chai-Shune. 1996. Voicing Underspecification in Taiwanese Word-Final Consonants. Paper presented at the Annual Meeting of the Linguistic Society of America, San Diego, CA.

Inkelas, S., and C. Zoll. 1999. Reduplication as Double Stem Selection. Paper presented at Phonology 2000 Symposium, Harvard/MIT.

Maddieson, Ian. 1984. *Patterns of Sound*. Cambridge: Cambridge University Press.

Marantz, Alec. 1982. Re Reduplication. *Linguistic Inquiry* 13:483–545.

McCarthy, John, and Alan Prince. 1986. Prosodic Morphology. Ms., University of Massachusetts at Amherst, and Brandeis University.

McCarthy, John, and Alan Prince. 1995. Faithfulness and Reduplicative Identity. In *University of Massachusetts Occasional Papers in Linguistics 18: Papers in Optimality Theory*, pp. 249–384. Amherst, MA: GLSA. ROA 60-0000, http://ruccs.rutgers.edu/roa.html.

Moravcsik, Edith. 1978. Reduplicative Constructions. In *Universals of Human Language, Vol. 3: Word Structure*, ed. J. Greenberg, pp. 297–334. Stanford, CA: Stanford University Press.

Prince, Alan, and Paul Smolensky. 1993. *Optimality Theory: Constraint Interaction in Generative Grammar*. To appear, MIT Press.

Raimy, E., and W. Idsardi. 1997. A Minimalist Approach to Reduplication in Optimality Theory. In *Proceedings of NELS 27*, pp. 369–382. Amherst, MA: GLSA.

Sagart, L. 1996. Vestiges of Old Chinese Derivational Affixes in Modern Chinese Dialects. Paper presented at the First International Symposium on Synchronic and Diachronic Perspectives on the Grammar of Sinitic Languages, University of Melbourne.

Sherrard, Nicholas. 1997. Blending Theory – Correspondence Theory with Multiple Inputs. Handout for paper presented at Linguistics Association of Great Britain, University of Essex.

Steriade, D. 1995. Underspecification and Markedness. In *The Handbook of Phonological Theory*, ed. John Goldsmith, pp. 114–174. Oxford: Blackwell.

Struijke, C. 2000. Why Constraint Conflict can Disappear in Reduplication. ROA-385-01100, http://ruccs.rutgers.edu/roa.html.

Trigo, L. 1988. *On the Phonological Derivation and Behavior of Nasal Glides*. PhD dissertation, MIT.

Yip, M. 1982. Reduplication and CV Skeleta in Chinese Secret Languages. *Linguistic Inquiry* 13:637–662.

Yip, M. 1993. The Interaction of Align, Parse-Place, and Echo in Reduplication. Paper presented at Rutgers Optimality Workshop 1.

Yip, M. 1994. Morpheme-Level Features: Chaoyang Syllable Structure and Nasalization. ROA-81-0000, http://ruccs.rutgers.edu/roa.html.

Yip, M. 1997. Dialect Variation in Nasalization: Alignment or Duration? In *University of Maryland Working Papers in Linguistics*, ed. V. Miglio and B. Moren, vol. 5, pp. 176–200.

Yip, M. 1998. Identity Avoidance in Phonology and Morphology. In *Morphology and its Relation to Phonology and Syntax*, ed. S. Lapointe, D. Brentari, and P. Farrell, pp. 216–246. Stanford, CA: CSLI Publications.

Yip, M. In press. Reduplication and Alliteration and Rhyme. *Glot International* 4.

Yip, M. To appear. The Role of Markedness in Onset Change. In *Proceedings of "On the Formal Way to Chinese Languages,"* ed. C. S. Liu and S. W. Tang. Stanford, CA: CSLI Publications.

Zhang, Sheng Yu. 1979a. Chaoyang fangyan de chongdieshi [Reduplication in the Chaoyang Dialect]. *Zhongguoyuwen* 2:106–114.

Zhang, Sheng Yu. 1979b. Chaoyang fangyan de liandu biandiao [Tone Sandhi in the Chaoyang Dialect]. *Fangyan* 2:93–121.

Zhang, Sheng Yu. 1980. Chaoyang fangyan de liandu biandiao [Tone Sandhi in the Chaoyang Dialect (II)]. *Fangyan* 2:123–136.

Zhang, Sheng Yu. 1982. Chaoyang fangyan de xiangshengzi chongdie shi [The Reduplicated Onomatopoeic Particles in the Chaoyang Dialect]. *Fangyan* 3:181–182.

Zheng, Yi De. 1983. Fuzhou fangyan danyin dongci chongdie shi [Reduplication of Mono-Syllabic Verbs in the Fuzhou Dialect]. *Zhongguo Yuwen* 2:30–39.

PART III

THE STRUCTURE OF THE GRAMMAR:
APPROACHES TO OPACITY

8

Local Conjunction and Extending Sympathy Theory: OCP Effects in Yucatec Maya

HARUKA FUKAZAWA

1. Introduction

This chapter will show that the Obligatory Contour Principle (OCP) (Leben 1973; Goldsmith 1976) effect demonstrated by Yucatec Maya provides evidence for two recent theoretical proposals in Optimality Theory (OT) (Prince and Smolensky 1993). First, the triggering constraint of the phonological alternation will be shown to be a kind of double OCP by Local Conjunction of constraints (Smolensky 1993, 1995, 1997). Second, the output of stop-initial clusters requires the use of Sympathy Theory (McCarthy 1999).

In Yucatec Maya, when a stop is followed by a homorganic stop (or affricate), it becomes [h], and when an affricate is followed by a homorganic stop (or affricate), it spirantizes into a homorganic fricative (Straight 1976).

First, I discuss what triggers the alternation of stops or affricates. When two adjacent segments share only the same place features, the alternation is not observed. Also, when they share only the stop feature, the alternation does not take place. I therefore assert that no single OCP constraint such as OCP[Place], OCP[stop], and so on, forces the alternation. Rather, I claim that it is a local conjunction, OCP[Place]&OCP[stop], that triggers the stop alternation.[1,2] Second, I demonstrate the constraint interaction that accounts for why the segment does not delete but is replaced by [h] in the case of stop alternation. Third, I discuss the asymmetry between the affricate alternation and the stop alternation. While only the stop feature changes in the case of affricates, both the manner and place features change in the stop alternation. Adopting Sympathy Theory (McCarthy in 1999), and I argue that the asymmetry can be explained only when sympathetic faithfulness relations are allowed in the grammar.

2. Yucatec Maya Consonant Clusters

This section presents the Yucatec Maya data. The data in (1) show phonological alternations observed in consonant clusters in the language.

(1) **Yucatec Maya** (Straight 1976):

      a. taaŋ **k p**ak'ik **k k**ool   → taaŋ **k p**ak'ik **h k**ool
                                        "we're planting our clearing."
      b. tun koli**k k'**aaš   → tun koli**h k'**aaš
                                         "he's clearing bush"
      c. leʔ iŋ w o**t č**o   → leʔ iŋ w o**h č**o
                                        "that house of mine/my house there"
      d. ʔu**c t** iŋ w ič   → ʔu**s t** iŋ w ič
                                        "I like it (lit. goodness is at my eye)."
      e. ʔu k'áat u kaŋ kàa**s**teyàanoh   → ʔu k'áat u kaŋ kàa**s**teyàanoh
                                        "He wants to learn Spanish."

Let us summarize what emerges from these data as follows:[3]

1) A stop becomes [h] before a homorganic stop or affricate (1a–c);[4]
2) An affricate becomes a homorganic fricative before a homorganic
    stop or affricate (1d);
3) A stop or an affricate preserves its original form before a nonhom-
    organic stop or affricate (1a);
4) A fricative preserves its original form before a homorganic stop (1e).

In the above data, "homorganic" refers only to major place feature.
Coronal obstruents count as homorganic regardless of their value for
[anterior]. Also, it does not matter whether the consonants differ in
glottalization (k or k').

3. An Analysis within the OT Framework

3.1. An Analysis with Single Constraints Does Not Work

This section first considers analyses that rank only single constraints and
shows why they do not work. Then, an analysis using local conjunction
is introduced, making clear why local conjunction is necessary in the
analysis of the Yucatec data.

    As I pointed out in Section 1, two kinds of OCP effects must be con-
sidered in Yucatec: One is on the [Place] feature, and the other is on the
[stop] feature. I also claimed that deletion of the [stop] feature is
observed as the result of the OCP. Within the OT framework, therefore,

there are at least three kinds of constraints interacting here: OCP[Place], OCP[stop] and MAX[stop].

Since we actually observe the effects of the OCP, we must assume that OCP constraints are relatively high ranked in this language. They must be satisfied at the expense of violating some lower-ranked constraint(s). Since one of the [stop] features deletes, it is assumed that the violated lower-ranked constraint is a featural faithfulness constraint for [stop], namely, MAX[stop]. Another constraint, MAX[Place] refers to the feature class Place following Padgett (1995), and so targets any subset of the class Place, such as Lab or Dor.

As the data in (1) showed, when a stop is followed by a homorganic stop, the first stop becomes [h].[5] For example, /**k** kool/ becomes [**h** kool] (1a). Therefore, I assume the ranking in (2).

(2)   OCP[Place], OCP[stop] >> MAX[Place], MAX[stop]

Let us examine these data in the tableau in (3).

(3) A stop and a homorganic stop:[6]

/ **k** kool/	OCP[Place]	OCP[stop]	MAX[Place]	MAX[stop]
☞ a. **h** kool			*	*
b. **k** kool	*!	*!		

Candidate (b), in which no alternation is observed, violates both of the two higher-ranked constraints, namely, OCP[Place] and OCP[stop]. Since both of them are high ranked, the violation of only one of them is enough for the candidate to lose. On the other hand, candidate (a), in which the alternation is observed, violates neither OCP[Place] nor OCP[stop]; therefore, it wins. The ranking in (2) correctly provides the optimal candidate. From tableau (3), we conclude that at least one of the OCPs must outrank MAX[Place] and MAX[stop] to account for the correct output.

Let us now look at other data: a stop and a nonhomorganic stop. In this sequence, no phonological alternation is observed. Therefore, we must assume that OCP[stop] is lower ranked than the faithfulness constraint. However, the ranking given in tableau (3) produces the incorrect result, as shown in (4). Candidate (b), in which no alternation is observed, incorrectly loses due to the fatal violation of OCP[stop], even though this is the actual output. From this tableau, we must conclude that OCP[stop] must be lower ranked than either MAX[Place] or MAX[stop].

*(4) A stop and a nonhomorganic stop:

/ **k** pak'ik/	OCP[Place]	OCP[stop]	MAX[Place]	MAX[stop]
*☞a. **h** pak'ik			*	*
b. **k** pak'ik		*!		

Let us examine one more example: a fricative and a homorganic stop. In this sequence, no phonological alternation is observed, either. Therefore, we must conclude that OCP[Place] does not outrank the faithfulness constraints; see (5). Again, candidate (b), in which no phonological alternation is observed, incorrectly loses due to the fatal violation of OCP[Place].

*(5) A fricative and a homorganic stop:

/kàas teyàanoh/	OCP[Place]	OCP[stop]	MAX[Place]	MAX[stop]
*☞ a. kàahteyàanoh			*	
b. kàasteyàanoh	*!			

We have a conclusion from tableau (3) that at least one of the OCPs should outrank MAX[Place] and MAX[stop], as stated in (6).

(6) Tableau (3) requires:

      Either (a)   OCP[Place] >> MAX[Place], MAX[stop]

      Or   (b)   OCP[stop] >> MAX[Place], MAX[stop]

However, OCP[stop] cannot outrank the faithfulness constraints based on (4); see (7).

(7) Tableau (4) requires:

               MAX[Place], MAX[stop] >> OCP[stop]

Finally, OCP[Place] cannot outrank the faithfulness constraint based on tableau (5); see (8). Thus, we must conclude that there is no valid ranking here to explain all the data above.

(8) Tableau (5) requires:

               MAX[Place], MAX[stop] >> OCP[Place]

Yucatec spirantization is not accounted for by ranking the individual constraints. This is because OCP[Place] as well as OCP[stop] can be violated singly, but not both at the same time. With the ranking of the individual constraints separately, we cannot obtain the correct analysis. In the next section, I will propose a constraint conjunction, OCP[Place]&OCP[stop], and discuss why the conjunction is necessary in the analysis.

3.2. Local Conjunction

Within the OT framework, different constraint rankings account for the different grammars in the world's languages. There are, however, some phonological phenomena that cannot be explained by the ranking of single constraints. These include Southern Palestinian Arabic RTR phenomena (McCarthy 1997), stress assignment in Diyari (Hewitt and Crowhurst 1996),[7] vowel length phenomena in the Wellagga dialect of Oromo (Alderete 1997), vowel raising phenomena in Nzɛbi (Kirchner 1996), and front vowel raising in the Northern Mantuan Italian dialect (Miglio 1999). In such cases, each researcher has reported that analyses of the data are possible only by introducing Local Conjunction.

Local Conjunction is defined as a combination of two single lower-ranked constraints that produces a violation of a higher one (Smolensky 1993, 1995, 1997). If constraint A and constraint B are each ranked lower than constraint C, a candidate can violate either of them so as to satisfy C, as in (9).

(9)   C >> A, B.

However, if a candidate violates both A and B, the conjunction of these two violations may force the violation of constraint C, as in (10).

(10)   A&B >> C >> A, B

(10) indicates that A and B are each separately violable so as to satisfy the higher-ranked constraint C; however, both of them are not violable at the same time – i.e., in the same domain.

Although several studies have focused on local conjunction, its scope and definition are still under debate. If local conjunction is a type of constraint, it must be in Universal Grammar (UG). However, if it is UG, it must be crosslinguistically valid. A question now arises: Are all possible local conjunctions truly in UG? If so, UG grows extremely large.

Fukazawa and Miglio (1998) propose that what is in UG is the possibility of local conjunction – in other words, the "&" operator for conjunction. However, the choice of which two constraints to be conjoined is language-specific. This proposal reduces the size of UG and seems to be corroborated by the crosslinguistic rarity of each particular type of local conjunction. Because of the nature of local conjunction, as the union of two lower-ranked constraints overriding hierarchically higher-ranked ones, it should be considered a last-resort option. In other words,

Local Conjunction should come into play only when every ranking of single constraints fails to explain the data in a language.

However, it seems necessary to restrict local conjunction even further. If any constraint can be conjoined with any other, then even the language-specific grammar becomes extremely unrestricted. Smolensky (1993, 1995, 1997) has pointed out one restriction of local conjunction: locality must be respected in Local Conjunction. The two constraints to be conjoined must be violated in the same specified domain at the same time. This is based upon the idea that constraint interaction is stronger locally than nonlocally.

This is still not a restriction on the type of constraints that may be conjoined. There must also be some strict control on the nature of the constraints to be conjoined. McCarthy (1997) suggests that the two constraints to be conjoined must be phonetically conjoinable. However, when we consider the constraints from the perspective of only the articulatory view, there might be several examples that are categorized into phonetically motivated/nonmotivated constraints. On the other hand, when we take the perceptual view into consideration, we might be able to consider all the constraints phonetically motivated. Thus, Fukazawa and Miglio (1998) make it clear that it is necessary to introduce more specific restrictions on conjunction and they propose that only two constraints belonging to the same constraint family[8] are conjoinable. This proposal is supported by the examination of several previous analyses of local conjunction.

In summary, whenever data may be analyzed with local conjunction, the following points should be taken into consideration:

1. Motivation: the ranking of single constraints fail to produce the correct analysis;
2. Restrictions: (a) locality must be respected;
   (b) phonetic conjoinability may be respected;
   (c) two constraints to be conjoined must belong to the SAME CONSTRAINT FAMILY.

On the basis of the idea of Local Conjunction, I will propose a local conjunction, OCP[Place] & OCP[stop], and discuss its validity and necessity in the analysis of Yucatec Maya.

3.3. OCP[Place] & OCP[stop]

In this section, I reexamine the data discussed earlier using local conjunction. The revised ranking I propose is given in (11).

(11)   OCP[Place]&OCP[stop]
```
                   _____|_____
                   |               |
              MAX[Place]    MAX[stop]
                   |_____|
                   _____|_____
                   |               |
              OCP[Place]     OCP[stop]
```

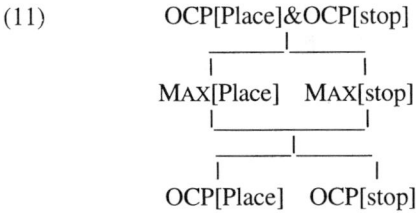

With this ranking, let us reexamine the data in tableaux (3), (4), and (5).

(3') A stop and a homorganic stop (revised version of tableau (3)):

/ k kool/	OCP[Place] &OCP[stop]	MAX[Place]	MAX[stop]
☞ a. **h kool**		*	*
b. **k kool**	*!		

In (3'), candidate (b) violates the conjunction because it violates both of the OCPs. This is a fatal violation. Thus, candidate (a) correctly wins. Candidate (b) also violates each single OCP constraint; however, this does not matter, since each single OCP[Place] or OCP[stop] is not ranked highly enough to be active, as shown in the tableau in (12).

(12)

/ k kool/	OCP[Place]& OCP[stop]	MAX [Place]	MAX [stop]	OCP [Place]	OCP [stop]
☞ a. **h kool**		*	*		
b. **k kool**	*!			*	*

Next, let us reexamine the sequence of stop and a nonhomorganic stop. In (4'), candidate (b) does not violate the conjunction, since it violates only OCP[stop]. Thus, it correctly wins. The violation of the single OCP[stop] does not matter, since OCP[stop] is lower ranked than the MAX[F] constraints. We can obtain the correct output by introducing the conjunction in (4') in contrast to *(4). A similar result is achieved with a sequence of a fricative and a homorganic stop, as shown in (5'). Candidate (b) in this tableau does not violate the conjunction, because it violates only OCP[Place]. Thus, candidate (b) is correctly optimal. Again, the violation of single OCP[Place] does not matter, since it is lower ranked than the two MAX[F] constraints.

(4') A stop and a non-homorganic stop (revised version of tableau *(4)):

/ k pak'ik/	OCP[Place]& OCP[stop]	MAX [Place]	MAX [stop]	OCP [Place]	OCP [stop]
a. **h pak'ik**		*!	*!		
☞ b. **k pak'ik**					*

(5') A fricative and a homorganic stop (revised version of tableau *(5):

/kàas teyàanoh/	OCP[Place]& OCP[stop]	MAX [Place]	MAX [stop]	OCP [Place]	OCP [stop]
a. kàahteyàanoh		*!			
☞ b. kàasteyàanoh				*	

We have observed that neither of the two single OCP constraints should be higher ranked than faithfulness constraints in the language. Nevertheless, some constraint for the OCP effect must account for the attested phonological alternation. I have therefore proposed that OCP[Place]&OCP[stop] is necessary to explain the Yucatec data.

3.4. How to Satisfy the Conjunction: The Ranking in Yucatec Maya

In Yucatec, the higher-ranked constraint that has to be satisfied is not a single OCP constraint (e.g., OCP[Place] or OCP[stop]), but a conjunction OCP[Place]&OCP[stop]. The conjunction is satisfied if either OCP[Place] or OCP[stop] is respected. To avoid changing both features, yet avoid a violation of the local conjunction, which single OCP should be satisfied?

I claim that only OCP[stop] is satisfied to satisfy the conjunction, and that OCP[Place] is violated. This claim is supported by the affricate alternation. In the affricate alternation, what is changed is not the Place feature but the manner feature. I therefore conclude that MAX[Place] must be satisfied.

This claim implies the following two points. One is that OCP[stop] outranks MAX[stop], which gives rise to deletion of the [stop] feature. The other is that MAX[Place] outranks OCP[Place], which prohibits deleting the Place feature.

Let us summarize the claim above with the ranking of these four constraints as in (13).

(13)   OCP[Place]&OCP[stop]
                    _____|_____
                    | |
            MAX[Place]   OCP[stop]
                | |
            OCP[Place]   MAX[stop]

First, the ranking MAX[Place] » OCP[Place] will be examined. In the case of the affricate alternation, only the manner feature is changed, and the place feature is kept, resulting in the violation of OCP[Place]. Therefore, MAX[Place] outranks OCP[Place], as in (14). Due to the higher-ranked constraint MAX[Place], candidate (14b) wins.

(14) MAX[Place] >> OCP[Place]:

/ʔuc t /	OCP[Place] &OCP[stop]	MAX[Place]	OCP[Place]
a. ʔuc t	*!		
☞ b. ʔus t			*
c. ʔuh t		*!	

Next, the ranking OCP[stop] » MAX[stop] will be examined. As tableau (15) shows, a stop becomes [h] rather than [ʔ] to satisfy the conjunction. This indicates that OCP[stop] must be satisfied at the expense of violating MAX[stop]. The ranking in (15) states that two stop features cannot be adjacent, to satisfy OCP[stop]; therefore, MAX[stop] is violated, resulting in MAX[stop] alternation. The winning candidate (a) actually carries the Place feature change. However, as I already pointed out in connection with (14), the faithfulness constraint for the place feature, MAX[Place], cannot be demoted. Thus, in order to explain the manner feature change in (15), there must be some other constraint interaction. I will deal with this issue by introducing Sympathy Theory in Section 4.

(15) OCP[stop] >> MAX[stop]:

/ k kool/	OCP[Place] &OCP[stop]	OCP[stop]	MAX[stop]
☞ a. h kool			*
b. ʔ kool		*!	
c. k kool	*!		

Thus, (14) and (15) make it clear that the feature [stop] deletes due to the constraints OCP[Place]&OCP[stop], and OCP[stop], which is ranked high enough to be active, while OCP[Place] is not ranked high enough to be active, as shown in (13).

Before going on, I must discuss the ranking of MAX[Place] in this language. I claim that MAX[Place] is not only higher ranked than OCP[Place] but also than the markedness constraints for the place feature. By adding the pharyngeal place feature, Lombardi (this volume) extends the Universal Hierarchy of the markedness constraint for the place features proposed by Prince and Smolensky (1993): *Lab, *Dor » *Cor » *Phar. If the markedness constraints for the place feature outranked the faithfulness constraint, the candidate with the most unmarked Place feature should always be optimal regardless of the input. In other words, all consonants should become pharyngeal; see (16).

*(16) *Lab, *Dor >> *Cor >> *Phar >> MAX[Place]:

/ʔuc t /	*Lab / *Dor	*Cor	*Phar	MAX[Place]
a. ʔus t		*!		
*☞b. ʔuh t			*	*

With this ranking, candidate (b) incorrectly wins. To obtain the correct optimal candidate, the constraints should be re-ranked as in (17).

(17) MAX[Place] >> *Lab, *Dor >> *Cor >> *Phar:

/ʔuc t /	MAX[Place]	*Lab / *Dor	*Cor	*Phar
☞a. ʔus t			*	
b. ʔuh t	*!			*

Thus, MAX[Place] must outrank the markedness constraint to account for the correct output. If MAX[Place] is highly ranked, a question immediately arises about changing the place feature of the stop segment in the sequence of a stop and a homorganic stop (or affricate). I will argue that changing the place feature of the stop is derived from the interaction of other constraints. This will be discussed in detail in Section 4.

I will reanalyze the data examined in (3′), (4′), and (5′) with the revised ranking in (13) in this section, beginning with (4′). As tableau (4″a) shows, the ranking in (13) will not provide the optimal candidate. Violation of MAX[stop] does not penalize candidate (4″a) unless OCP[stop] and MAX[Place] are tied. However, there is no evidence that they are. Thus, I conclude that another ranking MAX[Place] » OCP[stop] is necessary to account for the correct output in this tableau.

*(4″a) Wrong result: a stop and a nonhomorganic stop

/ k pak'ik/	OCP[Place] &OCP[stop]	OCP [stop]	MAX [Place]	OCP [Place]	MAX [stop]
*☞a. hpak'ik			*		*
b. kpak'ik		*!			

Let us reanalyze this tableau with the new ranking in (4″b).

(4″b) A stop and a nonhomorganic stop:

/ k pak'ik/	OCP[Place] &OCP[stop]	MAX [Place]	OCP [stop]	OCP [Place]	MAX [stop]
a. hpak'ik		*!			*
☞ b. kpak'ik			*		

Since MAX[Place] outranks OCP[stop], candidate (b) correctly wins. (18) gives the resulting revised version of (13) with the ranking MAX[Place] »

OCP[stop]. The ranking in (18) makes clear that the conjunction should be satisfied, and that keeping the place feature is better than keeping the manner feature.

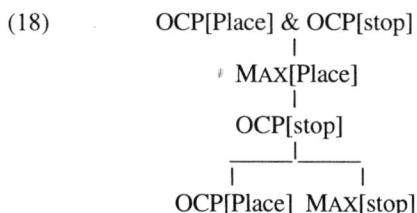

(18) OCP[Place] & OCP[stop]
                    |
          ˒ MAX[Place]
                    |
            OCP[stop]
        _____|_____
        | |
    OCP[Place]   MAX[stop]

In Yucatec Maya, the stop in the sequence does not delete even after deletion of the feature [stop]. Instead, it spirantizes into a fricative. Therefore, we assume that both HAVEMANNER and MAX-IO should be satisfied at the expense of violating some lower-ranked constraint – specifically, DEP[cont], stated in (19).

(19) (a) HAVEMANNER : Every segment must bear some manner feature.

(b) DEP[cont]: An output continuant feature must have an input correspondent.

To satisfy HAVEMANNER without violating MAX-IO, some manner feature, namely, [cont] must be inserted. I conclude, therefore, that DEP[cont] is lower ranked than HAVEMANNER or MAX-IO in Yucatec Maya. Let us observe how the ranking accounts for the actual data.

(20) A stop and a homorganic stop (affricate):

/ ot čo /	HAVEMANNER	MAX-IO	DEP[cont]
a.[9] ot čo ⍓ [stop]	*!		
b. o čo		*!	
☞ c. oh čo			*

Tableau (20) indicates that spirantization is preferred to deletion of the entire segment, giving the ranking in (21).

(21) The ranking for spirantization:

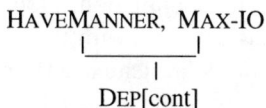

    HAVEMANNER, MAX-IO
     |_____|
           |
       DEP[cont]

Before discussing the interaction of other constraints, let us revise the ranking provided in (18) by adding the new ranking in (22).

(22) Ranking of constraints in Yucatec Maya (revised version of (18)):

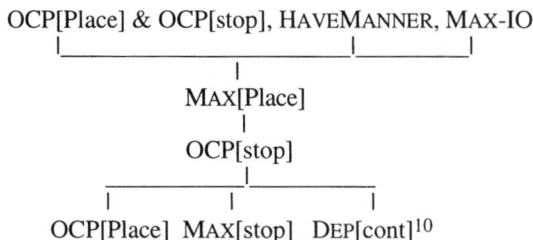

OCP[Place] & OCP[stop], HaveManner, Max-IO
|_____|_____|_____|
|
MAX[Place]
|
OCP[stop]
_____|_____
| | |
OCP[Place]   Max[stop]   Dep[cont][10]

In order to make it clear that HaveManner and Max-IO outrank Max[Place], and that Dep[cont] is lower ranked than OCP[stop], we should reanalyze spirantization with this new ranking, as shown in (23).[11]

(23) Spirantization of a stop in a homorganic cluster:

/ot čo /	OCP[pl.] & OCP[stop]	HAVE MANNER	MAX IO	MAX [Pl.]	OCP [stop]	OCP [Pl.]	MAX [stop]	DEP [cont]
a. ot čo	*!				*	*		
☞b oh čo				*			*	*
c. o čo			*!					
d. ot čo ✲ [stop]		*!				*	*	
e. oʔ čo				*	*!			

In (23), candidate (a) loses due to a violation of the conjunction. Violation of HaveManner penalizes candidate (d). Candidate (c) shows why deletion of the segment is impossible. Since violation of Max-IO penalizes (c), Max-IO must outrank Max[Place]. Candidate (e) illustrates why the stop becomes not the glottal stop but the glottal fricative. OCP[stop] violation penalizes this candidate. This indicates that OCP[stop] outranks Dep[cont]. Consequently, candidate (b), in which the stop spirantizes into a pharyngeal fricative, becomes optimal.

Let us next examine spirantization of an affricate in a homorganic sequence. Candidate (e) in (24) shows that hardening of the affricate will not help the situation, since it still violates the conjunction. Violation of Max-IO penalizes candidate (d). Thus, candidate (b), with the affricate spirantizing into the homorganic fricative, wins. Tableaux (23) and (24) are full explanations of the ranking of the constraints in (22). In Yucatec

Maya, keeping the input manner feature is not important in contrast to keeping the place feature due to the ranking.

(24) Spirantization of an affricate in a homorganic cluster:

/ʔuc t /	OCP[pl.] & OCP[stop]	HAVE MANNER	MAX IO	MAX [Pl.]	OCP [stop]	OCP [Pl.]	MAX [stop]	DEP [cont]
a.ʔuc t	*!				*	*		
☞ b.ʔus t						*	*	
c.ʔuh t				*!		*		
d.ʔu t			*!					
e.ʔut t	*!				*	*		

Let us summarize what we have observed so far. First, in the sequences of a stop and a nonhomorganic stop and of a fricative and a homorganic stop, no phonological alternation is observed. This is because the sequences themselves are well-formed given the ranking in (22). They do not violate the conjunction; therefore, the alternation is not triggered. Second, a stop or an affricate in a homorganic cluster would result in the violation of the higher-ranked local conjunction by violating two of the OCPs for the place and the manner features. Hence, the alternation takes place so as to satisfy the conjunction. Third, to satisfy the conjunction, one of the two members of the conjunction, OCP[stop], is satisfied. Hence, both a stop and an affricate spirantize by deleting the feature [stop], resulting in a violation of MAX[stop]. While only deleting the feature [stop] takes place in the affricate alternation, the [cont] feature is inserted in the stop alternation as well as the [stop] feature deletion. This is because the affricate originally bears the [cont] feature, which the stop does not.

In Yucatec Maya, the manner feature change is preferred to the place feature change. In other words, there is no need to change the place feature in Yucatec Maya grammar according to the ranking obtained so far. Nevertheless, the place feature as well as manner feature change in the stop alternation.

In the next section, I consider why the place feature changes in the case of stop alternation even though the ranking indicates that the stop alternation is not necessary. I discuss the asymmetry between the alternation of the stop and that of the affricate in the homorganic sequence. The stop in the homorganic sequence turns not into a homorganic fricative but into a pharyngeal fricative, while the affricate becomes a homorganic fricative. I claim that this asymmetry is derived from a new type of faithfulness relationship among candidates – Sympathy Theory (McCarthy 1999).

4. A Sympathy Theoretic Account of the Yucatec Alternation: /t/ → [h]

4.1. The Issue

In Section 3, the necessity of the conjunction, the way to satisfy the conjunction, and the necessity of introducing positional featural faithfulness were discussed. Now, we return to the problem pointed out in Section 3.4: why does the place feature of the stop in the sequence change to [phar] in spite of the highly ranked constraint, MAX[Place]?

We have not encountered any problems in the analysis of the stop alternation in the previous sections. This is because we have not discussed a candidate in which only the manner feature changes, and the place feature does not. In this section, I add this candidate to make it clear that a problem remains, and that the ranking given in Section 3.4 cannot account for the change in place.

First, let us observe why the ranking in (22) fails to account for the phenomenon with the additional candidate. The actual optimal candidate is (c). However, the ranking assumed so far incorrectly allows candidate (b) to win. If the ranking of MAX[Place] and OCP[Place] were reversed, candidate (c) would win. However, as already stated in Section 3.4, this reversal is impossible, because in the case of the affricate alternation, the place feature is kept, and the manner feature deletes.

*(25) A sequence of stop and a homorganic stop (or an affricate):

	/ ot čo /	OCP[Place] &OCP[stop]	MAX [Place]	OCP [stop]	OCP [Place]	MAX [stop]
a.	ot čo	*!		*	*	
*☞ b.	os čo				*	*
c.	oh čo		*!			*
d.	oʔ čo		*!	*		

Also, if this alternation were forced by the universal markedness hierarchy (*Lab, *Dor » *Cor » Phar), thus resulting in the emergence of unmarked structure, then candidate (c) would win, too. However, the analysis in Section 3.4 has already demonstrated that this argument is not possible, because MAX[Place] outranks the markedness constraints for the place features. In this language, not all consonants become pharyngeal.

In order to solve this problem, I introduce Sympathy Theory in the next section to discuss further constraint interactions.

4.2. Sympathy Theory

McCarthy (1999) proposes Sympathy Theory to solve the opacity problem in OT. Opacity means that a surface form is not what we expect it to be. Therefore, in order to explain the unexpected situation, we need some additional mechanism.

In rule-based theory, opacity is derived from a counterbleeding or counterfeeding rule order. In other words, the extra rule ordering gives rise to opacity. For example, in the analysis of Tiberian Hebrew in a rule-based theory, we observe a counterbleeding relation between the two rules, epenthesis in final clusters and ʔ-deletion in coda, as shown in (26). The order of the application of the two rules is crucial here. If we applied the ʔ-deletion rule first, then, the epenthesis rule would not apply; hence, the surface form would be [deš]. Thus, the counterbleeding rule order is inevitable to account for why the surface representation is not [deš], but [dešə].

(26)　　UR　　　　/dešʔ/

　　　　epenthesis　dešəʔ

　　　　ʔ-deletion　dešə

　　　　SR　　　　[dešə]

A case such as this leads to a problem when we analyze it in parallelist OT. Since a grammar consists of only the input and the output in OT, a simple constraint ranking cannot account for the phenomenon. Two constraint rankings of MAX-IO » DEP-IO and CodaCond » MAX-IO describe the phenomena of epenthesis in final clusters and ʔ-deletion in coda, respectively. Therefore, we establish one constraint ranking, CodaCond » MAX-IO » DEP-IO here. However, the ranking cannot produce the correct output as the tableau in (27) shows. Regardless of ranking, the actual output (a) cannot be a better candidate than the wrong winner (b) in (27), since (b) has a subset of the marks of (a). We cannot explain the actual output on the basis of the given constraint ranking.

(27)　　CodaCond >> MAX-IO >> DEP-IO

/dešʔ/	CodaCond	MAX-IO	DEP-IO
(☞) a.　dešə		*	*!
*☞ b.　deš		*	
c.　　dešəʔ	*!		

Sympathy Theory (McCarthy 1999) proposes that there is a new type of constraint interaction based on a faithfulness relationship between the optimal candidate and one of the failed candidates. When a failed candidate is the most harmonic with respect to some constraint, but cannot win due to a violation of a higher-ranked constraint, it can still allow another candidate, which is the most faithful to it in terms of some other constraint, to win through "sympathy." This nonoptimal, yet influential candidate is called the sympathy candidate. Phonological opacity is derived from such constraint interactions within OT since we never observe the sympathy candidate in the input or in the output.

We need Sympathy Theory to obtain the correct analysis of Tiberian Hebrew, because it is an instance of phonological opacity. A constraint, Aligh-R IO (Root, σ)[12] plays a crucial role to designate the sympathy candidate as the tableau in (28) shows. The sympathy candidate is indicated by ❀. Candidate (c) is the most harmonic candidate in terms of Aligh-R IO (Root, σ). However, it cannot be the optimal candidate due to its violation of the higher-ranked CodaCond constraint. Hence, it is designated as the sympathy candidate to let another candidate win. The opaque output is faithful to the sympathy candidate.

(28)   Designation of sympathy candidate (McCarthy 1999):

/dešʔ/	CodaCond	Max-IO	Dep-IO	Align-R $_{IO}$❀ (Root, σ)
opaque ☞ a. dešə		*	*	*
transparent ← b. deš		*		*
sympathetic ❀ c. dešəʔ	*!		*	

It is necessary to introduce an additional constraint, Max-❀O, to clarify how the sympathy candidate exerts its influence. This new constraint, stated in (29), is a kind of segmental faithfulness constraint which forces identity between the sympathy candidate and the output. McCarthy (1999) calls such a constraint a sympathy constraint. This sympathy constraint, Max-❀O, outranks Dep-IO in the language. In tableau (30), candidate (a) correctly wins since it best-satisfies the entire constraint ranking, including the sympathy constraint.

(29)   Max-❀O: every segment in the sympathy candidate (❀) should have a

correspondent in the output (O).

(30)　Constraint interaction with sympathy:

/dešʔ/	CodaCond	MAX-IO	MAX-❀O	DEP-IO	Align-R$_{IO}$❀ (Root, σ)
opaque ☞a. dešə		*	*	*	*
transparent ← b. deš		*	**!		*
sympathetic ❀c. dešə?	*!			*	

Thus, McCarthy (1999) succeeds in solving the opacity problem in OT with Sympathy Theory. All the examples that he provides are standard instances of the opacity problems in OT which are derived by serial derivation in rule-based theory.

Ito and Mester (1997) suggest that we should consider the conception of phonological opacity in parallelist OT. If Sympathy Theory is a fully generalized theory, then it must also explain other cases of opacity that are not just residual problems from a rule-based theory. They indicate in their analysis of German truncation that Sympathy Theory could account for all the grammars where some failed candidate, which is realized neither in the input nor in the output, plays an important role. The case of German that Ito and Mester analyze is not an opacity case derived by serial derivation but a type of prosodic morphological size restriction previously analyzed via Prosodic Circumscription (McCarthy and Prince 1990).

Building on Ito and Mester's suggestion, I propose that Sympathy Theory can be extended to account for an opaque phenomenon in OT that is not derived by serial derivation in rule-based theory. The evidence for my claim comes from a new analysis that focuses on the Yucatec Maya stop alternation discussed in this chapter. Neither rule-based theory nor OT has succeeded in elucidating this alternation. I claim that the alternation is also derived from phonological opacity in OT; hence, only OT with Sympathy Theory can lead to the correct analysis of the language.

4.3. Rule-Based and Bare OT Accounts of the Stop Alternation

The Yucatec stop alternation is not a standard case of opacity like those discussed by McCarthy (1999). The opacity cases he deals with are well explained in rule-based analyses. The intermediate stages in a serial derivation play crucial roles in accounting for such cases. As noted earlier, problems for those cases appear when we try to explain the data in parallelist OT, because we have only the input and the output. That is why McCarthy proposes Sympathy Theory. By contrast, the Yucatec stop alternation cannot be explained based on serial derivational analyses in rule-based theory, because no well-motivated rule can account for the change of the intermediate stage into the surface form.

Previous autosegmental analyses such as McCarthy (1988) and Lombardi (1990a,b) argue that the Yucatec alternation is OCP-motivated debuccalization. However, one major problem with those approaches is that they fail to explain why /t.t/ turns into [h.t], not [ʔ.t] as expected if debuccalization were the result of changing the place feature.

As indicated in Section 3.4, the alternation from /t.t/ into [h.t] involves two types of phonological changes: the place feature change and the manner feature change. [t] is both [stop] and [coronal], while [h] is [continuant] and [pharyngeal] (Lombardi 1990a,b). Therefore, there are two possible patterns in this stop alternation depending on the order of rule application, as shown in (31).

(31)   Changing place and manner features:

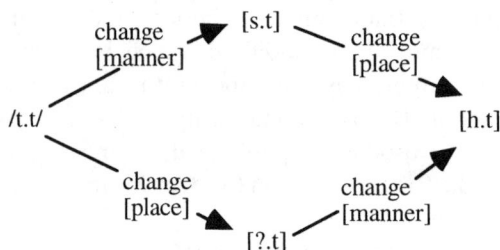

Now, a question arises. Since both [s.t] and [ʔ.t] in the intermediate stages of the alternations are permissible surface sequences in Yucatec Maya, we cannot justify the rules that turn /s.t/ into [h.t] or those that turn [ʔ.t] into [h.t]. Thus, a rule-based theory cannot account for the data without stipulating a special rule to change both the place and manner features simultaneously.[13]

This section has made it clear that the Yucatec stop alternation is not a standard case of opacity as described by McCarthy (1999). The intermediate stages in serial derivation play a crucial role in accounting for such cases. The problems for these cases appear when we try to explain the data in parallelist OT, because we have only the input and the output to refer to. On the other hand, the Yucatec stop alternation cannot be explained via a serial derivation within a rule-based theory because no rule exists that can account for the alternation from the intermediate stage to the surface form.

I have already proposed that a ranking MAX[Place], OCP[stop] »
MAX[stop], OCP[Place] is found in the language. The affricate alternation is the evidence for the fact that MAX[Place] is highly ranked. In the
sequence of an affricate and a stop, the affricate becomes not a pharyngeal fricative but a homorganic fricative. That is why the alternation is
changing the manner feature rather than changing the stop feature.
Therefore, I assume that MAX[Place] is higher ranked than MAX[stop],
as shown in (32). I have also determined the ranking MAX[Place] »
OCP[stop] in the analysis of the sequence of a stop and a nonhomorganic stop sequence. MAX[Place] must be higher ranked than OCP[stop]
to account for the correct winner. In (33), candidate (a) loses due to its
fatal violation of MAX[Place].

(32)   MAX[Place], OCP[stop] >>MAX[stop], OCP[Place]:

/ʔuc t /	OCP[Place] &OCP[stop]	MAX [Place]	OCP [stop]	MAX [stop]	OCP [Place]
a. ʔuc t	*!		*		*
☞ b. ʔus t				*	*
c. ʔuh t	*!			*	

(33) A stop and a nonhomorganic stop:

/k pak'ik/	OCP[Place] &OCP[stop]	MAX [Place]	OCP [stop]	OCP [Place]	MAX [stop]
a. hpak'ik		*!			*
☞ b. kpak'ik			*		

The relevant part of the ranking that I have established for the
language so far is summarized in (34).

(34)   Constraint Ranking in Yucatec Maya:

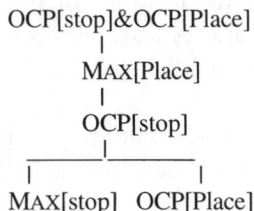

OCP[stop]&OCP[Place]
|
MAX[Place]
|
OCP[stop]
|
MAX[stop]   OCP[Place]

Since the ranking in (34) is established, we must assume that the stop
alternation is also the result of keeping the place feature and changing
only the manner feature due to its satisfaction of MAX[Place] and to its

violation of MAX[stop]. The ranking in (34) specifically predicts that the manner feature will change, but the place feature will not. However, we must recall the asymmetry between the affricate and the stop alternations illustrated in Section 3.4. In the affricate case, we observe that only the manner feature changes, while the change of the place feature, as well as that of the manner feature, is observed in the stop alternation, as (31) illustrates. The ranking in (34) cannot account for the asymmetry. As tableau (35) shows, the actual output, candidate (d), loses to candidate (c). With this ranking, the stop alternation should result in changing the manner feature like the affricate case.

(35) Stop alternation in the sequence of a stop and a homorganic stop (affricate):

	/ot. čo/	OCP[Place] & OCP[stop]	MAX [Place]	OCP [stop]	OCP [Place]	MAX [stop]
a.	ot. čo	*!		*	*	
b.	oʔ.čo		*!	*		
←c.	wrong winner os. čo				*	*
d.	desired winner oh. čo		*!			*

As a matter of fact, there is no chance for candidate (d) to win unless we stipulate some higher-ranked constraint that would penalize candidate (c). Promotion of OCP[Place] is impossible since OCP[Place] is violated in the optimal sequence of an affricate and a stop. Candidate (b) with only a change in the place feature and (c) with only a change in the manner feature violate faithfulness constraints for the place feature and for the manner feature, respectively. In contrast, candidate (d) changes both the place and the manner features and violates both faithfulness constraints. Therefore, candidates (b) and (c) are less unfaithful to the input than is candidate (d) in terms of these faithfulness constraints. Candidate (d) should always lose, because it has a superset of the marks of the less unfaithful candidates with respect to the faithfulness constraints.

Thus, the Yucatec data cannot be accounted for in OT without some extra mechanism. This section has demonstrated that neither a rule-based analysis nor an OT analysis with a simple constraint ranking can lead to a correct analysis of the Yucatec data. The next section discusses how Sympathy Theory successfully explains the phenomenon.

4.4. Sympathy Theory Account of the Alternation

The previous sections have shown that neither a rule-based theory nor OT with a simple constraint ranking can explain why the affricate alternation results in only changing the manner feature, while the stop alternation involves changing the place feature as well as changing the manner feature. This section discusses the application of Sympathy Theory in the analysis of this asymmetry.

As noted in Section 4.2, McCarthy (1999) proposes that phonological opacity in OT is derived from a new type of constraint interaction on the basis of a faithfulness relation between co-candidates. I claim that the Yucatec Maya stop alternation is an instance of such phonological opacity.[14] The actual output [h] (changing both the place and the manner features) is selected by virtue of its sympathetic relationship to the less unfaithful failed candidates [ʔ] (debuccalization). Since the failed candidate [ʔ] is realized neither in the input nor in the output, the selection of the optimal candidate is opaque. We observe the actual analysis based on Sympathy Theory in the following sections.

4.4.1. Selecting the sympathy candidate: DEP[cont]⊛. First of all, we must select the sympathy candidate and the designated constraint (the "flower-picker" constraint) that is responsible for the selection of a sympathy candidate.[15]

In the tableau in (36), DEP[cont] is the designated constraint. Only candidates (a) and (b) satisfy the designated constraint. Between (a) and (b), (b) best-satisfies the ranking. Hence, I conclude that candidate (b) is the sympathy candidate, because it is the most harmonic candidate with respect to the designated constraint, DEP[cont].

(36)   Selecting the sympathy candidate:

	/ot. čo/	OCP[pl.] & OCP[stop]	MAX [Place]	OCP [stop]	OCP [Place]	MAX [stop]	DEP⊛ [cont]
a.	ot.čo	*!		*	*		
☞b.	sympathetic o?.čo		*!	*			
←c	transparent os čo				*	*	*
d.	opaque oh.čo		*!			*	*

Before further discussing the selection of the winning candidate, I would like to explain why other constraints cannot become the designated constraint. First, MAX[Place] cannot become the designated constraint when we consider the sequence of the stop and the homorganic stop or affricate as in (36). If MAX[Place] were the designated constraint, then, candidate (c) becomes the sympathy candidate. Then, regardless of the ranking of all kinds of faithfulness constraints between the sympathy candidate and the output, candidate (c) would always become the optimal candidate. This is because (c) never violates any faithfulness constraints between the sympathy candidate and the output since it is both the sympathy and the optimal candidate by itself.

Consider the tableau in (37). Thus, if MAX[Place] were the designated constraint, then, the correct output – candidate (d) – could not be optimal.

*(37) Wrong selection of the designated constraint (1):

	/ot. čo/	OCP[pl.] & OCP[stop]	MAX[Place]	OCP [stop]	OCP [Place]	MAX [stop]	DEP [cont]
a.	ot.čo	*!		*	*		
b.	o?.čo		*!	*			
☞ c.	os.čo				*	*	*
d.	actual winner oh.čo		*!			*	*

Next, as long as we analyze only the stop alternation in the sequence, MAX[stop] as well could be the designated constraint. However, I determine only DEP[cont] can be the designated constraint on the basis of the analyses of other sequences such as the affricate alternation.

Let us examine the affricate alternation assuming that MAX[stop] were selected as the designated constraint. As tableau (38) shows, if MAX[stop] were the designated constraint, candidate (d) would become the sympathy candidate because it is the most harmonic candidate with respect to MAX[stop]. Then, there is no possible faithfulness constraint that can let the actual optimal candidate (b) win. I therefore conclude that DEP[cont] is the designated constraint in Yucatec Maya.

*(38) Wrong selection of the designated constraint(2):

/?uc t /	OCP[Place] &OCP[stop]	MAX [Place]	OCP[stop]	MAX [stop]	OCP[Place]
a. ?uc t	*!		*		*
actual winner b. ?us t				*	*
c. ?uh t		*!		*	
☞ d. ?u? t		*!	*		

4.4.2. An account of the winning candidate. This section discusses the rest of the analysis obtaining the correct output: namely, the selection of the sympathy constraint and the selection of the actual winner. According to McCarthy (1999), a sympathy constraint is a kind of faithfulness constraint for a correspondence relation between the sympathy candidate and the output. Here, I introduce a sympathy constraint: MAX[Place]✿O, which is a faithfulness constraint for the place feature between the sympathy candidate and the output. Since the sympathy constraint outranks MAX[Place]IO in the language, the actual output is correctly selected. In (39), candidate (d) correctly wins, because it best-satisfies the entire constraint ranking, including the sympathy constraint.

(39)   The entire ranking:

/ot. čo/	OCP[pl] & OCP[stop]	MAX [Pl.]✿O	MAX [Pl.]IO	OCP [stop]	OCP [Pl.]	MAX [stop]	DEP✿ [cont]
a. ot.čo	*!	*		*	*		
sympathetic ✿b. oʔ.čo			*	*!			
transparent ←c. os.čo		*!			*	*	*
opaque ☞d. oh.čo			*			*	*

We have seen in this section that selection of the actual output is opaque; therefore, we must apply a constraint ranking that includes the sympathy constraint to characterize the whole grammar.

4.5. Other Phenomena

We have observed that the grammar of Yucatec Maya consists of a constraint ranking with a sympathy constraint. Therefore, the ranking should explicate other phenomena as well as the stop alternation. In the following section, I will confirm the validity of the ranking by examining sequences of an affricate and a homorganic stop (affricate) and of a glottal stop and a nonhomorganic stop.

4.5.1. The affricate alternation with Sympathy Theory. In the sequence of an affricate and a stop (or affricate), the candidate in which only the [stop] feature changes is the most harmonic candidate with respect to the designated constraint DEP[cont]; therefore, it is the sympathy candidate. This candidate is also optimal because it best-satisfies the entire constraint ranking, including the sympathy constraint. In other words, in this case, the sympathetic relation has no particular effect. As (40) shows, in this sequence, candidate (c) is both sympathetic and optimal. This is an instance of transparent phonology, which is observed when the sympathy and optimal candidates are the same.

(40)   An affricate and a stop:

/ʔuc. t/	OCP[pl] & OCP[stop]	MAX [Pl.]⊛O	MAX [Pl.]IO	OCP [stop]	OCP [Pl.]	MAX [stop]	DEP⊛ [cont]
a. ʔuc. t	*!			*	*		
b. ʔuʔ. t		*!	*	*			*
sympathetic and optimal ⊛ ☞ c. ʔus. t					*	*	
d. ʔuh.t		*!	*			*	

4.5.2. A sequence of a glottal stop and a nonhomorganic stop. Another sequence we should examine is that of a glottal stop and a nonhomorganic stop such as in /ʔ.t/. As (41) shows, we do not observe any alternation.

(41) Sequence of a glottal stop and a nonhomorganic stop

(Straight 1976: 28 and 241):

teneʔ tín čam b'in h màan → teneʔ tín čam b'in h màan   'no gloss'

Since the nonhomorganic sequence is already well formed in Yucatec Maya, we do not observe any alternation. Therefore, the ranking established in Section 4.4 must also account for this phenomenon. However, as the tableau in (42) shows, the ranking does not account for this case. In (42), candidate (b) is the sympathy candidate, because it is the most harmonic candidate with respect to DEP[cont]. As a result candidate (c) is incorrectly optimal because it best-satisfies the entire constraint ranking.

(42) A wrong result:

/tene**ʔ** tín/	OCP[pl] & OCP [stop]	MAX [pl]⊛O	MAX [pl] IO	OCP [stop]	OCP [Pl.]	MAX [stop]	DEP⊛ [cont]
a. tenet tín	*!			*	*		
desired winner ⊛ b. tene**ʔ** tín				*!			
wrong winner *☞c. teneh tín						*	*

Since the correct output is candidate (b), we need to introduce an additional constraint to explain this case. I claim that the additional constraint is MAX[constricted glottis], which is a faithfulness constraint for the constricted glottis feature.

The table in (43) summarizes which obstruent has which feature. Lombardi (this volume) indicates that both [ʔ] and [h] have pharyngeal place features, and [ʔ] and [h] bear [stop] and [cont], respectively. Kenstowicz (1994:39) explains that we observe the absence of [constricted glottis] in a plain or aspirated stop and in a pharyngeal fricative [h], while the feature is present in an ejective or a glottal (pharyngeal) stop. [spread glottis] is absent in a plain, ejective, or glottal stop, while an aspirated stop and a pharyngeal fricative [h] bear the feature. On the basis of this observation, I analyze the glottal stop case with an additional faithfulness constraint, MAX[constricted glottis (constr. gl.)], stated in (44). Since the candidate with the glottal stop is optimal, I assume that MAX[constr. gl.] outranks OCP[stop].[16] Let us reexamine the sequence that was analyzed in (42). The designated candidate in (45) is (b) because it is the most harmonic candidate in terms of the designated constraint, DEP[cont]. Candidate (a) loses due to its violation of the conjunction. Candidate (c) loses to (b) due to the crucial ranking in which MAX[constr. gl.] outranks OCP[stop].

(43) The features in obstruents:

	[Place]	[stop]	[cont]	[spread glottis]	[constricted glottis]
[p] (plain)	lab	+	−	−	−
[p'] (ejective)	lab	+	−	−	+
[pʰ] (aspirated)	lab	+	−	+	−
[ʔ]	phar	+	−	−	+
[h]	phar	−	+	+	−

(44) MAX[constr. gl.]: every input [constr. gl.] feature

has an output correspondent.

(45) A glottal stop and a non-homorganic stop:

/teneʔ tín/	OCP[pl]& OCP[stop]	MAX [pl.] ⊛O	MAX [pl.] IO	MAX [co.gl.] IO	OCP [stop]	OCP [pl.]	MAX [stop]	DEP⊛ [cont]
a. tenet tín	*!	*	*	*	*			
☞⊛ b. teneʔ tín					*	*		
c. teneh tín				*!	*	*	*	*

With this ranking, I reexamine the sequence of a nonglottal stop and a homorganic stop. Since the nonglottal stop does not bear [constricted glottis], no segments of the input contain the feature [constricted glottis]. All the candidates in the tableau in (46) vacuously satisfy MAX[constr. gl.] so that the previous analysis without this constraint remains valid. Similarly, the proposed analysis of the sequence of an affricate and a stop is correct with the constraint, MAX[constr. gl.].

(46)   A stop and a homorganic stop:

/ot. čo/	OCP[pl.] & OCP [stop]	MAX [pl.]⊛O	MAX [pl]IO	MAX [co.gl.]IO	OCP [stop]	MAX [stop]	DEP⊛ [cont]
a. ot.čo	*!	*				*	
⊛ b. oʔ.čo			*		*!		
c. os.čo		*!					*
☞ d. oh.čo			*				*

5. Summary and Conclusion

I have argued that the stop alternation in Yucatec Maya is an instance of phonological opacity in OT; therefore, neither rule-based theory nor OT without Sympathy Theory can provide the correct analysis of the data. I have concluded that constraint ranking with the sympathy constraint can correctly account for all the phenomena of the OCP effects both on the [stop] and on the [Place] features in Yucatec Maya.

The actual output [h] in the alternation /t.t/ → [h.t] becomes optimal through the influence of the sympathetic candidate. As shown in (47), a candidate-to-candidate correspondence relation between [ʔ.t] and [h.t] accounts for the path for the alternation /t.t/ → [h.t].

(47) The path for the output:

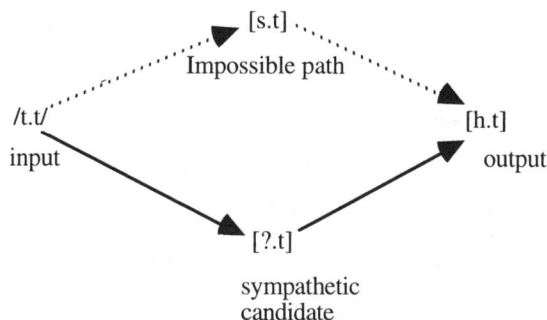

Sympathy Theory accounts for the following points in the language. First, DEP[cont] is the designated constraint responsible for the selection of the sympathy candidate. Second, the debuccalized candidate that fails by itself is the sympathy candidate in the stop alternation, because it is the most harmonic candidate with respect to the designated constraint, DEP[cont]. Third, the sympathy constraint that demands mapping between the sympathy candidate and the output is MAX[Place]✿O. This is a faithfulness constraint for the place feature between the sympathy candidate and the output. Lastly, the debuccalized and spirantized candidate correctly wins in the entire constraint ranking, including the sympathy constraint.

The Yucatec case is not a standard case of the problem of phonological opacity that arises from serial derivation in rule-based theory. However, the discussion in the section has made it clear that this is a new type of opacity in OT. I claim that Sympathy Theory can deal with such a case of opacity as well. My proposal that Sympathy Theory can be extended to more general opacity in OT makes the theory more universal and is supported by data that we could explain neither in rule-based theory nor in OT without Sympathy Theory. The OCP effects in Yucatec Maya thus provide evidence for two new devices in Optimality Theory: Local Conjunction and Extended Sympathy Theory.

Notes

I would like to thank the editor of this volume, Linda Lombardi, for the opportunity to contribute to this volume and for her beneficial comments. I would also like to thank Moira Yip for her helpful comments.
1. An alternative analysis that assumes a feature geometry in which Place dominates Manner (or vice versa) cannot account for the data. When Place

dominates Manner, OCP[Place] entails OCP[Manner], and vice versa. Thus the constraint OCP[Place] would prohibit adjacent segments that agree in Manner or Place alone in addition to those which share both, but only the latter are prohibited.

2. Frisch, Broe, and Pierrehumbert (in press) indicate that OCP effects are gradient: the more similar two consonants are, the stronger their cooccurrence restrictions. In a sense this is true in Yucatec since consonants that share both Place and Manner are subject to the OCP, but those less similar consonants that share only Place or only Manner are not. However, the OCP effect in Yucatec does not appear to support their additional claim that such effects are noncategorical.

3. Straight (1976) does not give examples of all clusters, but his descriptions are clear.

4. Following Lombardi (1990a,b), I assume that there are two kinds of manner features, [stop] and [continuant (cont)], which are independent features on separate and unordered tiers. I therefore assume that a stop, an affricate, and a fricative segments bear only [stop], both [stop] and [cont], and only [cont] features, respectively.

5. The first consonant in the cluster – that is, the consonant in coda position – always undergoes the change, although change in either consonant would satisfy the constraints here. This is due to high-ranked positional featural faithfulness (see Fukazawa 1999 for details).

6. Additional candidates with featural fusion, epenthesis, deletion from the onset, and impermissible segments such as [x] are ruled out by additional constraints that are not relevant to the present argument; see Fukazawa (1999). The preference for [h.t] over the candidate with [s.t] is discussed in Section 4.

7. Hewitt and Crowhurst (1996) propose a type of conjunction that differs from the definition used by Smolenksy and others; in comparison it is more like disjunction. I use Smolensky's definition here.

8. See Fukazawa and Miglio (1998) for discussion of the definition of constraint family.

9. Candidate (20a) is phonetically impossible; HAVEMANNER is probably unviolated in all languages so that it is a property of GEN. For detailed discussion, see Fukazawa (1999).

10. DEP[cont] is lower ranked than OCP[stop], because the continuant feature is not inserted in the sequence of a stop and a nonhomorganic stop such as [k.p], where OCP[stop] is violated.

11. With the ranking in this tableau, there is a better candidate, [osčo], which violates only the lower-ranked constraints, OCP[Place], MAX[stop], and DEP[cont]. I discuss the issue in Section 4.4.

12. Align-R IO: $]_{Root} =]_\sigma$ (all the right edge of the root coincides with the right edge of the syllable).

13. Paul Smolensky (p.c.) suggests that there is a logically possible way to explain this alternation as a case of feeding in serial derivation. First, a rule for deletion of the place feature from the stop segment applies when it is followed by homorganic stop. Next, another rule applies according

to which the placeless segment turns into [h]. However, as with the rules proposed in the text, it is unclear what the justification for this second rule would be instead of, for example, a rule turning the placeless segment into [?].

14. Paul Smolensky (p.c.) points out that OT would explain the alternation without any new theoretical device if we introduced a markedness hierarchy *[?] » *[h]. But this ranking seems unlikely since fricatives are probably in general more marked than stops. For example, many languages have more stops than fricatives in their sound systems.

15. McCarthy (1999) claims that only faithfulness constraints can be the designated constraint to choose the sympathy candidate, while Ito and Mester (1997) suggest that either faithfulness or markedness constraints can be the designated constraint. My analysis is consistent with McCarthy's proposal.

16. MAX[constr. gl.] must also outrank *[constr. gl.]. This ranking is needed in any case in Yucatec Maya, since its sound system contains glottalized stops.

References

Alderete, John. 1997. Dissimilation as Local Conjunction. *Proceedings of North Eastern Linguistics Society* 27:17–32.

Frisch, Stefan, Michael Broe, and Janet Pierrehumbert. In press. The Role of Similarity in Phonology: Explaining OCP-Place. *Proceedings of the 13th International Congress of Phonetic Sciences, 1995, Stockholm.*

Fukazawa, Haruka. 1999. Theoretical Implications of OCP Effects on Features in Optimality Theory. PhD dissertation, University of Maryland, College Park.

Fukazawa, Haruka, and Viola Miglio. 1998. Restricting Conjunction to Constraint Families. *Proceedings of Western Conference on Linguistics* 9: 102–117.

Goldsmith, John A. 1976. Autosegmental Phonology. PhD dissertation, MIT.

Hewitt, Mark, and Megan Crowhurst. 1996. Conjunctive Constraints and Templates in Optimality Theory. *Proceedings of North Eastern Linguistics Society* 26:101–116.

Ito, Junko, and Armin Mester. 1997. Sympathy Theory and German Truncations. *University of Maryland Working Papers in Linguistics* 5:117–138.

Kenstowicz, Michael. 1994. *Phonology in Generative Grammar.* Cambridge: Blackwell.

Kirchner, Robert. 1996. Synchronic Chain Shifts in Optimality Theory. *Linguistic Inquiry* 27:341–350.

Leben, William. 1973. Suprasegmental Phonology. PhD dissertation, MIT.

Lombardi, Linda. 1990a. The Nonlinear Organization of the Affricate. *Natural Language and Linguistic Theory* 8:375–425.

Lombardi, Linda. 1990b. On the Representation of the Affricate. *University of Massachusetts Occasional Papers* 13:87–135.

McCarthy, John. 1988. Feature Geometry and Dependency: A Review. *Phonetica* 43:84–108.

McCarthy, John. 1997. Process-Specific Constraints in Optimality Theory. *Linguistic Inquiry* 28:231–251.

McCarthy, John. 1999. Sympathy and Phonological Opacity. *Phonology* 16:331–339. ROA-315-0499, http://ruccs.rutgers.edu/roa.html.

McCarthy, John, and Alan Prince. 1990. Foot and Word in Prosodic Morphology: The Arabic Broken Plural. *Natural Language and Linguistic Theory* 8:209–282.

Miglio, Viola. 1999. Interactions Between Markedness and Faithfulness Constraints in Vowel Systems. PhD dissertation, University of Maryland, College Park.

NíChiosáin, Máire, and Jaye Padgett. 1997. Markedness, Segment Realization, and Locality in Spreading. Report No. LRC-97-01, Linguistics Research Center, University of California, Santa Cruz.

Padgett, Jaye. 1995. Feature Classes. *University of Massachusetts Occasional Papers* 18:385–420.

Prince, Alan, and Paul Smolensky. 1993. *Optimality Theory: Constraint Interactions in Generative Grammar.* To appear, MIT Press.

Smolensky, Paul. 1993. Harmony, Markedness, and Phonological Activity. Paper presented at Rutgers Optimality Workshop 1.

Smolensky, Paul. 1995. On the Internal Structure of the Constraint Component *Con* of UG. Talk presented at UCLA, April 7.

Smolensky, Paul. 1997. Constraint Interaction in Generative Grammar II: Local Conjunction. Paper presented at the Hopkins Optimality Theory Workshop/University of Maryland Mayfest 1997.

Straight, Henry Stephen. 1976. *The Acquisition of Maya Phonology: Variation in Yucatec Child Language.* New York: Garland.

9

Structure Preservation and Stratal Opacity in German

JUNKO ITO AND ARMIN MESTER

1. Introduction: Less Is More

One of the defining characteristics of the theory of Lexical Phonology, as developed in the work of Kiparsky (1982, 1985), Mohanan (1986), and Borowsky (1986, 1990), among others, was an approach that simultaneously stressed the separation and the unity of the lexical (word-level, structure-preserving) and postlexical (phrase-level, non-structure-preserving) phonology. The central idea was that even though the two constitute different modules of the grammar, the rules and their ordering are actually invariant across strata. If a rule is not seen to be active in a given stratum, this was ascribed to one of two factors: (i) the rule has been "turned off" at an earlier stratum or (ii) the rule does not yet apply because its output is blocked by the principle of structure preservation. The overall computation of phonological form is thus partitioned into a lexical and a postlexical part, with different canons of well-formedness holding at the two levels. In this chapter, we will show that within Optimality Theory (OT) (Prince and Smolensky 1993) this view remains correct in essential respects, even though the formal implementation differs in important ways. The resulting model, a type of stratal OT that we will also refer to as "Weak Parallelism," is parallelist in its basic operation, but explicitly recognizes the word phonology (lexical) and phrasal phonology (postlexical) as separate modules that operate in sequence.[1]

It will be seen that weakly parallel OT grammars give rise to a type of stratal opacity that receives no coherent analysis in Sympathy Theory (McCarthy 1999a; see also Fukazawa, this volume), an extension of standard OT dedicated to the treatment of phonological opacity.[2] Stratal opacity is distinct from a parallelist type of opacity that arises from constraint-conjunctive sources (see Ito and Mester, to appear). If this approach is on the right track, it offers the prospect of reducing all phonological opacity to other factors – a welcome result allowing us to maintain a simpler overall conception of the grammar without opacity-specific devices. Opacity is always the result of independently existing properties of the grammar, including both its overall architecture (lexical/postlexical serialism) and mechanisms internal to the constraint system (constraint conjunction, see Smolensky 1995).

The background discussion in Section 2 presents an overview of the sources of opacity in OT. The masking of dorsal fricative assimilation effects (responsible for the [ç] ~ [x] alternation) by allophonic R-vocalization in German constitutes the empirical focus of this chapter, and Section 3 illustrates the problem that this counterfeeding interaction poses for strictly parallel and transparent OT. Section 4 shows how a weakly parallel model of OT, distinguishing the lexical and the postlexical modules, straightforwardly accounts for the problematic interaction. Section 5 confronts Sympathy Theory with the counterfeeding problem. It turns out that, despite its initial apparent success, Sympathy faces insurmountable difficulties with the Richness-of-the-Base Hypothesis whenever, as in the case under investigation, the masking process of an opaque interaction is allophonic. The argument against Sympathy is extended in Section 6, where an additional process of German phonology, *g*-spirantization, is brought into the picture. The resulting doubly opaque interaction cannot be resolved by Sympathy even at the price of abandoning the Richness-of-the-Base Hypothesis and stipulating constraints on inputs. Section 7 concludes the chapter with a summary and a discussion of further consequences.

2. Weak Parallelism and Strict Parallelism

A phonological system is said to contain opacity to the extent that it contains generalizations that make crucial contributions to the overall computation of phonological form, but are not statable as truths about outputs. This raises important issues for OT, a theory of phonological form that is based on output constraints. Since opacity involves the masking of specific generalizations that hold within a specific phonological system (i.e., not of universal constraints from the universal constraint set), it cannot simply be reduced to constraint domination. Taken by itself, constraint domination (A » B » C » . . .) can give rise to complex and convoluted surface generalizations (C, except if B, except if A, . . .), but not to generalizations that are impossible to state as surface generalizations (see McCarthy 1999a for detailed discussion).

If OT with its output orientation is on the right track as an explanatory theory of phonology, how can opacity exist at all in phonological
systems? In what sense can there be generalizations that are true even
though they are not true of outputs? This problem is a real and pressing
one. We will argue that the proper answer does not involve the creation
of an opacity-specific mechanism grafted onto the basic model – be it
Sympathy or something else – but is already implicit in two structural
properties of the grammar: (a) constraint combinatorics, which creates
new composite constraints out of elementary ones, and (b) modular organization, in particular, the serial articulation into lexical and postlexical
phonology as separate modules. Loosely put, our proposal is that the
effects of some generalizations are masked and hidden on the surface
not because there is some component of the theory responsible for the
masking and hiding of generalizations, but rather as a side effect of both
parallel (1a) and serial (1b) elements of the theory.

(1) a. Parallel sources of opacity:

    i. [M&$_\ell$F] conjunctions (Ito and Mester to appear): The effects of a markedness

        constraint M are partially blocked because the relevant constraint is in reality not the

        pure markedness constraint M, but rather the Local markedness-cum-faithfulness

        conjunction M&$_\ell$F. This restricts the markedness effects to certain derived

        environments (Lubowicz 1998), resulting in opacity. Informally speaking, while

        derived β changed into γ, underived β does not:

        /α/ —⟶ [β] ⟶ [γ]

            /β/ ⇸ [γ]

    ii. [F&$_\ell$F] conjunctions (Kirchner 1996): Local conjunctions of faithfulness constraints

        result in the stepwise mapping characteristic of chain shifts. Informally speaking,

        while underlying α changed into β and underlying β into γ, derived β does not

        change into γ.

        /α/ ⟶ [β]

        /β/ ⟶ [γ]

        /α/ ⇸ [γ]

b. Serial sources of opacity

  Patterns established through the constraint ranking of the lexical module are masked

  by the effects of the partially different constraint ranking of the postlexical module.

Viewed from this vantage point, opacity is no more than an epiphenomenon, and developing a theory with specific opacity-generating devices, despite their ingenuity and descriptive success, is a questionable move at the level of explanatory adequacy. The sources of opacity are multiple and diverse, neither exclusively parallel nor exclusively serial; its proper treatment is therefore a strictly reductionist one. In particular, subsuming all opacity to a single factor is neither possible nor desirable, and attempts to place the explanatory burden entirely on one side, be they parallelist (McCarthy 1999a) or serialist (Kiparsky 1998), cannot succeed. Opaque patterns in outputs are rather the result of the way in which the whole grammar is configured. And to the extent that the overall architecture of an OT grammar contains both parallel and serial aspects, it comes as no surprise that opaque patterns in outputs reflect this by showing a mixture of parallel and serial factors.

The opacity implications of the theory of $[M\&_cF]$-conjunctions (1a) have been developed in detail in another paper (Ito and Mester, to appear), and we have little to add here.[3] In this paper, it is the stratal masking of generalizations (1b), in broad outline familiar from traditional phonology, that occupies our attention. Besides its opacity-related aspects, we will have occasion to explore the particular ways in which lexical and postlexical phonology show different constraint rankings.

With rule sequentialism no longer in serious consideration, some of the remaining options are outlined in (2)–(4). We adopt a basic distinction, as in (2) (dubbed Weak Parallelism), between lexical phonology and postlexical phonology as serially connected modules of the grammar, coupled with output–output relations (as developed in Benua 1997 and other work). We thus do not subscribe to Strict Parallelism (3), where no distinction is made between the lexical and postlexical modules of phonology. We are not familiar with an explicit proposal (let alone a worked-out analysis of a significant portion of the phonology of some language) along such strictly parallelist lines, but this is the approach literally implied by parallelist credos encountered in the recent literature. On the other hand, we also do not subscribe to the multilayered cascade of word-internal levels found in Full Serialism (4).[4]

(2) Weak Parallelism

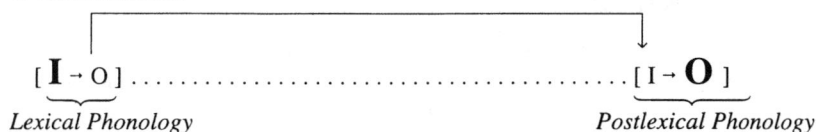

$$[\mathbf{I} \rightarrow \mathrm{O}] \dots\dots\dots\dots\dots\dots\dots\dots\dots\dots\dots\dots\dots\dots [\mathrm{I} \rightarrow \mathbf{O}]$$

Lexical Phonology   *Postlexical Phonology*

(3) Strict Parallelism

$$[\mathbf{I} \xrightarrow{\hspace{6cm}} \mathbf{O}]$$
$$P \; h \; o \; n \; o \; l \; o \; g \; y$$

(4) Full Serialism:

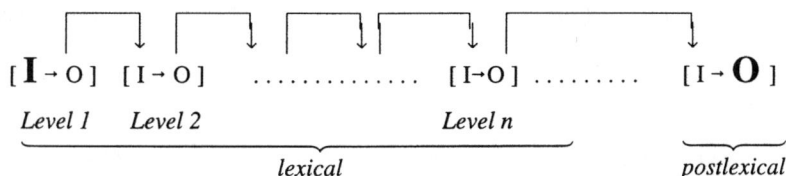

$$[\mathbf{I} \rightarrow \mathrm{O}] \quad [\mathrm{I} \rightarrow \mathrm{O}] \quad \dots\dots\dots \quad [\mathrm{I} \rightarrow \mathrm{O}] \quad \dots\dots \quad [\mathrm{I} \rightarrow \mathbf{O}]$$

Level 1   *Level 2*   *Level n*

                      lexical   *postlexical*

Multiple and serially connected word-internal levels made sense in the theoretical environment of Full Serialism's intellectual predecessor, namely classical Lexical Phonology and Morphology, where level and rule serialism were involved in virtually every explanation the theory was offering: cyclic versus noncyclic rule application at a level, the strict cycle condition, structure-building versus structure-changing operations, underspecification, and cyclic default rules, to name a few. All of these devices and principles were intrinsically connected with serialism and constituted its theoretical lifeline. Most of them, however, are long gone from the theoretical scene, having being replaced in OT by other – and superior – means of analysis and explanation, including local constraint conjunction, Output-to-Output faithfulness, and others. It would thus be surprising to find the multiple word-internal levels characteristic of classical Lexical-Phonological theory and practice still holding on to their former positions.

3. The Problem: Opaque [ç] in [+back] Contexts

The case of phonological opacity to be considered in this paper involves the process of ʀ-vocalization in German, which partially masks the context of a second alternation, namely, the dorsal fricative assimilation process responsible for the distribution of palatal [ç] and velar [x].

3.1. R-Vocalization

As shown in (5), R-vocalization replaces /R/ in syllable codas by [ɐ̯] –
in Moulton's words, a "lower mid unrounded vowel between central
and back" (1962:35). Its syllable peak counterpart [ɐ] (which arises,
derivationally speaking, out of contraction of [ɐ̯] with schwa) is found,
e.g., in the second syllable of *Mutter* ['mʊtɐ] 'mother'. Examples of R-
vocalization appear in (6), where onset [R], as in the plural form
[ty:Rən], corresponds to postnuclear [ɐ̯], as in the singular form [ty:ɐ̯].[5]

(5) **R-Vocalization:**   R → ɐ̯ / __ C₀]₀

(6)   **[R]**   **[ɐ̯]**

Türen	[.tyː.Rən.]	Tür	[.tyːɐ̯.]		*door, pl/sg*

Ohren	[.oː.Rən.]	Ohr	[.oːɐ̯.]	*ear, pl/sg*
Flure	[.fluː.Rə.]	Flur	[.fluːɐ̯.]	*corridor, pl/sg*
Meere	[.meː.Rə.]	Meer	[.meːɐ̯.]	*sea, pl/sg*
Tore	[.toː.Rə.]	Tor	[.toːɐ̯.]	*gate, pl/sg*
hören	[.høː.Rən.]	hört	[.høːɐ̯t.]	*hear, inf/3sg*
dürre	[.dY.Rə.]	dürrste	[.dYɐ̯s.tə.]	*dry, driest*
zerren	[.tsɛ.Rən.]	zerrt	[.tsɛɐ̯t.]	*pull, inf/3sg*
irren	[.I.Rən.]	irrt	[.Iɐ̯t.]	*err, inf/3sg*

Vocalized R contracts in various ways, sometimes optionally, sometimes obligatorily, with preceding low and lower-mid back vowels (i.e.,
[ɑː, ɑ, ɔ]), often resulting in a long version of the preceding vowel. This
is especially clear for [ɔ], where we find numerous examples such as *Horn*
[hɔɹn] 'horn', *Dorf* [dɔɹf] 'village', or *Wort* [vɔɹt] 'word' that testify to the
distributional generalization. Relevant alternations appear in cases like
(7), where [ɔː] (from /ɔR/) corresponds to [œɐ̯] (from /œR/, with /œ/
induced by umlaut).

(7)   **[ɔː]**   **[œɐ̯]**

Dorf	[.dɔːf.]	Dörfer	[.dœɐ̯.fɐ.]	*village, sg/pl*
Wort	[.vɔːt.]	Wörter	[.vœɐ̯.tɐ.]	*word, sg/pl*

For the low vowel [ɑ, ɑː], contraction appears optional, as the examples
in (8) show.

(8) scharren [.ʃɑ.ʀǝn.] scharr [.ʃɑɐ̯.] ~ [.ʃɑː.] *dig, inf/imp*

　　 Scharen [.ʃɑː.ʀǝn.] Schar [.ʃɑ(ː)ɐ̯.] ~ [.ʃɑː.] *crowd, pl/sg*

　　　　　　　　　　　 cf. Schah 　　　　　　　　 [.ʃɑː.] *shah*

　　　　　　　　　　　 Anarchie [ˌɑnɑɐ̯ˈçiː] ~ [ˌɑnɑːˈçiː] *anarchy*

The contractions in (7) and (8) are caused by constraints against sequences of all-too-similar vocoids (*[ɔɐ̯] and *[ɑɐ̯]); our formal treatment of R-vocalization abstracts away from these additional effects.

The analysis of the allophonic alternation between consonantal [ʀ] as the basic variant and vocalic [ɐ̯] in (9) follows standard lines. The vocalic variant violates a context-free markedness constraint against low glides (*ɐ̯) and appears only through the force of the top-ranked contextual constraint *CODA/R, a coda condition against uvular [ʀ] (more exactly, an M&ₗM conjunction *CODA&ₗ*R).[6] Faithfulness ranks lowest. [ɐ̯] is the closest vocalic counterpart of [ʀ] (see Krämer 1981), and we use IDENT(CONSONANTAL) as a stand-in for all faithfulness constraints violated in the ʀ → ɐ̯ change. Using [.tyːɐ̯.] ~ [.tyː.ʀǝn.] 'door, pl/sg' as an example, the correct forms are derived as in (10). The candidate with vocalic [ɐ̯] wins out in the singular, where the ʀ-candidate violates top-ranking *CODA/R (10a). But in the plural (10b), the segment in question comes to occupy onset position, making *CODA/R irrelevant. The decision comes down to the level of context-free markedness, where the ɐ̯-candidate, with its low glide, receives a fatal violation mark.

(9)　 *Coda/R 　　　　　　　 (markedness constraint against consonantal R in the coda)

　　 |

　　 *ɐ̯ 　　　　　　　　　　 (markedness constraint against low glide)

　　 |

　　 Ident(cons) 　　　　　 (faithfulness to input specifications for [consonantal])

(10) a.

/tyːR/ Tür 'door'	*Coda/R	*ɐ̯	Ident(cons)
☞　　 tyːɐ̯		*	*
tyːR	*!		

b.

/tyːR+ǝn/ Türen 'doors'	*Coda/R	*ɐ̯	Ident(cons)
.tyː.ɐ̯ǝn.		*!	*
☞　 .tyː.Rǝn.			

The fact that faithfulness (here, IDENT(CONS)) ranks lowest makes the process allophonic. Input specifications for [consonantal] are noncontrastive, as far as the distribution of [ʀ] and [ʁ̞] is concerned. Richness-of-the-Base (Prince and Smolensky 1993) demands, therefore, that it should be irrelevant for the selection of the correct output candidate whether /ʁ̞/ or /ʀ/ is posited in the input. Output constraints are sufficient to make the correct choice irrespective of input specifications. (11) shows that input specification as /ʁ̞/ or /ʀ/ indeed does not matter, and that the same results are obtained as before.

(11) a.

/tyːʁ̞/ Tür 'door'	*Coda/R	*ʁ̞	Ident(cons)
☞ tyːʁ̞		*	
tyːR	*!		*

b.

/tyːʁ̞+ən/ Türen 'doors'	*Coda/R	*ʁ̞	Ident(cons)
.tyː.ʁ̞ən.		*!	
☞ .tyː.Rən.			*

3.2. [ç ~ x] Allophony

The second alternation involved, the well-known dorsal fricative allophony in (12), concerns palatal [ç] (as in *möchte* [mœçtə] 'wants to') alternating with velar [x] after back vowels (as in *mochte* [mɔxtə] 'wanted to').[7]

(12)   Dorsal Fricative Allophony   ç → x   /[V, +back] __

	[ç]				[x]	
Licht	[lɪçt]	'light'		Bucht	[bʊxt]	'bay'
Nächte	[nɛçtə]	'nights'		Nacht	[nɑxt]	'night'
möchte	[mœçtə]	'wants to'		mochte	[mɔxtə]	'wanted to'
Bücher	[byːçʁ̞]	'books'		Buch	[buːx]	'book'
nächste	[nɛːçstə]	'next'		nach	[nɑːx]	'after'
Eiche	[ɑɪçə]	'oak'		Bauch	[bɑʊx]	'stomach'
euch	[ɔʏç]	'you'		auch	[ɑʊx]	'also'

Palatal [ç] is the basic variant and occurs, to the exclusion of [x], in initial position (13a) and postconsonantally (13b), i.e., everywhere except after back vowels.[8]

(13) a. [ç]e'mie   'chemistry'   *[x]emie

  [ç]i'rurg   'surgeon'   *[x]irurg

  '[ç]arisma   'charisma'   *[x]arisma

  '[ç]thonisch   'belonging to the earth' *[x]tonisch

b. sol[ç]   'such'   *sol[x]

  Kol'[ç]ose   'kolchoz'   *Kol[x]ose (but cf. Russian [kal'xos])

  man[ç]e   'some'   *man[x]e

  Bron'[ç]itis   'bronchitis'   *Bron[x]itis

  Kir[ç]e   'church'   *Kir[x]e

  dur[ç]   'through'   *dur[x]

Our basic analysis, which follows Merchant (1996) (see also literature cited there), establishes [ç] as the basic variant in relation to [x] by means of the two ranking relations in (14).[9] As has often been pointed out (see (11)), it is irrelevant for allophonic pairs such as [ç] ~ [x] which one of the two is posited in the input form: higher-ranking constraints obliterate the force of IO-Faithfulness, as far as the palatal/velar distinction is concerned. In conformity with Richness-of-the-Base, inputs are free to contain either /ç/ (as in (15a)) or /x/ (as in (15b)); the correct result is obtained with the ranking in (14) (this also holds for inputs with a segment underspecified for backness).

(14) $*x \gg \{*ç, \text{Ident(back)}\}$ /zɔlx/ → [zɔlç], *[zɔlx] 'such'

  /zɔlç/ → [zɔlç], *[zɔlx]

(15) a. With /ç/ as input:

/zɔlç/		*x	*ç	Ident(back)
	zɔlx	*!		
☞	zɔlç		*	*

b. With /x/ as input:

/zɔlx/		*x	*ç	Ident(back)
	zɔlx	*!		*
☞	zɔlç		*	

Completing the analysis, the contextual variant [x] emerges under the pressure of the top-ranking syntagmatic velarization constraint VEL (16), a member of the family of feature agreement conditions resulting in assimilation. (16) disallows a back vocoid followed by a voiceless palatal fricative.

(16)   VEL: *ç / [−cons, +back] ___   "[−cons, +back] must not be followed by [ç]."

The ranking in (17)[10] derives the overall distribution of the two dorsal fricatives, as illustrated in (18).

(17)   [ç~x] allophony: VEL
                                   |
                                  *x
                                   |
                             Ident(back)

(18) a. /x/ as input:

/buːx/		VEL	*x	Ident(back)
☞	buːx		*	
	buːç	*!		*

b. /ç/ as input:

/buːç/		VEL	*x	Ident(back)
☞	buːx		*	*
	buːç	*!		

3.3. Counterfeeding Interaction

Placing the two alternations under discussion side by side, we note a potential feeding relationship: ʀ-vocalization results in a [+back] vocoid, and dorsal fricative allophony produces a special allophone [x] after [+back] vocoids. The dorsal fricative exhibits opaque (counterfeeding) behavior in such interactions, as shown in (19), with the output sequence [ɐ̯ç]. Here we find the palatal variant [ç] in the context [−cons, +back]___, i.e., precisely where the variant [x] would be called for.

(19)   fürchten   [fʏɐ̯çtən]   'fear'   *[fʏɐ̯xtən]
       Lerche   [lɛɐ̯çə]   'lark'   *[lɛɐ̯xə]
       Pferch   [pfɛɐ̯ç]   'corral'   etc.
       Zwerchfell   [tsvɛɐ̯çfɛl]   'diaphragm'
       Kirche   [kɪɐ̯çə]   'church'
       Storch   [ʃtɔːç]   'stork'
       horchen   [hɔːçən]   'listen'
       Lurch   [lʊɐ̯ç]   'lizard'
       durch   [dʊɐ̯ç]   'through'

The distributional opacity is especially tangible in cases such as *Storch* [ʃtɔːç] 'stork' and *horchen* [hɔːçən] 'listen', with long [ɔː] through contraction (see (7) and (8)). All the examples in (19) show a dorsal fricative remaining palatal (front) in spite of a preceding back vocalic environment, i.e., behaving as if it stood in postconsonantal position.[11]

The basic interaction is shown in rule form in (20), where R-vocalization counterfeeds dorsal fricative assimilation (Wiese 1996: 257–258).

(20)   /dʊRç/ durch 'through'

      dorsal fricative assimilation: ç → x / [−cons, +bk] __   –

      R-vocalization: R →ɐ̯ / __ C₀]σ   ɐ̯

                                                  [dʊɐ̯ç]

The two constraint subhierarchies are repeated in (21).

(21)   [ç~x] allophony: [R~ɐ̯] allophony:

      VEL   *Coda/R

       | |

      *x   *ɐ̯

       | |

      Ident(back)   Ident(cons)

The two subhierarchies interact as in (22). Here *[dʊɐ̯x] emerges as the wrong winner (☞!!), which is not defeatable by elementary phonological means. It has no violations of the two high-ranking constraints (VEL and *CODA/R), whereas all other candidates, including the actual winner [dʊɐ̯ç] (☹), violate either one of these undominated constraints.

(22)   Transparent analysis, with incorrect winner:

/dʊRç/ 'through'	*Coda/R		*ɐ̯		Id(cns)	
		VEL		*x		Id(bk)
dʊRç	*!					
☹ dʊɐ̯ç		*!	*		*	
dʊRx	*!			*		*
☞!! dʊɐ̯x			*	*	*	*

4. The Lexical/Postlexical Divide

How, then, do we deal with this type of opacity problem in OT? As pointed out in the introduction, the answer is not likely to be found in some particular theoretical device whose exclusive function it would be to produce opaque patterns. Quite apart from problems of descriptive adequacy and completeness that existing proposals are beset with (see the discussion in Sections 5 and 6 and in Ito and Mester, to appear), the rationale for the very existence of such a device would remain obscure: Why would Universal Grammar contain a component that is exclusively concerned with the hiding of generalizations?

Given the architecture of an OT grammar assumed here, opacity effects can arise in (at least) two separate ways. First, the interaction of constraints in Optimality Theoretic phonology is not restricted to a ranking imposed on a given set of basic constraints, but the basic constraints can also interact by combining with each other, resulting in more complex constraints (as argued by Smolensky 1995 and others). This gives rise to parallel opacity effects. Second, traditional phonology is correct in making a basic distinction between lexical and postlexical phonology as different parts of grammar that are governed by partially different, and serially connected, constraint systems. This gives rise to stratal opacity.

Once we take the separation between the lexical and the postlexical modules of phonology seriously, the problematic interaction turns out to be a straightforward case of stratal opacity whose occurrence is arguably predictable on independent grounds (similar to some of the cases argued for in Kiparsky 1998). On the one hand, the [ç ~ x] alternation is a classic example of a lexically established allophonic distribution. Ever since Bloomfield (1930) its sensitivity to lexicon-internal morphological structure is well known, as shown by examples such as *Kuchen/Kuh-chen* ('cake'/'little cow' [kuːxən]/[kuːçən] (see also note 7), and by the general fact that the less restricted variant [ç] is the only one that appears morpheme-initially, irrespective of the backness of preceding vowels (*Indo*-[ç]*ina*, etc.). The two variants, palatal and velar, are acoustically and articulatorily far separated; we are not dealing with a gradient coarticulatory effect. The alternation is also never optional, even in fast or casual speech. Rather, the two variants [ç] and [x] themselves undergo further coarticulatory adjustment in the postlexical phonology. On the other hand, [ʀ ~ ʁ̥] allophony is a partially optional (see note 5) and strongly phonetically conditioned process. It shows no morphological sensitivities, and the allophone transcribed as [ʁ̥] is subject to an extensive degree of variation and malleability (Krämer 1981; Wedel, in preparation), as is typical of processes that are under detailed phonetic control. All these properties are hallmarks of the postlexical module.

Let us, then, follow traditional wisdom for a moment and consider the consequences of assigning [ç ~ x] allophony and [ʀ ~ ʁ̥] allophony to different modules of phonology, treating the first one as lexical and the second one as postlexical. The lexical constraint ranking is given in (23), where (23a) shows the constraints responsible for the distribution of [ɐ̯] and [ʀ], and (23b) the constraints responsible for [x] and [ç]. Turning to (23a) first, *ɐ̯ is ranked highest in the lexical phonology, above *CODA/R – therefore no *ɐ̯ appears in lexical outputs. This establishes the lexical segment inventory as containing consonantal [ʀ] but no vocalic [ɐ̯]. The overall effect recaptures the insight of Lexical Phonology that the lexical phonology is structure-preserving (see Kiparsky 1985 and numerous later works). The lexical segment inventory is not separately stipulated, but emerges directly from the lexical constraint ranking itself, which does double duty in accounting for alternations as well as defining the lexical inventory. The remainder of the subhierachy (23a) is straightforward: The ranking *CODA/R » *R is intrinsic since the conjoined constraint includes the simplex constraint *R,[12] and *R » IDENT(CONS) holds by M » F as a default ranking principle (see Hayes 1999; Ito and Mester 1999; Prince and Tesar 1999). Most aspects of the constraint hierarchy in (23b) have been justified above (see Section 3). *ç » IDENT(BACK) again holds by M » F default.

(23) a.　　*ɐ̯
　　　　　　　|
　　　　　*Coda/R (=*R&ₗ*Coda)
　　　　　　　|
　　　　　*R
　　　　　　　|
　　　　　Ident(cons)

b.　　VEL (= *ç /[+back, -cons]___)
　　　　|
　　　*x
　　　　|
　　　*ç
　　　　|
　　　Ident(back)

The ranking in the postlexical phonology is shown in (24), where "Φ" is used to highlight how postlexical ranking differs from lexical ranking. The postlexical phonology differs from the lexical phonology in two mutually independent respects. On the one hand, the contextual markedness constraint *CODA/R has moved above the context-free markedness constraint *ɐ̯. As a consequence, [ʀ ~ ɐ̯] allophony is postlexically operative. In the parlance of classical Lexical Phonology, structure preservation has been turned off, and [ɐ̯] is now found in codas in place of [ʀ]. On the other hand, the faithfulness constraint IDENT(BACK) has come to dominate the velarization constraint VEL. This is the OT correspondent of a rule being turned off: it freezes the effects of [ç ~ x] allophony in their lexical form, so that the alternation is an exclusively lexical phenomenon and is not at work at the postlexical level. A side effect of these two general properties of the postlexical phonology (heightened influence of contextual markedness and preservation of broad allophone distributions determined lexically) is that the results of lexical velarization are preserved irrespective of postlexical vocalization – in other words, opacity. Similar cases of opaque [ç] are found through phrasal vowel elision, such as *tu ich nicht* 'I don't do that' pronounced as [tuːɪçnɪç] (without elision) or, in fast speech, as [tuːçnɪç] (with elision), but never as *[tuːxnɪç]. This stratal scenario is the clue to the opaque appearance of [ç] in [+back] contexts.

(24)

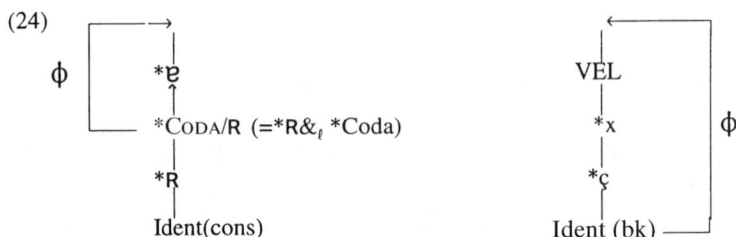

(23) and (24) show that the differences between lexical and postlexical phonology are not restricted to the ranking of faithfulness constraints, but also concern the ranking of markedness constraints with respect to each other (in particular, contextual and context-free markedness). The relation between the serially connected modules is thus a very different one from morpheme class distinctions within the phonological lexicon (native versus foreign, etc.): The latter is arguably reducible to differential faithfulness ranking (Ito and Mester 1995), which can in turn be given a strictly parallel Correspondence Theoretic analysis (Pater 1995; Fukazawa, Kitahara, and Ota 1998; Ito and Mester 1999). It makes sense that the lexical/postlexical phonology divide is of a very different nature from such vocabulary strata distinctions. It is based not on the series of contacts of a language with other languages (which is from a linguistic point of view accidental), but on substantive and universal facts relating both to domains (words versus phrases) and to the role of gradient phonetic factors.[13]

We now give a concrete illustration of this analysis by returning to the example [dʊʁç] 'through' familiar from (20)–(22). The structure-preserving effect of (23a) is that [ʁ] is banned from lexical outputs: only [ʀ] is found, in any position. This means, in particular, that the lexical output is [dʊʀç], not *[dʊʁx] or *[dʊʁç]. Completing the overall picture, (25) and (26) show how the two successive constraint systems of lexical and postlexical phonology result in the overall opaque mapping /dʊʀç, dʊʁç, dʊʀx, dʊʁx/ → [dʊʀç] → [dʊʁç]. Laying the groundwork for later argumentation, (25) highlights the fact that this result holds regardless of the way in which the input is specified for allophonically varying features. That is, it stands in full agreement with the Richness-of-the-Base Hypothesis.[14]

(25) Lexical:

a. /dʊRç/ b. /dʊRx/ c. /dʊɐ̯ç/ d. /dʊɐ̯x/	*ɐ̯	*Coda/R	*R	Id(cons)	VEL	*x	*ç	Id(back)
☞ dʊRç		*	*	$*_{c,d}$			*	$*_{b,d}$
dʊRx		*	*	$*_{c,d}$	*!	*		$*_{a,c}$
dʊɐ̯ç	*!			$*_{a,b}$	*!		*	$*_{b,d}$
dʊɐ̯x	*!			$*_{a,b}$	*!	*		$*_{a,c}$

(26) Postlexical:

/dʊRç/	*Coda/R	*ɐ̯	*R	Id(cons)	Id(back)	VEL	*x	*ç
dʊRç	*!		*					*
dʊRx	*!		*		*!	*	*	
☞ dʊɐ̯ç		*				*		*
dʊɐ̯x		*			*!	*	*	

While (25) shows the typical rich input structure, with all conceivable variants present for noncontrastive properties, lexical outputs are "phonemic," as far as [R ~ ɐ̯] is concerned: [dʊRç] is the winner, and no [ɐ̯] appears in any output, even if it is posited in the input. On the other hand, lexical outputs are by no means strictly phonemic, as shown by the [ç ~ x] relation, where both variants are already found in their appropriate places.

The postlexical phonology derives the result in a straightforward way, as shown in (26), where [dʊɐ̯ç] emerges as the winner: R-vocalization is postlexically in force because of *CODA/R » *ɐ̯ » IDENT(CONS), whereas postlexical outputs are conservative with regard to the distribution of [ç ~ x] because of IDENT(BACK) » VEL.[15]

In terms of the overall theory, we have arrived at a picture in which some crucial insights of Lexical Phonology have found a place in an OT model that makes a systematic and serial distinction between a lexical and a postlexical module of phonology. The two levels show different constraint rankings not only in terms of M-F relations, but also in terms of M-M relations. Concerning the latter, postlexical "processes" are turned on by promoting contextual markedness over context-free markedness, undoubtedly reflecting the strongly phonetic orientation of the phrasal system. In other cases, postlexical processes might be turned on by demoting relevant faithfulness constraints. Lexical outputs are characterized by "structure preservation" (limitation to a restricted inventory of elements and structures), which is, however, not an all-or-nothing principle, since in each individual case everything depends on the ranking relations of the constraints involved.

5. The Failure of Sympathy

Having demonstrated that weakly parallel OT provides a general and rather straightforward way to deal with opaque interactions with allophonic masking processes, it is time to turn to Sympathy Theory (McCarthy 1999a), one of the most interesting proposals put forth in recent OT work in the area of opacity. Can strictly parallelist OT, if enriched by Sympathy, come to terms with the problem posed by allophonic masking processes? Our ultimate conclusion will be negative, and we will build our case in a step-by-step fashion. After discussing background issues concerning the general coverage of Sympathy Theory in Section 5.1, we return to the German opacity problem involving allophonic alternations in Section 5.2.

5.1. Questions of Coverage

Modifying the relevant portions of Kiparsky's (1973:79) rule-based definition and building on McCarthy's recent work (see McCarthy 1999a), opaque patterns in outputs can be characterized in OT as in (27).

(27)   Let P be a phonological process induced by

• M: * A/C_D   a markedness constraint against A in the context C_D.

• F: $*(A_i,B_o)$ a faithfulness constraint against in-element A_i corresponding to out-

element B_o.

• M ≫ F $*A/C\_D$ dominates $*(A_i,B_o)$.

P is *opaque* (opposite: *transparent*) to the extent that there are outputs of the forms (i) CAD

("counterfeeding", see (28a)) or (ii) CBG, with B derived from A and A→B due to P

("counterbleeding", see (28b)).

A traditionally minded classification of opacity cases in ordered rule theory, distilled from Kiparsky (1973) and earlier work, appears in (28). In this collection, as explained in McCarthy (1999a), the category "counterfeeding" (28a) split into two subcases, "environment counterfeeding" and "focus counterfeeding." On the other hand, this distinction is not made for counterbleeding opacity (28b), since "focus counterbleeding" (28iv) is not part of the standard collection (we return to this case in Section 6). The counterfeeding interaction in the environment (28i) is a case of underapplication. The rule [A → B / C__D] does not apply – in OT terms, the M » F constraint interaction [*A/C__D » (A_i,B_o)] is not surface-true. Sympathy Theory deals with this variety by providing a means to make reference to the (losing) hyperfaithful candidate CAE (in this case, though not in general, identical to the input), in which the crucial environmental change E → D has not taken place. Sympathetic faithfulness then transfers this candidate's A (but not its E) to the output (see McCarthy 1998 for discussion and details of the technical execution).

(28)	in the environment		in the focus	
a.	(i)	/CAE/	(iii)	/CFD/
counterfeeding	$A→B/C\_D$	--	$A→B/C\_D$	--
	$E→D/\_\#$	......D	$F→A/C\_D$	...A...
		[CAD]		[CAD]
b.	(ii)	/CAD/	(iv)	/ C [+x,+y,+z] D /
counterbleeding	$A→B/C\_D$	...B...	$[+x,+y]→[-z] / C\_D$ ... [............−z] ...	
	$D→G/\_\#$	......G	$[+x]→[-y] / C\_D$ ... [...... −y...] ...	
		[CBG]	[C [+x−y−z] D]	

The diagnosis for environment counterbleeding (28ii) is overapplication – in OT terms, the environment of M:*A/C__D is not surface-apparent. The process is opaque since there are outputs of the form CBG, with out-element B corresponding to in-element A and with the change A → B due to M = *A/C__D, even though the output contains no D. Candidate CBG, the actual output, has an apparently gratuitous violation of $*(A_i,B_o)$, which remains fatal in comparison with CAG wherever $*(A_i,B_o)$ is ranked. Similar to the environment counterfeeding interaction, Sympathy Theory singles out the candidate CBD as the Sympathy candidate, and sympathetic faithfulness forces this candidate's B onto the overall winner CBG.

In processual parlance, the focus of a rule can be involved in opacity in two ways. The first case is focus counterfeeding (28iii), leading to underapplication. This is the well-known chain-shift scenario, in which the individual shifts F → A and A → B occur, but do not compose to take F all the way to B. From the perspective of Sympathy's claim to be a general model of opacity in OT, focus counterfeeding reveals a first crack in the theory since OT already has independent means to deal with it – Kirchner (1996) argues persuasively that focus counterfeeding is a constraint-conjunctive faithfulness effect preventing the two-step change F → A → B.[16] The markedness constraint *A/C__D is sandwiched between lower-ranking simple featural faithfulness (say, FAITH(FEATURE X) and FAITH(FEATURE Y)) and a higher-ranking conjoined faithfulness (i.e., FAITH(FEATURE X)&₁ₛFAITH(FEATURE Y)), ruling out the tautosegmental violation of both featural faithfulness constraints (see Kirchner 1996 for full exemplification). Sympathy is thus superfluous for this case of opacity.[17]

The three cases seen so far are presented and discussed in McCarthy (1998).[18] The last category – focus counterbleeding (28iv) – is not part of the traditional opacity setup, neither in Kiparsky's (1973) definition nor in McCarthy's (1999a) OT adaptation of it. However, the fact that the schematic derivational scenario given in (28iv) does not qualify as opaque in the usual sense should not be the criterion for phonological opacity. Rather, it suggests that mechanically transferring the notion of opacity from a derivationalist setting to OT has its limitations.[19] There are indeed cases of precisely this variety that create problems in OT in the sense that they are systematically missed by transparent constraint interactions. An actual example of focus counterbleeding will be discussed in Section 6.

5.2. Allophonic Masking Processes and Richness-of-the-Base

Having set the general stage for a Sympathy analysis, we now turn to the German opacity problem at hand. An appeal to Sympathy seems at first glance straightforward. Since this is a case of counterfeeding opacity, IO-IDENT(CONS) as selector singles out the faithful candidate [dʊʀç] (undoing R-vocalization, figuratively speaking), and the sympathetic faithfulness constraint ❀O-IDENT(BACK) transfers the [+back] property of the fricative from the ❀-candidate to the overall winner. The overall ranking accomplishing this is (29), where ❀O-IDENT(BACK) and *CODA/R both dominate VEL.

(29)   *Coda/R   ❀O-Ident(back)
              |‾‾‾‾‾‾‾‾‾‾‾‾‾‾‾‾‾‾‾‾‾‾‾‾‾‾
              | VEL
              | |
             *ɐ   *x
              ʀ |
         Ident(cons)❀   Ident(back)

Note the additional ranking [*Coda/R » VEL] that Sympathy needs to recruit in order to settle on [dʊʁ̥ç] (with opaque [ç]) as the winner instead of *[dʊʀç] (with opaque [ʀ]). The appearance of such additional rankings, necessitated by Sympathy, but without prior and independent motivation, is a general feature of Sympathy analyses (see Ito and Mester, to appear). Tableau (30) illustrates this analysis.

(30)

| /dʊʀç/ 'through' | | *Coda/R | | *ʁ̥ | | Id(cns)❀ | |
	❀O-Id(bk)		VEL		*x		Id(bk)
❀ dʊʀç		*!					
☞ dʊʁ̥ç			*	*		*	
dʊʀx	*!	*			*		*
dʊʁ̥x	*!			*	*	*	*

The Sympathy analysis in (29) thus appears to work, but appearances are deceptive. The analysis is flawed by a fatal dependency on noncontrastive properties of inputs. Sympathy relies on the fact that the input contains /ʀ/ and not [ʁ̥], which ceases to be harmless once it is recalled that both [ʀ ~ ʁ̥] and [ç ~ x] are allophonic relations. This is precisely where Richness-of-the-Base demands that input specifications be free. In particular, each one of the four input options /ʀç/, /ʁ̥ç/, /ʀx/, and /ʁ̥x/ should lead to the same optimal output. But this is not the case, given Sympathy's reliance on input ʀ. It derives phonotactically correct [ʁ̥ç] outputs for the ʀ-inputs /ʀç/ and /ʀx/ (30, 31), but the ʁ̥-inputs /ʁ̥ç/ and /ʁ̥x/ result in phonotactically impossible [ʁ̥x] outputs (32a,b).

(31)

/dʊʀx/	❀O-Id (bk)	*Coda/R	VEL	*ʁ̥	*x	IO-Id(cns)❀	IO-Id(bk)
❀ dʊʀç		*!					*
☞ dʊʁ̥ç			*	*		*	*
dʊʀx	*!	*			*		
dʊʁ̥x	*!			*	*	*	

(32)

a. /dʊʁ̥ç/	❀O-Id (bk)	*Coda/R	VEL	*ʁ̥	*x	IO-Id(cns)❀	IO-Id(bk)
dʊʀç	*!	*				*	
⊗ dʊʁ̥ç	*!		*	*			
dʊʀx		*!			*	*	*
☞!!❀dʊʁ̥x				*	*		*

b. /dʊɐ̯x/	❀O-Id(bk)	*Coda/R	VEL	*ɐ̯	*x	IO-Id(cns)❀	IO-Id(bk)
dʊRç	*!	*				*	*
☺ dʊɐ̯ç	*!		*	*			*
dʊRx		*!			*	*	
☞!!❀dʊɐ̯x				*	*		

The reason for the failure of Sympathy in (32) is easy to see. For inputs containing /ɐ̯/, it is impossible to recover some underlying /R/ through IO-Faithfulness in the process of ❀-candidate selection: no such /R/ is available. Looking beyond this specific case, whose details are irrelevant for the argument, we obtain the general conclusion in (33).

(33) **The argument from allophony:**

Consider an alternation P counterfed by another alternation Q:

P: A → B / C__D

Q: E → D / ...

No Sympathy analysis is possible for interactions of this kind whenever

(i) Q is allophonic and

(ii) crucially affects P's environment.[20]

In (33), the sympathetic way of ensuring opaque A in C__D (over transparent B) is via an IO-Faithfulness–based reference to C__E – but given that the relative distribution of the allophones D and E is free in inputs (Richness-of-the-Base), no probing via IO-Faithfulness secures this reference. This conclusion stands as long as two conditions hold: (i) Richness-of-the-Base remains a fundamental principle of OT, admitting rich inputs in cases of allophony,[21] and (ii) ❀-selectors are restricted, as proposed by McCarthy (1999a), to IO-Faithfulness constraints.[22]

A significant number of opaque interactions fall into the category dealt with in this paper, where a crucial factor in the environment involves an allophonically varying property and is therefore not accessible to Sympathy's faithfulness-guided probing of inputs. Another example from our own work (see the Sympathy analysis given in Ito and Mester 1997a) involves the opaque interaction of two processes in Japanese: (i) the well-known Rendaku Voicing in compounds (*tome* 'clip', *kami* + *dome* 'hair clip'), which is blocked in stems containing voiced obstruents (*taba* 'bundle', *hana* + *taba* 'flower bouquet', **hana* + *daba*), and (ii) Velar Nasalization, an allophonic process replacing word-medial /g/ by [ŋ] (/kagi/ → *kaŋi* 'key', vs. word-initial *geta* 'clogs'). In processual terms, Rendaku Voicing feeds Velar Nasalization in the focus of the rule (i.e., k → g → ŋ: *ori + kami* → *ori + gami* → *ori + ŋami*) and is itself counterfed by Velar Nasalization when the velar nasal replacing /g/ appears in the environment (*saka + toge* → *saka + toŋe* 'reverse thorn'). It is sufficient to note in the present context that a Sympathy analysis will stumble over the fact that only a reference to /g/ can prevent voicing of /t/ to [d] in [sakatoŋe], *[sakadoŋe], but that this reference cannot be relied on, since [g ~ ŋ] are allophonically distributed. The case is thus entirely parallel to the German case analyzed in detail in this paper (see Ito and Mester 2000 for a full analysis of the Japanese case).

It stands to reason, and we will see later on, that this result is not restricted to counterfeeding and actually holds in greater generality, affecting counterbleeding interactions as well. It is important here to look beyond the technical details in order to get to the heart of the problem, which is Sympathy Theory's central tenet that opacity arises through hyperfaithfulness to the input, implemented by having the Sympathy candidate selected by a faithfulness constraint F. This has nonvacuous effects only when the selector is a dominated (and hence violated) faithfulness constraint, so that the Sympathy candidate is more faithful to the input with respect to F than is the transparent winner (it cannot be less faithful, and if it is equally faithful, it coincides with the transparent winner). What the argument from allophony shows is that hyperfaithfulness in this sense cannot be the solution to the problem of opacity within OT. In an ironic twist, the very limitation of selectors to faithfulness that was intended to make Sympathy Theory restrictive turns out to curtail its ineffectiveness in a crucial way.

The flaw in Sympathy Theory that reveals itself in (33) transcends the area of opacity and affects the basic predictions that a grammar makes regarding contrasts and noncontrasts, one of its most fundamental tasks under any conception. Sympathy, via the special access provided by the selector status of low-ranking IO-Faithfulness constraints, has the power to tunnel through to irrelevant and arbitrary aspects of inputs. In this way, it subverts the noncontrastive status of allophonic variants such as [ç ~ x] or [ʀ ~ ʁ], in effect turning noncontrasts into contrasts. To illustrate, consider the two potential inputs /dʊʀç/ and /dʊʁç/, noncontrastive by hypothesis. The Sympathy-induced mappings /dʊʀç/ → [dʊʁç] and /dʊʁç/ → [dʊʁx] show that an OT grammar equipped with Sympathy is able to turn these into two different outputs. Sympathy has thus introduced a contrast between allophones (here, [ç] and [x]) through the back door, against all intentions.

6. Doubly Opaque Interactions

An analytically still more decisive argument emerges in situations where the correct opaque winner apparently cannot be selected by Sympathy, even granting some stipulation on inputs to the effect that they must contain /ʀ/ (and not /ɐ̯/) for output forms with coda [ɐ̯]. If this turns out to be true, it shows that Sympathy cannot be saved even by sacrificing Richness-of-the-Base.

The relevant cases are the Northern German *g*-spirantization examples in (34), which result in mappings such as /bʊʀg/ → [bʊɐ̯ç] 'castle'. Here, we are confronted with another source of distributionally opaque [ç]. Processually speaking, underlying /ʀg/ has turned into [ɐ̯ç] in a series of steps: ʀg]$_\sigma$ → ʀɣ]$_\sigma$ → ʀx]$_\sigma$ → ʀç]$_\sigma$ → ɐ̯ç]$_\sigma$. The background here is a general process of *g*-spirantization in syllable codas (analyzed in detail in Ito and Mester, to appear, where it is shown to present a different kind of opacity problem for Sympathy) resulting, in conjunction with coda devoicing and the constraint configuration in (21), in [x] after back vocoids, and [ç] otherwise. Underlying /g/ in these cases is supported by ubiquitous alternations such as [bɛɐ̯ç] ~ [bɛʁgə] 'mountain, sg/pl'. In rule terms, this case involves two opaque relations, as shown in (35).[23] (35) is doubly opaque: on the one hand, coda devoicing counterbleeds *g*-spirantization in the focus (this is an instance of the case missing from the classical collection of opacity cases discussed earlier; see (28)). On the other hand, ʀ-vocalization simultaneously counterfeeds the second branch of dorsal fricative allophony and counterbleeds its first branch in the environment.

(34) Hamburg   [hɑmbʊɐ̯ç]   (name of city); cf. hambu[ɐ̯gɪʃ] (adj.)

Berg   [bɛɐ̯ç]   'mountain'; cf. Ber[gə] (pl.)

Chirurg   [çɪRʊɐ̯ç]   'surgeon'; cf. Chiru[ɐ̯gən] (pl.)

birg   [bɪɐ̯ç]   'rescue', imp.

borg   [bɔːç]   'borrow', imp.

Georg   [ge ːɔːç]   (name)

(35)   /bʊʀg/ 'castle'

g-spirantization: g → ɣ / __]$_\sigma$ ......ɣ

coda devoicing: [−son] → [−voi] / __]$_\sigma$ x

dorsal fricative
                     [+dors,−son,+cnt,−voi]   ↗ [−bk]   .... ç

allophony: ↘ [+bk] / [−cns,+bk] __

R-vocalization: ʀ → ɐ̯ / __]$_\sigma$ ..... ɐ̯...

                                                             [dʊɐ̯ç]

Let us consider a Sympathy approach to this deeply opaque interaction. The two relevant markedness constraints are ranked intrinsically due to their conjunctive nature as in (36).[24] These two markedness constraints are accompanied by the usual entourage of appropriate selector, sympathetic, and ordinary faithfulness constraints in the tableau in (37) (from Ito and Mester, to appear), which represents an attempt to capture opaque *g*-spirantization by means of Sympathy. The central idea is that [hoːnɪɣ] is recruited as the Sympathy candidate (through IO-IDENT(VOI) as selector), and even though it cannot win in the overall competition (because of *CODA/VOIOBS), it transfers the fricative nature of its closing consonant to the winning output through ❀O-IDENT(CONT), where its place of articulation is adjusted (by the constraint configuration (21) responsible for [ç ~ x] allophony).

(36) *Coda/g   =[*Coda&*ₑ*VoiObs&*ₑ*Dorsal]: No voiced dorsal plosives in codas
  |
  *Coda/VoiObs =[*Coda&*ₑ*VoiObs]:   No voiced obstruents in codas

(37)

/hoːnIg/ 'honey'	*Coda/g	*Coda/ VoiObs	IO-Id(voi)❀	❀O- Id(cont)	IO-Id(cont)
[hoːnIg]	*!	*		*	
❀ [hoːnIɣ]		*!			*
[hoːnik]			*	*!	
☞ [hoːnIç]			*		*!

Fortified by the study of this sympathetic interaction, we are ready to turn to /bʊRg/ → [bʊʁç] with its doubly opaque [ç]: as a spirant opaquely derived from /g/ and as a palatal distributionally opaque in view of the preceding [ʁ]. In trying to account for the palatality of the opaque out-element [ç] (as opposed to a transparent velar [x]), a faithfulness-based link to the input correspondent, velar [g], holds little promise. Recall that the input is fixed as /g/ since this is a case of neutralization, with [g] and [ç ~ x] standing in contrast (*tauchen* [taʊxən] 'dive' vs. *taugen* [taʊgən] 'have value', *Gleichung* [glaɪçʊŋ] 'equation' vs. *Neigung* [naɪgʊŋ] 'inclination', etc.)

In (38), we make the Sympathy-favorable assumption that the input is fixed as the R-ful /bʊRg/ (as against /bʊʁg/). In other words, for the sake of the argument Richness-of-the-Base is suspended as a principle of grammar. The basic setup in (29) for opaque [ç] after [ʁ] is of course not yet equipped to derive the correct result with [ç], but rather produces a winner with transparent [k] (see (38) and the reference cited earlier for background and details). The sympathetic constraint configuration in (37) needs to be integrated with the one in (38), resulting in the double-Sympathy system in (39), where ❀ and ❖ refer to different Sympathy relations (❀ is responsible for opaque [ç] after [ʁ], ❖ for spirantization of /g/ in codas).

(38)

/bʊRg/	❀O-Id (bk)	*Coda/ VoiObs	*Coda/R	VEL	*ȩ̃	*x	IO-Id(cns)❀	IO-Id(bk)
bʊRg		*	*					
❀ bʊRk			*					
bʊRɣ		*	*					
bʊRx			*			*		
bʊRç	*		*					*
bʊȩ̃g		*			*		*	
☞ !!bʊȩ̃k					*		*	
bʊȩ̃ɣ		*			*		*	
bʊȩ̃x					*	*	*	
☹ bʊȩ̃ç	*			*	*		*	*

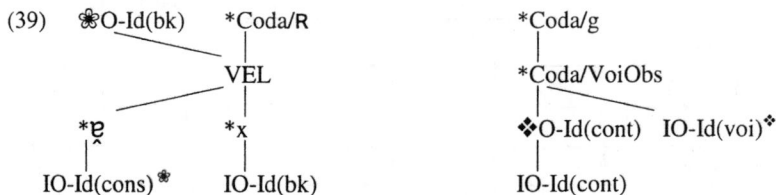

(39)

```
❀O-Id(bk)      *Coda/R                    *Coda/g
         \        |                          |
           VEL                         *Coda/VoiObs
         /        \                    /            \
 *ȩ̃         *x          ✤O-Id(cont)   IO-Id(voi)✤
  |           |                   |
IO-Id(cons)❀  IO-Id(bk)       IO-Id(cont)
```

Tableau (40), besides giving a feel for the complexity of this analysis, reveals a surprising result: The analysis is still not able to select the desired winner [bʊȩ̃ç] (designated by "☹"), but continues to produce *[bʊȩ̃k].

(40)

/bʊRg/	❀O-Id (bk)	*Coda/R	VEL	*ȩ̃	*x	IO-Id(cns)❀	IO-Id(bk)	*Coda/g	*Coda/VoiObs	IO-Id(voi)✤	✤O-Id(cnt)	IO-Id(cnt)
bʊRg		*						*	*		*	
❀ bʊRk		*								*	*	
bʊRɣ		*							*			*
bʊRx		*			*					*		*
bʊRç	*	*					*			*		*
bʊȩ̃g				*		*		*	*		*	
☞❀ !!bʊȩ̃k				*		*				*	*	
✤ bʊȩ̃ɣ				*		*			*			*
☞❀ !!bʊȩ̃x				*	*	*				*		*
☹ bʊȩ̃ç	*		*	*		*	*			*		*

Depending on whether the leftmost block of constraints (aiming to ensure [ç] after [ʁ] from /ʀ/) or the rightmost block of constraints (targeted towards coda [ç ~ x] from /g/), ranks higher, either [buʁk] (designated by ☞❄!!) or [buʁx] (designated by ☞✦!!) is selected as the winner.

As far as we can determine, the result in (40) reveals a fundamental inability of Sympathy to properly deal with such double-opacity cases. The ʀ-ful ❀-Sympathy candidate [buʀk] shows a final stop [k]; in contrast to the earlier cases with underlying /ç ~ x/, its ʀ is thus of no help in bringing about final palatality in the output through sympathetic faithfulness. On the other hand, the ʁ-ful ❖-Sympathy candidate [buʁɣ], while showing a final fricative, knows nothing about suppressing ʀ-vocalization and thus cannot contribute to final palatality either.

As the preceding remarks suggest, the malfunction appears to be due to the fact that the two prongs of double Sympathy do not communicate effectively, making it unsuitable as a model of double-opacity situations. Leaving it to practitioners of Sympathy to explore further analytical options that might overcome this problem,[25] we draw two preliminary conclusions.

(i) Incompleteness: Sympathy fails as a model for opacity cases where the environmental factor is involved in an allophonic alternation. The basic idea of Sympathy is here incompatible with Richness-of-the-Base.

(ii) Double opacity: Even if Richness-of-the-Base is sacrificed in favor of Sympathy in order to respond to (i), Sympathy Theory still encounters serious problems in double-opacity situations.

Concluding this section, it behooves us to show how the problematic double-opacity case /buʀg/ → [buʁç] falls into place in stratal OT. The essential property of this example is that it combines the stratal opacity of [ç] in post-[ʁ] contexts seen earlier with a different kind of opacity, namely, the parallelist kind of opacity instantiated by German *g*-spirantization. Parallel opacity is created though local constraint conjunctions of the forms M&$_\ell$F and F&$_\ell$F. As shown elsewhere (see Ito and Mester, to appear, for a detailed study of such M&$_\ell$F-cases), M&$_\ell$F conjunctions lead to opacity in the configuration M&$_\ell$F » C » M (where C is antagonistic to M). Here M, in conjunction with F, appears to apply only to derived elements (F-violators), not to underived elements. F&$_\ell$F conjunctions lead to opacity in the configuration F1&$_\ell$F2 » M » F1, F2 (where M is antagonistic to F1 and F2). Here M applies only to underived elements, not to derived elements. That is, elements that have changed in violation of F1 cannot go on to also violate F2, and vice versa.

This results in the familiar focus-counterfeeding chain-shift scenario explored by Kirchner (1996) and others.

Given what we have seen earlier, it is clear that the allophonic type of opaque interactions exemplified by the opaque [ç] after the [+back] vocoid [ʁ] in German cannot be reduced to the parallelist variety. In both M&$_\ell$F and F&$_\ell$F conjunctions, the crucial ingredient leading to opacity is F (IO-Faithfulness) – that is, a reference to the input. However, an allophonic masking process in an opaque interaction cannot be circumnavigated through reference to the input, here, to the underlying [ʀ] in a mapping like /dʊʀç/ → [dʊʁç]. This forestalls any constraint-conjunctive account involving faithfulness, just as it forestalls any Sympathy account.[26]

Without further discussion, we take from Ito and Mester (to appear) the analysis of *g*-spirantization involving the M&$_\ell$F conjunction *Coda/DorsPlos&$_\ell$Ident(voi) (ruling out dorsal plosives in codas that simultaneously violate voicing faithfulness; see the work cited for ranking justification and further discussion). The violation is avoided by means of spirantization (violation of lower-ranking Ident(cont)). This is shown in (41).

(41)   *Coda/VoiObs   =[*VoiObs&$_\ell$*Cod]
        |
        [*Coda/DorsPlos&$_\ell$Ident(voi)]   =[*Cod&$_\ell$*DorsPlos&$_\ell$Ident(voi)]
        |
        Ident(cont)
        |
        *Coda/DorsPlos   = [*Cod&$_\ell$*DorsPlos]
        |
        Ident(voi)

The workings of this analysis are illustrated in tableaux (42) and (43). (42) shows how input /g/ in the coda changes into output [ç] (because [k] violates *Coda/DorsPlos&$_\ell$Ident(voi)), whereas (43) shows how input /k/ survives unchanged in the coda.

(42)

/hoːnIg/	*Coda/ VoiObs	[*Coda/DorsPlos &$_\ell$Id(voi)]	Id(cnt)	*Coda/ DorsPlos	Id(voi)
[hoːnIg]	*!			*	
[hoːnIɣ]	*!		*		
[hoːnik]		*!		*	*
☞ [hoːnIç]			*		*

(43)

/plastIk/	*Coda/ VoiObs	[*Coda/DorsPlos &ₑId(voi)]	Id(cnt)	*Coda/ DorsPlos	Id(voi)
[plastIg]	*!			*	*
[plastIɣ]	*!		*		*
☞ [plastIk]	.			*	
[plastIç]			*!		

In (44), all three parts of the analysis are combined – the two sub-hierarchies of (24), with lexical/postlexical ranking differences resulting in serially opaque [ç] after [ɐ̯], and the spirantization hierarchy in (41) with its M&ₑF constraint resulting in parallelist opacity ([ç] instead of [k] for input /g/, but [k] for input /k/).

(44)

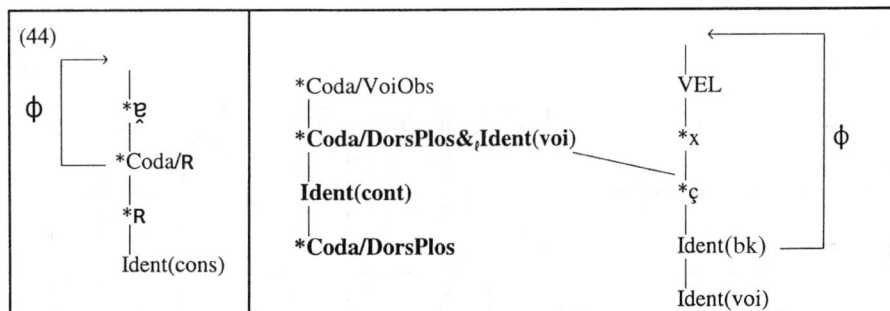

Tableaux (45) and (46) (where the ellipsis marks indicate the omission of irrelevant constraints) demonstrate that this analysis has no trouble deriving the total mapping /bʊʀɡ/ → [bʊɐ̯ç] (as well as the mapping /bʊɐ̯ɡ/ → [bʊɐ̯ç], with a different input variant). The fact that the overall winner is [bʊɐ̯ç] and not [bʊɐ̯k] follows from the ranking *CODA/DORSPLOS&ₑIDENT(VOI) » *ç, which connects two of the subhierarchies, as indicated in (44).

(45) Lexical:

/bʊRg/ /bʊ̰g̥/	*Coda/ VoiObs	*Coda/ DorsPlos &ₜId(voi)	Id (cnt)	...	*ʊ̰	*Coda/ R	...	VEL	*x	*ç	Id (bk)
bʊRg	*!			...		*	...				
bʊRk		*!		...		*	...				
bʊRɣ	*!		*	...		*	...				
bʊRx		*		...		*	...		*!		
☞ bʊRç		*		...		*	...			*	*
bʊ̰g̥	*!			...	*!		...				
bʊ̰k		*!		...	*!		...				
bʊ̰ɣ̥	*!		*	...	*!		...				
bʊ̰x		*		...	*!		...		*!		
bʊ̰ç		*		...	*!		...	*!		*	*

(46) Postlexical:

/bʊRç/	*Coda/ VoiObs	*Coda/ DorsPlos &ₜId(voi)	Id (cnt)	...	*Coda/ R	*ʊ̰	...	Id (bk)	VEL	*x	*ç
bʊRg	*!	*!	*	...	*!		...	*!			
bʊRk			*	...	*!		...	*!			
bʊRɣ	*!			...	*!		...	*!			
bʊRx				...	*!		...	*!		*	
bʊRç				...	*!		...				*
bʊ̰g̥	*!	*!	*	...	*		...	*!			
bʊ̰k			*	...	*		...	*!			
bʊ̰ɣ̥	*!			...	*		...	*!			
bʊ̰x				...	*		...	*!		*	
☞ bʊ̰ç				...	*		...		*		*

7. Summary and Further Consequences

We have argued in this chapter that Sympathy, as proposed by McCarthy (1999a), in spite of its initial promise, falls short of the goal of serving as a general model of opaque interactions within OT. While Sympathy's coverage of the various cases of opacity seems at first glance to be impressively complete, closer investigation has shown that this is far from being the case. In this chapter we have demonstrated that there are important classes of environment opacity cases that receive no adequate analysis by Sympathy (28i,ii). The main argument comes from a whole class of interactions that are bona fide cases of opacity but cannot be understood in terms of Sympathy at all. They involve alternations whose opacity is due to environment counterfeeding, with the environmental factor itself subject to an allophonic alternation.

What follows from the existence of such non-sympathetic opacity? In its narrowest interpretation, the result means that Sympathy Theory is not a complete model of opacity in OT. Taken more broadly, it suggests that the resolution of the whole opacity issue is to be sought elsewhere. Given that Sympathy needs to be complemented by other modes of analysis in order to deal with all cases of environment counterfeeding/counterbleeding (28i,iii) and is already superseded by F&$_c$F constraint conjunction for focus counterfeeding (28ii), the question of Sympathy's actual contribution becomes pressing.

We have seen in this chapter that a certain type of opacity encountered in natural languages, while intractable by the strictly parallelist means of Sympathy-enriched OT, finds a straightforward account in a theory that makes a systematic serial distinction between a lexical and a postlexical module of phonology. In a larger perspective, this weakly parallel model of OT incorporates in a natural way some key insights of classical Lexical Phonology connected to the ideas of turning off processes and rules and of structure preservation. Lexical outputs are characterized by structure preservation (limitation to a restricted inventory of elements and structures), which depends on the ranking relations of the relevant constraints involved. In the postlexical module, promoting contextual markedness over context-free markedness then results in the process being turned on. As we have seen, this gives rise to a stratal type of opacity, which exists independently of a parallelist type due to complex constraints created by some kinds of constraint conjunction. In special cases, the two types of opacity interact with each other, giving rise to multiply opaque patterns in outputs.

Notes

We would like to thank Linda Lombardi and Cheryl Zoll for detailed and constructive suggestions on an earlier version of this chapter. For useful comments, we are indebted to the members of the Special Research Project for the Typological Investigation of Languages and Cultures of the East and the West at Tsukuba University (July 1999), to the audience at the PAIK meeting at Kobe University (December 1999), and to the participants at the Workshop on Conflicting Rules in Phonology and Syntax at the University of Potsdam (December 1999). Special thanks are due to Luigi Burzio, Caroline Féry, Haruka Fukazawa, Shosuke Haraguchi, Bruce Hayes, Takeru Honma, René Kager, Mafuyu Kitahara, Haruo Kubozono, Gereon Müller, Akio Nasu, Sam Rosenthall, Philip Spaelti, Shin-ichi Tanaka, Markus Walter, Richard Wiese, Noriko Yamane, Teruo Yokotani, Yuko Yoshida, Hideki Zamma, and Draga Zec.

1. This type of stratal OT was first explored in some detail by McCarthy and Prince (1993) in their analysis of the prosodic morphology of Axininca Campa and has recently also been advocated by Kiparsky (1998). Within the larger field of optimization-based approaches to phonology, this approach has a precedent in the work of Goldsmith (1990:319–331, 1991).

2. While many differences in approach and outlook remain, the arguments given here complement those of Kiparsky (1998), where a comprehensive pan-Arabic syllable typology, with analyses of opaque interactions of epenthesis, syncope, and stress, crucially involves a serial separation of lexical phonology and postlexical phonology.

3. Except for taking note of the general pattern that emerges when the two cases in (1a) are placed side by side: [M&$_\ell$F] conjunctions lead to opacity-inducing restrictions of M to derived elements, whereas [F&$_\ell$F] conjunctions lead to opacity-inducing restrictions of some markedness constraint to underived elements.

4. The proliferation of word-internal levels was a problem persisting through-out the development of Lexical Phonology, where it was all too easy for ana-lysts to circumnavigate problems by postulating level distinctions without independent support. Part of the reason was that phonology was held responsible for all kinds of sound alternations, including cases nowadays generally analyzed as allomorph selection.

5. The examples in this paper are taken from the speech of the second author. Apart from some regional specifics, the forms are representative of the speech of most parts of Northern Germany. A full investigation of the dis-tribution of [ʀ] and [ɐ̯] – which we are not undertaking in the present context – would need to attend to various further details. In the style of speech under consideration here, all instances of coda ʀ are replaced by [ɐ̯], irrespective of the weight of the preceding nucleus. In more formal speech, there is a dis-tinction between obligatory vocalization after long V and diphthongs, as in the pronoun *wir* [viːɐ̯] 'we' (*[viːʀ]) and optional vocalization after a short V, as in *wirr* 'confused', where both vocalized [vɪɐ̯] and nonvocalized [vɪʀ] are encountered (see Krämer 1981; Hall 1993; Wiese 1996, and references cited there for details).

6. For discussion and analysis of similar types of coda conditions, see Smolensky (1995) and Ito and Mester (to appear).

7. For [ç ~ x], the derived contrasts of the *Kuchen* ~ *Kuh-chen* "cake/little cow" variety made famous by Bloomfield (1930) are grammatically and prosodically conditioned; see Borowsky (1990), Merchant (1996), and ref-erences cited there. Concerning the precise place of articulation of what we transcribe as [x], Wiese (1996) (referring to Kohler 1977) is undoubtedly right in pointing out that the segment in question in many contexts con-tains a uvular component – in particular, after the low vowel [ɑ] and option-

ally also after lax [ɔ] and [ʊ]. Since our interest here lies not in coarticulatory detail, but rather in the overall distinction between front and back articulation of the dorsal fricative, we continue to use [x] as a broad transcription.

8. As Hall (1992) observes, initial [x] is found only in a handful of unassimilated loans such as *Junta* or *José*. Word-initial orthographic <ch> is often pronounced [ʃ] or [k] (the latter case includes *Charisma* for many speakers).

9. The precise factors underlying the status of [ç] as the basic variant in relation to [x] in Standard German warrant further study: [x] is arguably the crosslinguistically more frequent segment, and dialects of German that do not participate in the dorsal fricative alternation invariably have [x] and not [ç] (cf. Swiss German [dɪx] 'you', [mɪx] 'me' for Standard German [dɪç], [mɪç]).

10. IDENT(BACK) here refers to consonantal backness. The vowel feature is protected by a higher-ranking constraint, possibly IDENT(VPLACE) (or different features are involved for consonants and vowels; see NíChiosáin and Padgett 1997, this volume, for discussion).

11. There are in fact dialects showing [x] in these contexts, with [kɪʁxə] for 'church', [hɔːxən] for 'listen', and so on. Such "transparent" dialects do not belong to Low German, whose consonantism is altogether different because it was not affected by the High German sound shifts (with forms such as [kɛʁkən] for 'church').

12. One advantage of such conjoined constraints is that their ranking in the constraint hierarchy is immediately restricted in certain respects. On the other hand, a nonconjoined coda condition could potentially be ranked anywhere in the hierarchy.

13. See Bermúdez-Otero (1999) for further discussion and motivation.

14. Faithfulness violation marks restricted to specific input variants are indexed in the appropriate way.

15. It should be clear that the stratal separation between lexical and postlexical phonology seen in (25) and (26) cannot be mimicked by means of OO-constraints, as in the work of Benua (1997) and others, since there is no phonetic output with coda ʀ that could serve as a reference point. This just echoes the point, made by McCarthy (1999a) and others, that opacity cannot be reduced to OO-effects.

16. An alternative conception, limited to distinctive feature oppositions, has been developed by Gnanadesikan (1997). We concentrate here on the constraint-conjunctive approach because it is more general and connects to many other issues in the theory. The general issues raised by it (e.g., how to define locality for violation clustering, how to impose limits on constraint combinatorics) are not specific to focus counterfeeding, but concern important questions that must be resolved by Optimality Theory in any case, irrespective of specific proposals how to construct complex constraints out of simple ones.

17. This is acknowledged in McCarthy (1999a:32–33), who regards the chain-shift case as irrelevant for Sympathy. At the descriptive level, this is of course true – OT already has ways of dealing with it. It is less clear when one takes

Sympathy Theory seriously as a general and comprehensive theory of opacity in OT. Furthermore, the availability of a constraint-conjunctive analysis does not automatically make a Sympathy approach unavailable. On the contrary, it is a straightforward matter to make the conjoined constraint the selector, and the Sympathy candidate will self-select as the overall winner under the pressure of an appropriate Sympathy constraint. This is troubling because Sympathy here appears superimposed on a constraint-conjunctive analysis that already deals with opacity without introducing any opacity-specific machinery. The latter point, of central importance for the level of explanation achieved, is here highlighted by the fact that the Sympathy analysis contains the constraint-conjunctive analysis as a proper subpart, thus raising the suspicion that perhaps all cases of opacity are actually due not to opacity-specific machinery such as Sympathy, but to independently existing parts of OT theory.

18. Space limitations prevent us from exemplifying these cases with tableaux. The reader is referred to McCarthy (1999a) for a more detailed exposition of the environment counterfeeding and environment counterbleeding cases.

19. This echoes a point made by Kager (1997:497) in earlier work: "one cannot, and should not, directly transfer the conceptual categories of rule-based theory into OT."

20. We saw earlier that when Q affects P's focus, we are dealing with the chain-shift scenario, where Sympathy is superfluous in any theory with a rich enough faithfulness component (allowing, for example, local conjunctions of markedness constraints). The allophonic argument against Sympathy also subverts any idea that rich faithfulness alone could deal with all cases of focus counterfeeding, since the opacity of any alternation P counterfed by another alternation Q, where Q is allophonic and crucially affects P's focus, is in principle beyond the reach of faithfulness. As an illustration, consider the following:

a.
$$A \rightarrow \left\{ \begin{array}{l} B_1/\_\_D_1 \\ B_2/\_\_D_2 \\ B_3/\_\_D_3 \end{array} \right\}$$

b.
$$\left\{ \begin{array}{l} B_3/\_\_B_4 \\ B_2/\_\_B_3 \\ B_1/\_\_B_2 \end{array} \right\} /C\_\_$$

In such cases, /A/ is the classical input for any B_{i+1} in an output of the form $[CB_{i+1}D_i]$, with any /B_n/ serving as an alternative input. This subverts the faithfulness-based account of chain shifts, which is dependent on the input being fixed as B_i. While this is sufficient to make the point as a *Gedankenexperiment*, actual examples are hard to come by, given the tight specifications that any actual case would have to meet. Cases like these, if they exist, could arise out of stratal scenarios, with (a) taking place in the lexical phonology and (b) in the postlexical phonology. In that case, the faithfulness-based account of the chain shift (b) would work postlexically, since the postlexical input, identical to the lexical output, would contain the required B_i elements.

21. Note that the Richness-of-the-Base is the desirable null hypothesis – all special legislation on inputs remains inferior and stipulative in comparison.
22. Ito and Mester (1997b) argue that for the analysis of German hypocoristics the ❀-selector must be an alignment constraint. Bermúdez-Otero (1999) provides further evidence that the selection of ❀-candidates cannot be confined to the class of IO Faithfulness constraints.
23. Note that over and above the fact that [ç] represents the basic variant (see (13)), there must be a rule turning (derived) [x] into [ç] everywhere except after back vowels.
24. See Ito and Mester (to appear) for further discussion and motivation for these constraints. Lombardi (this volume) presents interesting typological arguments against positing such coda conditions on voicing. We have nothing to add here, but merely note that we expect the eventual resolution of these problems to depend on further developments in the theory of feature faithfulness constraints. Consider, for instance, a theory where segment deletion/insertion always triggers Max/Dep-Feature violations, in addition to Max/Dep-Segment. In such a theory, segment-deleting/inserting candidates would in general be harmonically bounded by feature-changing candidates.
25. It is unclear whether the revised "cumulativity"-based approach to Sympathy in McCarthy (1999b) (intended to address "Duke of York"–related issues raised by Kiparsky 1998) changes matters in a decisive way. Our attempts to come up with a cumulativity analysis of multiple-opacity Yawelmani (from McCarthy 1999a) using any of the versions of cumulativity presented in McCarthy (1999b) have so far not been successful. As for the Richness-of-the-Base/allophony argument against Sympathy presented earlier, it appears to persist under cumulative Sympathy since the mode of Sympathy candidate selection remains unchanged.
26. One could try to take the bull by its horns and suggest an M&$_\ell$M account (this amounts to denying that we are dealing with a case of opacity). Thus, Ito and Mester (1998) pursue the brute-force strategy of positing *ҫ̬&$_\ell$*x (with the locality parameter set as adjacency) as the operative constraint conjunction. Besides its ad-hoc nature, the attempt remains unconvincing because it has trouble with basic questions of distribution, which lead to the piling on of further and further restrictions and qualifications (thus, the other order [xҫ̬] is fully well-formed, contractions as in /ʃtɔʀç/ → [ʃtɔːç], *[ʃtɔːx] complicate the picture, and so on).

References

Benua, Laura. 1997. Transderivational Identity: Phonological Relations between Words. PhD dissertation, University of Massachusetts, Amherst. ROA-259-0498, http://ruccs.rutgers.edu/roa.html.

Bermúdez-Otero, Ricardo. 1999. Constraint Interaction in Language Change: Quantity in English and Germanic. PhD dissertation, University of Manchester.

Bloomfield, Leonard. 1930. German ç and x. *Le maître phonétique* 3:27–28.

Borowsky, Toni. 1986. Topics in the Lexical Phonology of English. PhD dissertation, University of Massachusetts, Amherst.

Borowsky, Toni. 1990. On the word level. In *Studies in Lexical Phonology*, ed. S. Hargus and E. M. Kaisse, pp. 199–234. San Diego, CA: Academic.

Fukazawa, Haruka, Mafuyu Kitahara, and Mitsuhiko Ota. 1998. Lexical stratification and ranking invariance in constraint-based grammars. Ms., University of Maryland, College Park, Indiana University, and Georgetown University. ROA-267-0698, http://ruccs.rutgers.edu/roa.html.

Gnanadesikan, Amalia. 1997. Phonology with Ternary Scales. PhD dissertation, Department of Linguistics, University of Massachusetts, Amherst.

Goldsmith, John. 1990. *Autosegmental and Metrical Phonology*. Oxford: Blackwell.

Goldsmith, John. 1991. Phonology as an Intelligent System. In *Bridges between Psychology and Linguistics: A Swarthmore Festschrift for Lila Gleitman*, ed. D. J. Napoli and J. A. Kegl, pp. 247–267. Hillsdale, NJ: Erlbaum.

Hall, Tracy Alan. 1992. *Syllable Structure and Syllable-Related Processes in German*. Tübingen: Niemeyer.

Hall, Tracy Alan. 1993. The Phonology of German /R/. *Phonology* 6:1–18.

Hayes, Bruce. 1999. Phonological Acquisition in Optimality Theory: The Early Stages. Ms., UCLA. ROA-327-0699, http://ruccs.rutgers.edu/roa.html.

Ito, Junko, and Armin Mester. 1995. The Core-Periphery Structure of the Lexicon and Constraints on Reranking. In *Papers in Optimality Theory*, ed. J. Beckman, S. Urbanczyk, and L. Walsh, pp. 181–210. Amherst, MA: GLSA.

Ito, Junko, and Armin Mester. 1997a. Sympathy Theory and German Truncations. *University of Maryland Working Papers in Linguistics* 5:117–138. ROA-211-0897, http://ruccs.rutgers.edu/roa.html.

Ito, Junko, and Armin Mester. 1997b. Featural Sympathy. In *Phonology at Santa Cruz 5*, ed. D. Karvonen, M. Katayama, and R. Walker, pp. 29–36. Santa Cruz, CA: Linguistics Research Center, University of California, Santa Cruz.

Ito, Junko, and Armin Mester, 1998. [M&$_\ell$F] and [M&$_\ell$M] Conjunctions. Handout of paper presented at the Tübinger Silbenkonferenz.

Ito, Junko, and Armin Mester. 1999. The Phonological Lexicon. In *A Handbook of Japanese Linguistics*, ed. N. Tsujimura, pp. 62–100. Oxford: Blackwell.

Ito, Junko, and Armin Mester. 2000. Weak Parallelism and Modularity: Evidence from Japanese. Report of the Special Research Project on the Languages of the East and West, pp. 89–106. Tsukuba University.

Ito, Junko, and Armin Mester. To appear. On the Sources of Opacity in OT: Coda Processes in German. In *Structure and Typology of the Syllable*, ed. C. Fery and R. van de Vijver. Cambridge: Cambridge University Press. ROA-347-0999, http://ruccs.rutgers.edu/roa.html.

Kager, René. 1997. Rhythmic Vowel Deletion in Optimality Theory. In *Derivations and Constraints in Phonology*, ed. I. Roca, pp. 463–499. Oxford: Oxford University Press.

Kiparsky, Paul. 1973. Abstractness, Opacity and Global Rules. In *Three Dimensions of Linguistic Theory*, ed. O. Fujimura, pp. 57–86. Tokyo: TEC.

Kiparsky, Paul. 1982. Lexical Phonology and Morphology. In *Linguistics in the Morning Calm*, ed. I. S. Yang, pp. 3–91. Seoul: Hanshin.

Kiparsky, Paul. 1985. Some Consequences of Lexical Phonology. *Phonology* 2:85–138.

Kiparsky, Paul. 1998. Paradigm Effects and Opacity. Ms., Stanford University.

Kirchner, Robert. 1996. Synchronic Chain Shifts in Optimality Theory. *Linguistic Inquiry* 27:341–350.

Kohler, Klaus J. 1977. *Einführung in die Phonetik des Deutschen*. Berlin: E. Schmidt.

Krämer, Wolfgang. 1981. *Akustisch-Phonetische Untersuchungen zum Vokalischen /R/-Allophon des Deutschen*. Hamburg: Helmut Buske.

Lubowicz, Anna. 1998. Derived Environment Effects in OT. Ms., University of Massachusetts, Amherst. ROA 239-0198, http://ruccs.rutgers.edu/roa.html.

McCarthy, John J. 1999a. Sympathy and Phonological Opacity. *Phonology* 16:331–399. ROA-252-0398, http://ruccs.rutgers.edu/roa.html.

McCarthy, John J. 1999b. Sympathy, Cumulativity, and the Duke-of-York Gambit. Ms., University of Massachusetts, Amherst. ROA-315-0499, http://ruccs.rutgers.edu/roa.html.

McCarthy John J., and Alan Prince. 1993. Prosodic Morphology I: Constraint Satisfaction and Interaction. Ms., University of Massachusetts at Amherst, and Rutgers University. Report RUCCS TR-3.

Merchant, Jason. 1996. Alignment and Fricative Assimilation in German. *Linguistic Inquiry* 27:709–719.

Moulton, William G. 1962. *The Sounds of English and German*. Chicago: University of Chicago Press.

Pater, Joe. 1995. On the Nonuniformity of Weight-to-Stress and Stress Preservation Effects in English. Ms., McGill University. ROA-107-0000, http://ruccs.rutgers.edu/roa.html.

Prince, Alan S., and Paul Smolensky. 1993. Optimality Theory: Constraint Interaction in Generative Grammar. Ms., Rutgers University and University of Colorado, Boulder.

Prince, Alan S., and Bruce Tesar. 1999. Learning Phonotactic Distributions. Ms., Rutgers University. ROA-353-1099, http://ruccs.rutgers.edu/roa.html.

Smolensky, Paul. 1995. On the Structure of the Constraint Component Con of UG. Handout of paper presented at UCLA, April 7. ROA-86-0000, http://ruccs.rutgers.edu/roa.html.

Wedel, Andrew. In preparation. An Acoustic Study of Vocalized /R/ in German. Ms., University of California, Santa Cruz.

Wiese, Richard. 1996. *The Phonology of German*. Oxford: Clarendon.

Index